The Economic and Social Impact of AIDS in Europe

Editors: David FitzSimons, Vanessa Hardy and Keith Tolley

CASSELL

Published by Cassell PLC,
Wellington House,
125 Strand,
London WC2R 0BB

© National AIDS Trust 1995

First published 1995

All views presented here are those of the
authors and do not necessarily represent
the views of the National AIDS Trust or
the Editors. Neither NAT nor the Editors
can accept liability for any omissions or
incorrect statements made in the book.

ISBN
HB: 0 304 33157 0
PB: 0 304 33159 7

Printed and bound in Great Britain by
Redwood Books, Trowbridge, Wiltshire

Contents

CDC classification of HIV disease, 1987

Group	I	Acute infection
Group	**II**	Asymptomatic infection
Group	**III**	Persistent generalized lymphadenopathy
Group	**IV**	
	IV-a	Constitutional diseases such as weight loss, protracted fever, protracted diarrhoea (comparable but not similar to the earlier 'AIDS-related complex'): at least two of the following disorders should occur during a period of at least 3 months: – fever with temperature higher than 38°C (at least intermittent) – more than 10 per cent weight loss – persistent generalized lymphadenopathy – diarrhoea (at least intermittent) – fatigue with reduced physical functioning – night sweats
	IV-b	Neurological manifestations (myelopathy, peripheral neuropathy, AIDS dementia complex)
	IV-c1	AIDS-defining opportunistic infections (such as *Pneumocystis carinii* pneumonia, cerebral toxoplasmosis, *Candida* oesophagitis)
	IV-c2	Other secondary infections (such as oral hairy leukoplakia, oropharyngeal candidiasis, herpes zoster in a number of dermatoma)
	IV-d	AIDS-defining secondary malignancies (Kaposi's sarcoma, non-Hodgkin's lymphoma, primary brain lymphoma)
	IV-e	Other diseases (in particular auto-immune thrombocytopenia)

This table is included for illustrative purposes only: specific references should be checked to establish precisely what classification was used in a particular research project.

Preface

AIDS is predominantly a disease of the young. In Europe it mainly affects people aged 25–40 years,[1] economically the most important age group. Its impact goes far beyond the obvious consequences to the health of the individual who is HIV-positive and the cost of medical care. Prejudice and stigmatization have far-reaching effects: job losses, housing problems, ostracism by society, travel restrictions, etc. This discrimination carries an economic as well as social price.

This book arose out of a planned conference[2] which attempted to clarify the real and potential economic impact of AIDS in Europe for managers and officials in government, business and the social welfare systems. It sought to provide the evidence needed by policy-makers for the continuing need to commit resources to prevention efforts and research. Regrettably, the conference was cancelled. The marketing coincided with the promulgation by sections of the media of myths that there was no heterosexual HIV epidemic; that there was no AIDS epidemic in Africa; and that HIV did not cause AIDS.

The strength of the conference programme was such, however, that we thought it imperative to publish the presentations as soon as possible. This book contains 36 of the 90 proposed papers and represents a cross-section of European analysis – although it is not intended to be encyclopaedic.

The chapters on economic analysis represent the state of the art.[3] They demonstrate the lack of a common definition for cost analysis in Western Europe, let alone for the countries of Central and Eastern Europe. They also show that we are far from having an accurate estimate of costs, and that developments in this area are very piecemeal. Most of the current research deals only with hospital costs, added to which the different methodologies used make comparisons invalid. The very need for standardization in economic analysis is strongly argued in the chapters by Gyldmark and Tolley, and Kyriopoulos et al.

A number of the chapters provide estimates of the direct costs of medical care for patients with HIV or AIDS. However, direct costs should also include the costs of social and informal care. In current HIV/AIDS research in Europe, there appears to be little interest in estimating these costs. This is illustrated by the absence of contributions in this area to the original conference or for the book. Almost no research has been undertaken on the voluntary sector, although most national AIDS strategies emphasize its importance in playing a crucial service provision role. The need for such research is highlighted in the changing cost patterns of the increasing shift to out-patient care (the result of earlier diagnosis, greater medical expertise and better prophylaxis and treatment.) The chapter by Beck documents this shift in London.

Particularly worrying, given the clear social benefits of preventing the spread of HIV, is the extremely limited attention that has been paid to the costs and cost-effectiveness of prevention. Why is this so? The chapter by Le Galès et al. is an indication of how important this area could become as an effective aid for policy- makers. What their analysis leaves out, however, are the ethical considerations that need to be included in this kind of study. Whilst healthcare systems are increasingly sensitive to budgetary constraints, and decisions about cost-effectiveness inevitably have to be made, the long-term implications for the mental and physical well-being of the population also have to be taken into account when measuring 'costs'. Any economic analysis should, therefore, be seen as a tool – and not as the dictator of policy.

The exact magnitude of the direct and indirect cost of AIDS is difficult to assess or predict. Indirect costs, for example, would have to take account of factors such as loss of individual social and economic productivity. Hence the importance of research by people such as Jager et al. who are developing the use of scenario analysis as a means of linking epidemiological simulations of HIV/AIDS incidence with economic and socio-cultural indicators. In another chapter, Minder et al. have also tried to include socio-economic factors in their analysis of costs.

The emerging democracies of Eastern Europe stand at a crossroads: the opportunity exists in some countries to prevent HIV gaining a hold but this comes at a time when they face economic pressures, a brain-drain to the West, little popular faith in the state instruments, and other pressing and more visible public health problems. The contributions on Lithuania (Chaplinskas), northern Poland (Zielińska and Korczak-Rogoń), the Czech Republic (Stožický) and the Slovak Republic (Mayer) give a flavour of the issues involved in tackling HIV under these constraints.

A common theme throughout the chapters dealing with social issues is how discrimination, prejudice, abuse of human rights or simply plain ignorance is ultimately both costly and counterproductive in terms of reducing the spread of HIV. Policy-makers, whether in business or in government, need to think through the ramifications of imposing coercive or unsupportive policies. This is most clearly shown by Shtarkshall and Davidson's frank account of what happened when the Israeli government decided to screen immigrant Ethiopian Jews for HIV.

Although issues of housing, insurance and employment are predominantly considered from a UK perspective, similar debates and conclusions will apply within different national frameworks. Workplace discrimination has traditionally been tackled in Europe through legislation and employers' policies supported by staff education. However, there is scant legislation in Europe to protect the rights of people living with HIV. Most countries seem to rely on employers recognizing the value of committing resources to countering discrimination.

A few companies have responded to the public health and corporate challenge of HIV/AIDS with vigour, but alas all too few. The AIDS panic of the 1980s has now subsided and, as long as there are large pools of skilled unemployed people, companies will continue to view HIV/AIDS as a remote workplace problem. But as European HIV prevalence figures show,[4] it is an issue that employers will increasingly have to deal with. In a supportive environment people with HIV and AIDS can continue employment and remain economically productive members of society, as Faas's case studies demonstrate.

Multinational companies face additional responsibilities with operations in countries and regions where HIV prevalence rates are higher than in Europe. Inevitably, they will have to face the threat posed by HIV and its attendant scourge, tuberculosis, to the health of their staff, as well as the repercussions of HIV – discrimination, prejudice and loss of loved ones. HIV is already threatening the social and economic stability of several countries. In Rwanda the high toll of death through AIDS and tuberculosis is held to have been a contributory factor to the genocidal war. In eastern Africa HIV is affecting farming systems, including commercial sugar plantations, not only directly through illness in the workforce but indirectly through increasing spread of crop diseases and pests. However, Williams and Ray offer a positive and constructive report on what can be done through workplace initiatives in Africa.

Increasingly, multinational companies will have to pay attention to the impact of their activities on the communities in which they operate. Construction sites, for instance, will require many male labourers who, inevitably, will attract camp followers. Transport projects will open new arteries not just for trade but also for sexually transmitted diseases such as HIV. Companies have already begun to assess their impact on the environment: perhaps they should be addressing the issue of HIV/AIDS too.

We believe this book will make funding agencies and decision-makers see the need for further research and help identify the socio-economic areas most in need of investigation. These data are critical for appropriate policies for the future. The chapters bridge the gap between the economic issues on the one hand and the social implications on the other, offering a unique and truly European resource for a wide spectrum of readers, from sociologists to members of the business community.

The Editors would like to thank Britta Griffiths for her hard work on the conference programme, Jean Marray, the assistant editor, for her major contribution in helping to make this book a reality and Julian Meldrum (NAT) for his critical support and comments.

David W FitzSimons, Vanessa Hardy, Keith Tolley
England, December 1994

---

1 European Centre for the Epidemiological Monitoring of AIDS (WHO–EC Collaborating Centre on AIDS), Hôpital National de Saint-Maurice, 14 rue de val d'Osne, F-94410 Saint-Maurice, France.

2 The conference entitled the Socio-Economic Impact of AIDS in Europe should have taken place on 25–28 February 1994. It was organized by the National AIDS Trust (UK) and was co-sponsored by the Commission of the European Communities, the Council of Europe and the World Health Organization with the support of the Departments of Employment and Health in England and Wales. We would like to acknowledge their support. We would also like to recognize the contribution of the Speakers Selection Committee who helped to create the programme. They were Dr. Johannes Hallauer, WHO; Bernie Merkel, EC Directorate General V; Chris Staniland, Department of Health; Dr Graham Hart, Middlesex Hospital; Dr Alastair Gray, Wolfson College, Oxford; Keith Tolley, University of Nottingham; Dr Peter Davies, Project Sigma, London; Dr J.C. Jager, Centre of Public Health Forecasting, the Netherlands; David FitzSimons, CAB International; Peter Roth, Gray's Inn, London; Robert Hill, business consultant; Phil Blinkhorn, Ashdown Research; Dr Les Rudd, National AIDS Trust, Vanessa Hardy, National AIDS Trust; Tim Clement-Jones, Kingfisher plc. Copyright for the name of the conference is owned by Ashdown Research.

3 Wherever possible figures have been given in US$

4 European Centre for the Epidemiological Monitoring of AIDS (as above).

AIDS: Epidemic Update and Corporate Response

Dr Michael Merson

Executive Director, Global Programme on AIDS, World Health Organization, Geneva, Switzerland

In this chapter,[1] I shall first present an update of the current and future scope of the epidemic, and then discuss the impact of AIDS on the health and survival of individuals, families and communities, as well as on the economy of nations. Lastly, I shall outline the many things that the private sector can do to stem the tide of the epidemic. There is a great deal at stake in rolling back this epidemic, and the contribution of the private sector is crucial. I do not mean just business donations, but corporate leadership – business becoming equal partners in the international effort against AIDS.

Medical and epidemiological update

To begin with some basics, *AIDS* stands for acquired immunodeficiency syndrome. And, let there be no misunderstanding: AIDS is caused by *HIV*, the human immunodeficiency virus. People with AIDS are people who were infected with HIV.

Once HIV enters the body, it weakens the immune system so that the infected person can no longer fight off life-threatening illnesses such as tuberculosis or rare forms of pneumonia or meningitis – what are called opportunistic infections. Once infected, a person is infected for life, and capable of infecting others. Fortunately, HIV works slowly. Most viruses produce full-blown disease in a matter of days or weeks. The influenza virus, for example, causes 'flu in just five days. HIV is different. A few weeks after initial infection, people usually develop a short mild illness with fever and swollen glands, after which they look and feel healthy for years. During that time, however, the virus is quietly weakening their immune system by killing off CD4 cells – important white blood cells of the immune system. When the immune deficiency becomes severe enough, the person starts having symptoms like diarrhoea and fatigue. Then, many years after initial infection, people reach the final state of infection known as AIDS, in which they are unable to fight off the opportunistic infections that ultimately cause their death.

HIV spreads primarily through sexual intercourse, so AIDS is regarded as essentially a sexually transmitted disease (STD). The virus can be transmitted from a man to a woman, from a man to another man, and from a woman to a man. Having many sex partners increases the risk of infection, unless people use condoms consistently and correctly. But even people with one partner are at risk, if that partner has unprotected sex with other people. In some places the majority of women who are HIV-infected have only one partner – their husband.

Like other STDs, HIV can also be transmitted through transfused blood, and through the sharing of infected syringes or needles, for example by drug users. Finally, HIV can be passed by an infected woman to her foetus or baby – in the womb, during childbirth and during breast-feeding. Worldwide, these routes of transmission are all much less common than sexual intercourse.

It is also important to know how HIV *is not* transmitted. HIV is not spread though everyday contact of any kind, such as shaking hands with or hugging someone, eating or drinking from the same crockery, being sneezed on, or using the same door knobs, telephones or toilet seats. Hence, no one can acquire HIV infection by working next to an infected colleague in a factory or office. Unlike people suffering from a cold, or from measles, someone with HIV infection or AIDS is not casually contagious. Unless everyone understands this, ignorance may cause groundless fear and lead to discrimination against people who are known or thought to have HIV.

Is there a cure for this fatal, sexually transmitted disease? For now, the answer is no. While bacterial infections can be cured with antibiotics, science has not been as successful in curing viral diseases. Nevertheless, with proper treatment the lives of people with HIV infection can be prolonged and their well-being improved. Scientists are searching for better ways of preventing or treating the opportunistic infections of AIDS patients, and are trying to develop better antiviral drugs and drug combinations to combat the virus itself. Realistically, however, a cure is not on the horizon.

Traditionally, public health authorities fight viral diseases not with medicines but with vaccines. The greatest public health triumphs have come from vaccinating people against smallpox (now totally eradicated), polio, measles, and so on. But HIV strains are highly variable – both over time, and geographically, and this may be a significant obstacle to vaccine development. Broadly, there are at least seven major genetic subtypes of HIV around the world which may need to be included in any vaccine. As part of our role in coordinating international vaccine research, WHO is ensuring that vaccine manufacturers have access to virus strains not only from the industrialized world but from developing countries. As of today, over fifteen candidate vaccines have been developed. Some are already being tested in human volunteers to see if they are safe and produce an immune response, and large-scale trials of a few of these vaccines may begin soon. Realistically, however, we cannot expect to have a vaccine for mass use before the year 2000 – and this is an optimistic prediction.

That being the case, it is vital to see just where we are in the epidemic – which is sometimes described as a *pan*demic, because it is worldwide.

As of 1 July 1994, 190 countries have reported close to 1 million AIDS cases to WHO. But reporting is always incomplete, and we estimate that around 4 million adults and children have actually developed AIDS since the start of the epidemic. Most AIDS cases so far have been in Africa and in the industrialized countries of Europe and North America, where HIV first began its epidemic spread. Where the epidemic is more recent, fewer people have as yet developed AIDS.

But while AIDS cases are the visible part of the epidemic, they are also the smallest part. Remember the approximate ten-year latency period before AIDS develops in someone with HIV. This means that the AIDS statistics today tell us what the HIV situation was a decade ago. *Today's* HIV situation is that there have now been over 17 million HIV infections since the beginning of the epidemic – more than 16 million in teenagers and adults, over 1 million in children born to HIV-infected mothers. And while sub-Saharan Africa is still ahead, other regions are catching up.

The end of the epidemic is nowhere in sight. There is no doubt that it will extend well into the twenty-first century. By the year 2000, we project that the current global figure of over 17 million cumulative HIV infections will already have more than doubled, to between 30 to 40 million infections. The epidemic expansion will be most dramatic in Asia. Soon, more Asians will be infected each year than Africans. Cumulative infections in Asia – estimated at 0.5 million in early 1991 and at over 2.5 million today – are expected to rise to more than 10 million by the year 2000.

A few words are in order about the vulnerability of adolescents and young adults to HIV infection. About half of all infections so far have occurred in those between the ages of 15 and 24 – an important figure to remember when analysing the vulnerability of the workforce. Women get infected even earlier than men. Part of the reason for this may be biological – HIV seems to pass more readily through the immature vagina and cervix. Another is that young women tend to have sex with older men, who have been sexually active for longer and are more likely to be infected.

I come to the regional HIV trends (Figure 1).

In Western Europe, North America and Australasia over 1.5 million adults have been infected since the start of the epidemic. In these regions some progress has been made in prevention efforts. For example, the rate of new infections has dropped among homosexual and bisexual men, owing in part to effective AIDS education and condom promotion. In places with good needle-exchange and drug treatment programmes, HIV incidence is also low among injecting drug users. However, heterosexual transmission is rising steadily, especially among poor urban

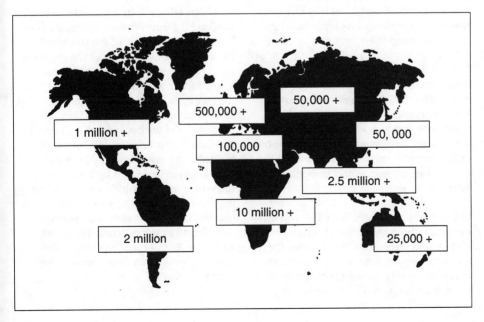

Figure 1
Estimated distribution of total adult HIV infections from late 1970s/early 1980s until mid 1994 WHO – Global Programme on AIDS

500,000 +

50,000 +

1 million +

50, 000

100,000

2.5 million +

10 million +

2 million

25,000 +

populations with high rates of drug injecting and STDs.

It must be stressed that STDs are now known to facilitate HIV transmission significantly. People with an untreated STD such as chancroid, syphilis or chlamydia are perhaps five to ten times more likely to become infected with HIV, or, if already infected with HIV, to pass the virus to someone else through sexual intercourse. This is why treatment of STDs – important in its own right – has also become a prime strategy for preventing HIV infection.

We estimate that the countries of central Asia and eastern Europe have so far had over 50,000 HIV infections, most of them acquired through sexual intercourse. But this figure is misleading because the potential for a major epidemic exists. These countries have many of the factors associated with rapid HIV spread through sex and drug use – economic crisis, rising unemployment, ethnic and religious conflicts, and the movement of civilian populations. The good news is that in April 1993, at a landmark meeting in Riga, Latvia, the region's health and finance ministers made the decision to invest heavily in prevention. That was an important turning point in a region which had long considered itself 'immune' to AIDS.

To date, there have been even more infections – around 100,000 – in another region where the AIDS threat seemed remote: North Africa and the Middle East. But there as everywhere else, AIDS is proving that it is not a disease of foreigners. Today, most transmission is occurring within the countries of the region and through sexual intercourse.

In Latin America, there have been an estimated 2 million infections in adults, most of them through sexual intercourse. On the positive side, we are seeing some evidence of sexual behaviour change in the form of declining STD rates, for example in Costa Rica. But certain Caribbean countries have some of the highest AIDS rates per capita in the world, and many people seeking treatment at STD clinics are infected with HIV. The future course of the epidemic in Latin America may depend above all on what happens in Brazil, its most populous country. Brazil already has more AIDS cases than any developing country outside Africa.

People with an STD have by definition been engaging in unprotected sexual intercourse, which means they have put themselves at risk of HIV infection too. Hence it is not surprising that their HIV rates are among the highest. To get an idea of the HIV rates in the wider 'general' population, we look at women who attend an antenatal clinic for pregnancy care. For example, HIV infection rates among pregnant women are beginning to climb in Honduras, are higher still in Haiti, and in cities in Uganda and Zambia are as high as 30 per cent. It is important to remember that in a population with so much infection among pregnant women, infection rates among STD patients can approach 50 per cent and among female prostitutes can reach 80 per cent.

In Africa, where there have been over 10 million HIV infections in adults, the central and eastern parts of the continent have been the main focus of the epidemic up to now. But HIV continues to spread southward, northward and westward on the continent – mainly through heterosexual intercourse which is why such a big proportion of the population is at risk. In Abidjan, in West Africa, HIV prevalence in adults increased from 1 per cent in 1986 to over 10 per cent by 1992. In Nigeria, where many people used to believe they were at little or no risk of HIV, infection levels of 15 per cent to 20 per cent were found in some female prostitute groups in 1992. I could cite even more alarming rates from Botswana and South Africa.

But no doubt the most alarming trends of all are those on the Asian continent, particularly south and south-east Asia.

In vulnerable population groups, such as injecting drug users, the increase in HIV infection has been simply explosive. This has been most striking in Myanmar, India and Thailand. But the same is now happening elsewhere. In Ho Chi Minh City, for example, HIV prevalence among drug injectors went from 2 per cent in late 1992 to over 30 per cent by the third quarter of 1993 – less than a year! Another vulnerable group is female sex workers, who inevitably risk high infection rates unless there is 100 per cent condom use. In just two years, their infection levels more than doubled in parts of Thailand and India. More recently, HIV infection has also been shown to be rising dramatically among female prostitutes in Cambodia.

What is essential to remember is that HIV never remains confined to any 'risk group' but eventually diffuses into the wider population. This is demonstrated in Thailand where, beginning in 1987, the epidemic started to spread from drug injectors to female prostitutes, to their young male clients (as documented by the HIV rates in military recruits) and finally to the regular partners of these men (as documented in pregnant women). In other words, as an epidemic matures, the net of HIV infection is cast wider and wider. At the start, the most vulnerable people are those who are practising the most high-risk behaviour. Then the net of infection gradually expands to include those one might not think of being particularly at risk – monogamous wives, for example. And ultimately, as we see in the mature epidemics in Africa, and now in northern Thailand, the lines begin to blur altogether between the 'risk groups' and the general population.

Before leaving the subject of HIV infection patterns, I want to emphasize that you do not need to *see* high HIV levels in a particular city or country to know that the people living there are at risk. Experience has shown repeatedly that mobility is a factor in HIV transmission. People who travel for work or migrate or move, whether within their own country or across national borders, are particularly vulnerable to HIV. Old family ties loosen or break, new sexual partnerships are formed, sometimes fleeting ones. The point is that wherever you have people on the move, HIV can take advantage of them unless they practise safer sex.

There is another factor to look at when evaluating the potential HIV threat. As I stated earlier, having an STD means you have been having unprotected intercourse and in addition makes you more likely to acquire or transmit HIV. So when there is an increase in STD cases, this tells us HIV cannot be far behind. This is what is happening in China today, for example. With tens of millions of people on the move to seek employment, and with increasing rates of STDs, I have great concern about the serious potential for HIV spread in that country.

Impact of AIDS

At present, the impact of AIDS is worst in parts of the world such as sub-Saharan Africa where many of the infected people have already progressed to illness and then death. As the same happens to infected people elsewhere, we shall see the same kind of impact.

First, the impact on health and life expectancy. As the number of AIDS cases grows, so does the burden it places on the health system. Hospital bed occupancy by AIDS patients is now more than 50 per cent in many African cities. But parts of Asia are catching up. I recently visited Chiang Mai province in northern Thailand and was amazed to see AIDS patients occupying around half the beds on the medical wards at the provincial hospital. One of the most common illnesses AIDS patients get is tuberculosis. In fact, virtually everywhere the epidemic of HIV infection has been followed by a worsening TB epidemic. This can be seen by visiting health facilities in many African countries, and increasingly in places like Bombay and Chiang Rai.

AIDS affects, above all, people who are young or in early middle age. With every premature death, years of potentially healthy life are lost – to the individual and to society. In Uganda, for example, the estimated potential productive years of life lost in the 20–49 year age group will triple this decade on account of AIDS. Even in the USA, AIDS has grown to be the leading cause of death in young men in over 60 cities.

Because AIDS affects the breadwinners, the mainstays of the family and the workforce, it is having a socio-economic impact out of all proportion to the numbers of people infected. In Africa, where HIV spreads mainly through heterosexual intercourse – as it does in Asia, Latin America and the Caribbean – virtually every adult dying of AIDS leaves behind family members who were depending on him or her for love, care and often financial support. By the year 2000, as many as 5–10 million children worldwide will have lost their mother or both parents to AIDS. And the situation for children will only get worse, considering that an estimated 13 million women will have been infected worldwide by the year 2000. AIDS deaths in young adults also leave elderly parents without support in their old age – and in many cases, burdened with the care of orphaned grandchildren.

By the time a person with AIDS dies, the family may be impoverished because of the costs in time and money of caring for and burying him or her. In Thailand, the healthcare costs alone for a person with AIDS are estimated to be one-third to one-half of the average annual family income.

Worldwide, according to a 1992 WHO study, medical care for a little over half a million people with AIDS cost almost $5,000 million. Over 90 per cent of those costs are in industrialized countries although they account for only 22 per cent of cases. Over the next six years, developing countries – including some of the poorest in the world – will spend close to $1,000 million on healthcare for AIDS patients.

These healthcare costs though they sound high are actually minor compared with the *other* costs to the economy of adults dying in the prime of their working years, depleting the workforce of invaluable manpower. On all continents – everywhere the indirect costs of the epidemic have been estimated – they turn out to be many times greater than the cost of healthcare. In Thailand, for example, a well-known study estimated the healthcare costs per AIDS patient at $1,500, as compared with the indirect costs to the economy calculated at $22,000 on average per death. The aggregate costs in Thailand are now estimated to total nearly $11,000 million by the year 2000, for a population of less than 60 million people. The epidemic in Thailand is ahead of that in most of Asia. Still, these figures give you an idea of the potential economic loss if the epidemic continues its rapid expansion among the more than 3,000 million Asians.

What can AIDS mean to a business enterprise? First, AIDS will divert national resources from infrastructure investment to healthcare. It will shrink consumer markets as personal income drops, and as an increasing proportion of that income has to be spent on hospital bills and drugs. AIDS will have a direct impact on the workforce, too. Just to take one example, in the last few years there has been a five-fold increase in deaths among employees of Barclays Bank Limited in Zambia. Most of those who died were under the age of 45 and their cause of death was often given as tuberculosis or pneumonia. These long illnesses and eventual deaths have had serious effects on the bank. Some of these are out-of-pocket costs – for example, escalating medical costs and survivor payments. Others may be less visible, including falling productivity of directly affected employees, and deteriorating staff morale in this environment of ever-increasing illness and death, where people simply wonder 'Who will be next?'.

To summarize, AIDS causes illness, disability and death among employees and their families. The direct outcome is increased healthcare costs, death benefits and pension costs. Productivity drops as workers stay home because of illness or to take care of ill relatives. The firm begins to lose people with precious training or skills, or valuable knowledge of the company. This not only disrupts production but leads to increased training and labour costs. At the same time, AIDS is likely to cause a drop in demand for a firm's products.

How great will the impact be on a given firm? That, of course, depends on many factors, including the infection rate in its workforce and in the wider community, how much in-house training new employees need, and how sensitive the firm is to the loss of key people. But no company will escape the impact of AIDS on its workforce, on its markets, on the national or international economy.

Taking up the AIDS challenge

So there is no cure and no vaccine on the horizon, at least not before the year 2000 – and by then the shape of the AIDS epidemic in much of the world will have been determined. Are we helpless without a 'magic bullet'?

The answer is, no. HIV *can* be stopped with information and education about AIDS, and with good support services that make condoms widely available and provide prompt care for the other STDs. Experience of the past decade shows that this works when it is done well and to scale.

For prevention to work, there are two behaviours to be encouraged. One is safer sex. Apart from no sex at all, the safest option in the AIDS era is fidelity, but only so long as both partners, and not just one, remain faithful. Non-penetrative sex is also very safe. Another form of safer sex is consistent and correct use of a condom every time for sexual intercourse, which means that people must have access to good-quality condoms and know how to use them correctly.

In Africa there has been a spectacular increase in condom use in countries where condoms were virtually unknown a decade ago. It may be of interest to business people that much of this increase was achieved by using standard marketing techniques, such as pretesting products with customers, attractive packaging, effective advertising, and a solid profit motive for the salesforce. When these marketing techniques are applied by the public sector to a socially useful product – like condoms – it is called 'social marketing'. Condom social marketing works.

The other behaviour we promote is seeking care for an STD, and this too requires a corresponding service. A good healthcare provider will not only treat an STD, but give advice about preventing further episodes – and about condom use.

Who needs to hear the safer-sex message, and how? To begin with, young people. It is clear from their infection rates that the young are a prime audience for the safer-sex message because many of them are sexually active. And the earlier they hear the message and get the opportunity to learn the necessary skills, the better. Perhaps the most important skill, especially for young girls, is how to say no to unsafe sex, especially to someone older or of greater status or power. Whether the information and skills are conveyed in school or outside doesn't really matter, so long as the young people learn what they need to. And school education does not encourage early sexual experimentation. On the contrary, it leads to a postponement of sexual activity and a reduction in teenage pregnancy – and for those who do have sex, the sexual practices are safer. These are important facts for parents and future employers to know.

We also need to target our AIDS information services to others who are particularly vulnerable to HIV infection. These usually include STD patients, homosexual and bisexual men, prostitutes and their clients, and injecting drug users. In business terms, this is called 'market segmentation'. Targeting always has to be done carefully because of the risk that the target groups will acquire a stigma. And stigmatized people do not heed prevention messages coming from authorities. The other risk of targeting is that people who do not belong to a targeted group – the so-called general public – can cling to the illusion of safety. Why should they bother with safer sex when the authorities are implying that only people targeted by prevention messages should be worried about AIDS?

For all these reasons, it is important that targeted efforts be complemented by prevention messages directed at the general population – through newspapers, radio, television and other media.

I am often asked what kind of a dent we can make in the global epidemic if national AIDS programmes around the world carry out all the basics of AIDS prevention, including programmes to prevent HIV spread through blood transfusions. On the basis of recent WHO studies, we estimate that basic prevention would avert more than half of all new HIV infections between now and the end of this decade. Because AIDS is fatal, that

means saving 10 million lives. The life-saving impact of prevention would be felt even more as we move into the twenty-first century because averting one infection *now* means preventing one person from acquiring HIV who can pass it on to others, who could in turn infect still others, in the familiar epidemic snowball.

So much for what national AIDS programmes can do about AIDS. What can individual businesses do? Let me make a few suggestions based on lessons we have learned through public health experience.

To begin with, businesses can set up an 'AIDS in the Workplace' programme. The two main components of such a programme should be, first, to ensure that people believed or known to have HIV infection or AIDS are treated fairly, humanely and without discrimination, and second, to prevent new infections among employees and their dependents. In other words, the goals are *non-discrimination*, *care and support* for those who are infected, and *prevention* of further infections. I want to stress that in practice these must be linked. Every action taken – be it the adoption of a corporate policy, or the provision of healthcare, or the establishment of regular AIDS education – will wind up serving both the people who are infected and those who are not. Most of the time, the employer will not even know who falls into which category; nor will people themselves, most probably. What is important is not to think in terms of 'them' and 'us', or set one group against the other. The goals of prevention and non-discrimination are linked in another way, too. Prevention efforts simply will not be credible to the workforce unless they are carried out in a supportive climate of non-discrimination.

Often the first thing to do when establishing a workforce programme is to be sure that senior management sets corporate policies on AIDS. Policies can, but need not, be in writing, so long as their spirit is adhered to. Some of the policies need to address issues of non-discrimination. For example, the National Leadership Coalition now brings together more than 200 US-based firms and other employers who subscribe to its famous 'Ten Principles'. The principles recognize the need for businesses to treat people with AIDS in the same way as people with any other serious condition; to have non-discriminatory employment practices; and to protect the confidentiality of employees' medical and insurance information. They also include a policy on AIDS prevention, by stating that AIDS education is to be provided to all staff.

To take another example, an 'AIDS Agreement' calling for protection of HIV-positive employees against discrimination and victimization was recently signed by the National Union of Mineworkers and the Chamber of Mines of South Africa. Barclays Bank Limited in Zimbabwe operates on a similar principle. In addition, they consider that the only medical criterion for recruitment and termination of employment is fitness to work – HIV infection does not in itself constitute lack of fitness to work.

Firms which adhere to the principle of non-discrimination give their HIV-infected employees suitable new work assignments as and when their health begins to weaken. Truck drivers can become guards, for example, and miners may be given supervisory functions. These same firms have, of course, already benefited from the services of HIV-positive staff during their many years of good health.

Apart from ensuring their freedom from discrimination, what else should a business do for its HIV-positive employees? For one, ensure their access to health services, whether directly through the company medical service or as part of a health insurance scheme. In either case, their health and insurance data must be pro-tected with full confidentiality. In addition, give them the needed support to be able to cope with their illness. In countries with a high prevalence of HIV infection, some firms I know give their employees time off to go for AIDS counselling. Some provide day care for children. Some ensure that their staff can take infected relatives to the hospital, either by providing car-pooling or by being flexible about working hours.

The other key component of a workplace programme on AIDS is prevention – protecting the workforce through information, education, and support services including condom distribution and STD care. These are the elements I described earlier as the basis of AIDS prevention. Again, senior management are the key here. AIDS prevention simply will not happen without their commitment, and in some places their courage in overcoming resistance to the discussion of sex. All the top managers of the company must understand the full ramifications of the epidemic – its impact on society and on business, the kinds of approaches to AIDS prevention that do and do not work.

There are a number of ways to do prevention which complement each other. You can display posters that convey information about HIV and AIDS. In the old days, AIDS prevention messages tried to frighten people into safer sex. We learned that this backfires – it does not induce people to change their behaviour. It simply makes them afraid of persons *with* AIDS. It is better to motivate people to practise safer sex through positive messages than through fear. Get professional communicators and educators to develop the posters and messages, and ensure that they are consistent with the social and cultural norms of the workforce and of the surrounding community.

Secondly, you can organize AIDS education sessions. Remember, just one session will never do it. People need convincing;

and once they have adopted safer behaviour, they need help in maintaining it.

If workers are to turn up and really participate in AIDS education, you need to get their commitment. One way to do that is through trade union structures, where they exist. However you do it, get your employees on board. Staff will feel involved if they help define the content of the education programme. It also helps them to get over the taboos on discussing sexuality and STDs. Those who are particularly motivated and respected by their colleagues can act as peer educators. Remember the special prevention needs of women – an important and growing part of the workforce. And as part of your education programme, do not forget to encourage a supportive and caring attitude towards people with HIV and AIDS.

As I explained earlier, a crucial part of AIDS prevention is condom promotion. The point has got to be that the condom is a life-saving device – there is no need to be embarrassed by it. In Switzerland, a rather conservative country, a highly successful condom promotion campaign has increased condom use fivefold without offending the population. I am not suggesting that a condom be served up with every soft drink in the company cafeteria, but you *must* make sure that condoms are readily accessible to all your employees. Some firms offer them free, but whether you do or not, make sure they are easy to get – from a vending machine in the toilets, from the company stores, from your news stand, in whatever way is appropriate. Also, there is no point encouraging people to use condoms without explaining how to use them. There are many booklets with condom instructions available; WHO has one that can be used as is or adapted.

Another essential support service for all staff is good-quality STD treatment – whether through the company medical service or as part of a good health insurance scheme. I cannot stress this too strongly: AIDS education is not enough. Without condom promotion and services for STD treatment, a workplace programme will never have the desired effect.

No doubt there will be some employers who will ask, why should I bother setting up a prevention programme? Won't pre-employment blood screening of job applicants keep infected individuals out and prevent AIDS in my workforce? The answer is no. A decade of experience shows that compulsory testing cannot achieve AIDS prevention in the workplace any more than it can outside it. And it sends your workers the wrong message, too – that HIV can be stopped at the door of the factory or office. That is simply untrue, and it will undermine the real prevention messages of your education programme.

Testing merely distracts attention from the real issue, which is how to help your existing employees avoid exposure to HIV. After all, no matter how big your annual turnover is, it is small in comparison to your overall workforce. A simple calculation will show that most new infections in the firm are bound to turn up among existing employees. So that is where you need to put your energy and resources – into preventing *those* infections through education and supporting services. Do not throw money away on a lot of testing.

When the Royal Garden Resorts in Thailand stopped testing employees, its General Manager explains, 'We took the money we saved and invested it in STD treatment and free condoms for employees'. The outcome was a 50 per cent decline in STDs, which meant lower STD treatment costs (not to mention more protection from AIDS) plus a boost in staff morale – all at no extra cost to the company.

One other question often asked by employers is whether it will 'look bad' if they are seen to be undertaking AIDS prevention activities for their workforce. Companies involved in tourism or food services in particular worry that it will bring them bad publicity. Again, experience shows that this kind of backlash simply does not materialize, either among employees or among customers. On the contrary, it looks bad for a firm if it does not move quickly enough on prevention! A regional manager for Northwest Airlines recently told me about *his* experience in doing AIDS education in the workplace: 'My employees come up and thank me – they're grateful, they say, "my employer cares about me".'

Let me conclude by saying a few words about the international corporate response to AIDS. Given all that is at stake in bringing this runaway epidemic under control, what can and should be done by the major corporations – individually, as a community, nationally and internationally?

First, individually, corporations can do a lot at home, that is, right on their own premises. I have outlined the main components of workplace programmes aimed at prevention, non-discrimination, care and support. Do these in the right way and you will reap major benefits in terms of a healthier workplace with better morale, with all the financial savings that translates into. This is a clear win–win–win situation. Everyone wins: your employees, your firm, your stockholders, and therefore you as a manager.

Secondly, corporations can act as a community. Corporations have an unparalleled opportunity to get together and share information, skills and direction. Get involved in an existing business coalition, like the Thailand Business Coalition on AIDS or the US-based National Leadership Coalition on AIDS. Start a new coalition, if there is none near you. Or piggy-back on an existing corporate struc-

ture. The Confederation of Indian Industries is showing interest in dealing with AIDS issues and has approached us for collaboration on how they might structure themselves for this. WHO and a number of our partner agencies are in a position to be helpful to business coalitions. You can use our technical information, adapt our prototype materials for your policy and education activities. You can use us as an honest broker, as a bridge between the government and your business community. And we can support you in regional networking.

Thirdly, corporations can act as community citizens, whether at the local or national level. You can make precious contributions in kind to your national AIDS programme – to mass media campaigns, for example, if that happens to be your area of expertise. Some of the best-known advertising firms in the world have designed stunningly effective AIDS campaigns. Or you can make a cash contribution to get a national mass media campaign off the ground, as ten companies did in São Paulo, Brazil. You can sponsor sporting events and benefit dinners in your community. Real estate agencies might be able to offer a space to house, say, an AIDS counselling centre. Telecommunications and computer industries can provide their national AIDS programme with some badly needed equipment.

More broadly, the corporate sector can help shape the national response to AIDS. I am talking about your leadership role as individuals and as representatives of the private sector. In either case, you are in a position to help set the national AIDS agenda. For example, the Thailand Business Coalition on AIDS got a grant from the national government to hold a meeting bringing together the business community and the ministries of health and labour. They debated issues of HIV testing in the workplace and in this way made a major contribution to the shaping of national policy. Remember, businesses need to be involved in the national response to AIDS because, like it or not, they are involved in the national epidemic – and in the global one as well, if they do business overseas. No matter what kind of enterprise you have, there is no way to 'insulate' your corporation from AIDS and its ripple effects.

Finally, corporations can become an equal partner in the international response to AIDS. Let me be frank. This is no short-term emergency; AIDS and its repercussions will be with us for decades to come. The epidemic is simply too complex and reaches into too many areas of society to be brought under control by any one type of organization or profession or sector. Public health people must do their part, governments too, the United Nations agencies – but the private sector has got to be involved. I am not only talking about the programmes you are developing in your workplaces or about your corporate contributions to the community, whether local, national or international. I am talking about your role as movers and shakers, as opinion leaders, as pace-setters – as the people that others listen to. We cannot respond to AIDS without you, nor you without us.

Conclusion

Wherever you look, the response to AIDS has lagged behind the epidemic curve. 'It can't happen here', 'It won't be as bad as over there' – the excuses for delay are always the same. And I can testify to this personally – the delay is always regretted. Three or four years later, once the AIDS cases begin to accumulate, the top political figures tell me how bitterly they regret having delayed. But by then, dealing with the problem is harder and more expensive, and there is no going back. I appeal to the business community – do not allow this to happen. Get involved *now* in the response to AIDS. Do what you always do best – stay alert, be proactive, take the smart decisions early. I can only agree with the Vice-President of Robinson Department Store who said, 'When it comes to AIDS, a good business person may save more lives than a good doctor'. With business as equal partners, with a vigorous international corporate response, we have a real chance to get ahead of the epidemic. It is an opportunity we cannot afford to miss.

---

[1]Based on an address presented by Dr Michael Merson at an AETNA/WHO Asia AIDS seminar, Hong Kong, on 14 April 1994.

Towards a Standardized Framework for Costing HIV and AIDS Treatment and Care in Europe

Keith Tolley

School of Public Health/Department of Economics, University of Nottingham, England

Marlene Gyldmark

Danish Hospital Institute, Copenhagen, Denmark

Introduction

'It is a mark of the educated man and a proof of his culture that in every subject he looks for only so much precision as its nature permits or its solution requires.'

Aristotle

AIDS has become a major public health problem in Europe, and the social and economic burden of the disease is likely to expand. Naturally, most attention has been directed to the medical and human aspects of the disease. But as the disease spreads to affect more people in society the socio-economic aspects of AIDS grow in importance. Treatment and care for the ill together with preventive activities consume large amounts of resources, but often the total amounts are unknown. In addition, the outcome of these efforts is unknown or only partly documented.

The cost of HIV and AIDS healthcare has been examined in a number of countries in Europe. Unfortunately, because of the differences in methods used these estimates are difficult to interpret and compare. For example, what does the information about the cost of treating AIDS in Spain really convey unless it can be compared in a meaningful way to the costs of treating AIDS in Denmark or France? More accurate cost measurement using a standardized costing framework can enable improved planning of care budgets both on an individual country level and at a multinational scale involving organizations such as the EU. However, to achieve such goals requires common and acceptable methods to be adopted by each cost study. In this chapter we examine the need for more standardized method of costing treatment and care for HIV/AIDS and suggest some ways forward towards the development and implementation of standard methods.

Existing cost studies and problems of comparison

A review of eleven early European studies of the costs of health and social treatment and care for HIV/AIDS patients was carried out by Tolley and Gyldmark (1993).[1] These are presented in Table 1.[2] We are currently expanding and updating this

Study	Original price year	Average cost per person-year ($) [a,b]
UK		
Johnson *et al.* (1986)	1985	15,000
Rees (1990)	1989	4,600[i]–28,200[ii]
Tolley *et al.* (1991)	1989	1,700[i]–9,100[ii]
Germany		
Drummond and Davies (1988)	1987	22,300
Hanpft *et al.* (1990)	1986	3,100[i]–13,000[ii]
Exner-Frierfeld (1989)	1987	3,700
Netherlands		
Borleffs *et al.* (1990)	1987	2,000[i]–19,000[ii]
Belgium		
Lambert and Carrin (1990)	1988	21,900
Spain		
Ginestal (1990)[c]	1987	25,400*–27,800**
France		
Debeaupuis and Tcheriatchoukine (1987)	1986	22,300
Greece		
Hatzakis and Trichopoulos (1990)	1988	70,400

Cost figures inflated to 1990 prices and converted from local currency using national healthcare-specific price indices and health-specific purchasing power parities .

[a] All costs are for AIDS patients except Rees, Tolley *et al.* Hanpft *et al.* and Borleffs where: [i]HIV-positive and [ii]AIDS. Where determined, the high cost estimates for each study have been used.

[b] All costs are for hospital in-patient treatment and care except Tolley *et al.* (social care costs only); Gschrey-Duver *et al.* (out-patient costs).

[c] Costs for two regions in Spain were: *Aranzazu; **Basurto.

table to include more recent cost estimates. All cost estimates (presented as costs per person-year) were converted into 1990 US$ using healthcare-specific purchasing power parities (PPPs). PPPs are an adjustment to allow for differences in the cost of living between countries which should enhance the comparability of the cost estimates.

The HIV/AIDS cost estimates ranged between $1,700 (social care per HIV-positive person-year) to $28,200 (hospital care per AIDS person-year), with the exception of a Greek study which produced a PPP adjusted cost estimate for the hospital treatment and care of AIDS patients of $70,400 per person-year (Table 1). The estimates in Table 1 raise several questions. Why is the estimate for Greece so high? Is it possible to detect trends in costs over time from the estimates? Is the concentration of cost estimates (as found in the review) between US$19,000 to US$28,000 per person-year a reliable estimate of the costs of hospital care for HIV/AIDS patients across Europe?

Unfortunately, such questions cannot be easily answered based on evidence from the cost studies undertaken to date. The problem is that there are large differences in the methods used to estimate costs in each study, which means that any direct comparison of cost estimates is not possible, despite the use of PPPs. In addition, the costing methods used in several of the studies are of too low quality to be used for policy purposes.

While technological development, changes in treatment routines and in patient case-mix will contribute to changing cost estimates, these causes can only be adequately detected and documented if cost estimates are based on the application of standard methods. In addition, such an approach to costing would be useful for broader cost-effectiveness evaluations of new approaches to the treatment of HIV/AIDS, such as early intervention drug therapy.

The use of a standard costing framework does not mean that the production of cost estimates are calculated according to 'cook-book recipes', which would have limited use due to the differences in healthcare organization and data sources across European countries. However, there are a number of areas in costs studies where methodological variation can be minimized or eliminated.

These areas cover:

- the range of the cost components included;
- the stage of diagnosis and diagnostic definition used;
- the method of data collection;
- the methods used to estimate unit costs.

Each area is examined in more detail below.

The cost components included

A problem with comparing studies such as those in Table 1 is that they generally include different cost components. Studies of hospital care may for instance focus on in-patient care only while some also, or only, include out-patient services. Within these components differences exist in the resources included. Typical examples are the exclusion of certain groups of drugs or laboratory services. The range of cost components and resources included often depends on the availability of data, sometimes to the extent that data are excluded even if they are highly relevant to the purpose of the study.

Stage of diagnosis and diagnostic definition

Differences in the HIV/AIDS stage of diagnosis and diagnostic definition used limits the comparability of cost estimates from different studies The problem is to control for variations in the severity of illness and hence differences in resource use associated with the study populations that do not use the same HIV/AIDS staging classification. A number of possibilities exist. Most previous cost studies have used either the Centers for Disease Control and Prevention (CDC) classification of HIV infection based on four groups of clinical condition (Acute infection, asymptomatic infection, Persistent Generalized Lymphadenopathy and AIDS – various conditions, opportunistic or secondary infections) or a prior definition of HIV–ARC–AIDS based on CD4 cell count (Centers for Disease Control 1987). A diagnostic staging system rarely used for costing purposes is the Walter Reed Classification.[3]

More recently, attempts have been made to use more flexible diagnostic staging systems for cost estimation purposes such as the Severity Classification System for AIDS Hospitalizations (SCSAH), which has been demonstrated in the US context to control for differences in patient severity of illness and hence resource utilization.[4] However, the SCSAH has not been adequately tested in the European context – we know of only one study that has applied the system for costing purposes.[5] Recent research in the UK has been undertaken with a sample of HIV-positive haemophiliac patients in the UK to apply CD4 cell count as a simple proxy for severity of illness to examine cost variation at different stages of HIV/AIDS infection.[6] More work is required to compare and contrast the relative merits of CD4 cell count and SCSAH as staging systems for HIV/AIDS cost estimation.[7]

The costs of treatment and care vary according to stages of the disease, this being largely related to differences in severity of illness.[8] However, many studies only provide a mean cost estimate for an AIDS diagnosis. Ideally, a cost study should include the whole course of treatment, that is from diagnosis of HIV-positivity to death, to get a complete picture of resource use. This is difficult unless a database is constructed that contains daily registrations of resource use for all HIV/AIDS patients (or an appropriate random sample) from the onset of the disease until death. This type of information is not readily available in many places at the present but with the onset of computerized patient files this level of detail will hopefully exist in the near future.

Finally, it is useful in costing to distinguish between 'risk' groups and other patient socio-demographic characteristics such as income and race. A few studies (all from the USA) have indicated variations in hospital resource use between IDUs (injecting drug users) and non-IDUs, by socio-economic status, or sex. However, this evidence is all US based where studies have had the advantage of relatively large HIV/AIDS patient sample sizes.[9] There is a need to create a sufficiently large sample of HIV/AIDS patients in order to examine resource use and cost variations in a European context. This would require multi-centre studies at the national and international level, the constraint being the problem of coordinating and financing such an exercise.

Method of data collection

Variations in costs of treating HIV/AIDS patients also occur as a result of different methods of resource use data collection. The choice of study and method of data collection is characterized by two aspects:

1. The choice of a prospective or retrospective study design for data collection, and

2. Whether data is collected using a 'bottom–up' or 'top–down' approach.

Figure 1 summarizes this relationship and the options for data collection.

With regard to the choice between

Data collection method	Retrospective	Prospective
Top-down	Use of hospital ledger	Not possible
Bottom-up	Use of data in patient files	Resource use recorded for each patient

Figure 1
Data collection methods

prospective and retrospective data collection, retrospective data are more prone to flaws than prospectively collected data, other things being equal. The use of prospective methods enables the researcher to include relevant and significant cost components and to ensure high validity in the survey methods. These outputs are partly precluded in retrospective data collections. However, it is only worth the extra expense of conducting a prospective data collection exercise if the retrospective data available is of insufficient quality for the type of cost estimate required. For example, if the objective of the costing is to produce a one-off estimate of in-patient costs of direct medical care for AIDS patients then retrospective data using medical case notes may provide sufficient detail to be able to estimate costs per patient. For an assessment of overall costs (including the use of a wide range of in-patient and out-patient resources, diagnostic tests, medications, and so on) which can be updated, then prospective data collection is likely to be important.

The cost estimates presented in Table 1 were mostly based on retrospective data. Some of the studies included only patients who had died and therefore presented estimates of mean costs covering resource use from AIDS diagnosis to death. This means that cost estimates based on a sample of patients who have died are likely to be higher than estimates that included living patients, as costs of treatment and care tend to increase

rapidly in the final stage prior to death. Once again, a breakdown of costs by stage of AIDS will reduce this problem.

Different cost estimates can be produced depending on whether a bottom–up or top–down method of data collection has been used. This bottom–up method requires the registration of all relevant resource inputs at the individual patient level (alternative comparison units can be used such as bed-days, or hospital wards – however, the use of the individual patient level enables comparison of the costs per patient day/year or lifetime costs per patient). The top–down method is used to allocate aggregate resources or costs to specific comparison units such as costs per patient-year. For example, at its most aggregated level this approach might involve the allocation of total hospital costs to department or patient level. Use of the method requires that there is some pre-existing knowledge about the causal relationship between the cost per patient and total costs. A problem with the top–down approach is that the allocation can be somewhat arbitrary and does not easily enable the identification of differences in resource use between patients due to factors such as stage of diagnosis, severity of illness, sex and age.

While the bottom–up data collection can be used with either prospective or retrospective data collection, the top–down approach can only be employed retrospectively, that is, when the total costs are already known.

The main disadvantage with using the top–down approach is that it is relatively inflexible and the relationships between resource use/costs, care activities, and patient characteristics is only weakly defined. The main advantage is that it is relatively easy to administer and requires less time to carry out than data collection at individual patient level. In contrast, the bottom–up approach is flexible as it allows the researcher to include relevant cost components (especially if prospective data collection has been conducted) and to assess variations in resource use according to different patient characteristics. A disadvantage is that the method can be time consuming and expensive to carry out, especially if conducted prospectively. In addition, there are some resource items which cannot be exclusively attached to individual patients, such as hospital overheads. These can be averaged out across all patients, although this is a somewhat arbitrary allocation procedure, or identified as a separate cost. As patient files become more accessible (through computerized data files) and contain more detailed information, some of the disadvantages of the bottom–up approach should be reduced.

Unit cost estimation

Identifying appropriate unit costs to apply to resource items identified was a major problem in the studies reviewed in Table 1, and is a problem common in most economic evaluations of healthcare interventions. Ideally, the unit costs should reflect the opportunity cost of a resource – this is an important concept in economic analysis which incorporates the notion of scarcity of resources. A positive opportunity cost exists if a resource (time or materials) has an alternative worthwhile use from the one it is being employed in. For example, the provision of zidovudine (AZT) therapy to one group of patients means that that drug may not be available to other patients. As the supply of the drug is not limitless it has an opportunity cost. This could be valued using the market price of the drug. Similarly, the time of a social worker spent in consultation with a client with AIDS has an opportunity cost as that time cannot be used to provide a service for other client groups such as elderly people. Opportunity cost is difficult and maybe impossible to measure accurately, and so that best approximations have to be made. However, in many early HIV/AIDS costs studies (especially in USA) inadequate proxy methods have been used – such as the use of general per diem rates to represent unit costs. A per diem rate is a figure used to represent the average cost per bed day in a ward or hospital, but this charge is unlikely to reflect with much accuracy the cost of providing treatment and care for HIV/AIDS patients. The problem is that the calculation of per diem rates is usually based on a mix of patients and not a homogeneous group of AIDS or HIV-positive patients. Hospital charges have also been used to estimate the costs of individual resource items. General charges for an in-patient stay are unlikely to reflect the true cost of treating an HIV/AIDS patient as, for instance, they will not include all the diagnostic procedures and therapies required for HIV/AIDS treatment and care. Even charges that are available for specific resource items such as a diagnostic test or a medication should be applied cautiously and with consideration given as to the extent to which these represent the true cost of the resource.

Towards a standardized cost framework

A standard framework for costing HIV/AIDS treatment and care should ideally be flexible so that structural and context variation due to the method of service delivery or the type of healthcare system in existence can be identified, whilst eliminating or reducing methodological bias in cost estimates produced from different studies. The standard framework should also help the researcher and policy-makers to consider carefully the aim of the study and so design a costing approach that is appropriate to achieve the stated objectives.

A standardized framework for costing could include all services related to the care of HIV/AIDS patients. This would cover all medical treatment, preventive services, statutory social services and voluntary services, care provided by the family and partners of the person with HIV/AIDS (i.e. informal carers), general HIV education and information and research. However, this scope represents the final aim. We focus on a narrower objective in this chapter – the development of a standardized framework for estimating the direct costs of health and social care for people with HIV/AIDS.

The first stage in the development of a standardized framework is to outline the areas in which standards can most readily and profitably be applied. Preliminary analysis has identified three broad areas:

- the production of a checklist of standard cost categories that should be included in a cost study;
- a standardized approach to data collection;
- standard principles for estimating the unit cost of service use.

When deciding how to apply standard methods in each of these three areas it is important to have a clear image of the purpose of the study (what is the aim of the study and which agencies and costs are to be included). Therefore, it is only possible to deal with general issues in the use of a standardized framework, as the final structure when applied will depend on the objectives of the costs study. This is why it is important that the instrument is sufficiently flexible to deal with different study objectives. Many previous HIV/AIDS costs studies have lacked a carefully specified study objective or perspective and have consequently produced poor quality and vague cost estimates. A standardized framework should help in the specification of clear and achievable costing objectives. One feasible approach would be the construction of a 'decision tree' in which the three main decisions to be made by the researcher would be to define:

1. The purpose of the study – this could be a cost study or, for example, a cost-effectiveness analysis.
2. The perspective of the analysis – the analysis could be conducted from several perspectives (or combination of perspectives), the choice of which determines the range of cost components included in the study.
3. The time horizon for the study – the level of detail and reliability of the results are likely to depend on the time period planned for data collection. The researchers must decide whether to conduct an evaluation which is short term (less than one year of data collection), medium term (one to two years of data collection) or long term (more than two years of data collection). The choice depends on the time and money resources available for evaluation and pressure being applied by policy-makers for results.

The decision-tree approach for planning a costs study is illustrated in Figure 2. The combination of decisions made using the tree will help determine the precise costing methods that are best to use.

Each area of potential standardization outlined above will be examined in more detail below.

Standard checklist of cost components

As indicated in Figure 2 the choice of a perspective for the study determines which cost components should be included in the analysis. A study of the

Figure 2
Decision-tree approach for a costs analysis

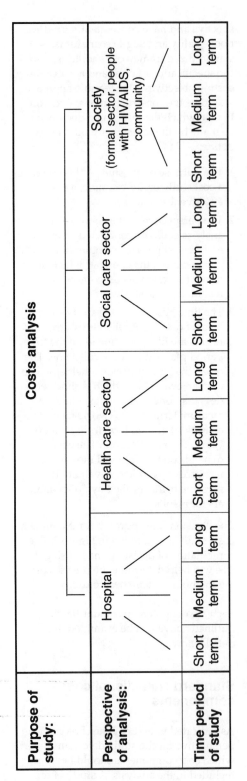

costs of health and social care from the society perspective would ideally include all possible cost components, for example costs to the hospital, social sector, personal costs incurred by the patients and family/partners. If costs were calculated from the perspective of the hospital only, medical costs would be included and not those incurred by patients and companions (e.g. time and travel to an out-patient clinic).

A standard checklist of cost components can be produced from which the appropriate costs for the perspective chosen in any HIV/AIDS cost study can be selected. The selected cost components should be explicitly listed so that it is possible to identify the range included to help comparisons with cost estimates from other studies. However, the choice should not only be determined by the purpose and perspective of a study. Special circumstances at the study site will also have an influence. For example, some drugs or services for HIV/AIDS patients may not be available in every country. In Denmark, for instance, voluntary work and informal care is a relatively small part of the care provided to HIV/AIDS patients while this service is much more important in the UK. Therefore, it is important to use a standard checklist of cost components as a guide and to explicitly indicate why and when a cost component is excluded or included in the cost calculation.

Standard methods for data collection

The next stage in the production of cost estimates for the care of HIV/AIDS patients is to determine the most appropriate and reliable method for data collection. Drawing on our discussion above the basic choices are whether to collect resource use data prospectively or retrospectively and whether to use a bottom–up or top–down approach to costing. Once again, it is important to consider the purpose and perspective of the analysis in deciding which approach to adopt.

For example, if the purpose of the study is to examine past trends in the cost of treatment and care and compare this with present costs then the estimates should be based on retrospective data. The data collection methods can be either top–down or bottom–up, depending on data availability. Patient medical records are frequently used for costing treatment and care. The quality and scope of these are therefore often crucial in the choice of data collection approach – if they are difficult to use and are not computerized and miss important resource information, then a top–down approach is likely to be necessary.

The perspective of the analysis will also influence the choice of data collection method. If the perspective of the study is the society then a bottom–up approach should be used as much of the relevant resource use data, for instance personal costs incurred by patients and family, cannot be obtained using a top–down approach.

Proponents of the top–down approach emphasize its easy and fast application, and use for estimating total current costs which is relevant for financial planning. However, the bottom–up approach, by focusing only on specific resource inputs used by each patient in the study, provides a better basis for examining the factors causing actual variations in average and marginal costs per patient and in total costs. In addition, the bottom–up approach facilitates the more precise monitoring of resource use data and so should, if carried out properly, provide more reliable and valid data. Therefore, careful use of the bottom–up approach enables the costs of treatment and care to be estimated with much greater accuracy than through the top–down approach.

A further consideration is whether efforts should be made to develop a centralized resource use database such as the DMI2 HIV/AIDS database in France.[10] This is a computerized system set up by the Ministry of Health to collect resource use data for HIV/AIDS hospital care from 42 hospitals across France. Such a system certainly has advantages in increasing the number of HIV/AIDS patients for whom standard data on resource use is collected. However, the cost and complexity of organizing and running the system may reduce its acceptability in other countries in Europe (however, a study is currently being funded to examine the feasibility of a central resource use and monitoring system for HIV/AIDS hospital care in the UK). In the development of any centralized resource use database for HIV/AIDS a key concern should be to ensure patient confidentiality is not breached.

Unit cost measurement

Use of the bottom–up approach poses particular problems in identifying appropriate unit costs to apply to the resource use data collected. The general principle that should be used in costing units of resource use is to calculate the opportunity cost (i.e. the alternative use value) of using these inputs for the treatment and care of HIV infected and AIDS patients. The problem with identifying relevant opportunity costs is that they critically depend on the study context and local circumstances. Whilst, as we pointed out earlier in this chapter, accurate estimation of opportunity costs is likely to be, in practice, an unrealistic objective, adherence by new cost studies to a standard set of principles for costing resource inputs would assist comparability and reduce the possibility of use of arbitrary or misleading unit costs.

One such principle is that the market price or charge for each type of resource input should be assessed to determine whether it offers a reasonable approximation of opportunity cost, for example hourly salary rate, drug prices. Using such data ideally requires competitive resource markets where prices are not artificially negotiated or otherwise distorted.

In any costs study if a set of prices has been used to estimate unit costs there should be a clear indication of their source and whether they include overheads or other fixed costs. There is no general rule for the inclusion of the latter as this will again depend upon the purpose and perspective of the study. For example, if the perspective adopted is that of the clinical department providing treatment and care and the costs estimates produced are to be used for internal charging purposes then overheads should not be included in the estimates. If the perspective is that of the hospital then it would be necessary to include overheads and hospital fixed costs. However, it is always advisable to report overheads and fixed costs separately in order to improve the comparability of studies.

Important to note is that per diem and aggregated hospital charge data should not be applied to estimate the costs of HIV/AIDS treatment and care without extreme caution. In every case they should be explicitly justified and, if necessary, adjusted to more adequately reflect the real cost of HIV/AIDS care. Profit motives, varying accounting and reimbursement practices can mean the use of per diems and hospital charges are unlikely to represent a good proxy of opportunity cost.

A further principle is that in evaluations where it is possible to examine the expansion (or contraction) of services, attention should be given to the identification of the marginal costs of treating additional HIV/AIDS patients. For example, if the capacity of a hospital was increased to provide beds for an additional ten AIDS patients, the marginal cost would be the extra cost of the additional doctor and nurse workload, additional procedures and medication and new capital costs (for example, if a new ward had to be converted). By examining marginal costs the extra resource requirements could be identified.

A standard framework

A preliminary and illustrative standard framework for cost studies is provided in Figure 3.[11] The rationale behind this model is to use the bottom–up approach which we feel will provide the most accurate and reliable cost estimates. This framework can be linked with the decision tree analysis of Figure 2 to provide a more complete guide to the requirements of an efficient approach to costing HIV/AIDS treatment and care. Almost all of the discussion above has related to the costing of hospital treatment and care, where most effort has been directed to date, and most scope exists for applying a standardized framework. However, Figure 3 includes a recognition of the importance of estimates of social care costs. Social care and informal care is used by people from across the spectrum of HIV/AIDS stages and is likely to represent a growing proportion of total care costs up to the next century. More emphasis needs to be given to the production of social care costs for HIV/AIDS in Europe.

Indirect cost estimation

A separate issue from the evaluation of the direct costs of treatment and care is the relevance of an assessment of indirect costs. HIV/AIDS has the potential to cause a major loss of human and economic productivity through premature death and morbidity – an assessment of the indirect cost can indicate how significant this loss could be. Owing to the seriousness and prolonged course of the

Figure 3
Illustrative standard cost framework:
Treatment and care for people with HIV infection or AIDS

Cost categories	Agencies involved	Type of cost	Type of resource	No. of units per patient per year	x	Unit cost measure	Total = cost
Hospital In-patient • AIDS unit • Intensive Care unit • Other wards / Out-patient • Day care • Other service	Health services	Direct	*Staff time* e.g. nursing doctors ancillary	[hours per day x in-patient stay; visits to out-patient x hours per visit]	x	[Salary or wage]	=$$
			Non-staff input e.g. medication (AZT) diagnostic tests other lab tests other drugs	[amounts/doses provided]	x	[Market or shadow price]	=$$
Other hospital		General	*Overheads...* hotel costs/ admin./ training	[apportionment]	x	[Unit cost]	=$$
General Practitioner *Other community medical services* • AIDS/STD clinic • Physiotherapy • Specialist services • Home nursing	Health services	Direct	*Staff*	[visits x hours per visit]	x	[Salary or wage]	=$$
			Non-staff	[amounts]	x	[Market or shadow price]	=$$
	Voluntary sector	General	*Overheads...* hotel costs/ admin./ training	[apportionment]	x	[Unit cost]	=$$
Social care/support • Domiciliary care • Residential • Other formal • Social support	Social Services	Direct	*Staff time* e.g. Social Workers Home Helps Occupational Therapists	[visits/use x hours per use]	x	[Salary or wage]	=$$
			Non-staff input e.g. home adaptation grants	[amounts provided]	x	[Market or shadow price]	=$$
		General	*Overheads...* hotel costs/ admin./ training	[apportionment]	x	[Unit cost]	=$$
Informal care	Partners/ Relatives	Direct	*Caring time*	[hours per day x days]	x	[Value of personal time]	=$$
			Travel and other expenses	[amounts e.g. hours travelling]	x	[Market price e.g. fare]	=$$
	Volunteers	Intangible	e.g. stress	[amounts]	x	[Shadow price]	=$$

This framework is not comprehensive of all possible categories, but is illustrative of the main cost sectors. In addition, it excludes the direct costs of prevention, research, information provision, non-patient specific counselling and so on. Intangible costs other than to informal carers and indirect costs (productivity losses/gains) have been excluded.

disease there are considerable cost consequences related to absence from the labour market, from participation in other socially worthwhile activities and loss of human life. In the US Scitovsky and Rice in a paper published in 1987 estimated an indirect cost for AIDS in 1991 of $55.6 billion (1984 prices),[12] although it is now generally recognized that this was an overestimate. No attempt has been made to estimate indirect costs for Europe or a linked body of countries such as those within the EU. A few of the chapters in this book contain attempts to estimate indirect costs in individual countries in Europe, although these are limited in scope. How valuable is it to produce an assessment of the indirect costs of HIV/AIDS in Europe or the EU?

One problem is that the identification and measurement of indirect costs is very difficult. In previous evaluations of the cost of illness due to different diseases it has only been possible to calculate crude estimates using simplistic methods such as the 'human capital' approach.[13] This is an attempt to measure total lost economic productivity by multiplying the working life years lost due to premature mortality or morbidity by expected foregone earnings, representing a proxy for lost productivity. The few evaluations that have attempted to measure the indirect costs of AIDS have adopted a form of this approach rather than attempting to measure the value of loss of social productivity and personal loss.

Assessment of indirect costs is dependent on the structure of the economy. In developing countries the loss of economic productivity due to HIV/AIDS is of great importance. This is because AIDS has had a larger overall impact across a wider cross-section of society including the most educated and skilled members of the population.[14] Using macroeconomic modelling techniques, predictions have been made that at worst the GDP of Tanzania will have been reduced by 15–25 per cent as a result of AIDS by the year 2010.[15] In the developed European countries, however, the current and future impact on economic productivity, is not so obvious, and it is not certain whether, given the crude methods used to estimate indirect costs, it provides useful information for planning HIV/AIDS treatment and care and prevention programmes. With this aim in mind priority should be given to producing better estimates of the costs of treatment and care and subsequently the assessment of the cost-effectiveness of different health and social care strategies for HIV/AIDS. Indirect cost estimation would be of greater benefit in the European context if losses of social productivity and human loss could be estimated.

Conclusion

As the quotation of Aristoteles at the beginning of this chapter stated, it is important to find a balance between precision and relevant considerations such as the use to which the information is going to be applied. Naturally, we want cost estimates to be as precise as possible but there is a limit to the price that should be paid in terms of cost and effort of data collection and unit costing. In the future we may be able to obtain greater precision throughout Europe through better computerized medical records but given the inherent problems in the calculation of costs, 100 per cent exactness in estimates will never be attained. However, this should not prevent the development of approaches that can help produce more reliable HIV/AIDS treatment and care cost estimates for comparison across sites and the analysis of cost trends.

The purpose of this chapter has been to present the need for a standardized approach to the estimation of HIV/AIDS treatment and care costs to help achieve greater precision and policy value. The standardized framework should be developed and applied in new studies in Europe to ensure that the twin objectives of minimum standards of quality and comparability are obtained. Comparability is of no use unless the cost estimate is based on a minimum acceptable level of quality. Whilst the focus of this chapter and previous cost studies has been on the cost of hospital care, it is important that the standardized framework is also developed to assist in the production of reliable cost estimates for out-of-hospital health and social care provided by the statutory agents and the voluntary sector. We will be turning our attention to this issue in the next stage of research.

A standard approach will help improve the cost estimates and enhance comparison of results from different cost studies. Moving towards this goal will enable better planning of resources for HIV/AIDS treatment and care at individual hospital/community, region, state or organizational (e.g. EU) levels. In addition, these estimates will be useful as a basis for cost projections at the individual country or EU level, using an appropriate epidemiological modelling technique such as scenario analysis to estimate the future prevalence and incidence of HIV/AIDS.[16] The authors are currently involved in an EU funded project to assess the feasibility of a standardized framework for cost estimation and projection in member countries, and are participating in EU sponsored research coordinated by the National Institute of Public Health and Environmental Protection in The Netherlands to examine the development of multinational scenarios of the economic impact of AIDS in Europe (see the chapter by Jager *et al.* in this book).

---

1 K. Tolley and M. Gyldmark, 'The treatment and care costs of people with HIV infection or AIDS: development of a standardized cost framework for Europe', *Health Policy*, 24, pp. 55–70, 1993.

2 Studies in Table 2:

A. Johnson, M.W. Adler and J.M. Crown, 'The Acquired Immunodeficiency Syndrome and epidemic of infection with human immunodeficiency virus: costs of care and prevention in an inner London district', *British Medical Journal*, 293, pp. 489–92, 1986.

M. Rees, 'Methodological and practical issues in estimating the direct costs of AIDS/HIV: England and Wales', *AIDS: The Challenge for Economic Analysis* (eds. M. Drummond and L. Davies), pp. 69–75. Health Services Management Centre, University of Birmingham.

K. Tolley, D. Robinson and A. Maynard, *HIV–AIDS and Social Care*, Discussion Paper 81. Centre for Health Economics, University of York, 1991.

M. Drummond and L. Davies, 'Treating AIDS: the economic issues', *Health Policy*, 10, pp. 1–19, 1988.

R. Hanpft, F. Reinecke and F. Beske, 'Comparing in-patient and out-patient costs for HIV, LAS and AIDS: methodology, results and consequences from a study in Germany', *Economic Aspects of AIDS and HIV Infection* (eds. D. Schwefel *et al.*), pp. 164–72. Springer-Verlag, Berlin, 1990.

H. Exner-Freisfeld and E.B. Helm, 'Ambulatory and in-patient costs for diagnosis and therapy of one AIDS patient at the Frankfurt University Clinic', *Öffentliche Gesundheitswesen*, 51, pp. 12–16, 1989.

J.C.C. Borleffs, J.C. Jager, M.J.J.C. Poos, M.G.W. Dijkgraaf, R.M.A. Geels, H. Vrehen and A.J.P. Schrijvers, 'Hospital costs for patients with HIV infection in a University Hospital in The Netherlands', *Health Policy*, 16, pp. 43–54, 1990.

J. Lambert and G. Carrin, 'Direct and indirect costs of AIDS in Belgium: a preliminary analysis', *Economic Aspects of AIDS and HIV Infection* (eds. D. Schwefel *et al.*), pp. 151–60. Springer-Verlag, Berlin, 1990.

J. Ginestal, 'The regional cost of AIDS in Spain', *Economic Aspects of AIDS and HIV Infection* (eds. D. Schwefel *et al.*), pp. 195–203. Springer-Verlag, Berlin, 1990.

J. Debeaupuis and J. Tcheriatchoukine, *Report on the cost of hospital treatment for AIDS*. Inspectorate General of Social Affairs, Paris, 1987.

A. Hatzakis and D. Trichopoulos, *AIDS: The Challenge for Economic Analysis*, pp. 75–81. Health Services Management Centre, University of Birmingham, 1990.

3 R.R. Redfield, D.C. Wright, E.C. Tramont, 'The Walter Reed staging classification for HTLV-III/LAV infection', *New England Journal of Medicine*, 314, p. 131, 1986.

4 B.J. Turner, J.V. Kelly and J.K. Ball, 'A severity classification system for AIDS hospitalizations', *Medical Care*, 27, 4, pp. 423–37, 1986.

5 A. Tramarin, F. Milocchi, K. Tolley, A. Vaglia, F. Marcolini, V. Manfrin and F. De Lalla, 'An economic evaluation of home care assistance for AIDS patients: a pilot study in a town in Northern Italy', *AIDS*, 6, pp. 1377–83, 1992.

6 J. Kennelly, A. Ghani, K. Tolley, C. Sabin, A. Maynard and C. Lee , 'Costs of treating haemophilic patients with HIV infection',

report to the Department of Health. Royal Free Hospital, London, 1994.

7 K. Tolley, A. Ghani, J. Kennelly, C. Lee, A. Tramarin, F. De Lalla, *Comparing the Costs of HIV/AIDS Treatment and Care: Examining the Relationship between Diagnostic Stages and Costs*, 'International Conference on the Econometrics of AIDS', University of Barcelona, Spain, 2–3 December 1993.

8 J.V. Kelly, J.K. Ball and B.J. Turner, 'Duration and costs of AIDS hospitalizations in New York. Variations by patient severity of illness and hospital type', *Medical Care*, 27, 12, pp. 1085–98, 1989.

9 C. Dismuke, B.F. Kiker, V.G. Sharif and R.P. Wilder, 'Economic aspects of hospital care for HIV/AIDS patients', paper presented at 'Health Economists Study Group', University of Newcastle, 6-8 July 1994.

V. Mor, J.A. Fleshman, M. Dresser and J. Piette, 'Variation in health service use among HIV infected patients', *Medical Care*, 30, 1, pp. 17–29, 1992.

10 G. Bez, E. Andre, J.M. Nadal, I. Tortay, R. Demeulemeester, M. Legrand and C. Pradier, 'DMI2: an information system built around the patient', poster PO-C26-3240, *IXth International Conference on AIDS*, Berlin, 6–11 June 1993.

11 K. Tolley and M. Gyldmark, 'The treatment and care costs of people with HIV infection or AIDS: development of a standardized cost framework for Europe', *Health Policy*, 24, pp. 55–70, 1993.

12 A.A. Scitovsky and D.P. Rice, *Estimates of the Direct and Indirect Costs of Acquired Immunodeficiency Syndrome in the United States, 1985, 1986 and 1991*, Public Health Reports, 102, 1, pp. 5–17, 1987.

13 D.P. Rice, *Estimating the Cost of Illness*. Department of Health, Education and Welfare, Publication No. 947-6, US Government Printing Office, Washington DC, 1966.

14 M. Ainsworth and M. Over, *The Economic Impact of AIDS: Shocks, Responses and Outcomes*, Technical Working Paper No. 1. The World Bank Africa Technical Department, Population, Health and Nutrition Division, Washington, USA, 1992.

15 J.T. Cuddington, 'Modelling the macroeconomic effects of AIDS, with an application to Tanzania', *The World Bank Economic Review*, 7, 2, pp. 173–89, 1993.

16 M.J. Postma, R. Leidl, A.M. Downs, J.

3Rovira, K. Tolley, M. Gyldmark and J.C. Jager, 'Economic impact of the AIDS epidemic in the European Community: towards multi-national scenarios on hospital care and costs', *AIDS*, 7, pp. 541–53, 1993.

Assessment of the Socio-economic Impact of AIDS: From National Towards Multinational Scenarios

Dr Johannes Jager and Dr Maarten Postma

National Institute of Public Health and Environmental Protection (RIVM), The Netherlands

Keith Tolley

University of Nottingham, England

Jo Kennelly

Royal Free Hospital and School of Medicine, London, England

The development of HIV-related health-care policies requires an international and multidisciplinary approach. An example of this is scenario analysis which combines epidemiological, health service, social, economic and biomedical research.[1] Mathematical modelling contributes to scenario construction and enables the projections of future impacts on society to be made.

To date, impact scenarios have largely been confined to regional and national projections with little use multinationally.[2] Workshops, however, have been held throughout Europe[3] and by WHO[4] to explore the construction of multinational impact scenarios, and a partial impact assessment for the European Union (EU) as a whole has been undertaken.[5] Further, it has been shown for multinational impact assessments that the use of standardized methods for the collection, processing and presentation of information on costs is very important.[6]

The aim of this chapter is to identify the important issues that will emerge in attempts to move on from the use of scenario analysis at the national level to the multinational level, such as the EU. The aim of this research is to produce three sets of multinational scenarios for HIV/AIDS: epidemiological scenarios, economic impact scenarios and socio-cultural impact scenarios. We begin by looking at current HIV/AIDS scenario methods. This is followed by a brief look at findings from research to develop socio-economic impact scenarios for The Netherlands and preliminary work at the EU level. In the final section, we address the methodological and practical issues in the further development of scenario analysis at the multinational level, namely the EU.

There are three basic steps undertaken in scenario analysis: building a conceptual model, defining baseline analyses and specification of basic variables and indicators (scenario construction) (Figure 1).

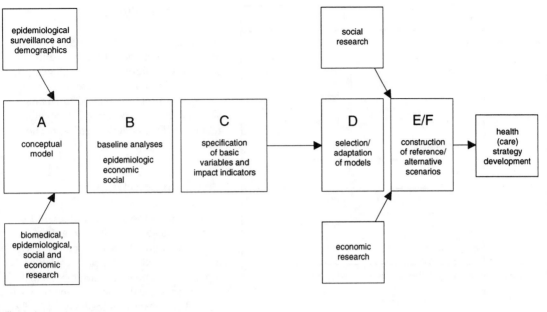

Figure 1
Contextual frame for AIDS scenario studies
A–F: the main steps of the analysis (see text) [After
Jager & Van den Boom (1)]

Conceptual model

The purpose of the conceptual model is to
identify the important components to be
studied and their likely interrelationships.
The conceptual basis of scenario analysis
is given in Figure 2. Here, the relationship
between the central components –
HIV/AIDS and society – is modelled.
Risk behaviour is seen as the basic determinant of infection and prevention is
aimed at avoidance of further HIV cases.
Medical treatment and care are shown to
influence the course of the epidemic. The
conceptual model indicates the main
requirements for baseline analysis and
scenario construction.

Figure 2
**Conceptual model for the Dutch AIDS scenario
study** [After Van den Boom *et al.* (2)]

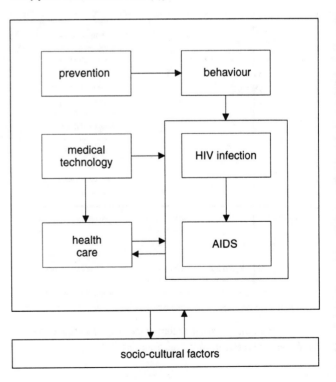

basic variable		indicator
epidemiology	behaviour	
	group size	HIV/AIDS incidence
	transmission probability	prevalence
	number of partners	– for 'overall' epidemic
	effects of prevention	– for subepidemics
	progression	
		mortality
	incubation time	potential years of life lost
	survival time	
economics	per person-year health care use	patient-related
	per person-year corresponding costs	hospital bed need
	organization of care	
		hospital costs: – care – treatment – medicines (AZT) – out-patient
		nursing home costs
		hours/costs of care: – district nurse – general practitioner – home help
		out-patient drugs
		general programme costs: – of testing – of other prevention – of research
socio-cultural	socio-sexological aspects	attitudes towards sexuality
	AIDS control options	societal response
	(psycho-) social aspects of care	discrimination/tolerance
	prevention strategy	access to social facilities

Table 1 **Basic variables and indicators in the fields of epidemiology, economics and sociology** [After: Van den Boom et al. (2)]

Baseline analysis

Baseline analysis is the collection of relevant epidemiological, economic and socio-cultural information for developing HIV/AIDS impact scenarios in these three fields over a set time period. Such analysis has been undertaken in the development of AIDS impact scenarios in The Netherlands to the year 2000.[7]

Scenario construction

Table 1 shows the basic variables and impact indicators involved in epidemiological, economic and socio-cultural scenario construction. The basic variables represent independent variables whilst the impact indicators are dependent variables. This means that the basic variables are expected to have different independent effects on the impact indicators. By varying the basic variables a range of impact scenarios can be produced. The conceptual model defines the relationship between the basic variables and impact indicators (i.e. between the independent and dependent variables). Using this approach the development of scenarios basically involves the use of 'what if' studies. For example, '*what* happens to future HIV incidence and AIDS mortality *if* transmission probability increases or decreases by x, y or z per cent.' Currently, several models for HIV/AIDS epidemiology are available.[8]

An epidemiological scenario, by providing estimates of the future pattern of HIV prevalence and incidence, provides the basis for producing economic and socio-cultural scenarios. The two main methods of linking epidemiological information with economic and socio-cultural data are the *incidence-based* and *prevalence-based* ones. Incidence-based modelling accounts all future consequences to the year of first occurrence; for example, potential years of life lost (PYLL) are designated to the year of death of an AIDS patient. Prevalence-based modelling designates the consequences to the year in which they occurred; for example, hospital costs are accounted to the relevant budget-year.

After selecting and building suitable epidemiological models the construction of a *reference* scenario and *alternative* epidemiological, economic and socio-cultural scenarios can be started. The reference scenario is based on the assumption of unchanged developments as described by baseline analysis. Therefore, the intensity of preventive efforts, its effectiveness, the epidemiological course of HIV infection, therapies, treatments and the effects of the latter two on disease progression are all assumed to remain stable over time. In addition, the absence of an effective vaccine in the future is assumed. In alternative scenarios the effects of deviations from the baseline parameter values, assumed in the reference scenario, are studied. For example, the impact on HIV prevalence of changes in risk behaviour, intensifying use of preventive methods, increasing efficacy of prevention techniques, changes in the incubation period of the disease, the introduction of new medications and therapy, and shifts in patterns of care (e.g. substitution of outpatient services for in-patient admissions) can be examined. From this analysis different scenarios can be used to examine a variety of economic and socio-cultural scenarios. At this point it should be stressed that scenarios differ from predictions and forecasts as they allow several possible impacts to be examined, whereas the latter focus on the production of only the most likely outcome.

There is a lack of empirical evidence with which to build reference and alternative scenarios. Hence the approach currently adopted is to identify the most recent data available from the scientific literature and to consult experts in the fields of mathematical modelling, epidemiology, health economics and social sciences.

Costs

In calculating the economic impact of AIDS the emphasis we have adopted in scenario analysis has been to focus on direct patient-related medical care costs incurred in the health system. The impact of non-medical (e.g. life insurance), general programme (e.g. research, prevention, public information, HIV testing facilities) and indirect costs[9] for HIV/AIDS has yet to be assessed fully using scenario analysis. These are important areas of future research. In the following section all costs have been presented in 1993 ECUs.

Economic scenario results

National scenarios – The Netherlands

In this section we examine in detail three health service cost impact scenarios to the year 2000 derived from the Dutch AIDS Study.[10] The first scenario is the *reference scenario* (R) based on unchanged epidemiological and social environment conditions during the 1990s (compared to the late 1980s). Therefore, for this scenario we assumed the prevalence of HIV-infection, the intensity and effectiveness of prevention initiatives, treatment patterns and the social environment would remain stable over time. The other two scenarios represent the alternative scenarios. We define one of these as the *subscenario* model (S). This describes a situation in which there are *no* new cases of infection between 1990 and 2000 so that the number of AIDS cases at any one time in the future is derived only from those persons infected before 1990. This means that the subscenario actually represents a part of the reference scenario.[11] The other alternative scenario we define as the *therapy* scenario (T) which demonstrates the consequences of prolonging mean survival by one year during the AIDS stage due to improvements in therapy from the year 1992. Both alternative scenarios should be compared to the pattern represented by the reference scenario.

The production of the health service cost scenarios requires a baseline estimate of the costs of HIV/AIDS medical care costs. The large proportion of the medical costs of HIV/AIDS in The Netherlands are related to the provision of hospital treatment and care. In The Netherlands, hospital resource use and costs data for HIV/AIDS have been collected through a prospective study conducted from 1987 at the University Hospital Utrecht (AZU).[12] This study has provided estimates of hospital costs per person-year (Table 2). The mean cost of 'hospital care', defined as inpatient stay costs such as nursing care, meals, general drug therapy, has been estimated at 8,940 ECUs per-person-year for the CDC-IV stage (AIDS), and 312 ECUs for CDC-II/III stage (pre-AIDS).[13] The mean cost of 'hospital cure', defined as consultations, specific AIDS drugs, diagnostic procedures, transfusions, etc, was estimated at 7,870 ECUs per person-year for the CDC-IV stage, and 2,990 ECUs for CDC-II/III stage (1993 prices). Cost estimates for other health service components have been produced in Table 2 – these represent the best estimates available from the literature, but are crude approximations. The details of the unit cost data used to derive the cost estimates in Table 2 are provided elsewhere.[14]

Table 2
Assumptions for healthcare utilization in various sectors per person year of AIDS (unless stated otherwise) in terms of resource use and monetary costs (in 1993 ECUs)
[After: Van den Boom et al. (3)]

Sector	Resource use estimate	Monetary costs (ECUs)
Hospital care	28.9 days[a]	8940[a]
	1.5 days[b]	312[b]
Hospital cure	various[a]	7870[a]
	various[b]	2990[b]
Nursing home	3.0 days	375
District nurse	10.5 hours	540
Home help	20.5 hours	615
Intensive home care	0.6 hours	65
Early treatment with zidovudine[b]	500 mg/day	4120
General practitioner	10 consultations	280
	6 consultations[c]	120[c]

[a]   Figure referring to CDC-IV
[b]   Figure referring to CDC-II/III
[c]   Figure referring to pre-AIDS.
      For early treatment, only information on zidovudine costs is available.

This cost data, disaggregated where possible by CDC stage, is used in each of the three scenarios R, S and T. For the reference scenario, linking the epidemiological data with the cost data from Table 2 produces an estimate of 39,800 ECUs for total medical care costs in The Netherlands in 1993 (Figure 3).[15] The costs of hospital care and treatment represent the main share at 85 per cent. Of the non-hospital costs only early treatment with zidovudine is a significant share at 9.5 per cent. The reference scenario estimates for 1995 and 2000 are 45,600 ECUs and 53,100 ECUs respectively.

These cost scenarios can be compared with those produced by the two alternative scenarios. Applying the same cost estimates in Table 2 to the S and T scenarios produces the pattern illustrated in Figure 3. In 1995 there are relatively small differences between the three scenario outcomes. By 2000 the S scenario produces an estimate of 31,000 ECUs, whilst the comparable estimate of costs for the T scenario is 58,900 ECUs. These provide the upper and lower bounds for the range of costs estimated to occur under different epidemiological assumptions up to the year 2000.

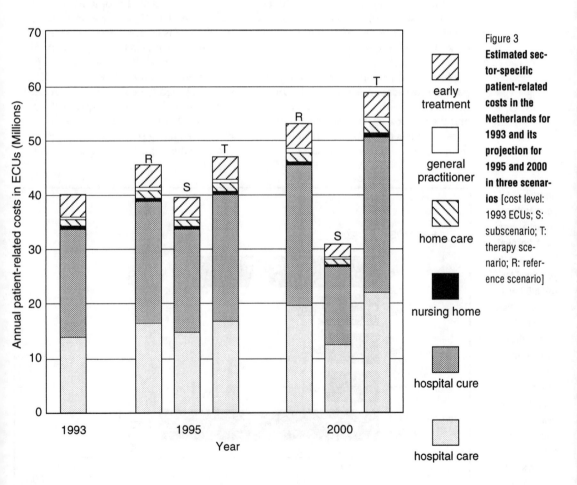

Figure 3
Estimated sector-specific patient-related costs in the Netherlands for 1993 and its projection for 1995 and 2000 in three scenarios [cost level: 1993 ECUs; S: subscenario; T: therapy scenario; R: reference scenario]

Closer examination of the cost patterns within each scenario reveal some interesting trends. All the scenarios demonstrate a decrease in the proportion of total costs represented by early treatment with zidovudine, General Practitioner costs and hospital treatment costs and an increase in hospital care costs and home care costs between 1993 and 2000. Nursing home care is estimated to have only a limited but stable impact on costs (of approximately 1 per cent of total costs) in all three scenarios. The cost patterns are solely due to differences in the epidemiological developments contained within each scenario. For example, the Dutch Government policy of substituting home care for hospital admission might be expected to further increase the share related to home care up to 2000.[16]

We have conducted further work to compare the cost scenarios for HIV/AIDS medical care with total healthcare costs, and the use of scenario analysis to compare estimates of HIV/AIDS hospital resource utilization with that for other

diseases in The Netherlands. We only present the results here – further details of methodology and assumptions used are provided in Postma et al.[17] Our scenarios indicate that HIV/AIDS medical care costs in The Netherlands are likely to be at least 0.18 per cent of total healthcare costs in 2000, but could be as much as 0.34 per cent. Figure 4 demonstrates that the impact of AIDS on hospital resource use is not expected to overtake other major diseases by the year 2000. Using hospital beds as an indicator of resource use to compare projections for different diseases, our analysis for The Netherlands has indicated a potential bed need for HIV/AIDS of 200 beds in 2000. In comparison, bed need for each of lung cancer, diabetes and pneumonia is estimated at approximately 600–700. The largest bed need is concentrated in the diseases of the circulatory system with up to 2,600 beds and 2,200 beds projected to be needed for coronary heart disease and stroke respectively in the year 2000. Other research we have conducted using scenario analysis to examine the impact of AIDS on the life

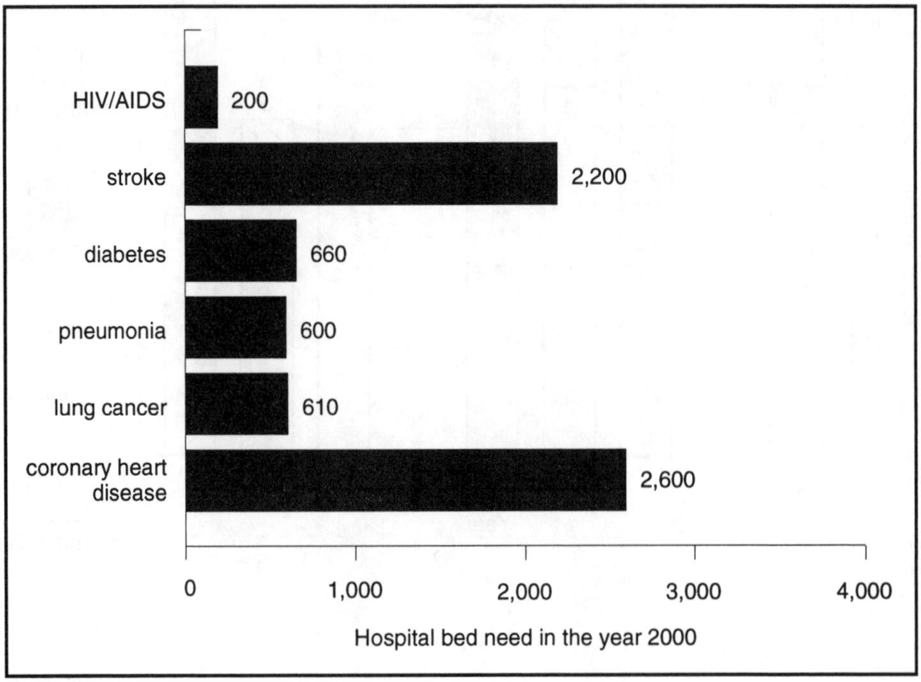

Figure 4
Comparative impact assessment: hospital bed need in the year 2000 for HIV/AIDS and five other diseases in The Netherlands.
[Source: Academic Hospital Utrecht for HIV/AIDS; SIG Health Care Information (Utrecht) for other diseases; data processed by authors]

insurance market in The Netherlands is presented elsewhere.[18]

Multinational scenarios

Whilst our work on the production of R, S and T scenarios for one country, The Netherlands, was conducted we also undertook preliminary work on the production of multinational scenarios to assess the impact of AIDS in the EU.[19] In this research scenarios are developed in which the spread of infection is simulated by a population dynamic model described in detail elsewhere.[20] In this, the EU population is divided into two groups according to risk of infection (high risk and low risk) which produces two alternative scenarios: L a low prevalence scenario with a constant survival time for AIDS of two years assumed, and H a high prevalence scenario with an assumed survival time estimated at three years (this

assumption increases prevalence). Scenarios of hospital cost are modelled by linking epidemiological simulations, based on available surveillance data, to estimates of patient-related costs available from European literature. Scenarios of hospital costs are made using a prevalence-based procedure which has the effect of producing higher future cost outcomes when linked with longer survival time as in scenario H. For estimating PYLL (potential years of life lost) an incidence-based procedure is used: that is, PYLL is accounted to the actual year of death.

Scenarios of hospital bed need, hospital costs and PYLL are presented for 1993 in Table 3. Baseline estimates of bed need and hospital treatment and care for full-blown AIDS were derived from European literature. Minimum and maximum estimates in the year 2000 for the L and H scenarios are based on current in-patient -day estimates

Cost category	indicator	year	scenario	min.	max.
Direct	hospital bed need	2000	L	970	2,920
		2000	H	4,340	13,010
	hospital costs (in millions)	2000	L	150.9	251.4
		2000	H	672.9	1,121.5
Indirect	PYLL (in thousands)	2000	L	203.8	262.0
		2000	H	404.8	520.5

Table 3 **Indicators for direct and indirect patient-related costs of AIDS:**
Projected hospital bed need, monetary hospital costs and potential years of life lost (PYLL) in the EU in 2000 in a high prevalence scenario (H) and low prevalence scenario (L).
Projections for 2000 are shown for a minimum and a maximum estimate of per person year (ppy) annual in-patient day need (30–90), ppy annual monetary hospital costs (15,000–25,000 ECUs) and PYLL per AIDS death (34–45 years) respectively

of 30[21] and 90 days per person-year[22] (Table 3). Similarly, estimates of current hospital costs per AIDS person-year of 15,000 and 25,000 ECUs, based on evidence from several studies in EU countries,[23] have been used to produce the scenarios of hospital costs for the year 2000 in Table 3.[24] The results illustrate an expected EU bed need of between 970 and 13,010 beds, and hospital costs of 150,900 to 1,121,500 million ECUs in the (twelve) EU countries. The wide range reflects the uncertainty associated with the in-patient days and cost estimates used to produce the scenarios.

Scenarios of PYLL have also been presented in Table 3. These represent a proxy of indirect cost of HIV/AIDS in the EU, although a monetary value of the life years lost has not been estimated. The maximum loss at the EU level is estimated at 520,500 years in 2000, which is 1.53 years per 1,000 EU inhabitants. This can be compared with other PYLL projections we have produced for three EU countries: The Netherlands, France and Germany.[25] This demonstrates that in the year 2000, whilst lung cancer might have PYLL four times per 1,000 that of AIDS and while that for suicide might be twice as high, both the PYLL due to road traffic accidents and other infectious diseases might be exceeded by that of AIDS.

Further development of multinational scenarios

Preliminary assessments of multinational scenario construction have been undertaken.[26] More recently, a working group funded by an EU 'Concerted Action' has been formed to enhance development of multinational scenarios. Participants of this group provide expertise from Europe in the fields of modelling, statistics and operations research, surveillance and epidemiology, health economics and health services research, social sciences and scenario analysis. The objectives of the group are threefold. First, to stimulate the integra-

tion of knowledge and skills from relevant disciplines: epidemiology, social sciences, health services research and economics. Second, to strengthen the link between data collection, mathematical modelling and impact assessment. Finally, to develop and apply a common methodology for AIDS scenario analysis at the EU level.

In developing scenario analysis from the national to multinational level of the EU, the group have identified several new factors which are likely to influence the impact of HIV/AIDS on society. In particular, they have highlighted the relevance of increased international mobility and relationships. Of particular importance is movement by people with HIV/AIDS, or by those 'at risk' of infection, between EU countries and between EU and non-EU countries (especially in Eastern Europe with the end of travel restrictions for people in those countries). In addition to holiday and work-related movement, it is possible that patients with HIV infection or AIDS will increasingly seek treatment in countries where they are not resident.

Another area in need of further investigation is the international differences in resource utilization and costs of HIV/AIDS treatment and care. Important factors that might affect utilisation and costs in each country are the structure of the healthcare system and the influence this has on the demand for and supply of health services, the level of economic development in a country and the availability of informal care and support. Research should include identifying differences and the reasons for these, and designing a standardized framework for allowing valid comparisons to be made.[27] Finally, the development of alternative scenarios will be strengthened by better data on the impact of possible interventions designed to slow down disease progression.[28]

Figure 5 provides an extension of the conceptual model of Figure 2. It integrates the additional topics outlined in the preceding paragraph. In this model health status is affected by a large number of factors including biological, social and lifestyle (drug use, sexual behaviour) risk factors and determinants. In addition, these determinants are influenced by prevention, care and treatment activities, EU and national healthcare policy. The resulting health status outcomes (i.e. prevalence of HIV infection and AIDS and AIDS mortality) provides the main source of demand

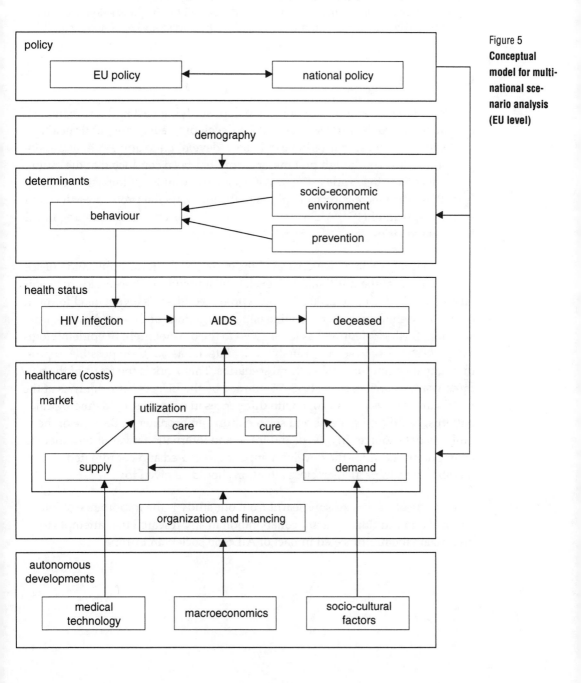

Figure 5
Conceptual model for multinational scenario analysis (EU level)

for health services. This demand is also influenced by the supply of healthcare facilities and other social developments such as the availability of informal help (e.g. 'buddies'). From this linking of demand and supply, the utilization and costs of services can be derived. Finally, the conceptual model illustrates that the organization and financing of healthcare delivery systems will affect the supply and demand of health service facilities and costs. The complete system is affected by autonomous developments: for example, in medical technology, the macro-economy and demography. An analogous conceptual model has recently been developed for the production of public health forecasts in The Netherlands.[29]

Conclusion

Scenario analysis represents a flexible tool for studying past and future impacts of healthcare problems on society and for developing adequate public health strategies. To date, scenarios have only been developed to any extent at the single country level, although preliminary work has been conducted at the multinational level using crude estimates of resource use and cost impact. Results from these, and increasing recognition of the international problems associated with the spread of HIV/AIDS, have raised the importance of developing multinational scenarios.

In this chapter we have demonstrated the current state in the application of scenario analysis at the multinational level. Whilst preliminary scenarios of hospital cost and bed need to 2000 have been produced, there is a vital need for more detailed baseline analysis to provide better projections of these indicators. In addition, further attention has to be given to the development of epidemiological models for use in scenario analysis. To date, it has not been possible to produce any meaningful socio-cultural scenarios. This work is the focus of the new three-year research project (1993–96) funded by the EU. Scenario analysis at the multinational level has to cope with differences in countries' epidemiological patterns, healthcare systems and socio-cultural environments. Because of the multiple data sources involved, and intra- and international variations, there is an important need for the development of a structured and coordinated methodology. In particular, close attention should be given to:

Finally, one of the key lessons learnt from our study is the importance of international and multidisciplinary collaboration in any research that attempts to investigate the multifaceted impact of AIDS on society in Europe.

Acknowledgements

This study is a result of the EU Concerted Action on 'Multinational Scenario Analysis Concerning the Epidemiological, Social and Economic Impacts of HIV/AIDS on Society' (grant PL 931723) within the framework of the Research and Technological Development Programme of the EU. This is part of the EU division of Biomedical and Health Research.

1 J.C. Jager, F.M.L.G. van den Boom, 'Scenario analysis, health policy, and decision making', *Modeling the AIDS Epidemic: Planning, Policy and Prediction* (eds. E.H. Kaplan and M.L Brandeau), pp. 237–52. Raven Press, New York, 1994.

2 F.M.L.G. van den Boom, J.C. Jager, D.P. Reinking, M.J. Postma, C.E.S. Albers, *AIDS up to the Year 2000: Epidemiological, Socio-cultural and Economic Scenario Analysis for The Netherlands.* Kluwer Academic Publishers Group, Dordrecht, 1992.

A.J. Dunning, W.I.M. Wils, *The Heart of the Future; the Future of the Heart.* Kluwer, Dordrecht, 1987.

G.M. Boas, 'Scenario-analyse economische aspecten coronaire hartziekten', thesis at the University of Limburg, 1994.

Ph.A. Idenburg, E. Kelting. R.V. Bijl, *Care for Mental Health in the Future.* Kluwer, Dordecht, 1991.

A.F. Casparie, H. Verkleij, D. Ruwaard *et al.*, *Chronic Diseases in the Year 2000*, vols. 1–3. Kluwer, Dordrecht, 1991–93.

R. Bijl, 'Constructie van toekomstscenario's. Beleidsgericht scenario-onderzoek, toegepast op het gebied van de geestelijke volksgezondheid en de geestelijke gezondheidszorg', thesis at the University of Utrecht, NcGV-reeks 91–19, 1991.

M. Beckman, R. Leidl, A. Mieick, W. Satzinger, U. Weber, *Szenarien für soziale Folgen von AIDS.* GSF Forschungszentrum für Umwelt und Gesundheit, Munich, 1991.

3 J.C. Jager, E.J. Ruitenberg (eds.), *Statistical Analysis and Mathematical Modelling of AIDS.* Oxford University Press, Oxford 1998.

J.C. Jager, E.J. Ruitenberg (eds.), *AIDS Impact Assessment: Modelling and Scenario Analysis.* Elsevier Science Publishers, Amsterdam, 1992.

D. Schwefel, R. Leidl, J. Rovira, M. F. Drummond (eds.), *Economic Aspects of AIDS and HIV Infection.* Springer-Verlag, Berlin, 1990.

4 World Health Organization, *Training Workshop on Scenario Building and Long-term Planning for AIDS, Madrid,* 19–21 September 1990.

5 R. Leidl, M.J. Postma, M.J.J.C. Poos, B. Magnoni d'Intignano, A.E. Baert, 'Construction of socio-economic AIDS-scenarios based on routine surveillance data', *AIDS Impact Assessment: Modelling and Scenario Analysis* (eds. J.C. Jager, E.J. Ruitenberg), pp. 269–87. Elsevier Science Publishers, Amsterdam, 1992.

M.J. Postma, R. Leidl, A.M. Downs, J. Rovira, K. Tolley, M. Gyldmark, J.C. Jager, 'Economic impact of the AIDS epidemic in the European Community: towards multinational scenarios on hospital care and cost', *AIDS*, 7, pp. 541–53, 1993.

6 K. Tolley, M. Gyldmark, 'The treatment and care costs of people with HIV infection or AIDS: development of a standardized cost framework for Europe', *Health Policy*, 24, pp. 55–70, 1993.

7 F.M.L.G. van den Boom, J.C. Jager, D.P. Reinking, M.J. Postma, C.E.S. Albers, *AIDS up to the Year 2000: Epidemiological, Socio-cultural and Economic Analysis for The Netherlands.* Kluwer Academic Publishers Group, Dordrecht, 1992.

D.P. Reinking, F.M.L.G. van den Boom, M.J. Postma, J.C. Jager, 'The socio-cultural and economic impact of AIDS on society: an outline of the scenario project in The Netherlands and the contribution of information from the social sciences,' *AIDS Impact Assessment: Modelling and Scenario Analysis* (eds. J.C.Jager and E.J. Ruitenberg), pp. 223–38. Elsevier Science Publishers, Amsterdam, 1992.

M.J. Postma, M.G.W. Dijkgraaf, J.C.C. Borleffs, D.P. Reinking, F.M.L.G. van den Boom, J.C. Jager, 'Omvang en kosten van ziekenhuiszorg voor HIV-geïnfecteerden; vergelijking en integratie van Nederlandse studies voor scenario-analyse [Hospital resource utilization by HIV-infected persons and corresponding costs: comparing and integrating Dutch studies for scenario analysis], *Tijdschrift voor Sociale Gezondheidszorg*, 70, pp. 186–96, 1992. In Dutch.

8 F.M.L.G. van den Boom, J.C. Jager, D.P. Reinking, M.J. Postma, C.E.S. Albers, *AIDS up to the Year 2000: Epidemiological, Socio-cultural and Eco-

nomic Analysis for The Netherlands. Kluwer Academic Publishers Group, Dordrecht, 1992.

J.W. Hay, 'Econometric issues in modelling the costs of AIDS', Health Policy, 11, pp. 125–45, 1989.

N.T.J. Bailey, 'Operational modelling of HIV/AIDS to assist public health policy making and control', AIDS Impact Assessment: Modelling and Scenario Analysis (eds. J.C. Jager, E.J. Ruitenberg), pp. 27–36. Elsevier Science Publishers, Amsterdam, 1992.

R.M. Anderson, 'The role of mathematical models in the study of HIV transmission and the epidemiology of AIDS', Journal of Acquired Immune Deficiency Syndromes, 1, pp 241–56, 1988.

V. Isham, 'Mathematical modelling of the transmission dynamics of HIV infection and AIDS: a review', Journal of the Royal Statistic Association, 151, 1, pp. 5–49, 1988.

J.A.M. van Druten, A.G.M. Reintjes, J.C. Jager, S.H. Helsterkamp, M.J.J.C. Poos, R.A. Coutinho, M.G.W. Dijkgraaf, E.J. Ruitenberg, 'HIV infection dynamics and intervention experiments in linked risk groups', Statistics in Medicine, 9, pp. 721–36, 1990.

M.E.E. Kretzschmar, D.P. Reinking, H. Brouwers, G. van Zessen, J.C. Jager, 'Network models: from paradigm to mathematical tool', Modeling the AIDS Epidemic: Planning, Policy and Prediction (eds. E. H. Kaplan and M.L. Brandeau), pp 561–84. Raven press, New York, 1994.

S.H. Heisterkamp, B.J. de Haan, J.C. Jager, J.A.M. van Druten, J.C.M. Hendriks, 'Short- and medium-term projections of the AIDS/HIV epidemic by a dynamic model with an application to the risk group of homosexual men in Amsterdam', Statistics in Medicine, 11, pp. 1425–41, 1992.

R. Leidl, 'Model-based scenarios to describe economic impacts of AIDS: the role of case-mix', Economic Aspects of AIDS and HIV Infection, Springer-Verlag, Berlin, pp. 282–94, 1990.

9 J. Rovira, 'Economic aspects of AIDS', Economic Aspects of AIDS and HIV Infection (eds. D.Schwefel, R. Leidl, J. Rovira and M.F. Drummond), pp. 49–56. Springer-Verlag, Berlin, 1990.

A.M. Johnson, 'Economic aspects of care and prevention of HIV infection and AIDS', Statisti-

cal Analysis and Mathematical Modelling of AIDS (eds. J.C. Jager and E.J. Ruitenburg), pp. 150–159. Oxford University Press, Oxford, 1988.

10 M.J. Postma, J.C. Jager, M.G.W. Dijkgraaf, J.C.C. Borleffs, 'AIDS-scenarios for The Netherlands: the impact on the health care system', Proceedings 'Econometrics of AIDS' conference, Barcelona, December 1993.

11 F.M.L.G. van den Boom, J.C. Jager, D.P. Reinking, M.J. Postma, C.E.S. Albers, AIDS up to the Year 2000: Epidemiological, Socio-cultural and Economic Analysis for The Netherlands. Kluwer Academic Publishers Group, Dordrecht, 1992.

12 M.G.W. Dijkgraaf, A.H.P. Luijben, J.C. Jager, A.J.P. Schrijvers, J.C.C. Borleffs, 'Trends in hospital resource utilisation by HIV-infected persons, January 1987–June 1990', Health Policy, 20, 1994.

J.C.C. Borleffs, J.C. Jager, M.J.J.C. Poos, M.G.W. Dijkgraaf, R.M.A. Geels, H. Vrehen, A.J.P. Schrijvers, 'Hospital costs for patients with HIV infection in a university hospital in The Netherlands', Health Policy, 16, pp. 43–54, 1990.

13 The stages CDC-II and CDC-III have been combined. We refer to the combined stage as CDC-II/III.

14 M.J. Postma, J.C. Jager, M.G.W. Dijkgraaf, J.C.C. Borleffs, 'AIDS-scenarios for The Netherlands: the impact on the health care system', Proceedings 'Econometrics of AIDS' conference, Barcelona, December 1993.

15 For this purpose we use per person-year CDC-IV hospital resource utilization and costs for expressing needs in the AIDS stage, whereas CDC-II/III figures are used for the pre-AIDS stage. Also, we use separate estimates for the early and final phases of AIDS stage (for details see Postma et al. note.10).

16 Beriedheid tot verandering. Commissie Structuur en Financiering Gezondheidszorg, The Hague, 1987.

17 M.J. Postma, J.C. Jager, M.G.W. Dijkgraaf, J.C.C. Borleffs, 'AIDS-scenarios for The Netherlands: the impact on the health care system', Proceedings 'Econometrics of AIDS' conference, Barcelona, December 1993.

18 M.G.W. Dijkgraaf, A.H.P. Luijben, J.C. Jager, A.J.P. Schrijvers, J.C.C. Borleffs, 'Trends in hos-

pital resource utilisation by HIV-infected persons, January 1987–June 1990', *Health Policy*, 20, 1994.

M.J. Postma, H. Houweling, S.H. Heisterkamp, J.C. Jager, 'Uitbreiding van het garantiefonds voor HIV-geïnfecteerden in relatie tot verwachte epidemiologische ontwikkelingen' [Extension of the life nsurance fund for HIV infected people in relation to expected epidemiological developments], report no 432501001. RIVM, Bilthoven, The Netherlands, *in press*. In Dutch.

19 M.J. Postma, R. Leidl, A.M. Downs, J. Rovira, K. Tolley, M. Gyldmark, J.C. Jager, 'Economic impact of the AIDS epidemic in the European Community: towards multinational scenarios on hospital care and cost', *AIDS*, 7, pp. 541–53, 1993.

20 R. Leidl, 'Model-based scenarios to describe economic impacts of AIDS: the role of case-mix', *Economic Aspects of AIDS and HIV Infection*, pp. 282–94. Springer-Verlag, Berlin, 1990.

21 M.G.W. Dijkgraaf, A.H.P. Luijben, J.C. Jager, A.J.P. Schrijvers, J.C.C. Borleffs, 'Trends in hospital resource utilisation by HIV-infected persons, January 1987–June 1990', *Health Policy*, 20, 1994.

22 J. Rovira, R. Leidl, 'Projecting personal health care costs of HIV/AIDS patients in Catalonia,' *Proceedings 'Econometrics of AIDS' conference*, Barcelona, December 1993.

23 M.J. Postma, R. Leidl, A.M. Downs, J. Rovira, K. Tolley, M. Gyldmark, J.C. Jager, 'Economic impact of the AIDS epidemic in the European Community: towards multinational scenarios on hospital care and cost', *AIDS* 7, pp. 541–53, 1993.

J. Rovira, R. Leidl, 'Projecting personal health care costs of HIV/AIDS patients in Catalonia', *Proceedings 'Econometrics of AIDS' Conference*, Barcelona, December 1993.

M.J. Postma, J.C. Jager, M.G.W. Dijkgraaf, J.C.C. Borleffs, K. Tolley, R.M. Leidl, 'AIDS-scenarios for The Netherlands; the economic impact on hospitals', *Health Policy* (forthcoming).

24 Monetary amounts are expressed in 1993 prices. To transform from the original currency cost figures, expressed in 1987 prices, use has been made of the following health price inflators for the period 1987–93:
 Spain: 1.37 (estimated from OECD figures: Organisation for Economic Co-operation and Development Health Data, database version 1.01, OECD, Paris, 1991.
The Netherlands: 1.24 (Ministry of Welfare, Health and Cultural Affairs [Ministerie van Welzijn, Volksgezondheid en Cultuur, WVC], *Financieel Overzicht Zorg 1993* [Financial Statement Healthcare]. WVC, The Hague, 1993. In Dutch.
For transforming to ECUs, the rates of 16 August 1994 are used (1 ECU = FL 2.13 = Pts 158).

25 J.C. Jager, M.J. Postma, R. Leidl, B. Magnoni d'Intignano, A.E. Baert, 'AIDS impact scenarios: questions for the years to come', *AIDS*, 11, pp. 1166–7, 1990.

26 R. Leidl, M.J. Postma, M.J.J.C. Poos, B. Magnoni d'Intignano, A.E. Baert, 'Construction of socio-economic AIDS-scenarios based on routine surveillance data', *AIDS Impact Assessment: Modelling and Scenario Analysis* (eds. J.C. Jager, E.J. Ruitenberg), pp. 269–87. Elsevier Science Publishers, Amsterdam, 1992.

 R. Leidl, M.J. Postma, A.M. Downs, J. Rovira, K. Tolley, M. Gyldmark, J.C. Jager, 'Economic impact of the AIDS epidemic in the European Community: towards multinational scenarios on hospital care and cost', *AIDS*, 7, pp. 541–53, 1993.

Ministry of Welfare, Health and Cultural Affairs [Ministerie van Welzijn, Volksgezondheid en Cultuur, WVC], *Financieel Overzicht Zorg 1993* [Financial Statement Healthcare]. WVC, The Hague, 1993. In Dutch.

27 K. Tolley, M. Gyldmark, 'The treatment and care costs of people with HIV infection or AIDS: development of a standardized cost framework for Europe', *Health Policy*, 24, pp. 55–70, 1993.

28 R. Leidl, 'A survey of the economic evaluation of early drug intervention in HIV infection', *Modeling the AIDS Epidemic: Planning, Policy and Prediction* (eds. E.H. Kaplan and M.L. Brandeau), pp. 253–71. Raven Press, New York, 1994.

29 D. Ruwaard, P.G.N. Kramers, A. van den Bergh Jeths, P.W. Achterberg (eds.), *Public Health Status and Forecasts. The Health Status of the Dutch Population over the Period 1950–2010.* SDU Uitgeverij, The Hague, 1994.

Estimates of HIV/AIDS Healthcare Expenditure in Greece: An Analytic Approach for Prospective Financing

Professor John Kyriopoulos, H. Kornarou, M. Gitona and V. Paparizos

Athens School of Public Health, Department of Health Economics, University of Athens, Greece

With the Acquired Immune Deficiency Syndrome (AIDS), society is confronted for the first time since the polio epidemic of the 1950s with a serious infectious disease of epidemic proportions to which medical science has, as yet, no answer: a disease involving not just large-scale human suffering but also enormous economic and social costs.[1]

Governments and international bodies are becoming increasingly concerned about the economic and social consequences of AIDS. The increase in the number of HIV-positive persons and AIDS cases results in additional consumption of healthcare services, placing a burden on the healthcare sector, which is forced to redistribute scarce health resources.

International experience on AIDS cost estimations has demonstrated that a major problem is the comparison of the results of studies concerning the socioeconomic impact of the AIDS epidemic. Despite the concern over the economic burden that the AIDS epidemic is imposing on the nation's health resources, hard data on the costs of treating persons with AIDS are still relatively scarce and incomplete in Greece.

Indeed Greece, compared to other European countries, has a very low prevalence of HIV, although the proportion of cases due to heterosexual transmission is relatively high.[2]

Economic impact of AIDS: the Greek experience

The first case of AIDS in Greece was identified in November 1983. By the end of 1993, 825 cases had been reported to the health authorities (under the CDC 1989 definition) and the first patient was hospitalized in 1986.

In Table 2, a summary of the findings from several Greek papers on the economic impact of AIDS is presented. In this Table all costs are in US dollars, at prices current in the year the study was conducted.

Filalithis (1987) produced an early estimate for the average cost per person at an upper limit of about $11,213.[3] An estimate for the daily cost of hospitalization was $150, with a mean hospitalization stay from 50 to 70 days. The Gross Domestic Product (GDP) in 1987 was $4,714 per capita, which means that the percentage of average annual AIDS cost per capita from this study – relative to the GDP per capita – was 159–239 per cent.

Diomidous and Sissouras (1990) studied 30 cases from two hospitals in Athens.[4] They estimate an average hospitalization stay of 25 days, hospitalization cost per day of $127, total hospital cost of $4,253, and lifetime cost of $6,880 per capita. The GDP per capita in 1988 was $5,117 and the per capita AIDS cost to per capita GDP was 124 per cent.

Hatzakis and Trichopoulos (1990) studied seven cases from a hospital in Athens.[5] They estimated annual in-patient and out-patient hospital care as well as lifetime cost. Average yearly cost per patient was found to be $38,482. The GDP in 1989 was $5,948 per capita and the average annual AIDS cost per capita was 647 per cent of the GDP.

Mokou et al. (1989) attempted to estimate the implication of AIDS costs on health expenditure.[6] The average yearly cost was estimated at $25,804, representing 435 per cent of the GDP per year and per capita.

Yfantopoulos (1990), in a sample of 20 cases, estimated the average yearly cost per patient according to long-term and short-term hospitalization.[7] The average yearly cost per person was $16,981–23,133 without the inclusion of the zidovudine (AZT) cost. The GDP per capita at that time was $6,589. On this basis, the average annual cost per capita was from 258 to 353 per cent of the GDP per capita.

Paparizos (1992) studied 60 AIDS patients (CDC stage IV) according to hospitaliza-

Year	1984	1985	1986	1987	1988	1989	1990	1991	1992	1993	Total
Homo–bisexual	1	5	11	23	51	44	70	85	76	85	451
IV Drug Users	–	–	1	–	3	5	6	10	5	8	38
Homo–bisexual & IVDU	–	–	–	1	–	–	1	2	1	–	5
Haemophiliacs	1	1	–	14	6	7	11	5	5	6	56
Transfusion Recipients	–	–	–	7	7	9	6	10	5	1	45
Heterosexual Contact	4	1	10	4	11	33	24	15	44	15	161
Mother to Child	–	–	–	1	1	1	2	–	1	14	20
Other	–	–	–	3	3	8	15	20	25	41	115
Total	6	7	22	53	82	107	135	147	162	170	891

Table 1 **Cases in Greece, by time series and by transmission category (31.12.93)**

Table 2
AIDS cost components in Greek studies

Year of Study	Cases	Average Hospital Days	Cost per Hospital Day $	Lifetime Cost $	Average Annual Cost per Capita $	GDP Per Capita $	Per Capita AIDS Cost to GDP per Capita (%)	Authors
1987			150		7,518–11,213	4,714	159–239	Filalithis
1988	30	25*	127	6,880	6,350	5,117	124	Diomidous, Sissouras
1989	7	110	275		38,482	5,948	647	Hatzakis, Trichopoulos
1989					25,804	5,948	435	Mokou et al.
1990	20		411		16,981–23,133	6,589	258–353	Yfantopoulos
1991	60	21.3*	229	25,299	17,489	6,427	272	Paparizos
1991					25,000–27,083	6,427	389–421	Gitona et al.
1992	47	93	158		30,188–32,511	6,589	458–496	Kyriopoulos et al.
1992	105	11.7*	481	24,160	8,428	6,647	127	Komarou
1993					18,192–34,000	7,100	256–478	Kyriopoulos, Niakas, Georgoussi

Note: In US dollars and prices current at time of study
* These figures are hospital days per in-patient admission. All other figures in this column are total hospital days per year.

tion cost, epidemiological features and natural course of the disease.[8] The average yearly cost per person was estimated at $17,489. In 1991 the GDP was $6,427. Consequently, the percentage of the average annual AIDS cost was 272 per cent of the GDP per capita.

Gitona et al. (1991) studied medical hospital costs.[9] The average annual cost per capita ranged from $25,000 to $27,083. Using the lower estimate, the percentage of AIDS cost to GDP was 389–421 per cent.

Kyriopoulos et al. (1992), in a sample of 47 cases, estimated per patient cost of zidovudine as $77.5 per day and an average, yearly cost per person of $30,188–32,511.[10] Moreover, for the period 1989–93 the direct medical cost ranged from $47- to $73 million and the total indirect cost range was from $48,933- to $72,772 million.

Kornarou (1992), in a sample of 105 cases, estimated average hospitalization stay at 11.7 days, the cost of daily hospitalization as $481, the total zidovudine cost as $549,275, lifetime cost as $24,160, average yearly cost per person as $8,428, and life expectancy from 22 to 30 months.[11] Moreover, the yearly indirect cost per person was estimated as $86,304. Although in 1992 the average annual AIDS cost per patient was $8,428 the GDP was $6,647, producing a percentage ratio of 127 per cent.

Kyriopoulos et al. (1993) estimated an average annual cost per capita of $18,192–34,000.[12] In 1993 the GDP was $7,100, so the AIDS cost per capita to GDP was 256–478 per cent.

Cost components

Each of the studies in Table 2 estimated the costs of hospital-based care. It is difficult to make any direct comparison of the various cost estimates among studies because of the different cost components included in each study and the different year of study. The Paparizos and Kornarou studies covered both in-patient and out-patient costs. The studies by Hatzakis and Trichopoulos, Kyriopoulos *et al.* (1992), Paparizos, and Kornarou have estimated the zidovudine (AZT) cost. The studies by Diomidous and Sissouras, Hatzakis and Trichopoulos, Paparizos, and Kornarou estimated that the lifetime cost per patient ranges from $6,880 to $41,689. Only Kyriopoulos,[13] Kyriopoulos *et al.* (1992) and Kornarou estimated the annual indirect socio-economic cost per patient, and this ranged from $35,573 to $86,304.

Evaluation of the studies

All the Greek studies have attempted to assess the treatment and care provided to people with HIV infection and AIDS since 1987 when the first case was reported. However, the various cost estimates produced are difficult to compare. The main results state that AIDS care creates a large burden on the healthcare budget, being a very expensive disease in the context of the Greek standard of living.

The cost estimates in Table 2 raise several questions. The relatively high cost in the Hatzakis and Trichopoulos study does not appear to be realistic. The sample studied is only seven cases. However, the Mokou *et al.* and Kyriopoulos *et al.* (1992 and 1993) studies are based on current and projected epidemiological scenarios and hypothetical care provision, using shadow prices[14] to estimate unit costs.

Only the Paparizos and Kornarou studies could be compared, as both are retrospective analyses and attempt to measure the true cost for a large sample. Average annual cost per patient is higher in the Paparizos study than in Kornarou, as in the former sample Kaposi's sarcoma was the main clinical feature. This diagnosis group is costly because of the drugs used.

A comparison of the results from these studies shows large deviations in the cost per patient. This is because the evaluations were conducted in different years, different methodologies were used and there are actual differences between the HIV/AIDS cases being studied.[15.] The factors which make an accurate comparison impossible include:

- differences in the stage of the disease in the patient, epidemiological classification of the patient (i.e. whether they are male/female, an injecting drug user, etc.) and the level of hospital care and treatment;
- variations between the prices used by the healthcare sector to estimate costs, and market prices;
- lack of data for hospital and other healthcare settings.

Differences in methodology used

Classification of patients according to HIV/AIDS definition used and stage of disease

There are many differences concerning the above parameters. Only the study by Paparizos refers to detailed data of diagnosis and stage of the disease. He also estimates the cost per stage of the disease. The study by Kyriopoulos et al. (1992) has a prospective study design but it omits the date of diagnosis. The Hatzakis and Trichopoulos study does not refer to the date of diagnosis either. All others try to present a lifetime cost using samples from specialized hospitals. So, comparison of the yearly costs per patient among the studies is difficult. Two studies – those of Kornarou and Paparizos – could be compared because they have similar parameters.

Data collection

Most of the Greek studies have used retrospective data collection. This is a major problem because of the lack of a computerized system containing patients' hospitalization records. So, the only way of monitoring data is through the file-records of the patients – which have a large amount of missing data. In addition, the process of collecting data can cause problems with the AIDS estimations. For example, the Hatzakis and Trichopoulos study has only seven cases, the Kyriopoulos et al. study (1992) concerns only two general hospitals and the Paparizos study has derived its sample from a dermatology clinic of an STD Hospital.

Cost components

There are a range of costs that must be considered (e.g. treatment costs, hospital costs, out-patient care costs). All the Greek studies consider only the direct costs falling on the formal (statutory) sector, even though the informal (voluntary, family) sector is quite active. Objections have been raised to the use of the traditional methods for calculating the indirect costs of AIDS/HIV. These involve calculating the numbers of years of working life lost due to morbidity and premature mortality and multiplying them by average labour participation rates and earnings. In the Kornarou and Kyriopoulos et al. (1992) studies objections have been raised concerning the inclusion of tax losses and insurance contributions as indirect costs of HIV/AIDS. They object that those kinds of losses are needed in every society in order to redistribute the income. They are transfer payments from one section of society (through the state) to another, and do not produce wealth for the society or increase the national income.

Evaluation of the cost

One of the most important, if not *the* most important problem in the studies is the lack of accurate price data in the health-care sector in Greece. As the state finances healthcare services, the lack of healthcare *market* price information makes cost estimation difficult. In particular, none of the studies has made any reference to the impact on marginal cost.[16] Only the Paparizos study uses resources combined with prices in order to estimate hospital cost. The prices come from the available hospital budget. The Hatzakis and Trichopoulos study uses average cost per AIDS patient per day, namely $275 (without zidovudine). The Kyriopoulos *et al.* study (1992) generally uses average cost per day, and the Kornarou study uses average cost per day for the two general hospitals. However, the average cost of hospitalization underestimates the cost of hospitalization of AIDS patients.[17] In addition, the real price of zidovudine is difficult to estimate because, in Greece, the National Drug Administration is the only supplier. Moreover, this drug is provided to the patients free of charge through hospitals.[18]

Prospective financing of healthcare

Despite their methodological variations, the review of the Greek studies in this chapter has demonstrated the great burden of the disease on the Greek healthcare sector. The percentage of average annual AIDS cost per capita compared to the GDP per capita is used as the basic parameter of cost estimation in working out a pattern for financing healthcare for AIDS patients. The determination and the integration of such parameters could obviously direct the implementation of a prospective financing mechanism. This could be based on a capitation system with funding according to stage of diagnosis and severity of illness criteria.

Prospective financing of healthcare for HIV patients must be based on the analysis of AIDS cost parameters as well as on the classification of the patients according to the CDC 1989 definition stage of the disease. It must be mentioned that the practical development of such a prepayment system would require detailed cost analysis of the care provided and other relevant regulatory, ethical and legislative arrangements concerning their acceptability by the users, providers and insurers. To use a proxy AIDS patients' cost analysis for the implementation of a prospective financing based on fixed capitation rates, it is necessary to have a breakdown of AIDS patients into homogeneous resource use groups, according to severity of illness. The use of a severity of classification breakdown to produce homogeneous resource use groups for cost estimation is constrained in cost studies by the need for a large sample size – which is often not going to be available.

More precisely, for the implementation of a system of prepayment for AIDS outpatient treatment, patients' characteristics, Greek health sector particularities and other variables, such as the forecasting models and patients' cost analysis that have been developed, must be used. It is believed that by using these criteria the production of homogeneous AIDS costs groups for their prospective financing could be achieved.[19]

The implementation of a prospective hospital financing mechanism in the Greek hospital sector does not seem very difficult for several reasons. Hospitals in Greece are mainly funded retrospectively by the social security system and prospectively by the state budget by using a non-diagnostically related budgeting technique that includes nursing, medical, administrative and hotel costs, as well as physicians' salaries.[20]

According to the results of our research on AIDS in-patients' cost components, the recognition of methodological difficulties and international experience on cost estimations, we recommend the reform of the existing hospital system and, as a consequence, of AIDS patient hospital care. The annual mixed budgeting technique can be easily transformed to a diagnostically related prospective payment system. In such a financing system the classification of the patients into homogeneous AIDS cost groups should be the criterion by which hospital resources are allocated. For the success of our proposal the managerial autonomy of AIDS departments/units is necessary.

It is believed that by the use of a common approach to the analytic AIDS-cost estimation the expected results should be the following:

- a crude but initial use of clinical budgeting techniques in Greece;

- the precise definition of AIDS patient homogeneous cost groups could direct policy-makers to the implementation of a hospital prospective-payment system, such as Diagnostic Related Groups (DRGs) or a similar classification method;

- the adoption of an out-patient and in-patient prospective financing method will ameliorate AIDS patients' management in the Greek national health service as well as achieve continuity in the provision of their healthcare;

- various motives for more efficient and effective reallocation of resources, focusing mainly on the use of alternative patterns of healthcare delivery to AIDS patients.

Conclusion

This chapter reviews the Greek HIV/AIDS costs studies and outlines the differences in methods used. Variations in the different estimations are due to the classification of the patients according to the HIV/AIDS definition used, the stage of the disease of the collected cases, the epidemiological type of the study, the range of clinical cost variables and other parameters. First findings show an increasing demand for health services relating to HIV/AIDS and, consequently, pressure on healthcare budgets to meet a range of health-policy priorities. According to the Greek studies, the economic cost of AIDS is continuously increasing but the lack of a standardized method to evaluate the cost of AIDS results in an underestimation of the real burden of the disease on the national economy and society.

The great diversity in methodologies calls for intensive multidimensional communication to coordinate current and proposed research efforts. Having discussed the existing national data, we recommend the use of a common methodology concerning the cost estimation of AIDS patients.[21]

Finally, it is obvious that the priority which should be given to the analysis of the economics of AIDS represents a challenge for the health policy decision-makers to promote management information on health services more generally in order to improve the organization and monitoring of performance of the Greek healthcare sector.

Acknowledgements

This paper is based on the studies of Filalithis, Diomidous and Sissouras, Hatzakis and Trichopoulos, Mokou *et al*, Yfantopoulos, Paparizos, Gitona *et al*, Kyriopoulos *et al*, Kornarou, and Kyriopoulos–Niakas–Georgoussi. We are grateful for the willing co-operation of these authors and for access to their papers.

1 M.F. Drummond, L.M. Davies, 'Topics for economic analysis', *AIDS: The Challenge for Economic Analysis* (eds. M.F. Drummond and L.M. Davies), pp. 2–7. University of Birmingham, 1990.

2 G. Papaevangelou, A. Roumeliotou, G. Stergiou, A. Nestoridou, E. Trichopoulou, G. Kallinikos, G. Rizos, H. Kornarou, 'HIV infection in Greek intravenous drug users', *European Journal of Epidemiology*, 7 (1), 88–90, 1991.

3 A. Filalithis, 'Socio-economic consequences of HIV/AIDS', paper presented at the Greek–French Symposium on AIDS, Iraklio, Crete, 25–27 June 1987. In Greek.

4 M. Diomidous, A. Sissouras, 'Planning for AIDS or HIV related services in Greece: first steps towards operational schemes', *Economic Aspects of AIDS and HIV Infection*, pp. 251–261. Health Systems Research, 1990.

5 A. Hatzakis, D. Trichopoulos, 'Methodological and practical issues in estimating the direct cost of AIDS/HIV: Greece', *AIDS: The Challenge for Economic Analysis* (eds. M.F. Drummond and L.M. Davies), pp. 76–80. University of Birmingham, 1990.

6 N. Mokou, D. Niakas, E. Georgoussi, A. Hatzakis, J. Kyriopoulos, 'Macroeconomic evaluation of AIDS cost in Greece, 1989–1993', paper presented at *1st Panhellenic Conference on AIDS*, Athens, 18–19 March 1989. In Greek.

7 J. Yfantopoulos, 'Economic impact of AIDS in Greece', *Proceedings of 2nd Panhellenic Conference on AIDS*, pp. 130–137. Hellenic Association for the Study and Control of AIDS, Thessaloniki, 1990. In Greek.

8 V. Paparizos, 'Study on the economic cost of hospital care for AIDS patients in Greece', doctoral thesis, University of Athens, 1992. In Greek.

9 M. Gitona, J. Kyriopoulos, E. Georgoussi, D. Niakas, G. Skoutelis, 'AIDS drect and indirect cost in Greece 1989–1993', paper presented at *VII International Conference on AIDS*, Florence, Italy, 16–21 June 1991.

10 J. Kyriopoulos, E. Georgoussi, A. Gennimata, D. Niakas, G. Skoutelis, 'AIDS cost in Greece: 1989–1993. Macroeconomic approach and estimations, *Health Review*, 4, pp. 35–38, 1992. In Greek.

11 H. Kornarou, 'Direct and indirect cost of AIDS in Greece', doctoral thesis, University of Athens, 1992. In Greek.

12 J. Kyriopoulos, D. Niakas, E. Georgoussi, 'AIDS cost in Greece: a prospective approach based on epidemiological scenarios of HIV/AIDS', *AIDS Economics and Management in Greece* (eds. J. Kyriopoulos, H. Kornarou, V. Paparizos), pp. 89–98. Centre for Health and Social Science, 1993. In Greek.

13 J. Kyriopoulos, 'Economic approach to AIDS. Methodological problems and research results', *Proceedings of 3rd Panhellenic Conference on AIDS*, pp. 71–80. Hellenic Association for the Study and Control of AIDS, Athens, 1991. In Greek.

14 Shadow prices: hypothetical prices, including hospitalization and other health service costs, estimated on the basis of healthcare market prices, given the non-realistic estimation of hospital output.

15 D. Niakas, J. Kyriopoulos, 'Methodological problems of empirical research approaches to AIDS cost and the creation of a cost estimation pattern in Greece', *AIDS Economics and Management in Greece* (eds. J. Kyriopoulos, H. Kornarou, V. Paparizos), pp. 157–178. Centre for Health Social Sciences, Athens, 1993. In Greek.

16 Marginal cost: cost of producing additional output. For example, if the capacity of a hospital was increased to provide beds for an additional ten AIDS patients, the marginal cost would be the extra cost of the additional doctor and nurse workload, additional procedures and medication and new capital costs (for example, if a new ward had to be converted). There are great difficulties in precisely measuring both the level of hospital output and the marginal cost of increasing this output.

17 J. Kyriopoulos, 'Economic approach to AIDS. Methodological problems and research results', *Proceedings of 3rd Panhellenic Conference on AIDS*, pp. 71–80. Hellenic Association for the Study and Control of AIDS, Athens, 1991. In Greek.

18 J. Kyriopoulos, D. Niakas, E. Georgoussi, 'AIDS cost in Greece: a prospective approach based on epidemiological scenarios of HIV/AIDS', *AIDS Economics and Management in Greece* (eds. J. Kyriopoulos, H. Kornarou, V. Paparizos), pp. 89–98. Centre for Health and Social Science, 1993. In Greek.

19 A reform concerning the introduction of a prospective financing system could be the implementation of capitation rates or case-mix budgeting techniques according to various clinical, diagnostic, etc, criteria. Most reforms in the developed countries are mainly focused on the adoption of alternative methods of financing healthcare.

20 J. Kyriopoulos, M. Gitona, H. Kornarou, 'Managed care programmes of AIDS patients and prospective financing', *AIDS Economics and Management in Greece* (eds. J. Kyriopoulos, H. Kornarou, V. Paparizos), pp. 149–156. Centre for Health Social Sciences, Athens, 1993. In Greek.

21 K. Tolley, M. Gyldmark, 'The treatment and care costs of people with HIV infection or AIDS: development of a standardised cost framework for Europe', *Health Policy*, 24, pp. 55–70, 1993.

D. Niakas, J. Kyriopoulos, 'Methodological problems of empirical research approaches to AIDS cost and the creation of a cost estimation pattern in Greece', *AIDS Economics and Management in Greece* (eds. J. Kyriopoulos, H. Kornarou, V. Paparizos), pp. 157–178. Centre for Health Social Sciences, Athens, 1993. In Greek.

An Approach to the Direct and Indirect Cost of AIDS in Greece

Professor George Papaevangelou, H. Kornarou, A. Roumeliotou, J. Yfantopoulos

Athens School of Public Health, University of Athens, Greece

In Greece, the future scenarios of the incidence of AIDS do not appear to be as terrifying as the worldwide picture. However, the prospective tendency of the epidemic is worrying.[1] The total number of AIDS cases in Greece reported by 31 December 1993 was 891, and at 31 December 1992 it was 721 – an increase of 170 cases in just one year. The epidemiological pattern of AIDS in Greece is shown in the following tables: Table 1 shows the distribution of AIDS cases by transmission category and sex; Table 2, the AIDS cases by disease category; Table 3, the AIDS cases by age and sex category; and Table 4 shows the time series of reported AIDS cases and deaths to 31 December 1993.

Table 1

AIDS cases by transmission category and sex in Greece (31–12–93) (Age>13)

Transmission category	Men		Women		Total	
	n	%	n	%	n	%
Homo/bisexual	451	57.9	–	–	451	51.8
IV Drug Users (IDUs)	27	3.5	11	12.0	38	4.4
Homo/bisexual IDUs	5	0.6	0	0.0	5	0.6
Transfusion Recipients	27	3.5	18	19.6	45	5.2
Haemophiliacs	56	7.2	0	0.0	56	6.4
Heterosexuals	116	14.9	45	48.9	161	18.5
Others	97	12.4	18	19.5	115	13.1
Total	779	100	92	100	871	100

Table 2
AIDS cases by disease category in Greece
(31–12–93)

Disease category	Cases	%
Opportunistic infections (OIs)	585	65.7
Kaposi's sarcoma	108	12.1
Kaposi's sarcoma + OIs	17	1.9
Lymphoma	25	2.8
Encephalopathy	58	6.5
HIV wasting syndrome	97	10.9
Interstitial pneumonia	1	0.1
Total	891	100.0

Table 3
AIDS cases by age, sex category in Greece
(31–12–93)
(Age>13)

Age Group	Men		Women		Total	
	n	%	n	%	n	%
13–14 Years	1	0.1	1	1.1	2	0.2
15–19	12	1.5	3	3.3	15	1.7
20–24	30	3.9	10	10.9	40	4.6
25–29	118	15.1	21	22.8	139	16.0
30–34	152	19.5	16	17.4	168	19.3
35–39	144	18.5	11	12.0	155	17.8
40–49	169	21.7	7	7.6	176	20.2
50–59	65	8.3	7	7.6	72	8.3
60+	59	7.6	10	10.9	69	7.9
Unknown	29	3.7	6	6.5	35	4.0
Total	779	100.0	92	100.0	871	100.0

Years	No. cases	Accumulated cases	Deaths
1984	6	6	6
1985	7	13	7
1986	22	35	17
1987	53	88	41
1988	82	170	42
1989	107	277	60
1990	135	412	32
1991	147	559	21
1992	162	721	30
1993	170	891	86
Total	891	–	342

Table 4
AIDS cases by time series in Greece
(31–12–93)

With numbers of HIV-positive persons increasing and survival times lengthening it is important to predict the further spread of the virus and also the needs of healthcare services, and to estimate the burden of the disease on the economic system. The economic consequences of AIDS are likely to lead to resources being diverted from other health policy priorities. An assessment of the annual costs of treatment and care per patient serves several purposes, including assisting health and social service purchasers to set budgets or reimbursements for HIV/AIDS care, and as data for use in economic evaluations of the relative cost-effectiveness of alternative HIV/AIDS services.

Economic estimation of the real cost of AIDS enables the burden on the national budget, on the healthcare sector and on the social security system to be identified.

This should also help clarify the need for a complete and coordinated programme of the organization, management and financing of healthcare services for HIV-positive persons.

The purpose of this paper is to evaluate the impact of AIDS upon the health, the insurance and the socio-economic sector in Greece.

Data

An attempt was made at the University of Athens to create the largest possible database of AIDS cases in Greece. In 1991, 71.2 per cent of the total number of AIDS cases in Greece had been hospitalized in Athens.[2] Out of 150 patient files from two General Hospitals in Athens with clinics specializing in AIDS, 105 cases, covering the period 1990–91, were finally collected for further analysis. The approach used to define HIV and AIDS is based on that of the American Centers for Disease Control and Prevention (CDC).

The lack of a computerized system storing hospital data on HIV-positive persons has meant that only retrospective analysis is possible. The database does not cover healthcare services provided by other public hospitals, private clinics or out-patient visits paid for out-of-pocket by the patient. Services provided by volunteers are also excluded. Table 5 presents the sample of HIV/AIDS cases by age and sex.

Methods

Ideally, estimation of the costs of treatment models for AIDS should be based on the marginal opportunity costs of resources used. This requires specification of the amount and type of resources used, and calculation of the value of those resources in terms of their best alternative use. However, the lack of appropriate data forces the use of other methods.

Table 5
Sample of HIV/AIDS cases by age and sex category

Age	Men	Women	Total	%
0–14	–	–	–	–
15–24	8	1	9	8.6
25–44	69	3	72	68.6
45–64	17	–	17	16.2
65+	1		1	0.9
Missing[a]	4	2	6	5.7
Total	99	6	105	100

[a] Age unknown

A costing model was developed to measure the direct and indirect cost components of the different types of therapies.[3] Data to be collected are divided into two categories.

Fixed data, including:

- demographics (sex, date of birth, residence, etc.);
- risk group and relevant medical history.

Variable data, including:

- diagnosis following 1989 CDC definitions;
- clinical parameters important in the follow-up of the HIV infection;
- utilization characteristics such as out-patient care, hospital admission, duration of hospital stay;
- treatments such as drug therapy (type and dosage) blood transfusions, CHOP scheme (chemotherapy);
- diagnostic examinations such as blood analysis, hematological, immunological and biochemical tests, diagnostic procedures, serological and microbiological studies.

Direct cost

Direct costs are all the costs of prevention, treatment, rehabilitation and long-term care due to the burden of the disease on public and private healthcare sectors as well as on the home and the community. Direct costs are borne (predominantly) by the healthcare system in the treatment of the disease and include activities such as in-patient and out-patient services, medications and laboratory tests.

Table 6 outlines the methods used to determine the costs of each kind of hospital activity. The personnel cost is calculated using an estimate of the salary and time input of the healthcare workers (doctor, nurse). The per patient expenditure for supplies and disposable medical equipment is added to the personnel cost in order to estimate the overall costs per hospital day. Some activities, such as the CHOP scheme (chemotherapy), T-lymphocyte subset, pentamidine, and diagnostic examinations resulting from HIV infection, have been estimated on the basis of fixed prices charged by hospitals. Blood transfusion has been estimated by Yfantopoulos and Politi at a maximum of $142 per unit.[4] Treatment costs for other medications as well as the costs of diagnostic examinations are based on shadow prices: these are estimates of the cost of items or activities and are used instead of market prices as either the latter undervalue these resources or relevant market price data were not available. Cost figures for all hospital activities are assumed to be constant over the two-year period of observation, using 1991 price levels. In subsequent analysis using this data, costs are expressed in 1991 US dollars.

In addition to hospital care, people with AIDS/HIV might receive counselling for emotional support; community and residential support services; and informal care services provided by family and friends. Owing to the lack of data on these aspects of care, it is impossible to produce accurate cost estimates.

Indirect cost

Using a narrow definition, the indirect costs to the economy of ill health reflect the value of those goods and services that could have been produced if a person had not fallen ill. Therefore, indirect costs measure the losses in worker pro-

Activities	Costing method
Out-patient care	Shadow prices
Hospitalization	
Medication	Shadow prices
Laboratory tests	Shadow prices
Hospice cost	Shadow prices
Blood transfusion	Estimated cost
CHOP scheme (chemotherapy)	Estimated cost
T-lymphocyte subset	Estimated cost
Pentamidine	Estimated cost
Zidovudine	Shadow prices
Examinations relevant to HIV+ condition	Estimated cost

Table 6
Source of costs for different hospital activities

[a] Shadow prices: as the hospital charges are an unrealistic indicator of true cost, we have used an estimated price fro certain items. These are known as 'shadow prices'.

[b] Estimated cost: cost calculated by the authors (see section on methodology).

ductivity that result from illness, disability and premature death.

In a wider sense, indirect costs accruing to society include social and personal time and income loss both to the individual and others who give up work or other activities in order to care for the person with HIV/AIDS.[5]

In our study we use the narrower definition to estimate indirect costs. The method we use is known as the 'Human Capital Method', which requires an estimate of the lost productivity due to premature death as a result of AIDS. Owing to lack of data, we have not attempted to measure the loss of 'domestic productivity' (i.e. that incurred by people who look after the home).

AIDS patients are likely to die many years before they would have died if they had not contracted HIV infection, although their life expectancy varies over a wide range. Consequently we have used a number of assumptions in order to calculate indirect costs:

- The productive age for men is 20–65 years old and for women 20–60 years old.
- Working life expectancies by age groups are 35 years for the age group 20–24 years old, 25 years for the age group 25–44 years old and five years for the age group 45–64 years old.

  According to the age of death for each person of our sample, we estimate the lost working life expectancy per death and from this we can estimate the loss of future productivity.

- Gross Domestic Product (GDP) per worker is used to estimate the annual loss of current (1990 year of observation) and future productivity. Actual salaries were not used because of lack of data.

Indirect costs are calculated by multiplying life years lost by estimated annual GDP loss per AIDS death. A basic principle of economic theory is that future

losses are not valued as highly as losses in the present time period. Therefore, life years lost in the future must be discounted to reflect this.

The formula we use to estimate the present value of indirect costs is:

$$Pr = \sum_{t=1}^{n} \frac{Qt}{(1+r)}t$$

or

$$Pr = Qt. \sum \frac{1}{(1+r)}n$$

In terms:

Pr	=	Present value
Q	=	GDP per worker in 1990
n	=	working life expectancy
r	=	the annual discount rate (1990, r = 18%)
Qt	=	GDP in 't' time period for each worker

It is important to note that our calculation of indirect cost is a low estimate because parameters such as quality of life during the illness and loss of productivity due to friends and family adopting a carer role could not be estimated.

Results

Direct cost

The study focuses on the cost of hospital in-patient and out-patient services.The lifetime aspects of cost were considered from the first HIV-positive diagnosis (time of infection) until death. Out of 105 cases, 38 patients who had died had a life expectancy of 22–30 months (the survival time of these patients is short because of late diagnosis). They used 578 packs of zidovudine (1 pack contains 100 capsules, each of 100 mg), made 426 out-patient hospital visits, and had 1,232 total number of in-patient hospital days. The mean length of stay in the hospital is 11.7 days per admission.

A breakdown of the hospital costs for AIDS patients demonstrated that the largest component was for drugs at 38.4 per cent of total costs. The operational cost of the AIDS Unit represented 14.7 per cent of total costs, laboratory tests were 5.5 per cent, personnel costs were 37.5 per cent and other miscellaneous costs were 3.8 per cent.

Table 7 outlines both lifetime hospital costs and annual costs per HIV/AIDS patient. The direct lifetime cost is based on data from the first HIV-positive diagnosis until death in 38 patients, but annual cost is based on the whole sample of 105 cases who have used healthcare services for two years. The lifetime cost per patient was estimated at $24,160 and the annual cost per case amounted to $8,428. Other estimations have shown average hospital costs for AIDS patients of $23,700 and $13,900 for HIV-positive patients.[6] Efforts have been made to estimate daily hospitalization costs by disease category:[7]

Kaposi's sarcoma (KS): average daily hospital cost = $220 per AIDS patient

PCP : average daily hospital cost = $210 per AIDS patient

KS and PCP: average daily hospital cost = $263 per AIDS patient

In addition, the average daily hospitalization cost of non-AIDS patients is $108 compared to an average daily cost of all patients with AIDS of between $226 and $476.[8]

Table 8 presents the cost of hospital out-patient care activities generated for patients with HIV infection: 56 HIV-positive persons visited the out-patient clinic 740 times, an average per person-year of 13.2. These visits were for check-up consultations and in order to receive zidovudine. Zidovudine is provided through hospitals to the patients free of charge and it is not sold on the market.

The cost of out-patient hospital care received by 56 HIV-positive individuals is estimated at $168 per person per visit with a breakdown into the following cost components: 61 per cent of the total cost is covered by drugs (mainly zidovudine), 32 per cent by personnel and 7 per cent by laboratory tests and other investigations performed.

Activity	Lifetime cost $	%	Annual cost $	%
Zidovudine (+ relevant examinations)	9,022	37.3	1,343	15.9
Out-patient care	963	4.0	1,122	13.3
In-patient care	14,175	58.7	5,963	70.8
Cost per person	24,160	100.0	8,428	100.0

Table 7
Hospital cost components of HIV/AIDS care in Greece (per person)

Table 8
Out-patient hos-
pital cost com-
ponents per
visit, per
HIV/AIDS case,
in Greece

Activity	Cost $	%
Drugs (+AZT)	102	61
Invasive treatment and Lab. tests	13	7
Personnel payment	53	32
Total	168	100

It is important to recognize that a disproportionate burden of the direct cost of
AIDS is falling on the public sector. Social
insurance is the only source of payment.
Moreover, social insurance is funded
mostly by the state budget and secondly
by social insurance contributions. Private
insurance is not a major funder of healthcare in Greece and is even less so in the
case of HIV/AIDS treatment and care.

Indirect cost

In order to study indirect cost we use data
from the 1990 economic year. At that time
the Gross Domestic Product per worker
was $11,774. In the observation year, 1990,
the total productivity losses from 105
HIV/AIDS cases were estimated at
$1,236,270. Consequently, the present
value of the lifetime indirect costs (based
on a narrow definition of lost work productivity) amounted to $6.2 million for
105 HIV/AIDS cases. Lifetime indirect
cost per person is therefore estimated at
up to $59,047.

Another study that estimated indirect
costs associated with HIV/AIDS in
Greece was that of Kyriopoulos et al.[9]
Using three epidemiological scenarios for
the five-year period 1989–93 they estimated indirect costs of $54.5–73.1 million
and a total cost of AIDS in Greece for that
period of $100.1–201.7 million. They pro-
duced an annual indirect cost estimate of
$35,573–86,304 per person.

These estimates of indirect cost demonstrate the large potential loss of economic
productivity due to AIDS. On top of this is
the larger loss of total social productivity
and the human consequences of AIDS
which means there can be no doubt about
the need for and importance of prevention.
Information and the promotion of safer
behaviour remain the only instruments for
countering HIV infection. The Ministry of
Health in Greece spends only $1,405,622 on
the seven AIDS Reference Centres in
Greece. If resources were increased, benefits would be felt in the near and distant
future both financially and in terms of the
human suffering prevented.

Discussion

The estimates presented above define the upper bounds for the cost of treatment included in our analysis, although because of data limitations these are underestimates of the total cost of the illness. We lack data on the cost of treatment provided at other hospitals and services provided by other private clinics, family and friends, and on social productivity losses.

It is important to underline that the main problem in assessing the cost of treatment of any disease, even AIDS, in Greece is the lack of a central information system which would facilitate data collection and permit a less biased estimation of the current cost profiles.

Moreover, with the present national health service system in Greece, the hospitalization cost is based on charges defined by the Ministry of Health. Consequently, the real cost components of the disease are often underestimated.

It is also important to use current data to estimate the cost of care because of rapid changes in treatment regimens for persons with human immunodeficiency virus (HIV) infection. New pharmaceutical products give better quality of life and longer life expectancy but mean that persons with HIV need to receive lifelong continuous out-patient and in-patient care from infection to death. Although the average length of stay in hospital has decreased, an increasing number of people with HIV infection are using services. The lack of home-care and voluntary healthcare services increases the frequency of hospitalization, resulting in an increase in the economic burden of the disease.

Improvements in preventive and therapeutic care continue to slow the rate of progression from HIV infection to serious complications and reduce the intensity of treatment for people with AIDS. HIV may be viewed in the future as a moderately expensive chronic illness.

The only means of acquiring information about all services received by a person with HIV is to conduct a survey among people with HIV infection. However, that is difficult in Greece because of the possibility of discrimination if a patient's health condition were to become publicly known.

Conclusion

The care provided to HIV-positive persons in Greece is hospital oriented and the cost per case reflects mainly hospitalization costs. In our study of HIV/AIDS patients[10] we have estimated the total direct lifetime costs of treatment and care as $24,160 per case (for 38 patients who had died). This is broken down as follows: $14,175 for in-patient care; $963 for out-patient care and $9,022 for zidovudine treatment. In addition, the lifetime indirect cost per case is estimated at $59,047. Possibly even higher daily and total costs per AIDS patient can be expected in the near future due to the increase of AIDS cases, the lengthening of life expectancy and the introduction of new and expensive drugs and therapeutic methods in AIDS treatment.

However, the findings of this study suggest that, since the cost of out-patient care is much less than the hospital cost, the further development of out-patient care could be more appropriate and cost-effective and more humane. The future priorities of health policies should be redefined and redirected towards preventive and out-patient treatments to minimize both the financial and social impact of AIDS.

Finally, the small size of the financial support for AIDS in the national budget raises questions about the need to alter the methods of organization administration and financing of AIDS healthcare services in Greece.[11]

1 G. Papaevangelou, *VIII International Conference of AIDS*, 19–24 July 1992, Amsterdam. Published in *Hellenic Archives of AIDS*, 5: 22–25. Hellenic Association for the Study and Control of AIDS, Athens, 1992.

2 A. Roumeliotou, *AIDS Prevention: 3rd Panhellenic Congress on AIDS*. BHTA publications, 1991.

3 D.P. Rice, *Estimating the Cost of Illness*, Health Economics, Series Bi 6. US Public Health Service, Washington DC, 1966.

J. Kyriopoulos, 'The competition in the market of health care services. International experience and Greek prospects', *Health Review*, 2, 5, 12: 41–46, 1991.

J. Yfantopoulos, 'Economic evaluation of healthcare services', report, University of Athens Nursing School, Athens, 1992.

Borletts, J.C.C., Jager, J.C., Poos, M.J.J.C., Dijkgraaf, M.G.W., Geels, R.M.A., Vrehen, H. and Schrijvers, A.J.P., 'Hospital cost for patients with HIV infection in a University Hospital in The Netherlands', *Health Policy*, 16:43–64, 1990, Elsevier Science Publishers B.V.

4 J. Yfantopoulos, C. Politi, *Blood Transfusion and the Challenge of AIDS in Greece. Medical and Economic Aspects*. BETA Medical Publishers, Athens, Greece, 1993.

5 A. Scitovsky, M. Cline, P. Lee, 'Medical care costs of patients with AIDS in San Francisco', *The Journal of the American Medical Association*, 256: 3103–6, 1986.

B. Bowen, 'The medical costs of AIDS in California', paper presented to the American Public Health Association, Las Vegas, October 1986.

K. Kizer, 'Acquired immune deficiency syndrome in California: a prescription for meeting the needs of 1990', report prepared by the California Department of Health Services, March 1986.

G.R. Seage, S. Landers, A. Barry *et al.* 'Medical care costs of AIDS in Massachusetts', *The Journal of the American Medical Association*, 256, 3107–9, 1986.

A. Scitovsky, D.P. Rice, J. Showstack *et al.*, 'Estimating the direct and indirect costs of acquired immune deficiency syndrome 1985, 1986 and 1990', *Public Health Report*, 102: 5–17; 1987.

C. Herlitz and B. Brorsson, 'The AIDS epidemic in Sweden: estimates of costs 1986, 1987 and 1990', *Scandinavian Journal of Social Medicine*, 17: 39–48, 1989.

J. Yfantopoulos, C. Politi, *Blood Transfusion and the Challenge of AIDS in Greece. Medical and Economic Aspects*. BETA Medical Publishers, Athens, Greece, 1993.

6 G. Papaevangelou, *VIII International Conference of AIDS*, 19–24 July 1992, Amsterdam. Published in *Hellenic Archives of AIDS*, 5: 22–25. Hellenic Association for the Study and Control of AIDS, Athens, 1992.

7 V. Paparizos, 'Study on the economic cost of hospital care for AIDS patients in Greece', doctorate thesis, University of Athens, Athens 1992.

8 *Ibid.*
H. Kornarou, 'Direct and indirect cost of AIDS in Greece', doctorate thesis, University of Athens, 1992. (In Greek).

9 J. Kyriopoulos, D. Niakas, E. Georgoussi, 'AIDS cost in Greece: a prospective approach based on epidemiological senarios of HIV/AIDS', *AIDS Economics and Management in Greece*, pp. 89–98. Centre for Health and Social Science, Athens School of Public Health, 1993.

10 As our study has produced a mean annual cost for 105 patients across the spectrum of HIV-positivity and AIDS, the range is likely to be very large according to actual diagnostic stage.

11 J. Kyriopoulos, H. Kornarou, V. Paparizos, *AIDS Economics and Management in Greece*. Centre for Health Social Sciences, Athens School of Public Health, 1993.

Epidemiological Projections of HIV in France: Estimates for the Indirect Economic Costs

Professor Denis-Clair Lambert

Department of Economics, University of Lyons, France

The simulation model

This chapter describes a model developed to estimate the potential indirect economic cost from premature mortality due to HIV/AIDS in France. A simulation of mortality trends for the French AIDS epidemic is based on HIV prevalence estimates and AIDS mortality rates derived from Hoskins' 1987 model for the USA.[1] HIV prevalence in France at the end of the 1980s has been estimated at between 100,000 and 200,000 cases.[2] The latest estimate for HIV prevalence for 1993 puts the number at the lower end of this range at between 120,000 and 130,000 cases.[3] A mid-point estimate from the 1989 estimates (150,000 cases) has been used for the indirect cost simulations in this chapter.

The simulations are based on recent HIV prevalence rates and so do not include cumulative AIDS cases, which by 30 July 1994 had reached 31,344 cases in France. However, adjustments for under-reporting mean that this figure may be nearer 36,000–40,000. The figure is questionable because of doubts about the validity of the criteria used to define AIDS and problems of under-reporting of AIDS cases. Short-run projections of HIV infection for the period 1989–93 produce results that differ little from the present estimates. Longer-term projections of HIV infection and deaths will have greater uncertainty and variation. Projections for the period 1970–2020 are based on a retrospective estimate of the first infections during the 1970s and cumulative annual mortality rates for each newly infected cohort, using an extreme assumption of 30 years survival (so that the 1990 cohort simulation is followed through to 2020).

The HIV/AIDS mortality projection has been used to estimate the indirect cost of mortality up to 2020. The indirect cost includes the estimated loss of private income and wealth for the individual and for the collective cohort of adults and children due to premature death as well as the direct medical costs. However, only the direct medical costs make an impact on the budget of the health authorities.

All prices used for the indirect cost of mortality are 1989 prices. Indirect costs up to 2020 are discounted by 3 per cent to account for the assumption of a lower present value of future costs. Nominal prices for the direct medical cost are produced by the AIDS division of the French Ministry of Health.

Model assumptions

Six transmission groups have been identified in the model. Three are dominant: homosexuals, injecting drug users (IDUs) and heterosexuals. Three other groups are: adults and children who have had blood transfusions; haemophiliacs; and children born to HIV-positive mothers, who remain HIV-positive (the majority of babies born of HIV-positive mothers are not infected but will initially have their mothers' HIV antibodies). Using the estimated prevalence for HIV in 1989 of 150,000 cases, two approaches to estimating the proportion of cases in each transmission group have been used:

Direct estimate method This produces the following percentages: homosexuals represent 54 per cent of cases, drug users 22 per cent of cases and heterosexual transmission represents 18 per cent of cases (Figure 1).

Back-calculation method (whereby transmission group percentages for HIV prevalence in 1989 are 'back-calculated' from current percentages for AIDS cases.) Using this method the transmission group pattern is very different from the direct estimates, drug users being the dominant group with 38 per cent of cases, heterosexuals representing 32 per cent of cases, and homosexual transmission amounting to only 25 per cent of cases (Figure 2).

The epidemiological scenarios

Four epidemiological scenarios have been defined for the HIV transmission rate, incorporating alternative mortality projections and methods of transmission group estimation (Table 1).

The distribution of HIV infection between the transmission groups in the future depends on the initial prevalence estimates for the dominant groups and the rate of progression of infection in each

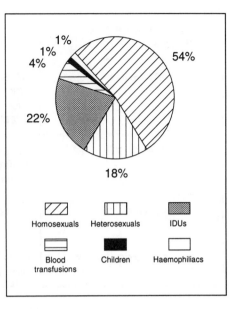

Figure 1
1989 direct estimate

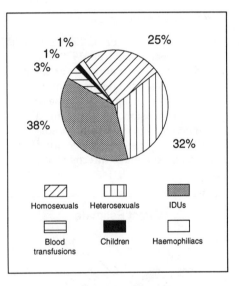

Figure 2
**1989
Back-calculation**

group. Two of the epidemiological scenarios (one using the direct estimate method, the other using back-calculation) are presented in Figure 3. Figure 3 illustrates that by the year 2020 heterosexual and IDU transmission could represent almost half of all cases (scenario IV, direct estimate method), and could be much higher (scenario I, back-calculation method).

Main assumptions HIV rate	
scenario I	pessimistic epidemic trends, based on back-calculation estimates of transmission groups (dominated by drug and hetero-sexual infection)
scenario II	pessimistic epidemic, based on direct estimate of transmission groups (dominated by homosexual infection)
scenario III	contained epidemic, based on back-calculation estimates
scenario IV	contained epidemic, based on direct estimate

Progression of the epidemic

The rate of progression of the epidemic is estimated using data from 1970–89, assuming a ten-year period from infection to AIDS-related death, with the first AIDS case appearing in 1983. The projected transmission rate of the infection is simulated using two possible scenarios of HIV increase: a 'pessimistic' infection rate and a 'contained' infection rate.

These were applied to the back-calculation and direct estimates of 1989 HIV prevalence. Figures 4 and 5 present the estimates for the two sub-models.[4] The aggregation of the six groups produces average growth rates for the 1990s of approximately 9 per cent for the pessimistic epidemic, and 4.5 per cent for the contained epidemic, and for 2010–20 a 1.5–0.5 per cent growth rate.

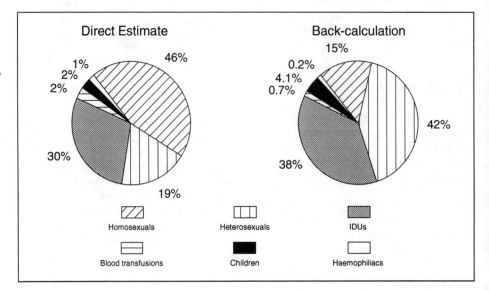

Changes in annual mortality

The estimates of annual mortality change due to AIDS vary according to the epidemiological scenario and sub-model used (Figure 6). In comparison with the contained infection sub-model (scenario III and IV) with an annual mortality of 10,000 cases in 1992, mortality under the pessimistic infection sub-model (scenario I and II) could be two or three times as high over the next two decades.

Direct cost of AIDS

The direct medical cost of HIV/AIDS has been estimated by the AIDS division of the French Ministry of Health. This includes costs of hospitalization, outpatient treatment, doctors and a large part of the prevention and research expenses. Most of the direct medical costs are met by the public sector. The budgetary impact for 1993 was approximately FFr 4,000 million (Figure 7), a small fraction of the total health service costs (FFr 600,000 million).

Estimating the indirect cost of premature mortality

A proportion of the indirect costs of premature mortality for HIV/AIDS can be attributed to the health budget in France. This is the amount of funds used for tort and other liabilities. The principal financial liability has been the compensation of individuals who have been infected through blood transfusion. This represents approximately FFr 4,000 million in 1993. This figure takes account of the different amounts of compensation paid to adults and children – whether haemophiliacs who received contaminated factor VIII blood products, or those who received infected blood transfusions – taking into account age, sex and potential life years lost. A separate simulation has been conducted for the four scenarios for the case of blood contamination and

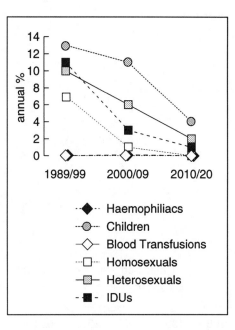

Figure 4

Pessimistic infection model annual increase in HIV prevalence

Calculated using direct estimates and back-calculation methods

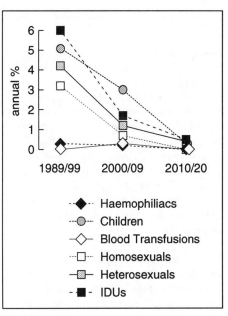

Figure 5

Contained epidemic annual increase in HIV prevalence

Calculated using direct estimates and back-calculation methods

the budgetary impact of providing indemnity.

The estimate of indirect cost is based on the potential working or active life years lost and estimated foregone average income over this time period. Wealth

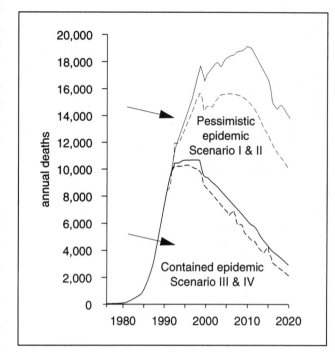

annual deaths

Pessimistic epidemic Scenario I & II

Contained epidemic Scenario III & IV

Figure 6
Annual AIDS mortality
France
1976/2020

losses and state transfer payments (e.g. taxes, welfare, pensions) have not been included. Projections of life years lost due to premature HIV/AIDS mortality are made for the years 1989–2020. Different values of economic loss are estimated for each transmission group. For instance, Figure 8 presents the economic loss for the single year 1992. An average per case estimate of FFr 1,846,000 is based on a conservative estimate of retirement at age 60 and 25 years of active life lost (median age at death of 35).

The human capital approach has been used to calculate indirect costs. Rice *et al.* estimated that the present value of lifetime earnings for an adult was twice the value of an infant's death.[5] Hence, for the simulation model, the value of human life is assumed to increase from the end of adolescence to a maximum for male adults aged between 30–40 at death, and declines to a lower level equivalent to that of infants for elderly persons. For 1992, this produces an estimate of indirect costs per case varying from FFr 901,000 for chil-

dren to FFr 2,451,100 for heterosexuals and homosexual adults. The important determinants of costs are: age at death, and the probability of being in work. Lower values are, therefore, estimated for people receiving blood transfusions (especially more elderly people); higher values are associated with younger haemophiliacs (Figure 8). However, the decrease in value of expected earnings after retirement is not an entirely valid assumption. The economic loss of a premature death is reduced if dependants are compensated by inheritance of wealth which can then be put to productive use.

National estimates of the indirect costs of HIV/AIDS in France for 1992

Based on scenario I, the estimated indirect cost of HIV/AIDS mortality is FFr 19,583 million (Figure 9). Using the back-calculation method, three-quarters of the indirect cost is estimated to be related to heterosexual and homosexual transmission cases.

The direct costs of HIV/AIDS in 1992 were estimated to be FFr 6,592 million. This consists of the costs of medical care (FFr 3,004 million), prevention and research (FFr 1,288 million) and compensation awards for individuals acquiring the virus through contaminated blood products (FFr 2,300 million). By adding these to the indirect costs, the total cost of HIV/AIDS is estimated to be FFr 26,175 million in 1992 (Figure 10).[6] Seventy-five per cent of total costs consist of indirect costs.

Simulation of future indirect cost

Owing to a projected increasing period between HIV infection and death from AIDS for the drug user, heterosexual and children transmission groups, and the contained trend for new cases of transmission through transfusion, a changing

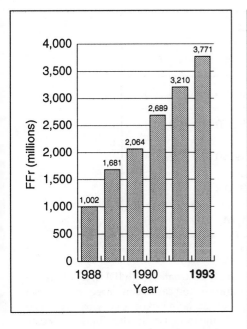

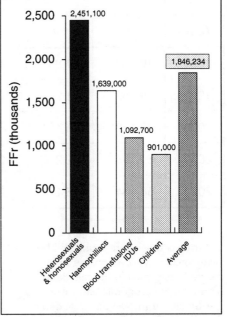

Figure 7 (left)
HIV/AIDS direct medical cost
France FFr (millions)

Figure 8 (right)
HIV/AIDS indirect costs per case
France 1992, FFr (thousands)

cost pattern exists for the four scenarios. First, based on the 'pessimistic infection' sub-model, the peak in mortality cost is predicted for the years 2000–10 to be five times greater than in 1989. Under the 'contained infection' sub-model, the maximum cost impact occurs in the present decade and declines during the next two decades. The 2020 mortality cost of scenario IV, however, represents only 17 per cent of that for scenario I.

Secondly, important differences exist in indirect costs according to transmission route (using either back-calculation or direct estimates). The global mortality cost depends on whether more life years were

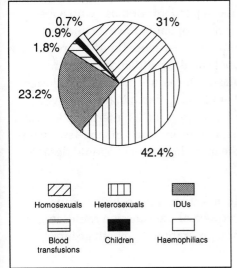

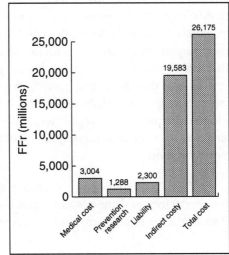

Figure 9 (left)
Distribution of HIV/AIDS indirect costs
France 1992, Scenario I
FFr 19,583 million

Figure 10 (right)
1992 Total cost of HIV/AIDS
France FFr (millions)

Table 2
Indirect cost of HIV/AIDS Mortality in France
FFr millions, present value discounted at 3 per cent to 1989 values

Years	Scenarios			
	I	II	III	IV
1989	10,856	11,843	10,856	11,843
1992	19,583	21,274	18,370	20,113
2000	38,122	36,401	21,650	22,352
2010	60,168	52,276	19,314	17,736
2020	58,164	45,172	11,744	9,666

lost from active heterosexual and homosexual males, who, according to the methodology used in the calculations, have a higher economic value due to a greater labour market participation rate than, for instance, drug users. Therefore, the relative shares of the HIV/AIDS mortality associated with IDUs, children, and transfusion cases, compared to heterosexual and homosexual cases, are responsible for the trends in the distribution of costs and mortality in the scenario projections.

Conclusions

Should health policy-makers use estimates and projections of the indirect economic and social costs of premature deaths, including new risks such as AIDS?

If a short-term outlook is adopted, there is little possibility of taking into account the economic losses incurred by the dependants of those who have died from AIDS, the insurance system and the economy. However, indirect costs have frequently been calculated in order to raise more funds to prevent and compensate for traffic accidents, alcoholism, drug addiction or deaths attributed to tobacco. The reason these catastrophic issues are treated as long-term risks is that there is no possibility of eradicating them; in the same vein are we sure that the AIDS epidemic is under control? If a long-term outlook is adopted for public health policies, AIDS should be included in long-term planning and the economic consequences of the mortality increase should deserve more attention.

In this French simulation, the spread of the infection appears high because of the importance of drug addiction and heterosexual transmission routes in France and the limited impact of prevention programmes on both groups.

There are two principal conclusions from this study:

- the next two decades will see increasing AIDS-related mortality rates, given the low survival patterns after fifteen years of HIV-positivity. AIDS is likely to remain one of the main life-threatening diseases for young adults – both for men and for women.

- the indirect cost of HIV/AIDS mortality estimated for 1992 (FFr 19,583 million) is several times the size of the total direct cost (medical costs, prevention, research and liability compensation) of FFr 6,592 million in 1992. Even if the human capital method was replaced by a more modest estimate of indirect cost for AIDS, based on those used by insurance companies for death compensation from roads accidents (in this approach losses are calculated for only four years of future estimated average earnings), the indirect annual cost of 10,000–20,000 HIV/AIDS deaths would still represent more than the direct cost of the disease.

---

1 I. Hoskins, *HIV Mortality*. Society of Actuaries, Illinois, August 1987.

2 J.B. Brunet, A.J. Valleron *et al*, 'La prévalence de l'infection par le VIH en France', *Bulletin Epidémiologique Hebdomadaire*, 37, 1990.

3 D. Costagliola, N. Rude and A.J. Valleron, 'Incidence cumulée et prévalence de l'infection à VIH en France à la fin de l'année 1989: estimation par rétrocalcul', *Revue Française d'Epidémiologie et de Santé Publique*, 1994.

4 Assumptions are applied both to back-calculation and direct estimate methods, but with different infection growth rates in the case of renewed and pessimistic trends. In the case of IDU transmission, the baseline estimates of cases for the two methods are: 32,018 cases for the direct estimate from 1989; and 55,261 cases for back-calculation from 1989. The annual infection growth rates assumptions are: contained epidemic to 1999 – 6 per cent; to 2009 – 0.5 per cent; pessimistic epidemic to 1999 – 11 per cent; to 2009 – 3.05 per cent; and to 2020 – 1 per cent.

Results for IDU transmission – number of cases per year

	1989	2000	2020
scenario I	55,261	167,241	244,516
scenario II	32,018	93,685	136,973
scenario III	55,261	100,943	127,399
scenario IV	32,018	58,486	73,837

5 D. Rice, W. Max and E. Mackenzie, 'The lifetime cost of injury', *Inquiry*, vol. 27, Winter 1990.

6 Y Souteyrand, 'Le prix d'un virus', *Autrement*, May 1992.

Sida et Soins, Chiffres Clés. Mission Sida, Direction des Hôpitaux, Paris, March 1994.

Projecting Individual Healthcare Costs of HIV/AIDS Patients in Catalonia

Dr Joan Rovira

SOIKOS, University of Barcelona, Spain

Dr Reiner Leidl

University of Limburg, The Netherlands

This chapter aims to identify the main data requirements for the projection of the heathcare costs of the HIV/AIDS epidemic and to illustrate the use of these data in a simulation model designed for such cost projections. The chapter is based on the results of a study commissioned by the AIDS Programme of the Department of Health of Catalonia. Among the objectives of the study were to develop the methodology and to provide an estimate of the individual healthcare costs of HIV/AIDS patients in Catalonia in 1990 and to obtain projections of future costs up to 1995. The study has three parts:

1. to estimate the average annual costs of healthcare for HIV/AIDS patients in different stages of the disease;
2. an estimation of the total annual costs of healthcare for HIV/AIDS patients in Catalonia in 1990;
3. the projection of those costs to 1995 under several possible scenarios.

We focus on the methods used to project costs and, owing to space constraints, limited attention will be given to the presentation and discussion of the quantitative results of the study. The methodology and results of the first part of the study have been published elsewhere.[1] The second part will be published in a forthcoming article.[2] They will only be summarized in this paper to highlight how they relate to the third part, the projection model.

The estimation of the average annual costs of healthcare for HIV/AIDS patients in different stages of the disease

To estimate and project the annual healthcare costs of AIDS, lifetime costs of the disease would ideally be needed. However, the time constraints of the study did not allow for a follow-up period of this length. Therefore, an alternative methodology was developed. We assumed that the disease can be represented by a staging model and we tried to calculate the cost per period (year) in each of the three following stages: (1) Early (asymptomatic HIV) stage; (2) intermediate stage; and (3) (full-blown) AIDS stage. By multiplying these costs by the duration of the corresponding stages, an estimation of the lifetime costs of the disease, as well as the annual prevalence costs in a given year, could be derived.

The results of this part of the study are based on a prospective nine month follow-up of 167 patients treated between 1 March 1990 and 30 November 1990 at the Hospital Príncipes de España (HPE), Barcelona. Data on resource use were recorded for each one of the subjects included in the study. The monetary unit costs (at 1989 prices) of the resources were based on an *ad hoc* extension of the hospital's cost accounting system, which provides cost data at the clinical department level. Those which could be individually assigned to patients (laboratory tests,

drugs, etc.) were valued on the basis of the unit costs data directly available from the hospital accounting system. A residual cost was estimated for the part of the costs relating to a hospital stay or an outpatient visit which could not be individually assigned.

Some of the results are shown in Tables 1 to 5. The database allows crossing any of the variables included to obtain disaggregate figures, for example the cost of zidovudine for homo–bisexual patients in the intermediate stage. The aggregate figures in Table 5, annual costs per individual, constitute the inputs to the next part of the study.

Stages	Person-days monitored	Number of admissions (in-patient)	Number of visits (out-patient)	Number of days in day-hospitalization[a]
Total	28,622	163	574	268
Early	9,054	3	85	0
Intermediate	4,944	22	116	0
AIDS	14,624	138	373	268

[a] Day-hospitalization is a new service provided by some hospitals. Patients are treated during the day in hospital, but spend the night at home.

Table 1 **Hospital resource use by diagnostic stage**

Stages	Number of admissions (in-patient)	Number of visits (out-patient)	Number of days in day-hospitalization
TOTAL	2.08	7.32	3.43
Early	0.12	3.43	0.00
Intermediate	1.62	6.56	0.00
AIDS	3.44	9.31	6.69

Table 2 **Annual hospital resource use per person by diagnostic stage**

Transmission group	Person-days monitored	Number of admissions (in-patient)	Number of visits (out-patient)	Number of days in day-hospitalization
Homo/bisexual (not IDU)	4,313	27	131	67
Heterosexual (not IDU)	1,866	15	50	38
Heterosexual (IDU)	21,750	114	379	163
Others	693	7	14	0

Table 3 Hospital resource use by transmission group

The estimation of the total annual costs of healthcare of AIDS patients in Catalonia in 1990.

The HPE is a National Health System (NHS) teaching hospital of the highest technological level (C level). Therefore its costs are higher than the corresponding costs of most of the types of hospital that treat AIDS patients in Catalonia. The procedure for estimating the average cost of healthcare for HIV/AIDS in Catalonia was as follows. We assumed that costs would vary according to ownership (NHS or non-NHS) and to level (A, AB, B, BC, or C). To derive estimates of the cost of AIDS patients treated in different hospitals from the cost figures obtained in the HPE study we used two basic assumptions:

• Tariffs (i.e. the *per diem* reimbursement of hospitalization paid by the NHS to a non-NHS hospital of a given level) reflect the actual costs of non-NHS hospitals. Most of these hospitals have been running budget deficits in the past years, hence tariffs may underestimate

Table 4 Annual hospital resource use per person by transmisson group

Transmission group	Number of admissions (in-patient)	Number of visits (out-patient)	Number of days in day-hospitalization
Total	2.08	7.32	3.43
Homo/bisexual (not IDU)	2.28	11.09	5.67
Heterosexual (not IDU)	2.93	9.78	7.43
Heterosexual (IDU)	1.91	6.36	2.74

the actual cost. However, the differences between tariffs and costs cannot be substantial as this would cause the deficits to grow continuously and place the hospitals in an untenable financial situation.

• The cost differentials by level among NHS hospitals are proportional to those among non-NHS hospitals.

Once the annual cost of healthcare of a patient treated in each type of hospital was estimated, we computed the average cost for Catalonia by weighting the former figures by the proportion of patients attending each type of hospital.

The distribution of patients by type of hospital was obtained from a hospital survey of AIDS patient admissions carried out in 1987 on a sample of eighteen hospitals, which accounted for about 90 per cent of all patients treated in Catalonia.

The projection of total costs to 1995 under several possible scenarios.

The projection of total cost was undertaken using the PCBAS model developed by Leidl.[3] The model provides deterministic simulations of the epidemic, which is modelled as consisting of two parallel epidemics: one in a 'low risk' group and the other in a 'higher risk' group of the population. The inputs of the model are the

size of the groups, the number of people infected in each group in the initial year, the growth of the infection in each group, the renewal rate in the 'high risk' group and the percentage of saturation, which sets a limit to the proportion of the population which can be infected. Additional assumptions have to be made regarding the transition probabilities between the stages of the disease as well as on the probabilities of survival. Finally, the economic variables have to be introduced in the form of annual costs per AIDS case.

By varying each set of parameters different simulated epidemics were produced. The results were then compared with the available empirical information on the epidemic to assess the validity of the model. In our case, the number of reported AIDS cases per year in Catalonia, corrected for reporting lags using the procedure proposed by Rosenberg,[4] was used to adjust the parameters of the model. There were, however, many parameter combinations that provide an acceptable fit to the observed data. Three sets of parameters were retained, representing three possible scenarios of the epidemic: a baseline scenario, a pessimistic scenario and an optimistic scenario.

The baseline scenario was that which provided the best fit to the observed data. The optimistic scenario assumes the same parameters as the baseline one, but assumes a zero incidence of HIV infec-

Stages	In-patient cost	Out-patient cost	Cost of days in day-hospitalization	Total
Early	11.8	65.0	–	76.8
Intermediate	851.5	297.6	–	1,149.1
AIDS	2,456.5	331.4	131.5	2,919.4

Table 5 **Annual patient cost (per thousand pesetas: 1989 prices)**

tions after 1991. The pessimistic scenario assumes a higher rate of growth in the 'low risk' group and a lower rate of growth in the 'high risk' group. This scenario still fits acceptably well with the observed data, while predicting an explosive growth of the epidemic in the long run.

Figures 1 to 5 illustrate simulations for several variables according to the three scenarios. Figure 1 shows a simulation for HIV incidence, which is the leading factor in defining the development of the epidemic. The differences among the three scenarios chosen are clearly illustrated. The differences are much less marked in

Figure 1
PC-based AIDS scenarios
Yearly incidence
HIV+

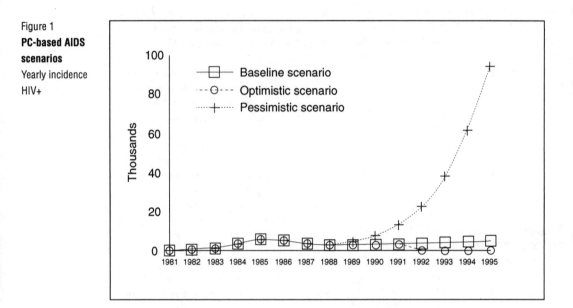

Figure 2
PC-based AIDS scenarios
AIDS – incidence

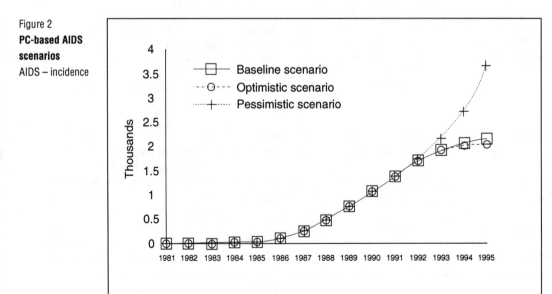

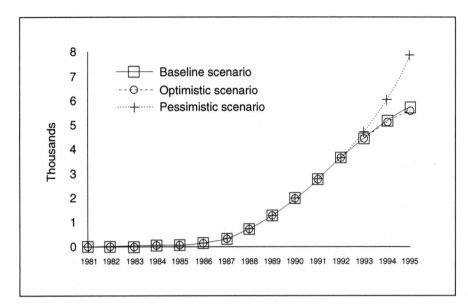

Figure 3
**PC-based AIDS
scenarios**
AIDS – preva-
lence

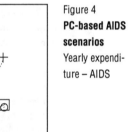

Figure 4
**PC-based AIDS
scenarios**
Yearly expendi-
ture – AIDS

the next figures, which present simulations for the incidence and the prevalence
of AIDS, and AIDS-related expenditures
and hospital beds requirements.

There were no similar data for HIV
patients, thus aggregate cost projections
were restricted to the AIDS stage The definitions of the pre-AIDS stages in the few
studies we could identify to provide infor-

mation to estimate the total costs of care
of these stages (i.e. for duration, cost per
time period, transition probabilities) do
not appear consistent.[5] Moreover, there is
no information on the distribution of pre-
AIDS patients among Catalan institutions,
similar to that recorded in the hospital
survey above. Therefore, we restricted the
estimate and projections of the aggregate
expenditure to the AIDS stage (Figure 4).

Figure 5
**PC-based AIDS
scenarios**
Hospital beds
needed yearly

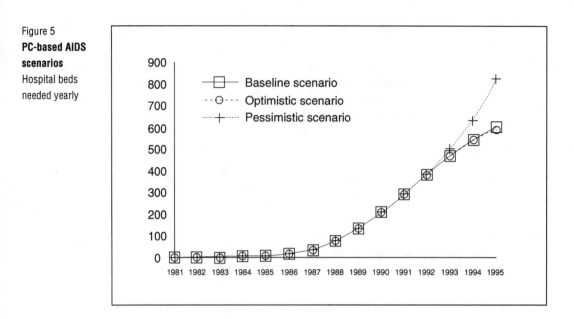

The trend in expenditure thus closely follows that of AIDS prevalence (Figure 3). However, it should be noted that it is precisely the number of individuals in the asymptomatic HIV and intermediate stages which shows the highest projected increases and, consequently, the highest potential for the future increase of total expenditure.

The adjustment required to link the average cost per patient found in the HPE cost study with the prevalence of recorded AIDS cases projected by the PCBAS model, had to be based on questionable assumptions supported by limited empirical evidence. Ideally, the projection of aggregate costs from prevalence data would use average costs per AIDS case obtained from a cohort follow-up study. However, the cost data available have usually been obtained from studies carried out in specific healthcare institutions, which cannot simply be linked to the prevalence data provided by epidemiological models such as the PCBAS.

In our estimation of total costs we adjusted the prevalence figures with an *ad hoc* utilization ratio based on data from the HPE. This ratio is the product of the number of patient days of observation in the HPE study and the average number of AIDS cases managed by the HPE AIDS out-patient clinic during the period of observation, multiplied by the length of that period, 270 days. The strong underlying assumptions are that:

- all existing AIDS cases in the area are included in the hospital records and are discontinued in case of death or migration and

- these patients receive care exclusively from the HPE.

These are certainly approximate and plausible assumptions, but they lack rigorous empirical evidence to support them.

Conclusions

We conclude that the Catalonia study provides a flexible approach to estimating and projecting the individual healthcare costs of HIV/AIDS patients. The methodology presented can be easily adapted to any setting, provided the data requirements are met. The accuracy and reliability of the estimates and projections obtained are of course questionable, owing to the lack of accuracy in the available information on which they are based. Still, they may be sufficient to reflect the order of magnitude, the relative values and the time trends of the phenomena analysed. Moreover, the study has served to identify the main informational limitations and, hence, the issues which require future empirical research to meet the needs of this type of analysis.

1 J. Rovira, G. López, A. Román, M. Santín, X. Badía. 'Els costos de l'assistència sanitària als malalts infectats per VIH i la SIDA: una aproximació empírica', *Salut Catalunya*, 6 (4): 139–44, 1992.

2 J. Rovira, A. Román, 'El coste de la asistencia sanitaria a pacientes con SIDA en Catalunya en 1990', unpublished report, Barcelona, 1992.

3 J. Rovira, R. Leidl, 'Estimación y proyecciones de los costes de atención sanitaria personal a los pacientes con VIH y SIDA en Cataluña mediante el modelo PC-BASED AIDS SCENARIOS (PCBAS)', (unpublished report), Barcelona, 1992.

R. Leidl, M.J. Postma, M.J.J.C. Poos, J.C. Jager, B. Majnoni d'Intignano, A.E. Baert, 'Construction of socioeconomic impact scenarios based on routine AIDS surveillance data', *AIDS-Impact Assessment, Modelling and Scenario Analysis* (eds. J.C. Jager, E. Ruitenberg), pp. 269–287. Elsevier, 1992.

R. Leidl, 'Konzeption, Eigenschaften und Anwendung eines deterministischen Modells der HIV-und-AIDS-Epidemie', *Gesundheit und Umwelt*, Reihe Med. Informatik, Biometrie und Epidemiologie Bd. 75 (eds. W. van Eimeren, K. Überla, K. Ulm), pp. 196–200. Springer, Berlin, 1992.

R. Leidl, 'Model-based scenarios to describe economic impacts of AIDS. The role of case-mix', *Economic Aspects of AIDS and HIV Infection* (eds. D. Schwefel, R. Leidl, J. Rovira, M.F. Drummond), pp. 282–294. Springer, Berlin, Heidelberg, 1990.

4 P.S. Rosenberg, 'A simple correction of AIDS surveillance data for reporting delays', *Journal of the Acquired Immune Deficiency Syndrome*, 3: 49–54, 1990.

5 J. Rovira, G. López, A. Román, M. Santín, X. Badía, 'Els costos de l' assistència sanitària als malalts infectats per VIH i la SIDA: una aproximació empírica', *Salut Catalunya*, 6 (4): 139–44, 1992.

The Cost of Hospital Care for HIV-infected Patients: The Impact of Changing Survival Patterns and Use of Services in the London of the 1980s

Dr Eddy Beck

St Mary's Hospital Medical School, London, England

This chapter describes the use of services by HIV-infected individuals and associated costs at various stages in the course of their HIV infection, based on a number of studies performed at St Mary's Hospital, London. These studies demonstrated changes in the use and cost of HIV-related hospital service provision, which were accompanied by changing mortality and morbidity patterns of people with HIV disease during the 1980s. St Mary's is an inner London hospital and a national AIDS referral centre. To date, 10 per cent of the UK AIDS case-load has been treated at St Mary's.

Changing mortality and morbidity patterns

Once an individual is infected with HIV, a symptom free period occurs between the time of infection and the development of HIV disease. HIV disease constitutes the symptomatic phase of HIV-infection and covers a spectrum of symptoms and signs ranging from minor manifestations of immunosuppression, like oral candidiasis or oral hairy leukoplakia, to non-specific constitutional symptoms (weight loss/night sweats) and other specific AIDS-defining opportunistic infections or tumours, like *Pneumocystis carinii* pneu-

monia (PCP) and Kaposi's sarcoma (KS).[1] Important questions concerning the natural history of HIV infection currently remain unanswered, including whether or not all infected individuals inevitably develop symptomatic disease and the average duration between time of infection and developing symptomatic disease for those who progress. The median time interval between HIV infection and the development of AIDS is currently thought to be about 11 years.

Mortality patterns for people with HIV disease have changed during the second half of the 1980s. In the early part of that decade, median survival from time of diagnosis of AIDS in the UK was 13.5 months (for the first 178 AIDS cases reported to the Communicable Diseases Surveillance Centre (CDSC)).[2] Other studies observed median survival times of 12.4 months[3] and 10.4 months[4] for patients diagnosed with AIDS before 1987, with similar survival patterns observed in the US AIDS patients diagnosed before 1987.[5]

For AIDS patients managed at St Mary's from 1982 to 1989 important changes in morbidity and mortality patterns were revealed.[6] Median survival for patients diagnosed with AIDS between 1984 and 1986 was 9–10 months, which increased to

20 months in patients diagnosed since 1987,[7] an improvement which has been sustained since then.[8] Similar phenomena were observed elsewhere in the UK, the US, Denmark, Australia and The Netherlands.[9] This change occurred around the time of the introduction of zidovudine for patients with symptomatic disease in 1987, the introduction of which was thought to contribute to the improvement in life-expectancy for people with AIDS. For patients diagnosed with AIDS between April and December 1987 at St Mary's Hospital, those treated with zidovudine had a significantly better survival at 12 months and 24 months.[10] These data, however, also confirmed findings from other studies which reported that the beneficial effects of zidovudine diminish with the duration of treatment.

These improvements were primarily due to a reduction in mortality associated with PCP,[11] while the mortality attributable to more intractable opportunistic infections and tumours increased.[12] At St Mary's, there was a marked reduction in deaths due to PCP, which caused 46 per cent of deaths in 1986 but only 3 per cent in 1989. By 1989, KS was responsible for 32 per cent of deaths so that it, with non-Hodgkin lymphoma, largely replaced PCP as the major cause of death. As many of these changes occurred around the time of the introduction of zidovudine and PCP prophylaxis, many workers attributed the changed mortality and morbidity patterns to these particular interventions.[13] The evidence for the effectiveness of these interventions partly rests on this temporal association and partly on the results of clinical trials which showed that both interventions prolonged the survival of AIDS patients.[14]

Changing patterns of service utilization and associated costs

Data on service utilization were collected and average costs calculated for AIDS patients treated at St Mary's Hospital between 1982 and 1989. Demographic data and data on use and outcome of in-patient and out-patient services were collected from individual case notes. The stage of HIV infection was defined using a classification system based on the 1987 CDC[15] and 1989 CDSC[16] notification systems: the three categories defined were asymptomatic HIV infection, symptomatic non-AIDS HIV disease and AIDS-defining HIV disease. Patients at each stage of HIV infection and diagnosed with AIDS before 1987 were compared with patients diagnosed since 1987. This not only takes the improved survival patterns into consideration that have occurred since 1987, but 1987 was also the year that zidovudine was introduced into routine clinical practice.

Service utilization data, available on individual patients for each visit or admission, were aggregated and mean units of service consumption per patient-year calculated.[17] HIV-related workload and associated costs were estimated for each of the 37 departments at St Mary's involved in HIV-related care. Unit costs per in-patient day, out-patient visit and of each test, procedure or treatment could be calculated from this survey. Average drug costs were calculated for average daily prescription dosages by using average St Mary's Hospital pharmacy costs. Average daily prescription dosages were obtained in consultation with the HIV pharmacist for the specialized drugs and from the *British National Formulary*[18] for the routine compounds. Original 1989/90 prices were adjusted for inflation for the1992/93 financial year. More detailed methods by which these costs were obtained are described elsewhere.[19]

The single most important finding over this period was the pronounced shift from an in-patient based to an out-patient based service. This was associated with earlier patient presentation and improved survival from the time of AIDS diagnosis.

For asymptomatic HIV-infected patients, a reduction in the mean number of in-patient admissions and days was observed. This included a reduction in the number of tests and procedures performed and in-patient drug days[20] prescribed per asymptomatic patient-year for patients who developed AIDS since 1987 compared with patients diagnosed with AIDS before 1987. Out-patient service utilization was comparable between the two groups in terms of number of out-patient visits and tests performed, though fewer out-patient procedures were performed and drug-days prescribed for patients diagnosed with AIDS since 1987.

The overall HIV-related in-patient costs per asymptomatic patient-year amounted to £637 for patients diagnosed with AIDS before 1987 compared with £307 for the patients diagnosed with AIDS since 1987. HIV-related out-patient expenditure was also comparable between the two groups: £774 per asymptomatic patient-year for patients diagnosed with AIDS before 1987 compared with £662 for patients diagnosed with AIDS since 1987. This brought the overall HIV-related expenditure to £1,411 per asymptomatic patient-year for patients diagnosed with AIDS before 1987 compared with £969 for patients diagnosed with AIDS since 1987; the reduction in cost per asymptomatic patient-year was mainly due to reduced in-patient service expenditure.

For patients with symptomatic non-AIDS disease, the mean number of in-patient episodes and days, in-patient tests and procedures performed and in-patient drug-days prescribed had all declined for patients diagnosed with AIDS since 1987 compared with patients diagnosed with AIDS before 1987; only the mean number of transfusions performed increased for the more recent patients. Out-patient related service utilization increased in terms of number of out-patient visits, out-patient tests performed and drug-days prescribed.

HIV-related in-patient expenditure per symptomatic non-AIDS patient-year was £3,359 for patients diagnosed with AIDS before 1987 compared with £1,808 for patients diagnosed with AIDS since 1987. Increased use of out-patient services was reflected in increased HIV-related out-patient expenditure, which amounted to £1,034 per symptomatic non-AIDS patient for patients diagnosed with AIDS before 1987 compared with £2,108 for patients diagnosed with AIDS since 1987. Overall HIV-related expenditure amounted to £4,393 per symptomatic non-AIDS patient-year for patients diagnosed with AIDS before 1987 compared with £3,916 for patients diagnosed with AIDS since 1987; reduced in-patient expenditure was largely off-set by increased out-patient expenditure, especially due to the increased number of visits and drug costs.

For those people who had developed an AIDS-defining condition, the mean number of in-patient visits per AIDS patient-year remained constant for the two groups, while the mean numbers of in-patient days, tests and procedures performed, in-patient transfusions administered and drug-days prescribed per AIDS patient-year were less for patients diagnosed with AIDS since 1987 compared with patients diagnosed with AIDS before 1987. Out-patient service utilization increased when comparing the two groups; the average numbers of out-patient visits, tests performed and drug-days prescribed all increased for patients diagnosed with AIDS since 1987 compared with patients diagnosed with AIDS before 1987.

HIV-related in-patient expenditure amounted to £14,220 per AIDS patient-year for patients diagnosed with AIDS before 1987 compared with £12,705 per AIDS patient-year for those patients diagnosed with AIDS since 1987. Associated HIV-related out-patient expenditure similarly increased from £2,636 per AIDS patient-year for those diagnosed with AIDS before 1987 compared with £4,747 per AIDS

Year	Asymptomatic					Symptomatic non-AIDS					AIDS				
	Care Costs %	Total Tests %	Total Drugs %	Other %	Total £	Care Costs %	Total Tests %	Total Drugs %	Other %	Total £	Care Costs %	Total Tests %	Total Drugs %	Other %	Total £
1983	56.5	42.6	0.9	0.0	655	38.9	61.1	0.0	0.0	6,557	83.0	10.0	6.7	0.3	43,953
1984	74.3	21.7	3.2	0.8	1,066	74.2	15.6	9.0	0.2	3,500	83.2	7.8	8.8	0.2	29,057
1985	75.1	14.6	10.2	0.1	1,226	88.1	6.8	5.0	0.1	5,848	81.0	8.8	9.9	0.3	18,667
1986	80.2	14.7	5.0	0.1	1,090	72.7	9.4	17.9	0.0	2,801	80.4	8.3	11.0	0.3	17,247
1987	76.7	16.8	6.4	0.1	999	66.0	10.3	23.5	0.2	4,201	68.8	8.4	22.6	0.2	17,248
1988	78.9	12.5	8.6	0.0	975	64.6	8.1	27.2	0.1	3,938	65.6	6.9	27.3	0.2	15,716
1989	67.6	15.3	17.1	0.0	1,156	61.9	8.0	30.0	0.1	3,785	64.8	5.6	29.4	0.2	16,305
Total	76.1	15.3	8.5	0.1	1,056	68.6	8.7	22.6	0.1	3,914	70.8	7.4	21.6	0.2	17,297

a Other activities include surgical procedures and expenditure on infusions.

Table 1
Direct hospital expenditure on in-patient days and out-patient visits (care costs), tests, drugs and other[a] activities as a percentage of total cost per disease category per patient-year by year (1992/93 prices).

patient-year for patients diagnosed with AIDS since 1987; this was mainly due to more frequent out-patient visits and increased drug costs. Overall HIV-related expenditure amounted to £16,856 per AIDS patient-year for patients diagnosed with AIDS before 1987 compared with £17,452 per AIDS patient-year for patients diagnosed with AIDS since 1987.

Over time, the proportion spent on care costs decreased, while the proportion spent on drugs increased, especially for people with HIV disease. Thus expenditure on drugs per symptomatic non-AIDS patient-year increased from 9 per cent in 1984 to 30 per cent in 1989 (Table). Similarly, drug expenditure per AIDS patient-year increased proportionally from 7 per cent in 1983 to 29 per cent in 1989 (Table). Increased expenditure on drugs was off-set by the shift from an in-patient based to an out-patient based service. To what extent these trends will continue to compensate each other in future remains to be seen,[21] especially with the anticipated introduction of new anti-viral agents and future use of combination anti-viral treatment.[22]

Changing mortality patterns and services utilization

The median survival time from the date of AIDS diagnosis for patients diagnosed with AIDS before 1987 was 14.6 months compared with 21.0 months for patients diagnosed with AIDS since 1987. However, 60 per cent of patients diagnosed with AIDS before 1987 presented with AIDS on their first HIV-related visit, compared with only 30 per cent of patients diagnosed since 1987. The median interval between the diagnosis of HIV infection and the diagnosis of AIDS was 8.8 months for patients diagnosed with AIDS since 1987, whereas more than 50 per cent of patients diagnosed with AIDS before 1987 were not previously known to be HIV-positive.[23]

Improved survival of AIDS patients was predominantly due to the reduced case-fatality associated with PCP. Evidence from the US demonstrated that hospitals with different numbers of AIDS patients had different case-fatality rates for patients with episodes of PCP.[24] Most of these between-centre comparisons attributed the different mortality patterns to the greater clinical proficiency of the physicians working in high volume and high experience AIDS centres versus low volume and low experience AIDS centres.[25] That improved clinical expertise contributed to the improved case-fatality of episodes of PCP over time at St Mary's is suggested by the fact that during the late 1980s the severity of pneumonia for fatal episodes of PCP increased (as indicated by the significant increase in the alveolar-arterial oxygen gradient of fatal episodes).[26] However, between 1983 and 1990, patients with their first episode of PCP treated at St Mary's Hospital presented with less extensive pneumonia at diagnosis (again indicated by their alveolar-arterial oxygen gradient on admission); this occurred independently of zidovudine therapy or PCP prophylaxis. Patients were being treated at an earlier stage in their disease course, which in turn was due either to earlier patient presentation, or to earlier medical diagnosis or both.[27]

A non-fatal outcome of an AIDS-defining (index) episode of PCP and subsequent long-term survival was significantly related to the degree of immunosuppression and the severity of PCP on admission. Additionally, haemoglobin on admission, time interval from the diagnosis of HIV infection to the diagnosis of first episode of PCP, age on admission and year of diagnosis were also significantly related to episode outcome. As the time interval between the diagnosis of HIV infection and the index diagnosis of PCP increased, individuals were more likely to present with less severe PCP, as indicated by their reduced alveolar-arterial oxygen gradient. Furthermore, this time interval was also directly related to the number of out-patient visits and respiratory investigations which patients received before their index episode of PCP: the longer this time interval the more likely that these patients had been seen in out-patients before their index episode of PCP and the more likely they were to have had respiratory functions test performed on an out-patient basis.[28]

The reduction in case-fatality associated with index episodes of PCP occurred because of the interplay between increased service utilization and treatment before the first episode of PCP, reduced case-severity of PCP on admission and appropriate treatment during the admission with all these variables being interdependent on each other.

Lifetime expenditure on HIV service provision

A major implication of these data is that early access to medical services, regular medical follow-up and early intervention, when developing symptomatic disease, are beneficial for short-term and long-term survival for individuals with HIV infection, independently of anti-viral therapy and PCP prophylaxis. For individuals who were followed up from time of HIV infection, the median lifetime hospital costs to death would amount to £48,510, not taking into consideration the opportunity costs for professionals treating HIV-infected individuals.[29] To the hospital costs need to be added the costs of statutory primary and community care services for these patients, which will increase the life-time costs to £63,905.[30] The costs of the voluntary sector service provision will further raise overall lifetime costs to £80,239.[31] This figure (US$117,600) is very similar to a recent US estimate of lifetime cost of treating a person with HIV infection, which amounted to $119,000.[32]

Conclusion

The English estimates produced in this paper, like Hellinger's [32], provide maximum estimates because regular follow-ups from the time of infection till death are assumed. It would, therefore, be far too simplistic to say that for each person in whom HIV infection is prevented £80,000 was averted on HIV service provision to the National Health Service. It does, however, provide us with the order of magnitude of potential savings on the lifetime use of health service resources – 61 per cent generated by direct hospital costs – by the successful prevention of HIV infection. These economic reasons, in conjunction with humanitarian reasons, provide a solid rationale for continuing efforts to maintain and expand those prevention programmes which have been found to be successful in reducing HIV transmission. It further demonstrates the complementary nature of HIV prevention programmes and treating HIV-infected individuals, both of which constitute integral aspects of any comprehensive approach to combating the HIV pandemic.

1 Centres for Disease Control, 'Revision of the CDC surveillance case definition for Acquired Immunodeficiency Syndrome', *Morbidity and Mortality Weekly Report*, 36: 3S-15S, 1987.

2 G. Mascara, M. McEvoy, 'Length of survival of patients with acquired immunodeficiency syndrome in the United Kingdom', British Medical Journal, 292: 1727–9, 1987.

3 G.K. Reeves, S.E. Overton, 'Preliminary survival analysis of UK AIDS data', Lancet, I: 880, 1988.

4 S.E. Whitmore-Overton, H.E. Tillett, B.G. Evans and G.M. Allardice, 'Improved survival from diagnosis of AIDS in adult cases in the United Kingdom and bias due to reporting delays', AIDS, 7: 415–20, 1993.

5 G.K. Reeves, S.E. Overton, 'Preliminary survival analysis of UK AIDS data', Lancet, I: 880, 1988.

A.R. Moss, G. McCallum, P.A. Volberding, P. Bacchetti and S. Dritz, 'Mortality associated with mode of presentation in the Acquired Immune Deficiency Syndrome', Journal of the National Cancer Institute, 73: 1281–4, 1984.

P. Bachetti, D. Osmond, R.E. Chaisson et al. 'Survival patterns of the first 500 patients with AIDS in San Francisco', Journal of Infectious Diseases, 57: 1044–7, 1988.

R. Rothenberg, M. Woelfel, R. Stoneburner, J. Milberg, R. Parker and B. Truman, 'Survival with the Acquired Immunodeficiency Syndrome', New England Journal of Medicine, 317: 1297–1302, 1987.

6 B.S. Peters, E.J. Beck, D.G. Coleman et al. 'Changing disease patterns in patients with AIDS in a referral centre in the United Kingdom: the changing face of AIDS', British Medical Journal, 302: 203–7, 1991.

7 Ibid.

8 D.G. Coleman, E.J. Beck, B.S. Peters, J.R.W. Harris and A.J. Pinching, 'Changing disease patterns in AIDS', British Medical Journal, 304: 839, 1992.

9 S.E. Whitmore-Overton, H.E. Tillett, B.G. Evans and G.M. Allardice, 'Improved survival from diagnosis of AIDS in adult cases in the United Kingdom and bias due to reporting delays', AIDS, 7: 415–20, 1993.

R. Rothenberg, M. Woelfel, R. Stoneburner, J. Milberg, R. Parker and B. Truman, 'Survival with the Acquired Immunodeficiency Syndrome', New England Journal of Medicine, 317: 1297–1302, 1987.

B.S. Peters, E.J. Beck, D.G. Coleman et al. 'Changing disease patterns in patients with AIDS in a referral centre in the United Kingdom: the changing face of AIDS', British Medical Journal, 302: 203–7, 1991.

D.G. Coleman, E.J. Beck, B.S. Peters, J.R.W. Harris and A.J. Pinching, 'Changing disease patterns in AIDS', British Medical Journal, 304: 839, 1992.

C. Pedersen, J. Gerstoft , P. Tauris et al. 'Trends in survival of Danish AIDS patients from 1981 to 1989', AIDS, 4: 1111–16, 1990.

P.J. Solomon, 'The survival distribution of Australian AIDS patients', Projections of Acquired Immune Deficiency Syndrome in Australia (eds. P.J. Solomon, C. Fazekas de St Groth and S.R. Wilson), pp. 61–70. National Centre for Epidemiology and Population Health Working Papers, Australian National University, Canberra, April 1990.

R.J. Bindels, R.M.J. Poos, J.T. Jong, J.W. Mulder, H.J.C. Jager and R.A. Coutinho, 'Trends in mortality among AIDS patients in Amsterdam, 1982–1989', AIDS, 5: 853–8, 1991.

10 B.S. Peters, E.J. Beck, D.G. Coleman, F. Moss, J.R.W. Harris, A.J. Pinching, 'The role of zidovudine in increased survival in AIDS patients', abstract Th.C.696, VI International Conference on AIDS, San Francisco, USA, June 1990.

11 B.S. Peters, E.J. Beck, D.G. Coleman et al. 'Changing disease patterns in patients with AIDS in a referral centre in the United Kingdom: the changing face of AIDS', British Medical Journal, 302: 203–7, 1991.

R.J. Bindels, R.M.J. Poos, J.T. Jong, J.W. Mulder, H.J.C. Jager and R.A. Coutinho, 'Trends in mortality among AIDS patients in Amsterdam, 1982–1989', AIDS, 5: 853–8, 1991.

J.E. Harris, 'Improved short-term survival of AIDS patients initially diagnosed with Pneumocystis carinii pneumonia, 1984 through

1987', Journal of the American Medical Association, 263: 397–401, 1990.

G.F. Lemp, S.F. Payne, D. Neal, T. Temelso and G.W. Rutherford, 'Survival Trends for Patients with AIDS', Journal of the American Medical Association, 263: 402–6, 1990.

R.D. Moore, J. Hidalgo, B.W. Sugland and R.E. Chaisson, 'Zidovudine and the natural history of the Acquired Immunodeficiency Syndrome', New England Journal of Medicine, 324: 1412–16, 1991.

W.E. Lafferty, D. Glidden and S.G. Hopkins, 'Survival trends of people with AIDS in Washington State', American Journal of Public Health, 81: 217–9, 1991.

G.F. Lemp, A.M. Hirozawa, J.B. Cohen et al. 'Survival for women and men with AIDS', Journal of Infectious Diseases, 166: 74–9, 1992.

12 B.S. Peters, E.J. Beck, D.G. Coleman et al. 'Changing disease patterns in patients with AIDS in a referral centre in the United Kingdom: the changing face of AIDS', British Medical Journal, 302: 203–7, 1991.

13 Ibid.

R.J. Bindels, R.M.J. Poos, J.T. Jong, J.W. Mulder, H.J.C. Jager and R.A. Coutinho, 'Trends in mortality among AIDS patients in Amsterdam, 1982–1989', AIDS, 5: 853–8, 1991.

R.D. Moore, J. Hidalgo, B.W. Sugland and R.E. Chaisson, 'Zidovudine and the natural history of the Acquired Immunodeficiency Syndrome', New England Journal of Medicine, 324: 1412–16, 1991.

W.E. Lafferty, D. Glidden and S.G. Hopkins, 'Survival trends of people with AIDS in Washington State', American Journal of Public Health, 81: 217–9, 1991.

G.F. Lemp, A.M. Hirozawa, J.B. Cohen et al. 'Survival for women and men with AIDS', Journal of Infectious Diseases, 166: 74–9, 1992.

P.J. Solomon, S.R. Wilson, C.E. Swanson, D.A. Cooper, 'Effect of zidovudine on survival of patients with AIDS in Australia', Medical Journal of Australia, 153: 254–7, 1990.

14 E. Dournon, S. Matheron, W. Rozenbaum et al. 'Effects of zidovudine in 365 consecutive patients with AIDS or AIDS-related complex', Lancet, II: 1297–1302, 1988.

M.A. Fischl, D.D. Richman, M.H. Grieco et al. 'The efficacy of azidothymidine (AZT) in the treatment of patients with AIDS and AIDS-related complex', New England Journal of Medicine, 317: 185–91, 1987.

M. Fischl, G. Dickinson and L. La Vioe, 'Safety and efficacy of sulfamethoxazole and trimethoprim chemoprophylaxis for Pneumocystis carinii pneumonia in AIDS', Journal of the American Medical Association, 259: 1185-9, 1988.

N.M.H. Graham, S.L. Zegler, L.P. Park et al. 'Effect of zidovudine and Pneumocystis carinii pneumonia prophylaxis on progression of HIV-1 infection to AIDS', Lancet, 338: 265–69, 1991.

15 Centres for Disease Control, 'Revision of the CDC surveillance case definition for Acquired Immunodeficiency Syndrome', Morbidity and Mortality Weekly Report, 36: 3S–15S, 1987.

16 CDSC, 'AIDS surveillance and HIV death clinical report form', PHLS Communicable Disease Surveillance Centre, London, April 1989.

17 One 'patient-year' was defined as a 365-day period of follow-up at St Mary's Hospital, falling within any of the three clinical categories described above.

18 British Medical Association/Royal Pharmaceutical Society of Great Britain, British National Formulary, Number 20. The Pharmaceutical Press, London, September 1990.

19 E.J. Beck, C. McKevitt, J. Kennelly, L. Whitaker, J. Wadsworth and D.L. Miller, Hospital Service Provision for People with HIV-Infection and AIDS: A Report for the Department of Health, 1991. Academic Department of Public Health, St Mary's Hospital Medical School, London, December 1991.

20 The number of days on which drugs were prescribed were summed: a 'drug-day' constituted one day on which one drug was prescribed.

21 E.J. Beck, L. Whitaker, J. Kennelly et al. Changing presentation and survival, service utilization and costs for AIDS patients: insights from a London referral centre, AIDS, 1994, 8: 379–84.

22 E. De Clercq, 'Basic approaches to anti-retro-viral therapy', Journal of AIDS, 4: 207–18, 1991.

23 E.J. Beck, J. Kennelly, C. McKevitt et al. 'Changing use of hospital services and costs at a London AIDS referral centre 1983–1989', AIDS, 8: 367–77, 1994.

24 C.L. Bennett, J.B. Garfinkle, S. Greenfield et al. 'The relation between hospital experience and in-hospital mortality for patients with AIDS-related PCP', Journal of the American Medical Association, 261: 2975–9, 1989.

C.L. Bennett, P. Gertler, P.A. Guze, J.B. Garfinkle, D.E. Kanouse and S. Greenfield, 'The relation between resource use and in-hospital mortality for patients with Acquired Immun-odeficiency Syndrome-related Pneumocystis carinii pneumonia', Archives of Internal Medicine, 150: 1447–1452, 1990.

E.S. Stone, G.R. Seage, T. Hertz and A.M. Epstein, 'The relation between hospital experience and mortality for patients with AIDS', Journal of the American Medical Association, 268: 2655–61, 1992.

25 Ibid.

26 E.J. Beck, P.D. French, M.H. Helbert et al. 'Empirically treated Pneumocystis pneumonia in London 1983–1989', International Journal of STD & AIDS, 3: 285–7, 1992.

27 E.J. Beck, P.D. French, M.H. Helbert et al. Improved outcome of Pneumocystis carinii pneumonia in AIDS Patients: a multifactorial treatment effect, International Journal of STD and AIDS, 3: 182–7, 1992.

28 E.J. Beck, B.S. Peters, E. Kupek et al. 'Access to medical services, episode outcome and long-term survival of index episodes PCP', abstract PO-B10-1439, IX International Conference on AIDS, Berlin, Germany, June 1993.

29 These calculations assumed that HIV-infected individuals were followed up from time of seroconversion and that the median time interval from time of HIV infection to AIDS is eleven years, one year of which is spent with symptomatic non-AIDS disease, and that the median interval from time of AIDS diagnosis to death is two years.

30 D.L. Miller, J. Wadsworth, E.J. Beck, A.M. Renton et al. Utilization, Needs and Costs of Community Services for People with HIV Infection: A London based Prospective Study. Academic Department of Public Health, St Mary's Hospital Medical School, London 1994.

31 Ibid.

32 F.J. Hellinger, 'The lifetime cost of treating a person with HIV', Journal of the American Medical Association, 270: 474–8, 1993.

The Cost of Medical Treatment of Out-patients with HIV Infection: Results from a Swiss Survey

Dr Christoph Minder, C. Junker and G. Nal

Department of Social and Preventive Medicine, University of Berne, Switzerland

During the first half of 1992, a comprehensive study of needs, resources, costs and well-being of HIV-positive and AIDS patients was undertaken in the *canton* of Berne, Switzerland.[1] The aim of this study was to obtain information from HIV-infected persons and their carers on their financial and living situation, their needs, the support they were obtaining both from private and professional sources as well as on financial limitations due to the disease (either in connection with reduced income or from increased expenses). Information on caring activities, time and money spent for caring, needs for support and personal well-being were obtained from carers selected by the interviewees.

A sub-study was conducted with 55 patients of the Medical Out-patient Clinic of the Insel University Hospital in Berne. For these patients additional information on their medical status and treatment in the first half of the year 1992 was obtained. This chapter presents information useful for cost estimates of out-patient treatment obtained from this substudy. The discussion will also cover some general points regarding available cost estimates for HIV/AIDS and their limitations.

Material and methods

Study design: In co-operation with the staff of the Medical Out-patient Clinic an interviewer contacted HIV-positive patients who arrived at the clinic for a medical consultation or for treatment (time period 19/3/92 to 2/6/1992). The clinic serves patients from all walks of life. It has, however, a rather large share of injecting drug users (IDUs). Recruitment is illustrated in Table 1.

In addition to these 49 interviews we had a short medical questionnaire for six patients who did not complete the questionnaire. While a sample size of 55 (46 male and 8 female respondents – sex was not recorded for one patient) is not adequate to obtain reliable estimates, we report our findings here because results from larger studies are not yet available.

Cost estimation: The financing system of Swiss hospitals is based on the 'fee-for-service principle'. Fees are periodically negotiated between hospitals, government and health insurance companies. Health insurance is private with government subsidies for basic insurance. In 1990, there were as many health insurance policies as Swiss residents,[2] indicating high coverage.

Table 1
Recruitment for questionnaires

Total number of possible contacts			152	(100%)			
Not realized	– patient did not show up	38					
	– patient had already been contacted in another place	28					
	– no interview for medical reasons (doctor's advice)	8					
	– organizational mishaps	3					
Total number of missed contacts			77	(51%)			
Total number of realized contacts			75	(49%)	75	(100%)	
Refusals	– psychological reasons	5					
	– 'no time'	4					
	– language problems	6					
	– no reason given	11					
	Total refusals				26	(35%)	
Completed questionnaires					49	(65%)	

Six additional patients provided partial information (see text)

In spring 1993 the medical records for the first half of 1992 of the 55 study patients were analysed. The AIDS specialist of the clinic provided us with a list of procedures that would eventually be required in the diagnosis and treatment of HIV and AIDS patients (appendix). Costing was undertaken using tax points and tax point values in use at the hospital at the time.[3] Hospitalization cost was based on the payment schedule of basic health insurance, and cost of medication on the recommendations of the Swiss Commission for AIDS. For this chapter, costs were converted into 1992 US$ per patient per year.

Results

Socio-demography and health: Table 2 shows the sample characteristics according to sex, working status, social standing, and self-reported injected drug consumption at the time of the interview.

Health status was described by the Walter Reed (WR) classification.[4] As there were only five, seven and six persons respectively in stages 1, 2 and 3, these were grouped together.

Cost: The cost estimates were an aggregate of unit costs for medical advice (con-

Item	Categories	
Sex	male	46
	female	8
	unknown	1
Employment status	working	29
	jobless	25
	unknown	1
SES	academics/executives	8
	employees & trades persons	20
	semi & unskilled	19
	unknown	8
Injected drug consumption	reported	4
	not reported	48
	unknown	3
WR stage[a]	1 to 3	18
	4 to 6	37
	unknown	0

Table 2
Socio-demographic characteristics of the sample

[a] WR = Walter Reed classification: stages 1–2 are pre-AIDS; stages 4–6 correspond to AIDS; stage 3 is mixed

sultation, counselling), laboratory costs (blood chemistry, bacteriology, X-rays, CTs, etc.) and medication (zidovudine, didanosine, pentamidine, fluconazole, antibiotics: see appendix). Table 3 presents the direct medical cost of one year of treatment, calculated on the basis of the contents of the patient's records of the first half of 1992. These cost estimates may have been biased by the failure to cover treatment and medication elsewhere. The cost estimates also contained a small number of short hospitalizations, as may have occurred for patients normally frequenting out-patient services.

Comparing the column 'mean cost' to the column (within group) 'standard deviation' in Table 3, it is evident that they were of the same size, whatever classifi-

Description	n	mean cost	standard deviation	P-value[a]
All probands	55	7,300	8,958	–
Walter Reed Stage				
WR 1–3	18	4,010	4,082	
				0.02
WR 4–6	37	8,900	10,220	
Work status				
working	29	6,968	8,061	
				0.7
jobless	25	7916	10,618	
(3 missing)				
Socio-economic status				
academics & executives	8	11,148	12,126	
employees & tradesmen	20	6,235	5,412	0.056
semi & unskilled	19	4,500	4,512	
(8 missing)				
Injected drug consumption (self-reported)				
yes	4	3,496	3,864	
				0.12
no	48	7,666	9,392	
(3 missing)				

[a] 2 groups: t-Tests; for Socio-economic status: Bartholomew's test of significance (see J.L. Fleiss, *Statistical Methods for Rates and Proportions*, (2nd edition), ed. J. Wiley, 1981, pp.147–149).

Table 3 **Direct medical cost of out-patient treatment. Mean costs per year in US$ (1992).**

cation was used. This was indicative of immense variability in direct medical costs between individuals. Similar conditions, whether medical (WR status), social (injecting drug use) or socio-economic (SES, work status), did not result in similar cost. To obtain reliable cost estimates a much larger sample would be needed. The reason for this variability cannot be attributed to the sampling design, as data collected on income did not show the same degree of variability (results not presented).

The last column 'p-values' refers to statistical tests between the exhibited groups. There were statistically confirmed cost differences according to HIV status, with mean cost more than doubling when moving from 'WR 1–3' to 'WR 4–6'. Mean cost varied also by SES, with high socio-economic status HIV-positive people obtaining medical help costing twice as much as that of the lower strata. There was possibly a tendency to more expensive medical treatment for non-IDUs, although numbers are too small to reach a conclusion.

Conclusions

Table 3 indicates that there is a significant effect of clinical stage on cost. However, cost for stages WR 1 to WR 3 seems to be fairly high, indicating a potential for cost-saving measures. The sizeable cost gradient by socio-economic status may be indicative of overuse of medical services by the better- off patients. Thus, the data point to a potential for cost reduction. Politically, it might be hard to achieve such savings, as in Switzerland the principle that the individual has the right to choose their doctor still holds. Overuse of medical services by individuals might be identified by close analysis of their use of health insurance. So far, little has been attempted in this direction.

Our cost estimates for asymptomatic patients (US$4,010) and ambulatory costs for AIDS patients (US$8,900) are fairly close to Hellinger's US estimates of $5,150 and $8,000 for 1991.[5]

Based on a seven-year lag from infection to the manifestation of AIDS and a three-year average survival time for AIDS patients, an estimate of the total cost of each HIV case would amount to about US$55,000 (SD± US$21,000), not including the terminal hospitalization. This estimate is fairly close to the one given by Hellinger [6] if one considers that we exclude longer hospitalizations here. However, detailed cost extrapolations are beyond the scope of this chapter.

We feel that our study has paved the way for larger studies incorporating larger numbers of HIV-infected persons and AIDS patients, like the ACSU Survey.[7] However, care should be taken to include sufficient information about psychological, personal, social and economic conditions since several important factors influencing cost seem to be undefined today.

Discussion

Representativity: As Table 1 indicates, the reasons for not having interviewed certain HIV-positive visitors to the clinic were largely that the patients did not show up or did not want to participate. There are reasons to believe that injecting drug users are less likely to participate in a survey, so there may be a bias, although the interviewer was instructed to pay the patient a small sum if that could induce him/her to participate. We therefore do not believe that the incurred bias is serious. If it does exist it is likely to have led to an underestimate of costs: patients too ill to be interviewed may have higher costs.

Social factors affecting cost: The immense variability made it very difficult to identify factors influencing costs. However, Table 3 showed that direct medical costs were influenced by disease status, social standing and possibly by actual injected drug consumption. The finding on SES was somewhat uncomfortable for a healthcare system claiming to disregard social differences.

The large variability of the costs that appears unrelated to the use of different classifications in Table 3 was indicative of the complexity of the case of people with AIDS. Tabulations by a simple index of social integration, by time elapsed since seroconversion became known, or by a range of psychological variables such as mental pain and life satisfaction, showed considerable cost differences (data not shown). This indicated that personal factors may play a decisive role in the determination of costs. In addition, chance events, such as the type of opportunistic infection each individual had, may produce variability.

We nevertheless consider these findings to be important clues to possibilities for cost control and reduction. It is obviously not sufficient to know the clinical status of a patient to determine the medical cost he or she will incur. Rather, personal characteristics seem to be influential.

Other work: We end with a comment on other cost estimates cited in the literature. We have thoroughly studied 26 articles dating from 1986 to 1993 and did not find a single detailed account of how actual costs were determined.[8] Most papers present extrapolations based on a combination of published and newly acquired epidemiological and global cost data (compare Hellinger [9]). Specialized investigations, such as those of Scitovski and Rice,[10] are the exception.

We think extrapolation from data of such variability as we have found will not produce valid figures unless cost estimates are based on sample sizes of several hundred patients. Presently accepted cost estimates may easily be off by a factor of 2 or 3 and the confidence intervals (were they ever computed) of these estimates would be huge. It also seems implausible that cost data from one country can be easily used in the context of another one because psychological and social factors as well as the healthcare systems vary too much between countries.

Medical examination	Number of tax points	Tax point value (US$)	Cost in US$
visit	13	2.63	34.23
consultation	20	2.63	52.70
analysis of blood	13	0.63	8.23
thrombocytes (blood platelet)	8	0.63	5.07
thorax x-rays	14	2.63	36.70
sonography	25	2.63	65.83
cranial CT	199.5	2.63	525.35
anaerobic stool	25	0.87	21.70
parasite, pathogenic stool	33	0.87	28.60
culture, blood bacteriologic	40	0.87	34.70
culture, blood-tuberculosis	76	0.87	65.70
creatinine-kinase	15	0.63	9.50
alkaline phosphatase, GOT, GPT	30	0.63	19.00
clearance, amylase	15	0.63	9.50
LDH-HBDH-activities	12	0.63	7.60
endogenous creatinine clearance	10	0.63	6.30
CD4+-antigen	95	0.63	60.17
p24-antigen	30	0.87	26.00
beta2-micro-globulin	30	0.63	19.00
hepatitis B serology	50	0.87	43.33
toxoplasmosis serology	60	0.87	52.00
cytomegalovirus serology	60	0.87	52.00
Syphilis serology	15	0.87	13.00
diagnostic set	275	0.87	283.33
medication			per year
AZT			3,971.00
ddI			5,958.00
pentamidine			520.00
fluconazole			964.0
antibiotics (TMP/SMX)			149.00
hospitalisation Insel Hospital/day			193.00

Appendix: costs for ambulant treatment of HIV-positive and AIDS patients Medical Policlinic, Insel Hospital, Berne, Switzerland

Acknowledgements
We would like to thank the Swiss National Science Foundation (grant no. 4026–026866) for financial support, which made this study possible. We would also like to thank A. Gasser, D. Hausser, C. Küchler, M-L. Blessing-Küchler and J. von Overbeck for their willingness to support the study and discuss the issues arising. We also thank the interviewer, D. dell'Ava, and the participating doctors, nurses, hospital officials, social workers and AIDS activists for their support and the sharing of their views.

1 M-L. Blessing-Küchler, A. Gasser, H. Kronenberg, Ch.E. Minder, G. Nal, 'Expenses, needs and resources of HIV-infected persons, AIDS patients and their care givers', final report, National Research Programme 26C, project no. 4026–026866, 1993.

2 Das Gesundheitswesen in der Schweiz: Leistungen, Kosten, Preise (ed. L. Salinas). Pharma Information, Edition 1993.

3 Tax points are negotiated between doctors, health insurers and the government rather infrequently (once every five to ten years); intermediate cost adjustments are handled by renegotiating tax point values.

4 The Walter Reed classification was in widespread use for classifying HIV disease before the CDC classification came into use; stages 4–6 correspond to AIDS, while 1–3 are mostly ARC manifestations: R. Redfield et al. 'The Walter Reed Staging Classification for HTL V–III, LAV Infection', New England Journal of Medicine, 314: 131–132, 1986.

5 F.J. Hellinger, 'Forecasting the medical care costs of the HIV epidemic: 1991–1994', Inquiry, 28, pp. 213–225, 1991.

6 Ibid.

7 C.L. Schur, M.L. Berk, Health Insurance Coverage of Persons With HIV-Related Illness: Data from the AIDS Costs and Services Utilzation Survey (ACSUS) screener. ACSUS Report No 2, Agency for Health Care Policy and Research pub. no. 94–0009, Rockville MD, 1994.

8 Note added in proof: The AIDS Cost and Services Utilization Survey, which has come to our attention only recently, seems to make an exception here. Its study design is similar to ours. It covers, however, more subjects, but with less information per subject.

9 F.J. Hellinger, 'Forecasting the Medical Care Costs of the HIV Epidemic: 1991–1994', Inquiry, 28, pp. 213–225, 1991.

10 A. Scitovski, D. Rice, 'Estimates of the direct and indirect costs of Acquired Immunodeficiency Syndrome in the United States 1985, 1986 and 1991', Public Health Reports, 102, pp. 5–17, USA, 1987.

Economic Evaluation of HIV Prenatal Screening in France: Results of a Cost–Benefit Analysis[1]

Dr Catherine Le Galès and Dr V. Seror

Centre for Research on Health Economics, INSERM Unit 357, CNRS UMR 9932

Dr C. Courpotin

Pediatrics Department, Hôpital Trousseau, Paris.

Dr M.J. Mayaux

Research in Epidemiology, INSERM Unit 292

Prof P. Reinert

Pediatrics Department, C.H.I.C., Créteil.

Dr J. Tricoire

Pediatrics Department, Hôpital Purpan, Toulouse.

HIV prenatal screening allows pregnant women the possibility of knowing their serological status and of terminating their pregnancy if they so wish (in case of seropositivity):[2] it also offers the possibility of early medical intervention for children born of seropositive mothers. In both these ways HIV prenatal screening represents a technically efficient prevention activity. Despite its partial nature, evidence points towards the growth of this preventive practice in France. Although the frequency of the screening performed at the beginning of pregnancy varies from one area to another, a 1987–89 national study reckoned that, at the time, two pregnant women out of three were screened.[3] A 1992 survey, carried out in the Provence–Alpes–Côte-d'Azur area's maternity hospitals, concluded that nearly 40 per cent of hospitals studied were practising systematic prenatal screening.[4]

In an earlier stage of our research, which analysed the cost-effectiveness of HIV prenatal screening, we had shown how the cost-effectiveness ratios varied, depending on whether the strategies were systematic or targeted at risk factors. It appeared that a targeted prenatal screening based on clinical interviews on risk factors was more cost-effective than a generalized screening (the average cost for each seropositive pregnant women discovered being five times lower). Nonetheless, a generalized screening resulted in the identification of additional cases of infection, at an extra cost which does not appear totally unreasonable (from US$52,356 to $87,260[5] for each additional screened case).[6]

The main purpose of the present research, which corresponds to one of the recommendations of the French 'Haut Comité de la Santé Publique' (1992), is to study the economic justification of prenatal screening according to the prevalence of infection in the population group concerned, and to question ourselves about the judiciousness of a national policy decision to organize the prevention of materno-foetal transmission in France. A cost–benefit analysis is presented for the healthcare system, with consideration of benefit limited to potential cost savings from the averted care of HIV cases prevented. The ethical considerations of treating abortion as a socially acceptable preventive measure are not part of this analysis.

Methodology

The costs of HIV prenatal screening are compared with the monetary benefits, the latter measured as avoided medical costs. This approach has methodological limitations, but was chosen because of the limited information available to conduct a more comprehensive cost–benefit analysis.[7] For practical reasons the analysis is also limited to measurement of the costs and benefits from the standpoint of the welfare insurance system.

A technical model of the cost–benefit of HIV prenatal screening is presented in this section.

An estimation of $N(Po)$ (number of newborn children with HIV infection risk) can be calculated with the equation (1):

Let :

$N(PW)$ be the annual number of pregnant women and

P be the prevalence rate of HIV infection among pregnant women followed up for pregnancy

Then :

$$N(Po) = N(PW) . P \qquad (1)$$

If Tv is the HIV materno-foetal transmission rate, then N_{HIV} (the number of children with HIV infection) is equal to :

$$N_{HIV} = N(Po) . Tv \qquad (2)$$

Based on the prenatal screening policy compliance rate, and the number of seropositive women who will decide to bring their pregnancy full term, a number of HIV-positive children – $N'(Po)$ – will actually be born (Figure 1). This number is equal to the sum of seropositive women who did not receive screening, HIV-positive women who were falsely declared negative at the conclusion of testing,[8] and those women who, knowing they were seropositive, chose not to terminate their pregnancy. This is represented by the equation:

$N'(Po) =$
  $[N(PW) . P . (1-C)]$
  $+ [N(PW) . P . C . R_{FN}]$
  $+ [N(PW) . P . C . (1-R_{FN}) . (1-A)]$

  and $N'(Po) \leq N(Po)$ $\qquad (3)$

With :

R_{FN} : the false negative rate with ELISA after a double technique

C : % of prenatal screening compliance

A : % of pregnancies ending by a termination

Likewise, N'_{HIV} – number of infected children who will be born following a screening policy – will be equal to :

$N'_{HIV} = N'(Po) \cdot Tv$ with
$N'_{HIV} \leq N_{HIV}$ (4)

The setting up of a prenatal screening policy results in the direct medical costs associated with the provision of serologic tests for HIV infection C(DP):

$C(DP) = (N(PW) \cdot C \cdot C_E) + [N(PW) \cdot C \cdot C_{WB} \cdot [P(1 - R_{FN}) + (1-P) R_{FP}]]$
(5)

where :

     C_E is the cost of ELISA serological test

   C_{WB} is the cost of confirmation test (Western-Blot test)

   R_{FN},   the false negative rate with ELISA after a double technique

R_{FP},   the false positive rate with ELISA.[9]

As a result of the screening, a certain number of women learning of their seropositivity will decide not to carry on with their pregnancy: $(N_{HIV} - N'_{HIV})$ births of infected children will therefore not take place. In addition, a proportion of births of non-infected children $(N_{nHIV} - N'_{nHIV})$ will also not take place as illustrated in the equation:

$N(Po) - N'(Po) =$
$[N_{HIV} + N_{nHIV}] - [N'_{HIV} + N'_{nHIV}]$

$= [N(PW) \cdot P \cdot (1-R_{FN}) \cdot C \cdot A \cdot Tv]$
$+ [N(PW) \cdot P \cdot (1-R_{FN}) \cdot C \cdot A \cdot (1 -Tv)]$

These children's direct medical costs, C(MC), will therefore be avoided :

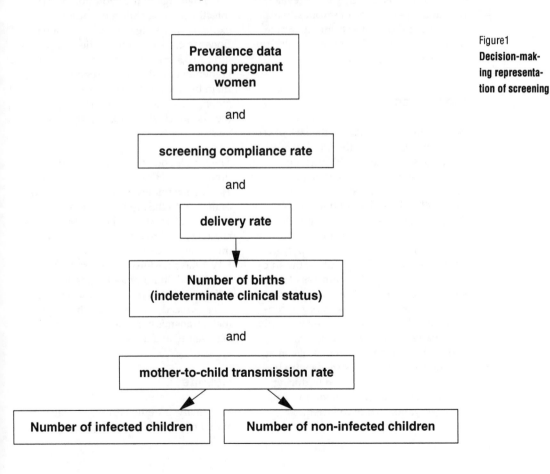

Figure1
Decision-making representation of screening

$$C(MC) =$$
$$C_{HIV} [N'_{HIV} - N_{HIV}]$$
$$+ C_{nHIV} [N'_{nHIV} - N_{nHIV}] \qquad (6)$$

$$C(MC) =$$
$$C_{HIV} [N(PW) . P . (1-R_{FN}) . C . A . Tv]$$
$$+ C_{nHIV} [N(PW) . P . (1 - R_{FN}) . C . A .$$
$$(1 - Tv)]$$

The equations in this section are a technical representation of a very simple point – from an economic viewpoint (or more strictly, from the perspective of the welfare insurance system), a screening policy would be acceptable if the potential medical cost savings were greater than or equal to the costs of prenatal screening, that is, $C(DP) \leq C(MC)$. The actual cost–benefit of an HIV prenatal screening programme will therefore depend on the values of parameters exogenous to the economic model, which are P, prevalence rate, and I, percentage of seropositive women deciding not to bring their pregnancy to full term. We investigate this further later in the chapter.

Data collection

In order to compensate for the lack of economic information on the medical and social consequences of HIV infection among children, a multi-centre prospective survey was carried out during 1990–1991. This collected data on the direct medical resource use connected to the medical follow-up of children born of infected mothers. In the survey protocol, all children followed up during the study period were included regardless of their level of use of medical services.[10] For each patient, an exhaustive inventory of contacts from departments inside the hospital – out-patient, day hospitalization, in-patient, home care – as well as of contacts outside the hospital was made with the help of questionnaires filled in during each meeting with the patient. In total, 820 observations were collected.

A detailed analysis was made of patients' characteristics and service utilization (age, length of resource use, frequency of hospital contacts by type) and of the main direct cost components (medical investigations and prescribed treatments, outpatients' consultations, day hospitalization and standard hospitalization), using a homogeneous HIV/AIDS disease stage classification.[11]

The medical resource use analysis, carried out within the framework of this study, is not sufficient on its own to evaluate the medical costs during the life of children born to mothers infected with HIV. Therefore, it is a matter of turning a cross-disciplinary approach into a longtitudinal approach, which requires information on the natural history of the disease among children. The need for good epidemiological knowledge of the evolution of HIV infection among children[12] probably explains why so few economic evaluations are carried out in the field of paediatric AIDS. However, an analysis of the epidemiological literature enables the main trends of the infection's evolution among younger children to be expressed (i.e. the survival rate during the first years).

The simulation of HIV infection in children born of HIV-positive mothers (Table 1) has been undertaken as part of a collaboration with the French team in charge of the paediatric AIDS cohort.[13] Since January 1986, the French prospective study of infants born of seropositive women with HIV-1 has registered all information on the clinical, immunological, and serologic follow-up of 196 infected children. This has produced evidence that the materno-foetal transmission rate is somewhere between 10 and 20 per cent.[14]

Results

Data analysis demonstrated a large variability of medical practices, clearly

		Birth	6 mths	12 mths	18 mths	24 mths	30 mths	36 mths	42 mths	4 years	5 years	6 years
Infected Pop°												
	Number of Indeterminate infection status (Po)	69	34	0								
	Asymptomatic	126	77	74	57	47	40	36	36	36	36	27
Clinical Status	Symptomatic	0	57	85	89	89	90	92	90	86	72	64
	AIDS	1	14	19	28	34	34	34	30	34	45	63
	Deaths	0	14	4	4	4	5	2	6	0	3	0
Cumulated deaths		0	14	18	22	26	32	33	39	39	42	42
Non-infected Pop°												
Transmission rate: 20%												
	Number of indeterminate infection status (Po)	784	784	784	784							
	Non-infected					784	784	784	784	784	784	784

Medical stage	Po		Non-infected (Px)		P1b
	Centre 1	Centre 2	Centre 1	Centre 2	Centre 1
Number of patients	46	13	37	9	7
Number of observations	172	30	95	11	63
Length of undertaking (days)	8,893	2,484	9,226	1,902	2,419
Average age at first observation (month)	5.35	5.30	19.40	33.78	8.34
Average length of undertaking at first observation (month)	3.22	3.38	15.40	25.31	7.57
Monthly average hospital contacts frequency	0.58	0.36	0.31	0.17	0.78
Average cost per hospital contact (in US$)	581.39	287.10	483.20	238.32	496.04
CI[95%] [...	462.42	140.56	410.56	69.62	291.71
...]	702.27	442.97	557.10	448.27	695.80

Note: Po (indeterminate serological status) and P1b (HIV+ infant with biological anomalies and no clinical symptoms) based on the CDC classification.

Table 2 **Results of the analysis of patients' medical resource use (continued opposite)**

reflected by the cost per hospital contact (Table 2). This pattern has occurred despite the fact that more than half of the patients (55.56 per cent) were involved in a therapeutic protocol. Thus, depending on whether a Po clinical-stage child is followed up by Centre 1 or Centre 2, the average medical contact frequency will vary from about once every two months to once every quarter – a lower contact frequency producing a significantly higher average cost per contact: from $140.6 to $443 for Centre 2, and from $462.4 to $702.3 for Centre 1.

It is clear that, depending on local conditions, for equivalent disease stages there is much variation in service utilization patterns for paediatric patients. For example, hospital-based day care in one centre might produce diagnoses and a timetable of care that is radically different to that of another centre where the patient receives the same therapy through an out-patient clinic or in-patient stay. However, at the time of the economic evaluation, these differences in service provision had been resolved, so that possible differences in medical costs cannot be attributed to this 'artefact'.

For the most part, the variability observed finds its source in the the way the patients were recruited. Thus, the recruiting by Centre 1 of a large proportion of neonates (newborn infants) for whom serologic status is not yet known can be partly explained by its links with the departments of obstetrics and gynaecology in maternity hospitals. Moreover, the analysis demonstrates the development of medical practices towards an earlier medical intervention for children born of HIV-positive mothers, as well as the variability of hospitals' service delivery. Variations exist in the propensity to prescribe and the frequency of certain biological procedures. For instance, the part of a diagnostic examination constituted by the simultaneous prescription of a culture and a PCR represents 75.8 per cent of the cost per medical contact for a Po stage patient being followed up by Centre 1, but only 17.6 per cent in Centre 2; day hospitalization represents 32.2 per cent of the cost per contact of a P2a stage patient in Centre 1; in Centre 2 it is 56 per cent and in Centre 3, 72.1 per cent.

By combining cost values per patient, per contact and per stage from Table 2 with the clinical evolution described in Table 1, it is possible to calculate a direct cost per patient. This is based on an assumption of a fifteen-year lifetime for HIV-infected children and the use of a 5 per cent discount rate. This reflects the assumption that costs incurred in the future have a lower present value than if they had been incurred today. The higher the discount rate the lower is the present value of future costs. The total lifelong medical cost of a child born of a mother with AIDS ranges between $11,705 and $21,222 (supposing a materno-foetal transmission rate of 20 per cent, and between $7,417 and $13,421 with a 10 per cent rate). This total cost reaches a range of $46,073–83,665 if the child is actually infected. These calculations show the importance of the costs incurred in identification of serologic status, since the average direct cost of a non-infected child's medical resource use is $3,124–5,602. A particular constraint of the avoided costs' approach is that direct medical cost calculations are based on an estimate of the average length of life. However, this is the best approach available as an epidemiological follow-up of paediatric AIDS cases to provide data on older patients is not yet possible.

There is less uncertainty regarding the cost of screening, as the biological protocol has been ratified for many years: it includes a double ELISA test, followed in the case of a positive or uncertain result by a Western Blot test. The characteristics (sensitivity, specificity) are well established, and the unit costs of biological tests are set by the welfare insurance system. The cost of HIV screening in a popu-

Table 2 **continued**

Medical stage	P2a			AIDS		
	Centre 1	Centre 2	Centre 3	Centre 1	Centre 2	Centre 3
Number of patients	17	8	3	11	14	5
Number of observations	136	15	21	112	98	42
Length of undertaking (days)	5,245	1,480	554	3,951	2,177	986
Average age at first observation (month)	43.52	64.46	54.90	52.74	45.68	62.34
Average length of undertaking at first observation (month)	16.94	36.88	15.00	34.36	18.29	21.80
Monthly average hospital contacts frequency	0.78	0.30	1.14	0.85	1.35	1.28
Average cost per hospital contact (in US$)	571.55	343.62	976.73	665.64	743.04	933.57
CI[95%] [...	422.19	9.54	728.42	524.15	621.32	797.11
...]	734.36	790.40	1,273.34	824.67	884.57	1,083.38

Note: P2a (general symptoms) and AIDS based on the CDC classification.

lation of 100,000, with an HIV prevalence of 4 per 1,000, reaches $2,172,775.

These several elements allow us to use our cost–benefit model to evaluate the net benefit (i.e. benefit minus costs) of a prenatal screening programme according to the two parameters exogenous to the economic analysis: HIV prevalence and the decision by seropositive women to terminate their pregnancy (Figure 2). We mentioned earlier the uncertainty which characterizes the calculation of direct medical costs. However, using our cost and benefit estimates for a 50 per cent pregnancy termination rate (T – a value commonly assumed as being close to real practices), the net benefit is nullified for a prevalence of between 2.06 and 3.75 per 1,000 (with an assumed prenatal screening compliance rate of 100 per cent). This value is much lower than the one observed in areas with high prevalence, like Provence–Alpes–Côte-d'Azur (4.2 per 1,000[15]) or Ile-de-France,[16] even if these areas themselves include geographic zones where the risk of HIV infection varies widely.[17] On the other hand, if it is assumed that the materno-foetal transmission rate would not reach 20 per cent, as previously, but 10 per cent, the confidence interval of optimal prevalence becomes 3.28–5.97 per 1,000: very close, therefore, to the average for areas of France considered to be most affected by HIV infection. At this lower transmission, only in those areas with higher prevalence would an HIV prenatal screening programme be economically justified according to the welfare system perspective we have adopted.

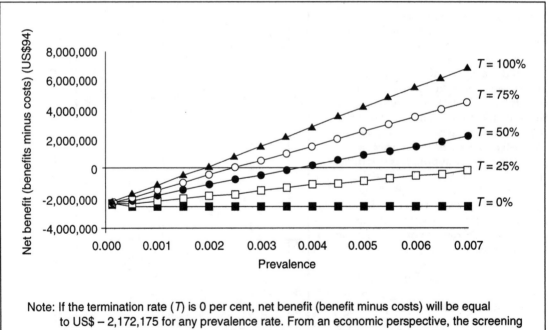

Note: If the termination rate (T) is 0 per cent, net benefit (benefit minus costs) will be equal to US$ – 2,172,175 for any prevalence rate. From an economic perspective, the screening policy is justified at the point at which benefits are equal to or exceed costs.

Figure 2 Net benefit of HIV prenatal screening depending on prevalence and pregnancy termination rate
Calculations are based on average estimations of direct costs observed for each clinical stage and for all centres

Discussion

Of course, our conclusions from the application of the cost–benefit model are extremely sensitive to the pregnancy termination rate value (Table 3). If this rate was 100 per cent, a prevalence contained between 1.03 and 1.87 per 1,000 would be enough to remove a net benefit. Variation in the results due to the technical characteristics of the screening method (sensitivity, specificity) is negligible (i.e. less than 2 per cent difference for optimal prevalence values: 3.80 instead of 3.75 per 1,000 for the upper limit; 2.09 instead of 2.06 for the lower limit). On the other hand, considering the variability of medical practices across the centres, and the differences in medical costs this produces, it is not surprising that if the cost–benefit analysis had relied on just one centre (for instance Centre 1), our conclusions would have been appreciably different: the optimal prevalence levels becoming higher and the estimation's intervals narrower (Table 4).

The precise scope of the avoided-costs measure of benefit can be debated. It can quite appropriately be considered that the only costs that would be avoided through the use of HIV prenatal screening are the direct medical costs of children actually HIV-positive, and not those of all children whatever their probable infection (Case 1). In this case, prenatal screening would therefore only start to be economically justified if the cost–benefit ratio is as in equation 7:

Case 1 :
$$C(PS) \leq CHIV\ [N'HIV - NHIV] \quad (7)$$

Furthermore, we can also consider a case in which the pregnancy termination of non-infected children will reduce the benefits of screening by terminating otherwise healthy children (Case 2). The cost–benefit equation then becomes:

Case 2 :
$$C(PS) \leq C_{HIV}\ [N'_{HIV} - N_{HIV}] \\ - C_{nHIV}\ [N'_{nHIV} - N_{nHIV}] \quad (8)$$

These new definitions of benefit lead to the removal of a net economic benefit at higher prevalence levels. So, with benefit measured as in Case 1, HIV prenatal screening in France is only justified in the areas where the prevalence of infection among pregnant women is at least contained between 2.62 and 4.79 per 1,000, assuming that 50 per cent of women found to be HIV-positive decide to terminate their pregnancy. A far more restrictive definition of benefit (as in Case 2) would then imply prevalence levels far above those actually observed in France: from 3.59 to 6.59 per 1,000.

Table 3
Variability of optimal prevalence[a] (per 1,000) for the calculation of avoided direct medical costs across centres

Pregnancy termination rate	Costs derived from the 3 centres data analysis		Costs derived from Centre 1 analysis	
25%	4.15	7.59	4.65	8.05
50%	2.06	3.76	2.31	3.98
75%	1.37	2.50	1.54	2.64
100%	1.03	1.87	1.15	1.98

[a] Optimal prevalence is defined as the one which nullifies net benefit.

Pregnancy termination rate	Benefit of screening = direct medical costs avoided					
	of infected and non-infected cases		of infected cases only		of infected cases minus non-infected cases	
25%	4.15	7.59	5.28	9.69	7.25	13.41
50%	2.06	3.76	2.62	4.79	3.59	6.59
75%	1.37	2.50	1.74	3.18	2.39	4.37
100%	1.03	1.87	1.31	2.38	1.79	3.27

Mother to child transmission rate: 20%

Table 4 **Variability of optimal prevalence (per 1,000) according to the definition of the measure of benefit**

Conclusion

The uncertainties which characterize this economic analysis and which it shares, to a lesser degree, with the few works published in this field,[18] requires the conclusions to be treated with caution. Likewise, the limits of the measurement of benefit within the framework of the avoided cost's approach have been widely accepted and must not be underestimated. This framework does not include either indirect costs or intangible effects. In fact, we have shown in a previous research the potential importance of the reassuring effect of a true negative test in the prenatal context.[19] On the other hand, insufficient knowledge of the disease's history among children requires a certain circumspection.

Nevertheless, this research shows the importance of evaluating the effect of the variability in the performance of a prevention programme, such as HIV prenatal screening, according to the prevalence among designated populations. It also shows the limits of a prevention policy that does not integrate this element, especially if the 'optimistic' hypothesis of a 10 per cent materno-foetal transmission rate was confirmed. Recent evidence from US and European research provides tentative evidence for other interventions, such as caesarean section, that could influence the results of the cost–benefit analysis reported in this chapter.[20]

1 This research has had the support of the Agence Nationale de Recherche sur le SIDA, Paris.

2 Although all children born to HIV-positive mothers are HIV-positive at birth, only a minority are in fact infected with the virus. By the age of approximately eighteen months children produce their own antibodies rather than continuing to bear their mother's.

3 BEH n°6-1991 in Haut Comité de la Santé Publique: Avis sur le dépistage de l'infection à VIH, Paris, March 1992.

4 Y. Obadia, D. Rey, J.P. Moatti, E. Couturier, Y Brossard, J.B. Brunet, 'Politique de sérodépistage du VIH en région PACA (Provence–Alpes–Côte d'Azur). Différences entre les taux de séroprévalence et les politiques pratiquées en fonction des modes de terminaison de la grossesse', Rev. Epidémiol. Santé Publique, 41, S17–S20, 1993.

5 All costs have been converted to US$ using a 1993–94 exchange rate of FFr 5.73: $1

6 C. Le Galès, J.P. Moatti et al, 'Cost-effectiveness of HIV screening of pregnant women in hospitals of the Paris area', European Journal of Obstetrics-Gynaecology and Reproductive Biology, 37, pp. 25–33, 1990.

7 There exists no systematic (or ad hoc) collection of economic information about the medical resource use of children born of seropositive mothers. We are aware of thus limiting the disease's incidence to the technical relationships between patients, their families, and the medical staff, while reality is much more complex than this.

8 Some HIV tests will appear negative whereas, in fact, the individual is HIV-positive but has developed insufficient antibodies to HIV for them to show up in the test. Alternative tests for the genetic material of the virus and for viral proteins can be used in this context.

9 The Western Blot technique is used for the test; its sensitivity, as well as its specificity, is assumed to equal 100 per cent.

10 100 children were followed up in Centre 1 over a period of twelve months (15 October 1990–15 October 1991); 46 children were followed up in Centre 2 for six months (1 April–30 September 1991); and nine children were followed up in Centre 3 for six months (1 March–31 August 1991).

11 Categorization of patients has been conducted in conformity with Atlanta's CDC paediatric nomenclature.

12 Time spent in the clinical stages of the disease (CDC of Atlanta) and the probability of transition to stages of greater illness severity.

13 S. Blanche, C. Rouzioux, M.L. Ghihard-Moscato, F. Veber, M.J. Mayaux et al, 'A prospective study of infants born to women seropositive for human immunodeficiency virus type 1', The New England Journal of Medicine, 320 (25): 1643–1648, 1989.

14 S. Blanche, F. Veber et al. (French 'HIV in the Newborn' Study Group), 'Prospective study of infants born to mother seropositive with HIV1', Vth International Conference on AIDS, Montreal, Quebec, Canada, 1989.

European Collaborative Study, 'Children born to women with HIV-1 infection: natural history and risk of transmission', Lancet, 337, n°8736, 253–60, 1991.

Y. Obadia, D. Rey, J.P. Moatti, E. Couturier, Y Brossard, J.B. Brunet, 'Politique de sérodépistage du VIH en région PACA (Provence–Alpes–Côte d'Azur). Différences entre les taux de séroprévalence et les politiques pratiquées en fonction des modes de terminaison de la grossesse', Rev. Epidémiol. Santé Publique, 41, S17–S20, 1993.

15 Y. Obadia, D. Rey, J.P. Moatti, E. Couturier, Y Brossard, J.B. Brunet, 'Politique de sérodépistage du VIH en région PACA (Provence–Alpes–Côte d'Azur). Différences entre les taux de séroprévalence et les politiques pratiquées en fonction des modes de terminaison de la grossesse', Rev. Epidémiol. Santé Publique, 41, S17–S20, 1993.

16 E. Couturier, Y. Brossard et al, 'HIV infection at outcome of pregnancy in the Paris area, France', Lancet, 340, pp. 707–9, 1992.

17 E. Couturier, C. Larsen, J.B. Brunet, 'Prévalence de l'infection a VIH chez les femmes enceintes en Ile-de-France et en région PACA (Provence–Alpes–Côte-d'Azur): enquête Prévagest', Rev. Epidémiol. Santé Publique, 41,

S15–S16, 1993.**18** M. Brandeau, D. Owens, C. Sox and R. Watcher, 'Screening of women of childbearing age for human immunodeficiency virus. A cost–benefit analysis', Archives of Internal Medicine, 152, pp. 2229–37, 1992.

19 J.P. Moatti, C. Le Galès, V. Seror, E. Papiernik and R. Henrion, 'Social acceptability of HIV screening among pregnant women', AIDS Care, 2 (3), pp. 213–22, 1990.

20 The European Collaborative Study, 'Caesarean section and risk of vertical transmission of HIV-1 infection', The Lancet, 343, pp. 1464–1467, June 1994.

'Zidovudine for the prevention of HIV transmission from mother to infant', Morbidity and Mortality Weekly Report, 43, 16, pp. 285–287, 1994.

Resourcing Healthcare for AIDS and HIV Infection in England, 1983–1993: Uncertainty and Hindsight

Dr Alastair Gray

Centre for Socio-Legal Studies, Wolfson College, University of Oxford, England

The cost of providing healthcare for people who are HIV-positive or who have AIDS has been a contentious subject in the United Kingdom since the earliest days of the epidemic. Initially, funding was criticized as misdirected and too low, and it was argued that the costs were likely to be extremely high unless prompt action was taken to stem the spread of the epidemic. However, once a formal mechanism for allocating money to health authorities to deal with HIV and AIDS had been established, criticisms began to be made that too much was being spent, or that the monies allocated for AIDS/HIV-related services had been diverted into other services. As early as 1987 comments were reported suggesting that a number of health authorities had committed centrally allocated AIDS funds to other projects (*The Times*, 27 October 1987). Such criticisms became more commonplace after the initial projections of the spread of the disease had been revised downwards, and were given formal voice in 1991 when the National Audit Office reported that the virtual doubling of AIDS allocations to Regional Health Authorities (RHAs) between 1988/89 and 1989/90 had resulted in an underspend of at least $23.1 million,[1] that some monies had been directed into other activities, and that resources should be monitored more carefully.[2]

More recently, levels of spending on HIV and AIDS have come under sustained attack, with a series of hostile Parliamentary Questions (for example in April 1993), press articles and correspondence. On 28 April 1993 a Parliamentary Answer indicated that the cumulative total of government funding for HIV/AIDS for the financial years 1986/87 to 1992/93 had totalled $1,364.9 million, including money spent on '…medical treatment and care, training of health and social care workers, infection control, surveillance, protection of the blood supply, HIV testing and counselling, funding of voluntary sector projects, local authority support services, research, and public education and prevention campaigns' (*Hansard*, 28 April 1993, col. 451). Press reports entitled 'Brake on bandwagon' (*The Sunday Times*, 9 May 1993), 'The high cost of the AIDS panic' (*The Times*, 6 May 1993), and 'AIDS: much better if we had been honest from the start' (*Daily Telegraph*, 5 May 1993) convey much of the flavour of the response to this information. Criticisms have also been made of the methods of resource allocation and in particular the encouragement these have given to treatment and care instead of prevention of infection.[3]

Many of these criticisms of funding of AIDS and HIV carry the implication that in the UK there has been a substantial discrepancy between allocation and actual expenditure, either in total or in relation to specific areas of provision. More particularly, some of these criticisms have implied that resources allocated for HIV/AIDS were too high even in relation to information available at the time (*Daily Telegraph*, 5 May 1993: *as above*). This chapter examines these contentions.

Methods

The level of Department of Health funding of hospital and community health services for HIV and AIDS in England was identified over the period 1987/88 to 1993/94. This was then compared with the annual levels of funding that would have been predicted over this period on the basis of prevailing estimates of treatment costs and current official projections of numbers affected by HIV and AIDS. Thirdly, actual expenditure on direct care of people with AIDS and HIV infection was estimated by combining retrospective data on treatment costs with estimates of the actual prevalence of AIDS and HIV infection over the period from 1983 to 1993.

Data

Costs per case

There are two principal methods of estimating the expenditure impact of HIV/AIDS: one is to multiply the numbers of individuals at different stages of the disease by the estimated average cost of caring for individuals at different stages of the disease, thus producing a 'bottom-up' estimate of present expenditure. This may then be projected into the future, usually by assuming that care costs remain constant while the numbers affected follow a path or paths predicted

by epidemiological modelling. There are numerous examples of this approach; a typical recent American example is given by Hellinger (1992).[4] This bottom-up method may involve extrapolating unit costs from a relatively small sample of patients who may not be representative of all patients, or from a particular geographical area which may not be typical of all areas. It may also exclude certain costs such as overheads or population based services which are not easy to attribute to individual cases.

Bottom-up estimates of treatment costs per AIDS case in the UK of $15,400–30,800 were being quoted in the health service press as early as 1985.[5] The same range was quoted in a number of places in 1986, again without a formal source, and was still being quoted in 1987. In December 1986 the Communicable Disease Surveillance Centre made projections of the total treatment cost of the epidemic based on a figure of $30,800 per patient, and at the beginning of 1987 a cost per case of $15,400–30,800 was still being widely quoted.

In August 1986 Johnson et al. published an estimated average lifetime cost of inpatient care for an AIDS patient of $10,531,[6] but this was criticized by Rees,[7] who argued that Johnson et al. had produced an underestimate by using a methodology which over-represented patients with short survival times and under-represented patients with longer survival times, thereby introducing a bias to the data – a time-censored cost problem. Rees predicted an overall in-patient cost per case of between $26,796 and $30,800, and a figure within this range was quoted by the Minister of Health soon after (*The Times*, 16 May 1987). A later estimate by Rees with the Economic Advisers Office of the Department of Health estimated a cost per case of $39,003, or $31,151 per annum.[8] Also in 1987 Cunningham and Griffiths produced an estimate of the cost of a hypothetical package of care for people with AIDS,[9] although this was sometimes quoted and used as an estimate of actual care.

Further work by Rees sponsored by the Department of Health in three District Health Authorities (DHAs)[10] produced a total cost per AIDS case per year ranging from $22,593 to $27,982. Rees's work also yielded the first estimates of care costs specific to HIV cases. Finally, in 1994 Beck et al. published the results of a study of costs by disease stage and year of treatment over the period 1983–1989.[11]

An alternative, 'top–down' approach, is to identify the resources allocated to services associated with AIDS and HIV by central or local government or by healthcare providers.[12] This approach also has limitations, and may wrongly estimate actual expenditure on HIV/AIDS, either because the funds set aside for such purposes are used in other ways, resulting in an overestimate of the resource costs, or because the funds set aside do not fully compensate providers for the actual additional costs they have incurred as a consequence of HIV/AIDS.

Variants of the top–down approach have been discussed and illustrated by Rees in the micro-context of costing within a DHA. For example, in Brighton, Rees showed that only 44 per cent of total district expenditure which could be attributed to AIDS/HIV was directly spent on the AIDS patients, and a further 13 per cent on HIV non-AIDS patients, with the remaining 43 per cent being accounted for by research, education, drug misuse programmes, infection control and administration.[13] In Oxfordshire, Rees found that direct treatment of AIDS patients accounted for only 17 per cent of the identified total expenditure, with a further 16 per cent on direct treatment of those infected with HIV, leaving two-thirds of total attributable expenditure accounted for by non-direct treatment costs such as counselling, testing, administration,

research and teaching.[14] Finally, in Riverside Health District Rees found that almost 60 per cent of all identified costs were related to direct treatment of AIDS patients, with a further 15 per cent related to direct treatment of those infected with HIV.[15]

Table 1 summarises this series of estimates and guesses of the treatment costs associated with AIDS and HIV cases. Unless otherwise stated, costs are valued according to the study year.

The two features of Table 1 which are particularly striking are first, the lack of estimates during the period 1985–89 of care costs for those infected with HIV but who did not have AIDS, and second, the broad consensus in 'guesstimates' and empirical estimates over most of the period covered around a figure of approximately $23,100–30,800 per annum for the direct treatment costs of someone with AIDS.

Projected and actual numbers with HIV/AIDS

The first officially sponsored predictions of HIV infection and AIDS in England and Wales were published in December 1988, by a Working Group chaired by David Cox and commissioned by the Department of Health.[16] The terms of reference of the Working Group were primarily to make predictions for a two- to five-year period of incidence and prevalence of AIDS and HIV cases. A range of methods and variants were illustrated, and a recommended basis for planning was given for the years 1987–92. In February 1990, the planning projections made in the Cox Report were more than halved by a Working Group of the Public Health Laboratory Service (PHLS) chaired by Professor N.E. Day.[17] Finally, in 1993 a second report from the PHLS Working Group made projections for the period to 1997, further revising downwards the estimates of the first Day Report.[18] The base-

Table 1
Estimated costs per AIDS and HIV case, 1985–1994

Year information refers to	Year information published	Estimated cost of health care per case	Source/comment
AIDS			
1985	1986	$15,400–30,800 pa	Unknown, see Times 3/2/86; HSSJ 6/3/86 p. 300; BMJ 1987 294 p. 455
1986	1986	$15,400–30,800 pa	Unknown
1986	1986	$10,531 lifetime	Johnson et al.
1987	1987	$26,796–30,800 lifetime	Rees
1987	1987	$41,665 pa	Cunningham and Griffiths
1987	1987	$27,104 lifetime	DoH
1987	1988	$31,151 pa	Rees/DoH (Rees and Roberts)
1987/88	1988	$22,593 pa	Riverside (DoH/Rees)
1988/89	1989	$26,479 pa	Oxfordshire (DoH/Rees)
1989/90	1989	$27,982 pa	Brighton (DoH/Rees)
1989/90	1994	$20,367 pa	Beck 1989/90 costs
HIV			
1988/89	1989	$4,312	Oxfordshire (DoH/Rees)
1989/90	1989	$1,848	Brighton (DoH/Rees) all known non–AIDS HIV positive
1989/90	1994	$1,445 asymptomatic $4,728 symptomatic non-AIDS	Beck 1989/90 costs

line projections of new AIDS cases from these three reports (each of which was accompanied by low and high variants illustrating the degree of uncertainty), and the actual numbers of new AIDS cases, are shown in Table 2.

In addition to these official projections, a number of other projections of the course of the epidemic have been made. Early attempts to predict future numbers of AIDS cases in the UK were made by McEvoy and Tillett in September 1985, who suggested planning for 1,800 new patients and 700 survivors by 1988.[19] These estimates were revised upwards in November 1986.[20] Medium- to long-term projections of the likely spread of AIDS in

the UK have been produced by an Institute of Actuaries AIDS Working Party which was constituted in 1987. These have covered periods up to approximately 30 years into the future using a wide range of different scenarios.[21]

Some estimation is also required to obtain figures on the actual prevalence of AIDS and HIV infection over the period 1983–93. The number of AIDS cases alive was estimated from the annual number of reports and survival data. To simplify, it was assumed that annual survival was one year for the period 1983–86, 18 months in 1987, and 24 months from 1988 onwards. (This is approximately in line with the actuarial lifetable analysis pre-

Year	Actual	DoH 1988 (Cox)	PHLS 1990 (Day)	PHLS 1993 (Day)
1983	26			
1984	76			
1985	152			
1986	290			
1987	634	800		
1988	715	1,250		
1989	780	1,800	1,070	
1990	1,197	2,350	1,300	
1991	1,264	2,950	1,600	
1992	1,397	3,600	2,000	1,840
1993	1,495		2,700	2,110
1994				2,265
1995				2,375
1996				2,430
1997				2,440

Table 2
Actual and projected numbers of new AIDS cases per year, 1983–1997, in England and Wales

Sources: Actual PHLS AIDS/HIV Quarterly Surveillance Tables, No. 22 to end of December 1993, Table 3 Projections: *see text*

sented in the second Day Report,[22] which has median survival times of 10–11 months in 1986 or earlier, 17–18 months in 1987, and 19–20 months in 1988). Consequently, prevalence was calculated as equivalent to the annual new cases reported from 1983–1986, annual new cases plus 50 per cent of previous year's cases for 1987, and annual new cases plus previous year's cases for 1988–1993.

Prevalence of severe HIV infection was estimated using the prevalence ratios of severe HIV disease to AIDS cases reported in PHLS for the period 1983–91.[23] Finally, the prevalent number of other HIV infections was taken from the average of the 1991 basic (R6B) and low (R6C) scenarios using the back-calculation method [24] presented by the Institute of Actuaries,[25] minus severe HIV infections.

Expenditure allocations for health care

The public expenditure impact of HIV/AIDS has been spread over a large number of government departments, including the Department of Health, the Home Office, the Department for Education, the Department of Employment, the Overseas Development Administration, and others. In this exercise, the main focus of interest is on government funding of *healthcare* services related to AIDS/HIV. The first general allocation of funds to health authorities by the Department of Health for the provision of services related to HIV and AIDS was made in the financial year 1987/88. Subsequently, these allocations have been made annually in line with a formula, which has itself changed over time.

These funds to Regional Health Authorities have been distributed with the general guidance that they be spent in pursuit of the government's broad policy aims concerning the prevention of the spread of HIV infection and the provision of treat-

ment, counselling and support for those infected or at risk.[26] From 1989/90 funds were split into direct treatment and non-treatment components, with general guidance on the use of funds, but there was no enforced requirement on managers at regional or district level to ensure funds allocated for community prevention or health education initiatives were actually used for these purposes.[27]

In 1992/93 and 1993/94 stricter procedures were introduced for auditing and reporting back the use of funds for particular years.[28] In 1993/94, for example, 61 per cent of the allocation was intended for direct treatment, 24 per cent for indirect care (including testing, counselling and capital equipment), 10 per cent for local provision and 5 per cent for drug misuse services.

Table 3 shows the actual amount allocated each year from 1987/88 to 1993/94. The estimated amount allocated for direct patient care has been calculated at 60 per cent of the total allocation. This proportion was used because it was the average proportion prevailing in the latest three years, when guidance has been most specific; it is of course possible that guidance was not adhered to, or that the proportion differed in earlier years, in which case the actual amount devoted to direct patient care would have been higher or lower than this figure. This would clearly affect the results of this study. Total and direct patient care allocations are also shown in constant 1993 prices, adjusted using the NHS Hospital and Community Health Services Pay and Prices Index.

Results

Table 4 shows estimates of the actual numbers of people in England and Wales with AIDS, severe infection and other HIV infection over the period 1983–93 (estimated as described above), the retrospectively estimated average cost per per-

Table 3 **Allocations of funds by the Department of Health to Regional Health Authorities for HIV/AIDS services, 1987/8 to 1993/4, England**

Year ending March	Total allocation		Allocation for direct patient care	
	Actual (current prices) $ million	Present value (Constant 1993 prices) $ million	Actual (current prices) $ million	Present value (Constant 1993 prices) $ million
1988	38.7	58.9	23.2	35.4
1989	90.9	118.1	54.5	70.9
1990	187.9	243.6	112.7	146.1
1991	194.0	231.4	116.4	138.9
1992	211.4	229.1	126.9	137.4
1993	279.4	285.5	167.6	171.3
1994	330.0	330.0	200.2	200.2
Total	1,332.3	1,496.6	801.5	900.2

son of providing healthcare in each year over the same period,[29] and the implied levels of total expenditure derived from combining unit costs and affected population. All figures are given in 1993/94 constant prices.

It can be seen that if the estimated prevalence figures are accurate and if the retrospectively calculated costs of providing care are accurate and typical of care provided in a wide range of different settings, then the actual expenditure on direct care for AIDS and HIV care over the period 1983–93 would have totalled $478 million. Of this total, $363 million, or 76 per cent, was attributable to AIDS care, $89 million (19 per cent) to severe HIV care, and $26 million (5 per cent) to other HIV care.

This figure of $478 million compares with an estimated total of $901 million allocated for direct patient care over the same period, and of $1,497 million allocated to all forms of AIDS/HIV services. In other words, around 32 per cent of the total allocation for all forms of AIDS/HIV services, or 53 per cent of the allocation for direct patient care, would actually have been spent on direct treatment if the estimates of prevalence and Beck *et al.*'s retrospective estimates of actual treatment costs over the period 1983–89 are accurate.

When placed in the context of what was known at the time rather than what has retrospectively been calculated about treatment costs over the period 1983–93, a somewhat different picture emerges. As a comparison of Table 4 with Table 1 shows, in most years the retrospective estimates of treatment costs by Beck *et al.* are generally lower than those estimated at the time (a difference partly attributable to coverage, in that the Beck *et al.* figures relate only to hospital care and do not include community-based health services). This is reflected in Figure 1, which shows the Department of Health allocation for direct patient care plotted against the estimated resource requirements calculated on the basis of actual prevalence and low and high prevailing estimates of treatment costs as set out in Table 1.

The actual allocation remains slightly above the anticipated resource requirements, but the difference is relatively small. Moreover, for at least two years (1985/86 and 1986/87) expenditure is being incurred with no compensating allocation. Over the period as a whole, the total resource requirement calculated on this basis ranges from $622 million to $812 million, compared with $901 million actually allocated.

Finally, Figure 2 shows estimated resource requirements for each year in the period 1987/88 to 1993/94 based on prevailing knowledge about treatment costs and the most current projections of prevalence for the year in question. In other words, in the Figure 2 situation resource requirements have been calculated on the 'best' information available at the time the allocation was decided, with no benefit of hindsight.

In this instance, estimated resource requirements vary from $799 million to $1,024 million over the period, against $901 million actually allocated. It should be noted that the high–low range reflects only uncertainty over treatment costs and not uncertainty over the projections themselves, which as noted earlier were framed within wide confidence intervals and would therefore have widened the likely resource requirement range very substantially if taken into account.

Year	Prevalence (cases alive)			Cost per case ($)			Total cost ($ million)			
	AIDS	Severe HIV	Other HIV	AIDS	Severe HIV	Other HIV	AIDS	Severe HIV	Other HIV	Total
1983	25	83	4,451	71,205	10,621	1,063	1.8	0.9	0.1	2.8
1984	75	188	7,045	47,072	5,670	1,726	3.5	1.1	0.3	4.9
1985	150	300	9,740	30,241	9,474	1,985	4.5	2.8	0.6	8.0
1986	300	450	12,297	27,939	4,538	1,766	8.3	2.0	0.8	11.2
1987	700	840	14,815	27,942	6,805	1,618	19.6	5.7	1.4	26.6
1988	1,012	1,015	17,604	25,461	6,380	1,580	25.7	6.5	1.5	33.9
1989	1,465	1,469	20,032	26,416	6,132	1,874	38.7	9.1	2.8	50.5
1990	1,947	1,953	22,248	26,416	6,132	1,874	51.4	12.0	3.7	67.0
1991	2,430	2,437	24,228	26,416	6,132	1,874	64.2	14.9	4.6	83.8
1992	2,629	2,637	26,385	26,416	6,132	1,874	69.5	16.2	4.9	90.6
1993	2,853	2,862	28,487	26,416	6,132	1,874	75.3	17.6	5.4	98.3
Total							362.5	88.8	26.1	477.6

Table 4 **Direct health expenditure on HIV and AIDS care 1983–1993 based on estimated prevalence of HIV infection and AIDS and retrospective patient cost data, 1993/94 prices ($), England**

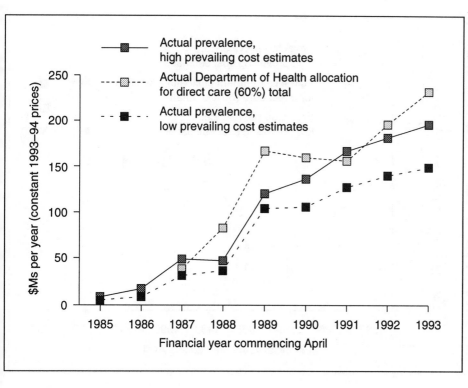

Figure 1
Department of
Health alloca-
tions for direct
AIDS/HIV patient
care compared
with expenditure
requirements
using prevailing
AIDS/HIV preva-
lence and
patient treat-
ment cost esti-
mates

Discussion

This paper has described and compared different ways of estimating the total
public expenditure implications of HIV/AIDS in England over the period
1983–93. The results indicate that in retrospect there has been a discrepancy
between what was provided for direct treatment costs and what a reasonable
back-calculation suggests was required and was actually used for this purpose.
However, as the level of retrospective information concerning costs and prevalence is reduced and calculations are performed using information available at
the time, so the resource requirements move closer to what was actually provided. What appears discrepant in the relatively precise refractor of hindsight
seems more appropriate through the veil of uncertainty prevailing at the time.

In effect, Table 4 shows resource requirements for direct treatment of HIV/AIDS
with full hindsight over costs and prevalence; Figure 1 shows resource requirements with hindsight over prevalence but not costs, and Figure 2 shows resource
requirements with no hindsight. The convergence towards what was actually provided is quite clear. Allocated public expenditure has tended to follow the path
predicted by short-term projections of the epidemic and prevailing cost data,
rather than the actual path as revealed retrospectively by epidemiological surveillance and cost studies. This demonstrates how important it is to have accurate
cost information underpinning policy decisions concerning resource allocations.

Figure 2
Department of Health allocations for direct AIDS/HIV patient care compared with expenditure requirements using projected AIDS/HIV prevalence and patient treatment cost estimates

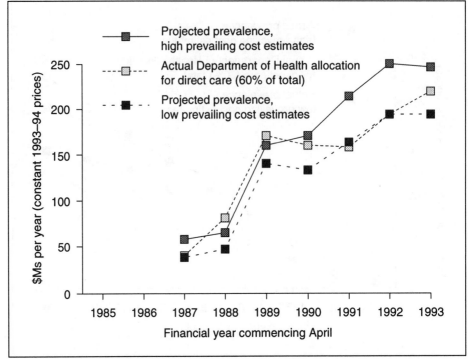

No more than three years elapsed between each of three official working parties constituted to predict future incidence and prevalence of AIDS and HIV in England and Wales, and each adopted a short projection horizon of no more than six years. Consequently it is clear that over the period 1983–93 the planning basis for dealing with the epidemic – including resourcing the response to it – was based on projections which were short-term and regularly updated. The predictions of the Institute of Actuaries AIDS Working Party, the only serious source of medium- to long-term predictions of AIDS cases in the UK, were not used as a basis for medium- to long-term cost projections and do not appear to have played a part in year-to-year resource allocations by the Department of Health. Official responses to the cost of the epidemic have been almost exclusively short-term, being confined to an allocation for the forthcoming year with perhaps some indication of intention for the year after: in other words, a planning horizon of no more than two years and usually one year.

Conclusions

It has been argued that the UK's funding policies for HIV and AIDS have been unsatisfactory, in that prevention of infection has been given far less attention than has treatment and care despite the fact that few effective treatments have been available.[30]

While it is clear that the basis of some early statements of the likely cost of AIDS and HIV in England was hard to discern even at the time,[31] it is much less clear that the allocation of funds for treatment associated with AIDS and HIV has ever been grossly out of line with reasonable estimates based on available information of prevalence and healthcare utilization by those affected. Although some estimates of the spread of the epidemic turned out to be inaccurate, the more heroic inaccuracies were usually in the medium to long term, whilst funding decisions have in practice been constrained to the next financial year. If direct treatment allocations have indeed been in excess of a retrospective calculation of actual resource requirements for direct care (a conclusion which may be altered by new data on retrospective costs), then a higher portion than previously thought of the total AIDS/HIV allocation has been available for other purposes, including prevention and infection control. If this has been the case, attention could usefully be focused on resource management and allocation decisions at the local rather than the national level.

Acknowledgements

Some aspects of this paper have been developed from an earlier programme of research at the AIDS Social History programme, London School of Hygiene and Tropical Medicine, which was funded by the Nuffield Provincial Hospitals Trust, and I am grateful to all concerned for support. Sushil Jathanna and Keith Tolley were kind enough to provide useful comments on an earlier draft; all remaining errors are solely my responsibility.

1 All costs have been converted to US$ using a 1993–94 exchange rate of US$1.54: £1.

2 National Audit Office, HIV and AIDS Related Health Services. HMSO, London, 1991.

3 M. McCarthy, S. Layzell, 'Funding policies for HIV and AIDS: time for change', British Medical Journal 307: 367: 369, 1993.

4 F. J. Hellinger, 'Forecasts of the costs of medical care for persons with HIV: 1992–1995', Inquiry, 29 (3): 356–65, Fall 1992.

5 Health and Social Services Journal, p. 1506, 28 November 1985.

6 A. M. Johnson, M.W. Adler and J.M. Crown, 'The acquired immune deficiency syndrome and epidemic of infection with human immunodeficiency virus costs of care and prevention in an inner London district', British Medical Journal, 293: 489–92, 1986.

7 M. Rees, 'Survival time, length of stay and the costing of AIDS in patients', unpublished, 1987.

8 M. Rees and B. Roberts, 'Quality Adjusted Life Years (QALYs) and the cost of AIDS patients', John Hunter Clinic, St Stephen's Hospital, London SW10 9TH. Unpublished 1988.

9 D. Cunningham and S.F. Griffiths, 'AIDS: counting the cost', British Medical Journal, 295: 921–22, 1987.

10 M. Rees, B. Roberts, S. Brindle, AIDS/HIV: The Cost of the Service in Riverside. Department of Health, London, April 1988.

M. Rees, The Cost of AIDS/HIV in the Oxfordshire Health District. Department of Health, London, February 1989.

M. Rees, The Cost of AIDS/HIV in the Brighton District. Department of Health, London, November 1989.

11 E.J. Beck, J. Kennelly, C. McKevitt et al. 'Changing use of hospital services and costs at a London AIDS referral centre, 1983–1989', AIDS, 8, 3: 367–377, 1994.

12 K. Tolley and A. Maynard, Government Funding of HIV–AIDS Medical and Social Care, Discussion Paper 70. Centre for Health Economics, University of York, 1990.

A. Gray, Economic Aspects of AIDS and HIV Infection in the UK, Discussion Paper No. 2. London School of Hygiene and Tropical Medicine, Department of Public Health and Health Policy, London, 1991.

13 M. Rees, The Cost of AIDS/HIV in the Brighton District. Department of Health, London, November 1989.

14 M. Rees, The Cost of AIDS/HIV in the Oxfordshire Health District. Department of Health, London, February 1989.

15 M. Rees, B. Roberts, S. Brindle, AIDS/HIV: the Cost of the Service in Riverside. Department of Health, London, April 1988.

16 Department of Health, Short-term Prediction of HIV Infection and AIDS in England and Wales: Report of a Working Group (Cox Report). HMSO, London, 1988.

17 PHLS, 'Acquired Immune Deficiency Syndrome in England and Wales to End 1993: Projections Using Data to End September 1989. Report of a Working Group Convened by the Director of the Public Health Laboratory Service (Day Report)', Communicable Disease Report, (Suppl) 1990.

18 PHLS, 'The Incidence and Prevalence of AIDS and Other Severe HIV disease in England and Wales for 1992–1997: Projections Using Data to the End of June 1992. Report of a Working Group Convened by the Director of the Public Health Laboratory Service (Day Report)', Communicable Disease Report, (Suppl) 1993.

19 M. McEvoy and H. Tillett, 'Some problems in the prediction of future numbers of cases of acquired immunodeficiency syndrome in the UK', Lancet, ii: 541–2, 1985.

20 H.E. Tillett and M. McEvoy, 'Reassessment of predicted numbers of AIDS cases in the UK', Lancet 1986, ii: 1104.

21 Institute of Actuaries, Aids Working Party, AIDS Bulletin No. 1, August 1987. Institute of Actuaries, Staple Inn Hall, High Holburn, London, WC1V 7QJ.

Institute of Actuaries, Aids Working Party, Aids Bulletin No. 2, December 1987.

Institute of Actuaries, Aids Working Party, The Implications of AIDS for Life Assurance Companies, supplement to Bulletin No. 2 of the AIDS Working Party, February 1988.

Institute of Actuaries, Aids Working Party, AIDS Bulletin No. 3, June 1988.

Institute of Actuaries, Aids Working Party, AIDS Bulletin No. 4, March 1989.

Institute of Actuaries, Aids Working Party, AIDS Bulletin No. 5, March 1991.

22 Table 3: PHLS, 'The Incidence and Prevalence of AIDS and Other Severe HIV Disease in England and Wales for 1992–1997: Projections Using Data to the End of June 1992. Report of a Working Group Convened by the Director of the Public Health Laboratory Service (Day Report)', Communicable Disease Report, (Suppl) 1993.

23 PHLS, 'The Incidence and Prevalence of AIDS and Other Severe HIV Disease in England and Wales for 1992–1997: Projections Using Data to the End of June 1992. Report of a Working Group Convened by the Director of the Public Health Laboratory Service (Day Report)', Communicable Disease Report, (Suppl) 1993.

24 Back-projection works by making use of the known number of new AIDS cases and information on the incubation period of the disease to estimate the number of new infections in past years.

25 Institute of Actuaries, 1991, Appendix 2.5.

26 National Audit Office, HIV and AIDS Related Health Services, p. 14. HMSO, London, 1991.

27 K. Tolley and A. Maynard, Government Funding of HIV–AIDS Medical and Social Care. Centre for Health Economics, University of York, Discussion Paper 70, 1990.

28 Department of Health, HIV/AIDS Allocation, EL (93) 19. Department of Health, Leeds, March 1993.

Department of Health, HIV/AIDS Allocation, EL (94) 11. Department of Health, Leeds, February 1994.

29 E. J. Beck, J. Kennelly, C. McKevitt et al. 'Changing use of hospital services and costs at a London AIDS referral centre, 1983–1989', AIDS , 8, 3: 367–377, 1994. See Table 1.

30 M. McCarthy, S. Layzell, 'Funding policies for HIV and AIDS: time for change', British Medical Journal 307: 367: 369, 1993.

31 A. Gray, Economic Aspects of AIDS and HIV Infection in the UK. London School of Hygiene and Tropical Medicine, Department of Public Health and Health Policy, Discussion Paper No. 2, 1991.

Back to Basics: Securing Funding for Voluntary HIV Services

John Nicholson

Director, George House Trust, Manchester, England

The voluntary sector throughout Europe plays a vital part both in HIV prevention and the care of people living with HIV. The cost of this sector is extremely difficult to quantify because of the huge contribution of unpaid voluntary workers. In countries such as the UK, the voluntary sector is frequently seen as a major provider of cost-effective community care services for people living with HIV, and has received funding from the state for this purpose.

However, uncertainty around funding makes it extremely difficult for voluntary organizations to plan for the long-term provision of this care. This chapter takes the experience of George House Trust as a way of illustrating the problems caused to services by the insecurity of funding and by having to apply to many different bodies (even within the public sector) for relatively small amounts of money.

George House Trust is one of a number of HIV voluntary organizations which now have to seek funding from a much larger number of funders than hitherto because of recent changes in funding mechanisms and allocations by the state for statutory health and social services. Other examples in the UK include Aled Richards Trust, Bristol, Body Positive North East, New-castle and several of the London-wide agencies.

George House Trust (GHT), in the role of North West HIV service provision and development agency, supports over 300 people living with HIV each year, in sixteen local authority areas and eighteen health authority areas (and the latter are not coterminous). 15,000 episodes of care each year include emotional support in people's own homes (befriending and support for a wide range of carers, partners, relatives and dependants); peer support in GHT itself (the facilitating of groups and services for HIV-positive women, drug users, gay men, black people); and financial support through hardship grants and respite care funding. Yet the £250,000 of public sector money originating from the Department of Health which GHT received in 1993/94 came from negotiations with 237 senior officers and 34 different financial routes. None of GHT's current funding is guaranteed beyond the end of financial year 1994/95.

The experience described is not untypical of voluntary organizations serving populations of more than one local district; nor is the experience improving as a result of supposed clarification of purchaser–provider arrangements.

The argument in this chapter is not so much for more funding for voluntary HIV service providers as for meaningful recognition of the importance of their role within overall community service provision, and financial security for their core functions. At the same time, other countries who see or who are developing the voluntary sector as a major service provider should learn from the experience in the UK, including the practical implications of operating the sector in this way.

Voluntary services are quality services

The numbers of people living with HIV are growing – worldwide and in Britain – and growing in all communities. The needs of people affected by HIV are more diverse, increasingly so, and they include those of carers, parents, children and dependants.

A growing number want to continue to live, and to die, in their own homes. And as people live longer, often thanks to better treatment of opportunistic infections, their community care needs are extending similarly.

Community care services can include :

- emotional support, such as one-to-one befriending, or 'buddying', in people's own homes, as well as support for carers and dependents, and through the facilitating of peer support or self-help groups;
- practical home care support, through night-sitting, childcare, transport to hospital or day services, complementary therapies, respite care;
- financial support, through hardship or respite funding, and through meeting day-to-day costs of food and transport.

All these vital voluntary services need to be planned and delivered in confidential and accessible, non-discriminatory ways. Statutory services cannot always be flexi-ble enough to provide the variety of choices or respond to differing needs. Voluntary services, on the other hand, cannot fulfil all the needs of someone wanting to live at home. Unless there is a comprehensive framework of statutory social and health care services, the voluntary support on its own cannot maintain the whole community care package that is needed. The aim therefore has to be that of quality community services, voluntary and statutory, rather than services on the cheap or services to let the public sector (or purse) off the hook.

GHT's surveys[1] of statutory sector planning documents throughout the North Western Region have, however, shown that community services in particular are not guaranteed by Health Authority Purchasing Plans, Local Authority Community Care Plans, or Department of Social Security benefits. GHT has consequently promoted joint approaches – looking to commission community care services across health and local authorities as well as voluntary and users' organizations.

The policy commitment to funding of non-governmental HIV organizations

The British Government has made clear its policy commitments to the HIV voluntary sector and to community care services for people living with HIV disease. These commitments run consistently through the National Health Service (NHS) and Community Care Act 1990,[2] the *Health of the Nation* White Paper[3] and the NHS Management Executive Circulars for Health Authorities on their HIV/AIDS allocations, especially EL (92) 18, EL (93) 19 and EL (94)11,[4] the first two of which contain specific guidelines for local authorities' AIDS Support Grant allocations.

For example, the Government guidance to the AIDS Support Grant which has been awarded by the Department of Health to local authorities, calls for:

'proper integration of the voluntary sector into strategic planning'

as well as evidence of financial support for the voluntary sector.

The NHS Management Executive Circulars on HIV/AIDS allocations all call for ensuring HIV services are integral to contracts, and are therefore safeguarded within corporate contracts when designated budgets cease, stressing how purchasing authorities should support voluntary organizations, including their core costs.

Most recently, Circular EL (94) 11 made clear, in its section 'Importance of the Voluntary Sector':

'With the removal of topslicing[5] it will be even more important to ensure that the voluntary sector is able to continue to contribute to the mixed economy of care at least to the same degree as now. Purchasers will need to ensure that they include the voluntary sector in consultations on their annual purchasing plans, and that they provide adequate financial support for core costs as well as service level agreements/contracts for services. Authorities should also offer help to the voluntary sector in coping with the requirements of contracting.'

At the same time the Government has devolved decision-making to the district health authorities and local authorities 'to determine local priorities in the light of local circumstances'. Department of Health letters on this subject have indicated that there are considerable allocations made by Government to health and local authorities, and that guidance to these authorities on the use of their allocations 'stresses the need to support the voluntary sector at an appropriate level'.

Given these Government commitments, the voluntary sector contribution should be secure. However, in practice the Government's expression of support is often counteracted by the results of the simultaneous delegation of decision-making. Voluntary organizations in the regions are in fact constantly seeking core managerial and administrative assistance from a large number of potential purchasers at the same time as (or instead of) carrying out their key functions. There are no extra resources for joint working, and no mechanisms in place to ensure that the Government can effectively monitor local activity, either on funding the voluntary sector or involving it in joint working.

The experience of HIV funding in the North Western Region, 1990 to 1994

The North Western Region (Greater Manchester and Lancashire) has consistently had the highest recorded level of HIV in England outside the London regions. (This is still true for the new North West, following merger of the North Western with Cheshire, Merseyside and part of Cumbria on 1 April 1994.) To provide services to meet this need, North Western Health and Local Authorities received between them around £12 million from the Department of Health in 1993/94, although this was reduced by £700,000 in the health sector (and 'ring-fencing' ended for HIV treatment and care on 1 April 1994) and reduced by £400,000 (out of £1 million) for the Local Authorities for 1994/95.

Up to 31 March 1994, there were nineteen (district) health authorities, which were to combine to form ten, six in Greater Manchester, four in Lancashire. There were ten Greater Manchester Family Health Service Authorities coterminous with local authorities and one coterminous with Lancashire County Council (which itself awaits boundary changes for shire county areas). A similar pattern existed for the

Figure 1
**Local Authority
and Health
Authority bound-
aries**

Local Authority boundaries

Health Authority boundaries prior to April 1994

Health Authority boundaries from April 1994

0   100 Km

former Mersey Region, but the number of constituent authorities was smaller than for the North Western.

The numbers of people living with HIV are not spread evenly throughout the region. They are mostly concentrated in or around the regional urban centre – Manchester and parts of its immediately surrounding districts. Isolated pockets of relatively high prevalence exist outside this, such as in Blackpool. Yet in inner city health districts there is a funding system based on (under-represented) population numbers rather than on the (well-documented) needs of local people.

Both for statutory and non-statutory services the argument is strong for direct regional commissioning of HIV community care services in this region, carried out jointly across the sectors. However, there is currently no agreement as to how community services, in health, local authority and voluntary sectors, are likely to be purchased across a new regional area for a relatively small, discrete client group, which is neither visible nor evenly spread – nor necessarily remaining in the districts where resident when first diagnosed HIV-positive.

The current interest in locality planning and purchasing creates further potential difficulties for HIV services. People with HIV are not going to show themselves in numbers at local public meetings, and are likely to be invisible in many related health-needs assessment processes. Consequently there is a greater necessity for purchasers to work together to identify the levels and types of community care needs for people living with HIV, separate from the 'local is best' approach.[6]

Section 64 funding

Section 64 allocations are the only direct, three-year Department of Health funding available for voluntary organizations. At present these are awarded to cover the core costs of 'national (or regional) voluntary organisations'. In fact for HIV it is only London-based organizations (often described as 'national') which receive any assistance from this source, and even *they* are receiving cuts.

George House Trust, a region-wide HIV voluntary organization for the North West, provides services across a geographical region from Derbyshire, Staffordshire and Cheshire to Cumbria and Yorkshire, as well as its prime area of Greater Manchester and Lancashire.

GHT's applications for Section 64 assistance have all been rejected on the grounds that the organization was 'not national'. The North West has no support from the Department of Health's only source of direct funding. There is therefore no security for North West voluntary core managerial and administration costs.

AIDS Support Grant

The AIDS Support Grant (ASG) has been awarded by the Department of Health to social service-providing local authorities on an annual basis and is due to run until 1 April 1995. The allocation for 1993/94 shows 67 per cent of this goes to London.

Local authorities have been guided to maintain support for the voluntary sector – although the Department of Health is now (July 1994) suggesting that there is no requirement for this in 1994/95. All local authorities have been required to match this Department of Health grant with a contribution of their own, all of this money to be spent specifically on HIV work. The ASG formed 70 per cent of the total monies, with local authorities providing 30 per cent. Department of Health monitoring of this is felt to have been inadequate – figures for the actual rather than budgeted 1993/94 expenditure are still unobtainable in July 1994.

Greater Manchester and Lancashire

Ten of the eleven local authorities in the North Western Region (i.e. all but Manchester) received the same amount for 1993/94 as for 1992/93 – less 20 per cent in cash terms. This totalled £279,000 for the whole of the North Western Region, less Manchester. Strangely, this ASG cash was also routed from the Department of Health to the North Western Regional Health Authority (NWRHA) which allocated it to Local Authorities in December 1993. Local authorities therefore did not physically receive the money until towards the end of the financial year. Extra 'Healthy Alliance' cash (i.e. roughly the 20 per cent cut, explicitly for joint working) was then allocated by the NWRHA, per capita, to district health authorities with no mechanism for ensuring local authority or voluntary involvement in its spending.

Inquiries were made to the Department of Health as to how these local authorities would be able to fund the voluntary sector at the same level as previously. These elicited the response that cuts would have to be made, in contravention of the Department's own guidelines.

For 1994/95 six of these Greater Manchester councils had their allocation cut to £10,000 or less, and three had a slight increase – yet the Department's guidelines still expected support to be provided to the voluntary sector.

The eleventh North Western local authority, Manchester, received a 1993/94 cash standstill, at £709,000, and then an indicative cut to just £300,000 for 1994/95. Manchester's allocation had specifically recognized its role at the regional centre. This reflected the number of people with HIV disease who live in or are attracted to move towards Manchester as the regional centre.

GHT's experience of discussions with local authorities shows that all authorities outside Manchester expect Manchester to pay for the majority of any region-wide voluntary activity which is based in Manchester. This would justify a regional role allocation to Manchester. Manchester Council, however, feels that region-wide voluntary activity should be supported by all districts across the region, despite their much lower allocations and despite the numbers of people with HIV disease living in and moving towards the regional centre represented by Manchester itself. Either way Manchester Council has not put in the real support which is needed for the services received – by Manchester residents – whether that is on the basis of Manchester residence or on the basis of Manchester's role as the regional centre.

At 1 December 1993 there had been *no* ASG allocation for 1993/94 made by any of these Local Authorities to GHT or its voluntary support services for people living with HIV disease in the North West.

North Western Regional Health Authority

The NWRHA had around £10 million available for recurrent HIV expenditure in 1993/94. The direction from the Department of Health was, however, increasingly clearly towards delegation of allocations to districts, for the latter to act as purchasing authorities in their own right. This brings to an end most, if not all, direct funding from a regional level.

Yet people living with HIV disease are not spread evenly throughout the region. They are mostly concentrated in or around the regional centre, that is, Manchester and parts of its immediately surrounding districts. Both for statutory and non-statutory services there is an argument for direct commissioning of HIV specialisms for at least the Greater Manchester part of the region.

This is particularly true as a result of the 'per capita equalization' which is being introduced for district funding. The poorest health authorities are the ones with the highest levels of health needs anyway. These are the ones with the highest numbers of people with HIV. And these are the ones who will lose most by equalization of resources. (It is also the case that population numbers are under-recorded in these districts. Mobility, homelessness, refugees, local tax evasion and electoral non-registration have all added to the under-representation in inner city areas; and this is particularly true of Manchester and nearby Salford.)

The NHS Management Executive Circulars (especially EL (92) 18 and EL (93) 19) emphasized the importance of funding those voluntary organizations whose work covers more than one district: 'It is essential that voluntary groups are given appropriate and adequate support' (EL (92) 18); 'Regions should therefore ensure that:...Region-wide voluntary agencies receive adequate financial support and help in managing their organisations' (EL (93) 19); 'Purchasers will need to ensure that they provide adequate financial support for core costs...'(EL (94) 11).

The NWRHA's own Advisory Committee on HIV and AIDS agreed from 1991 that there should be a direct funding relationship between the NWRHA and the region-wide voluntary sector. The Community Care Strategy prepared by a range of statutory and voluntary agencies for the NWRHA also set out regional commissioning and joint involvement in HIV purchasing and providing.

But the NWRHA was unable to dictate to districts how to spend their own allocations. AIDS Control Act 1990 returns showed almost all Authorities admitting to their use of voluntary services, but the existing HIV allocations from the NWRHA could not force Authorities to support the voluntary sector, locally or regionally, for these services.

In practice, George House Trust expects to need £375,000 a year from 1994/95 onwards in order to provide the same level of services for people living with HIV disease throughout the North Western Region. Between 1990 and 1994 almost half of this money came from the NWRHA, through specified allocations to two Manchester districts.

However, a direct funding relationship between GHT and the NWRHA was never achieved and there remains no certainty as to how GHT allocations originating from the former NWRHA will be dispersed in the long term. The new RHA has already delegated funding direct to districts, against the NWRHA Advisory Committee recommendations and Community Care Strategy.

District health authorities

There were nineteen health authorities in the North Western Region. GHT has worked with and provided services for residents of all of these – and in addition for residents of Cumbria, Derbyshire, Staffordshire, Cheshire and Yorkshire Authorities. The North Western Authorities combine to form ten Purchasing Consortia from the start of April 1994. All these health authorities have been continually approached with a view to securing 'Service Agreements' accordingly.

The funding history is as follows:

- in 1990/91 no district funded GHT with its own money (i.e. no district provided any money to GHT other than acting as brokers for Regional grants, as described above);

- in 1991/92 three districts found small sums of money, totalling £4,500;

- in 1992/93 three districts allocated GHT £9,000 between them from a Regional Health Authority allocation, while four districts allocated a total of £6,500 between them from their own resources. In addition, one Cheshire health authority donated £1,000.

- for 1993/94 GHT was aware at 1 December 1993 (two-thirds of the way through the financial year) of allocations of £20,500, from eight different health authorities. With one district there was a 'Service Agreement' for £5,000, lasting until 1994/95.

Of nineteen NWRHA districts, eleven had provided GHT with no funding of their own in the entire period 1990–94.

Purchasing plans: community care and *The Health of the Nation* White Paper

HIV is a new issue. Few budgets have included HIV community services in a mainstream way. Every additional allocation has had to be fought for – whether for voluntary or statutory service provision.

The Community Care Act has not led to any specific money for people with HIV. Although the Government specified that 85 per cent of local authority expenditure on community care should go to the 'independent sector', the main emphasis was on frail elderly, and no community care money has found its way to HIV services, let alone voluntary HIV services, in this region. (There have been some Joint Finance allocations to HIV voluntary organizations, but these have come through general voluntary sector bidding, not through Community Care planning as such.) Similarly, *The Health of the Nation* White Paper proposed 'Healthy Alliances' but without resource identification to back these up. There is no evidence of general *Health of the Nation* initiatives leading to funding for HIV services in this region.

Voluntary organizations will need to exist if they are to be in healthy alliances.

GHT has worked hard to get HIV into Community Care Plans and HIV commu-

nity services into Purchasing Plans, as can be seen from the publication, *Making HIV Community Care a Reality*.[7] But, as the latter showed, this has not happened easily. GHT funding is not automatically in mainstream budgets, and every success has required a long-argued fundraising enterprise, targeted particularly to the needs of the particular authority in question. The time spent on this has been at the expense of carrying out the actual existing work of GHT services themselves (which, like all services for people with HIV, has never been simple in the first place).

Yet all North Western Health Authorities have used GHT services, to the extent of over 10,000 episodes of care per year for their residents, at an average cost of £240,000 per year from 1990 to 1994. The financial support outlined above in no way approximates to the real costs of the services used. The attempt to gain 'Service Agreements' has been made almost entirely on the part of GHT, and has received little interest from the Health Authorities themselves right up to the imminent end of ring-fencing – which is not surprising, given the low level of funding actually provided.

Any perception by districts that regional funding could cover GHT costs would be misplaced. At the same time, any perception by the Department of Health that individual districts are likely to bridge the funding gap would be equally unsound.

The process of contractual relationships

Given the difficult experience described above, does the process of integration of the voluntary sector into contractual relationships, as emphasized by the legislation on community care and the Department of Health guidelines and circulars, not then offer an improved prospect for the future?

GHT participated fully in statutory sector and inter-agency committees and planning structures over the period 1990–94. For example, GHT represented the voluntary sector on the NWRHA *Health of the Nation* Regional Implementation Group and on the inter-sectoral Chief Officers' Community Care Executive Management Group in Manchester, as well as on all levels of HIV committees up to the NWRHA Regional Advisory Committee on HIV and AIDS.

GHT also led the way in bringing health authorities, local authorities and voluntary and user organizations together in joint HIV planning in several districts, and published two reports on the theme of joint planning,[8] community care and HIV disease – the second after a survey of all North Western Authorities during the course of 1992. As an individual agency GHT believes it has shown itself willing to produce the required contractual approach which was set out in the terms of the NHS and Community Care Act 1990 and the guidelines issued by the Department of Health for HIV-specific allocations.

Financial mechanisms

In March 1994, George House Trust was attempting to negotiate funding relationships for 1994/95 and beyond with 26 different health authorities and thirteen different local authorities (ten metropolitan district councils and three county councils). GHT was a participant in most of the available HIV committee structures in which these discussions took place – although, of course, in some authorities there was no involvement, let alone integration, of the HIV voluntary sector in strategic planning or financial allocation. Manchester City Council was the most obvious example of this.

During 1993/94 GHT calculated that it could eventually receive £250,000 of Department of Health HIV-specific money – through 34 different financial routes, and involving communication with 83 different individual statutory sector officers, both in Treasurers' Departments and in departments which authorized the grants involved. This communication was in addition to contacts with the Department of Health AIDS Unit, and individual officers in those Authorities where funding did not eventually materialize from GHT communications.

GHT requested financial assistance from some 237 individual senior officers in the health and local authorities in the region during 1993/94. This was mostly in addition to the individual officers who eventually authorized or released any financial allocations which were made to GHT.

With Health Authority Purchasing Consortia due to be formed on 1 April 1994, GHT had concluded no Service Agreements with individual districts, let alone consortia of Health Authorities, at the time of writing (1 March 1994).

The future

Whilst GHT managed in fact to survive during 1993/94, this was as a result of its own fundraising, slippage and one-off grants, not from income it could rely on at the start of the financial year. As the gap widens between Department of Health funding and the real costs of maintaining services, there is no guarantee that GHT will be able to continue in the same way for 1994/95 and beyond. In other words, GHT services will have to cease if there is no financial surety in the very near future.

The needs of people with HIV disease have, however, not diminished. The costs of GHT services, which are constantly striving to meet those needs, are unlikely to diminish, and could not fall below their present levels without a loss of services. Many of these are already over-stretched and have existed beyond any financial underwriting, largely reliant on unpaid voluntary labour for their survival.

An overall problem for HIV services is the general lack of a defined specification against which services could be purchased. Some health authorities in the North West have started to develop HIV Service Specifications, in some cases connected to Sexual Health Strategies, but it remains unclear whether these will be securely linked to Purchasing Plans, and if so, how. This is particularly difficult given the health authority mergers, which put individual district Specifications potentially in competition with each other. It is also not clear whether such Service Specifications should emanate from health authorities, or local authorities, or through a joint process; and none of these necessarily lead directly to purchasing intentions or to contractual arrangements as a result.

Another argument has been raised for contracting on a cost-per-case basis. In districts with small numbers of people who are HIV-positive, it is more attractive to some purchasers to produce this more individualistic relationship with providers – although the problems associated with extra-contractual referrals have not been resolved, and pose a threat to all anonymous self-referral services, such as HIV testing clinics.

On the other hand, the purchase of an individual care package for a person with HIV disease offers to some districts an opportunity to develop a rounded assessment and care management approach. This could result in a care plan which could be coordinated through joint working across the sectors, and purchased through contractual arrangements for the care packages themselves.

Whether at the level of the individual care package, or of the overall region-wide services, there is an evident lack of an agreed HIV Service Specification against which purchasing and contracting could take place. The NWRHA Framework[9] could form the basis for such a specification, but this would require a number of purchasers to agree to use the Framework in this way (or indeed to use any other similar mechanism). This is especially important for the future of region-wide services which could not be purchased through any one district alone.

Conclusions

First, the Government commitment to support the voluntary sector is clear in legislative terms, but appears incapable of being fulfilled at the local level to which the decision-making has been delegated.

Secondly, the amounts of money available from the Department of Health for assisting people living with HIV disease have not been inconsiderable, albeit time limited to some extent, but are not being allocated locally with anything more than the most short-term approach, and are being distributed through a large number of different funding channels.

Thirdly, the objective of making region-wide HIV voluntary organizations financially and administratively secure (as detailed in NHS Management Executive Circulars, the White Paper *Caring for People*,[10] etc., is not being met. This then reduces the effectiveness of these organizations, potentially if not actually leading to a waste of resources and to unnecessarily long periods of time spent by them in chasing their own financing.

Informal, unfinanced, insecure voluntary services continue to prop up HIV community care. But for how long?

There is a strong sense that HIV services have been allowed to develop on their own – because there has been specific funding until now, which could supposedly not be used by anyone else for anything else. But this acceptance will not survive when all funding and services are mainstream. Ring-fencing has kept services going, but has put HIV on a limb. The end of ring-fencing means that the limb is about to be cut off.

This chapter therefore argues not so much for *more* funding for voluntary HIV service providers, as for financial *security* for their core functions. Much voluntary sector funding originates from the Department of Health, but it comes through many hands. Far better would be one simple, direct relationship, whether with the Department or with a consortium of purchasers.

Such a relationship, for the core costs, on a three-year funding basis, would enable organizations to exist, structurally, without spending too much time negotiating with a wide variety of small and disconnected purchasers from different sectors. This would begin to make a reality of the British Government's stated commitment to support voluntary organizations and the voluntary provision of community care for people living with HIV.

---

1 N. Turner, J. Nicholson, *Making HIV Community Care a Reality*. George House Trust, Manchester, 1993. For GHT survey, see p. 2.

2 National Health Service and Community Care Act, 1990.

3 Department of Health, The Health of the Nation: A Strategy for Health in England. HMSO, London, 1992.

4 Department of Health, 'Allocation for HIV and AIDS Work', Executive Letter EL (92) 18. NHS Management Executive, London, 1992. Guidance on allocations for 1992/93 attached as Annex A.

Department of Health, 'Allocation for HIV and AIDS Work', Executive Letter EL (93) 19. NHS Management Executive, Leeds, 1993. Guidance

on allocations for 1993/4 attached as Annex A.

Department of Health, 'Allocation for HIV and AIDS Work', Executive Letter EL (94) 11. NHS Management Executive, Leeds, 1994.

5 Topslicing is when a regional authority sets aside a portion of the grant that it would otherwise distribute to local district authorities within the region to make direct grants to region-wide voluntary organizations to provide local services.

6 N. Turner, J. Nicholson, P. Dunne, Securing the Future of HIV Services. George House Trust, Manchester, 1994.

7 N. Turner, J. Nicholson, Making HIV Community Care a Reality. George House Trust, Manchester, 1993.

8 N. Turner, J. Nicholson, Joint Planning, Community Care & HIV Disease. George House Trust, Manchester, 1991.

N. Turner, J. Nicholson, Making HIV Community Care a Reality. George House Trust, Manchester, 1993.

9 Framework for HIV and AIDS. North Western Regional Health Authority, 1990 (revised 1994).

10 Department of Health, Caring for People: Community Care in the Next Decade and Beyond. HMSO, London, 1989.

The Organization of AIDS Prevention in Eastern Switzerland and the Principality of Liechtenstein: Approaches to Increase Efficiency

Dr Bernhard Güntert and Willy Oggier

Research Group for Management in Health Services, University of St. Gallen, Switzerland

The problem

In Switzerland all three governmental levels (federal, cantonal and municipal) are involved in AIDS prevention. While there is considerable clarity about the services and the costs of federal activities, there are no reliable data available at the cantonal and the municipal level. The available data from cantons and municipalities are not compatible because different accounting practices are used.

The same is true for private organizations involved in AIDS prevention.[1] Little knowledge exists about the relationship between the public sector and the prevention projects undertaken by these organizations. A further difficulty is that many of the activities of private organizations use volunteers and are provided free of charge. Some of these organizations receive financial support from public administration, whilst others finance themselves completely. Without the involvement of private organizations, many governmental institutions would be forced to carry out those tasks themselves.

Despite incomplete data, the aim of this chapter is to discuss the effectiveness and efficiency of AIDS prevention in six cantons of eastern Switzerland and the Principality of Liechtenstein. In terms of healthcare, particular attention has been paid to the Canton of St. Gallen.

Methodology

A survey of AIDS prevention services was carried out in the Cantonal Departments of Education and the Cantonal Health Departments of the six cantons of eastern Switzerland – Appenzell-Innerrhoden, Appenzell-Ausserrhoden, Graubünden, St. Gallen, Schaffhausen and Thurgau – as well as the Principality of Liechtenstein. The activities in the two departments, and the manner by which the prevention tasks were carried out, were noted. An examination of how far the tasks were delegated to other authorities or private institutions was also carried out. The extent and distribution of the capital invested at the cantonal level was analysed. And the survey also included an investigation of the personnel in public administration or in private organizations involved in AIDS prevention.

In parallel, another survey was carried out among the private organizations in the region that had an active role in AIDS prevention. The organizations' range of activities, coordination of their AIDS prevention programmes, resources, available personnel and the level of public funding were documented.[2]

The distribution of duties between federal and cantonal government[3]

The legal foundation for AIDS prevention in Switzerland is a law on epidemic diseases (Epidemiengesetz 1963). According to this law the federal government is responsible for the following activities:

- controlling epidemic diseases
- setting up a strategy of prevention
- providing information and education for the Swiss population
- coordination and support of cantonal and regional activities
- special activities for target groups (e.g. prevention within the armed forces, prevention with asylum seekers in reception centres)
- assistance with training of staff employed for AIDS prevention
- the social security insurance system
- evaluation of the various activities
- coordination of research

The cantons are responsible for treatment and nursing care of individuals with HIV or AIDS. They also decide on preventive measures to be provided through the health departments (e.g. drug prevention and prevention in schools). Generally, the cantons delegate some of these duties to the municipalities, while being responsible for the health system as a whole.

The delegation of public duties

Public duties do not necessarily have to be carried out by the cantonal administration. They are entitled to delegate public duties to state departments or to private organizations. If private organizations are providing the services, competition can be used to promote innovation and improve cost containment.

The following suggested guidelines should be considered to facilitate this process of delegation:

- Delegation to private organizations should only take place in areas where suppliers are competing; otherwise a public monopoly will be replaced by a private one. Generally, the private monopoly can be less easily controlled by democratic means.
- The public institutions have to define exactly which tasks they want to delegate to private third parties. Therefore a formulation of clear performance contracts is needed. Those have to be advertised publicly. Normally the order should be placed with the most promising service provider who meets the requirements.
- Assurance is required that private organizations will fulfil standards in the performance contract in terms of services, quality and cost control.
- The fulfilment of standards is to be controlled by the administration. If those standards are not followed, sanctions have to be implemented (e.g. price cuts, immediate call for new tenders for the performance contract).
- The duties to be carried out have to be reviewed on a regular basis and the constraints of the contracts regularly and widely publicized. This would prevent any decrease in cost-efficiency and keep competition alive.

If the requirements are not sufficiently covered by the private organizations, the public administration should take over the duties.

To fulfil its own duties in AIDS prevention the Federal Government has to become active, particularly in the areas of epidemic control, strategic planning, coordination and evaluation of activities, but also in the promotion and support of new projects, which could be expanded to a national level at a later date.

The cantonal departments can fulfil a public duty themselves or delegate it to third parties. Delegation to an external organization can either be to municipalities or to private organizations. A number of options for delegation exist:

1. The cantonal department does not delegate anything;

2. It delegates everything to the municipalities;

3. It delegates only a part of its activities to the municipalities;

4. It delegates everything to private organizations;

5. It delegates only a part of its activities to private organizations and, of course, a combination of 3 and 5.

In the six cantons of eastern Switzerland and the Principality of Liechtenstein the delegation practices presented in Table 1 are found:

Table 1
The delegation practices of the Cantonal Health Departments

	AI	AR	GR	SG	SH	TG	FL
CHD does not delegate							•
CHD delegates everything to the communities							
CHD delegates a part to the communities							
partly (<50% of cantonal expenses)			•				
majority (>50% of cantonal expenses)					•	•	
CHD delegates all of its activities to private organizations							•
CHD delegates a part of its activities to private organizations	•	•	•	•		•	
CHD undertakes all tasks itself							

Key
CHD = Cantonal Health Departments
AI = Appenzell-Innerrhoden
AR = Appenzell-Ausserrhoden
GR = Graubünden
SG = St. Gallen
SH = Schaffhausen
TG = Thurgau
FL = Principality of Liechtenstein

With the exception of the Principality of Liechtenstein all six cantons of eastern Switzerland fulfil certain tasks within the scope of AIDS prevention. The Principality of Liechtenstein represents a special case because the organization AIDS-Help Liechtenstein is a privately organized institution within the public administration. In the cantons, on the other hand, regional 'AIDS-Help' organizations are also private institutions, but contain representatives of the cantons on their managing committee. Those in the Cantonal Health Departments who were working in such roles judged the coordination with private organizations exceptionally good.

In addition to the survey of the Cantonal Health Departments, a survey of the Departments of Education of the six cantons of eastern Switzerland and the Principality of Liechtenstein was conducted. The results relating to their delegation policy are presented in Table 2:

All Cantonal Departments of Education (CDEs) have at least a partially direct role in preventing AIDS. Compared to the situation in the Cantonal Departments of Health, the federalistic structure of the CDEs is visible, especially in cantons which delegate a considerable part of their duties to the communities.

	AI	AR	GR	SG	SH	TG	FL
CDE does not delegate							
CDE delegates everything to the communities							
CDE delegates a part to the communities							
partly (<50% of cantonal expenses)	•	•		•			•
majority (>50% of cantonal expenses)							•
CDE delegates all of its activities to private organizations							
CDE delegates a part of its activities to private organizations	•		•	•			
CDE undertakes all tasks itself					•		

Table 2
The allocation of practices of the Cantonal Departments of Education (CDE)

Key: see Table 1 opposite

The Cantonal Departments of Education rate coordination with the Cantonal Health Departments as most important. This can be explained by the fact that both departments know the regional and local circumstances very well, are situated quite close together and therefore are able to react in a flexible way. In addition, especially in the small cantons, this mutual 'acquaintance' is certainly of substantial importance in ensuring good working relationships.

In general, in the area of preventing AIDS the Cantonal Departments of Health and Departments of Education delegate several duties to third parties. These are either lower levels in the public administration, especially schools or municipalities, or private institutions. However, it cannot be concluded that this produces an efficient and effective practice of allocation. It is very likely that private organizations hardly face any competition in their fields of activity and therefore are able to realize monopoly profits.

To examine efficiency and effectiveness in the organizational structure of AIDS prevention activities, an attempt has to be made to examine the delegation of public duties in the field of AIDS prevention through the following case study. This demonstrates that the formulation of the performance contracts is a crucial point.

Case study: the service instruction in the Canton of St. Gallen

The supply of services by organizations caring for and supporting AIDS patients is influenced by various factors. Those can either be defined by the environment or result from internal circumstances. The influencing factors are partly static, partly dynamic, as illustrated in Table 3.

The purpose of performance contracts is:

• to support an optimal use of the

resources within the HIV and AIDS patient care system;

• to guarantee the coordination of the activities of different suppliers;

• to define the scope of the management of organization;

• to provide the basis for public funding.

Thus performance contracts are useful to coordinate supply, in that they state well-aimed priorities whilst allowing for consideration of regional diversity. In doing so, structures are created to reduce complexity by influencing the behaviour and the reaction to dynamic factors. To be effective, performance contracts have to:

• be clearly defined;

• be accepted;

• include sanctions for situations where the objectives have not been met.

The basis for defining a performance contract for AIDS-Hilfe St. Gallen-Appenzell was the federal epidemic law and the cantonal health law. In the health law of the Canton of St. Gallen Article 3, lit. d, it is stated that the Department of Health can take temporary measures influencing health policy in order to prevent contagious diseases and other threats to health. Furthermore, the Department of Health is responsible for the execution of federal, intercantonal and cantonal regulations insofar as no other institution explicitly has this responsibility.

On 1 February 1991 a performance contract drawn up between the Healthcare Department and AIDS-Hilfe St. Gallen-Appenzell (AHSA) came into effect. The agreement regulates:

• the transfer of public duties in the domain of AIDS prevention to AHSA

• the co-operation between the Canton of St Gallen and the AHSA;

• the financial support of AHSA by the Canton of St Gallen; and

• supervision of AHSA by the Canton of St Gallen.

The agreement only provides a summary description of the activities required for AIDS prevention. A detailed performance contract does not exist. In the agreement's appendix an attempt has been made to define the terms 'direct prevention' and 'indirect prevention'.

As a result of this agreement AHSA has been subsidized with a fixed amount. The money is given to support general AIDS prevention measures. The canton is not subsidizing the care provided for people with HIV/AIDS by AHSA, which makes up only a small part of total expenditures. In 1993 the governmental subscription ran up to SFr 288,000.

No assessment of the organization's achievements is undertaken by the Cantonal Department of Health or any other department. The AHSA is obliged to hand in an annual report, containing a financial report, the auditors' report and the budget for the following year (including a detailed payroll budget and a formal application for the subsidies of the Canton of St. Gallen). A certain level of control of the activities is guaranteed by the seat which the Cantonal Department of Health holds on AHSA's managing committee. However, the representative of the Cantonal Health Department is only one of nine members of the managing committee, and does not have a right to veto.

The agreement leaves the AHSA quite autonomous to define its activities and to cope with dynamic and changing influences and demands.

	structural/static	dynamic
environmental influences	healthcare and public welfare legislation	prevalence of HIV
	concepts of support	mobility of persons with HIV
	body responsible for the organization	demand for services
	financial systems	admission practices of physicians, nurses and others
internal influences	job plan	competence
	infrastructure and facilities	commitment
	organization and management structure	own priorities
		relation to the surrounding care system
		quality of services

Table 3
Factors affecting services by organizations caring and supporting people with AIDS

Under ideal circumstances the expected results and the necessary resources in order to achieve the objectives should be defined in the performance contract. Since the effects of HIV and AIDS prevention cannot be measured properly, management control is undertaken through guidelines and resource allocation. We believe that a useful framework for the development of performance contracts for healthcare organizations should contain the following components:

- objective and purpose of the organization
- main services used
- primary and secondary services
- financial framework
- management control and quality assurance
- organizational preconditions
- possibilities of development and change
- possibilities for sanctioning

By examining the agreement between AHSA and the Canton of St. Gallen using these criteria, several discrepancies can be found. The agreement does contain an objective and a purpose, and it also defines the main service ('direct' and 'indirect' prevention) in the appendix, as well as the financial frame and further agreements on additional financing possibilities. But a detailed service description, which is essential for coordination between different service providers, is not made. Further references to management control and quality assurance, organizational instructions and sanctioning possibilities (in the case of performance contracts not being followed) are missing.

The condition that the Canton of St. Gallen is not allowed to enter an agreement with any agency other than AHSA has to be analysed critically. Fundamentally, performance contracts should be worked out with all the co-operating partners. If this is not undertaken, AHSA would be in a monopoly situation in the cantons of St. Gallen, Appenzell-Ausserrhoden and Appenzell-Innerrhoden, which in the long term could have adverse effects on the costs and on quality of the services.[4]

Case study: public funding of private organizations

To show the importance of the public sector – the influence of the federal government, the cantons and the communities – on the activities of private organizations two additional questions were introduced:

- What is the share of the public sector involvement (federal government, cantons and communities) in AIDS prevention in terms of percentage of total funds allocated to any particular private organization?
- How many jobs relating to AIDS prevention are directly financed (one full-time job = 100 per cent) by the public sector?

The public sector contribution in Table 4 may be overstated, as it includes activities other than AIDS prevention. For an exact definition of the various activities, a detailed examination of the accounts of the private organizations would be necessary.

Table 4 shows clearly that private organizations either receive a considerable amount (at least 40 per cent of their funding in 14 out of 25 organizations in 1992, and 13 out of 25 in 1993) or no funding at all. This could be an indicator of efficient resource allocation by the public administration, as no small amounts (10 per cent or less of the budget means) are being allocated to private organizations. This allows the public administration to execute management control on the private providers. This is important as a clear evaluation of the services is not possible.

A similar situation can be found with regard to public financing of jobs in the private organizations. The public admin-

	account 1992		budget 1993	
1% - 9%				
0% - 19%				
20% - 29%				
30% - 39%				
40% - 49%	••	2	•	1
50% - 59%	•	1	••	2
60% - 69%				
70% - 79%	•	1	••	2
80% - 89%	••••••	6	•••••	5
90% - 99%	•	1	•	1
100%	•••	3	••	2
		14		13

Table 4
Percentage of total funding of private organizations allocated by the public sector

1 dot equals 1 mention in the survey

istration either finances at least 80 per cent of jobs in each organization or none at all. These figures also lead to the assumption that the allocation of jobs is efficient, as small amounts of money represented by a low percentage of jobs being funded (10 per cent, 20 per cent, 30 per cent) are avoided.

Apart from the activities that are supported by the public administration, private organizations carry out many self-financed duties, funded by donations. However, much more important is the contribution of volunteers, which helps to keep total expenses at a low level.

Result and conclusions

In general, the following are the main results of the survey conducted in the six eastern cantons of Switzerland and the Principality of Liechtenstein:

- In some cantons (Schaffhausen, Thurgau) no performance contracts at all exist between the cantonal authorities and the private organizations that participate in AIDS prevention. In cases such as these performance contracts should be worked out.

- In the cases where performance contracts exist (Appenzell-Innerrhoden, Appenzell-Ausserrhoden, Graubünden, St. Gallen), the contracts have been organized inefficiently in several ways. There is a need for an appropriate improvement in these contracts.

- Very low levels of public funding or support for specific jobs in private organizations have been avoided. This appears to be an efficient approach to funding although no conclusion can be reached on the quality of services provided through their funding. Besides continuous monitoring of the use of allocated funds, more attention needs to be given to quality assurance.

1 The term 'private organization' covers all non-governmental organizations, irrespective of their legal status or their purpose, and includes private for-profit companies as well as not-for-profit voluntary organizations.

2 Willy Oggier, Bernard Güntert, Die AIDS-Präventionsanstrengungen in sechs ostschweiz-erischen Kantonen und im Fürstentum Liechtenstein, St. Gallen, 1994.

3 Bundesamt für Gesundheitswesen/Eidgenös-sische Kommission für AIDS-Fragen, HIV-Prävention in der Schweiz – Ziele, Strategien, Massnahmen, p. 231, Berne, 1993.

4 Marie-Claire Mathey, Inge Schröder, Kan-tonale Strategien der AIDS-Prävention und -Bekämpfung, Schlussbericht 1988. Cahiers de Recherches et de Documentation de l'Institut universitaire de médicine sociale et préventive, No. 39, p. 18, Lausanne, 1989.

Impact of AIDS Costs on the Health Budget of the Czech Republic

Dr Alexandr Stožický

Director, Czech Medical Association J.E. Purkyně, Prague

The Czech Republic has existed as an independent state since 1 January 1993, following the division of the Czech and Slovak Federal Republic, and has 10.3 million inhabitants in an area of 78,900 km². It is physically one of the smaller European countries (twenty-first in size and fourteenth by number of inhabitants). Its economic position, measured by GDP per inhabitant, amounts to US$8,900, ranking the Czech Republic eighteenth among European countries but in the vanguard of the reformed countries of Central and Eastern Europe.

The age structure of the population reveals irregularities between males and females depicted in the 'age pyramid' (Figure 1). Life expectancy at birth in 1992 was 68.5 years for men and 76.1 years for women (compared with 68.1 and 75.3 years, respectively, in 1988). In this regard the Czech Republic lags behind advanced European countries by six to seven years. The pattern of causes of death has remained unchanged for a long time. The most frequent causes are diseases of the circulatory system, followed by neoplasms (tumours), poisonings, respiratory system diseases and digestive system diseases. These five conditions accounted for 94 per cent of all deaths. The mortality rate for men of productive age is twice that of Western countries, and the rates for cardiovascular diseases and malignant tumours are among the worst in Europe. There is an extremely high incidence of serious chronic diseases such as hypertension, ischaemic heart disease, acute myocardial infarction, neuroses, gastric and duodenal ulcerations and diabetes.

HIV Testing

Since 1986 all blood donors and donations have been obligatorily screened for HIV antibodies; by 1993 some 2.5 million tests had been done, among which six were positive and one was from a patient with AIDS.

In the whole Czech Republic some 3.4 million tests have been done. Of these, 170 were positive for HIV antibodies (0.005 per cent) and 45 were from patients with symptoms of AIDS. Some 54,000 foreigners, students, and workers were tested: 84 were found to be infected with HIV (0.16 per cent) and one patient was found to have AIDS. The prevalence rate for foreign residents was significantly higher (32 times) than that for the whole population of the Czech Republic.

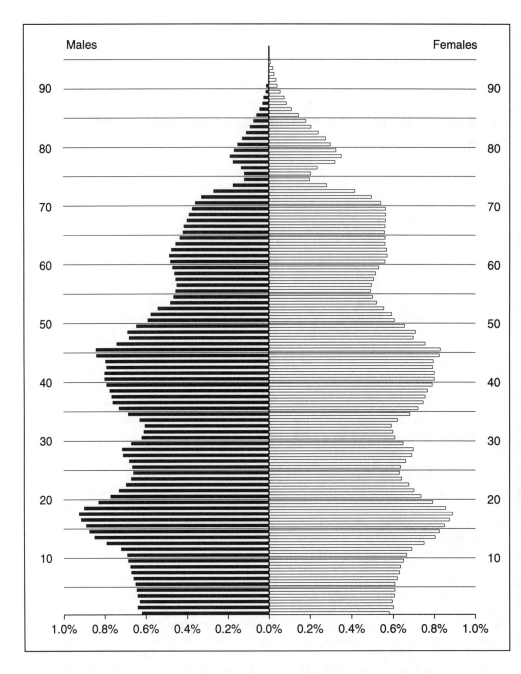

Males   Females

Figure 1
**Age structure of
population to
1/7/92**
Czech Health
Statistics Year-
book 1992

The pattern of the epidemic

There has been a steady development of
HIV infection and AIDS in the Czech
Republic in the period 1986–93 (see Figure
2). The cumulative number of HIV infections reached 170 in the year 1993 – 3.5

times more than in the year 1987; the number of reported AIDS cases grew from two
in 1987 to 46 in 1993 (a 32-fold increase).

Figure 3 further breaks down the data into
HIV infections and gender. Over the
period 1987–93 the number of cases in

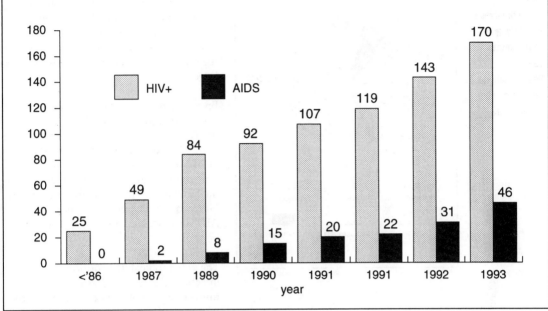

Figure 2 **HIV/AIDS in the Czech Republic [1986–1993] cumulative numbers**
Source: National Reference Laboratory - AIDS

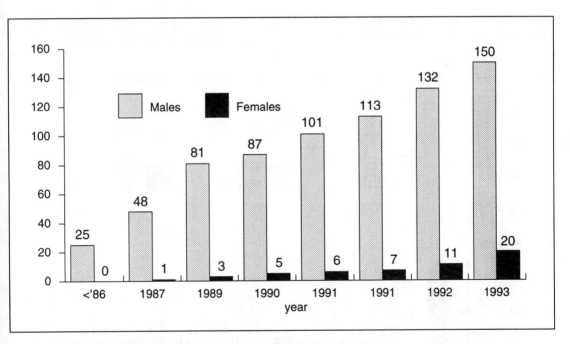

Figure 3 **HIV in the Czech Republic [1986–1993] cumulative numbers**
Source: National Reference Laboratory - AIDS

Figure 4
HIV in the Czech Republic as of 31 December 1993
Source: National Reference Laboratory - AIDS

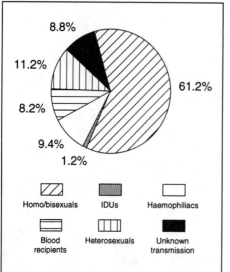

increased 3.1 times and that for females twenty times. While males accounted for 48.6 per cent and females for 51.4 per cent of the population in 1992, in that year thirteen times as many males as females were infected.

Breakdown by transmission category is shown in Figure 4, indicating that more than 60 per cent of all cases were amongst homo/bisexual men. Figure 5 further breaks down cases by clinical stage and transmission group, with homo/bisexual men making up the majority in all stages: HIV-positive 56.4 per cent, people with AIDS 66.7 per cent and AIDS deaths 81.5 per cent.

The geographical distribution of HIV infection (Figure 6) shows nearly two-thirds of cases (64.7 per cent) in the capital, Prague (1.2 million inhabitants).

Healthcare costs

Figure 5 **HIV+ by clinical stage Czech. Rep., as of 32 December 1993**
Source: National Reference Laboratory - AIDS

The costs of patients with AIDS are estimated to amount to $23,500 (700,000 Czech crowns) per year. Part of these costs are

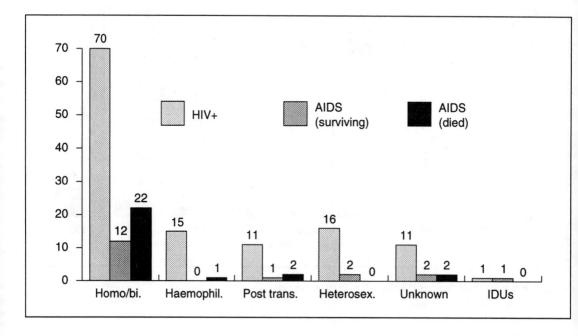

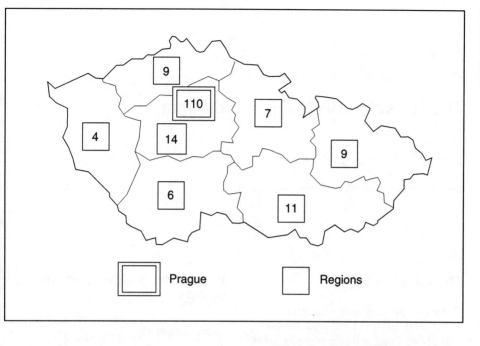

Figure 6
HIV Infection in Czech Republic
as of 31 December 1993

financed by health insurance companies (as are those for other illnesses) and the rest (e.g. drugs) is financed from the state budget. The total budget for healthcare services in the Czech Republic for the year 1993 was about $2,087 million (62,600 million Czech crowns), that is, 7 per cent of the GDP.

The Ministry of Health is prepared to compensate 30 people who were infected with HIV through blood transfusion – including sixteen haemophiliacs – with about $25,000 (750,000 crowns) per person. The treatment of HIV-positive and AIDS patients is very expensive in the Czech Republic too, and given the projected growth in the numbers of infected patients, one can only expect further growth in economic demands. This will call for the close co-operation of both governmental and non-governmental institutions, above all in the field of AIDS prevention and care for HIV-infected people.

Conclusion

Given the epidemic trends in other countries and the changing socio-economic conditions in the Czech Republic, it is reasonable to expect that the relatively low number of HIV-infected patients at present will increase in the next few years .

Acknowledgements
Figures 2–6 were created in the National AIDS Reference Laboratory (NRL) of the National Institute for Public Health in Prague. The author would like to thank Dr M. Brůčková for her help and kindness.

The Impact of HIV/AIDS in Lithuania

Dr Saulius Chaplinskas

Director, Lithuanian AIDS Centre, Vilnius

The AIDS Centre

There are currently only a handful of known HIV cases in Lithuania. However, a steady and planned beginning to AIDS prevention work has been under way since 1989 with the establishment of the AIDS Prevention Centre. Its remit covers prevention and care, and it is both responsible to and is financed by the Ministry of Health. The Centre has conducted two national AIDS prevention programmes: one in 1990–91 and the second in 1992–93, but neither was formally approved by the government, the Supreme Soviet or the Parliament of Lithuania. These included the first 'Condom Festival' which so shocked society in 1991, creating a sudden social change after which the mass media started to speak openly about sexuality, sexually transmitted diseases (STDs), drugs and prostitution.

Since the Centre's inception the government has changed four times. And this fact, together with the lack of status of the AIDS prevention programmes as government programmes, means that the concept of implementation of a national AIDS prevention programme has been changing too.

Prevention work with specific groups

Homosexual men

The Centre has gradually established the first contacts with homosexual men and drug users. While homosexual intercourse was still illegal and subject to punishment, the AIDS Centre was the only government organization openly supporting (illegal) groups of homosexual men and encouraging them to propagate safer sex messages and practices amongst themselves. The activities of the AIDS Centre, together with pressure from the West, also contributed to the repeal of laws against homosexuality in the middle of 1993.

Drug users

Some 550 drug users are officially registered in Lithuania but it is estimated that there are actually about 10,000–12,000 such people. However, although there has been a state narcotics service for some time, it is probable that injecting drug use problems are being pushed backstage, with action being confined to the registration of drug addicts and to single cases of detoxification. The main problems are seen as alcohol abuse and smoking. The drugs injected in Lithuania are the home-made opiate preparations from poppies which are plentiful in the country. The import or export of drugs is not popular, with the communities of drug addicts being very closed; they rarely communicate with one another or with foreign drug users. Moreover, the search for drugs and the criminal activities are linked; possession of drugs is still illegal.

For injecting drug users the AIDS Centre has launched a needle/syringe exchange programme, together with an AIDS prevention campaign through peer education. In 1992 we established the only social rehabilitation department for drug users in Lithuania, which acts on the basis of DAY TOP principles.[1]

Prisoners

In prisons forced homosexuality and drug addiction are commonplace and the risk of infection with HIV during homosexual intercourse or injecting drug use is high. In the past, financial and juridical problems made AIDS prevention measures in prisons (the provision of condoms and the distribution of clean syringes) impossible, but the situation is now changing. Condoms can be obtained free of charge in prison waiting rooms, or can be bought in prison shops.

In 1993 one HIV-positive person was detected in Vilnius prison. He is now free.

Prostitutes

The present economic situation is very favourable for the growth of prostitution. The Centre's staff have forged contacts with female prostitutes, and the trust engendered has made it possible to start the first research into the health of these women, as well as social investigations and educational work. The levels of knowledge and care about health are not sufficient. We are aware that condoms are not being used regularly with clients. Male prostitution, however, remains a somewhat less known occurrence.

Health education for state workers

The former Soviet system of education on hygiene for many state workers was oriented to teaching about illnesses and how to avoid them, not about health education and healthcare. It consisted only of lectures and other ineffective educational methods. This approach completely failed to engage individuals and has not shown any results. Knowing that, we were forced to look for ways in which we could achieve a more positive effect in the existing situation. We are aware that we have done not much in the sphere of AIDS education, but the first steps encourage us to believe that it will be effective. Following our example, other medical branches are planning similar programmes for themselves.

Socio-cultural factors influencing the Centre's work

Religion

Most Lithuanian believers profess Roman Catholicism (about 80 per cent) but some 30 denominations are registered, although most of them do not have many adherents. Some senior Catholic priests state that the activities of the AIDS Centre destroy the Church's work. But while they see no possibility for collaboration, they do not interfere in the Centre's activities.

Sexual activity

Sociological surveys in Lithuania have shown recently that almost 44.6 per cent of sixteen-year-old girls and 33.3 per cent of seventeen-year-old boys have made their sexual debut. One such survey was carried out in 1993: 650 Vilnius high-school students between the ages of fifteen and eighteen were interviewed on the basis of a questionnaire prepared by the AIDS Centre.

Condoms are not popular in Lithuania and lubricants are not well known. Our investigations have showed that only 2.5 per cent of sexually active people use condoms. The opinion that 'to have intercourse using a condom is the same as to smell a rose wearing a gasmask' still prevails.

Voluntary sector

The concept of volunteers and of active non-governmental organizations is something new in Lithuania. Their establishment is unrealistic at present without private capital or support from governmental organizations. Being aware of their importance in AIDS prevention, we have begun to support their activities. For example, the Gays Support Group, established as a department of the AIDS Centre, became an independent organization – the Movement for Sexual Equality – after the Penal Code was reformed. With some support from sponsors an independent newspaper for gays and their friends *Naglis* has appeared. Still within the structure of the AIDS Centre there is the Positive Group. The Centre has also taken part in establishing an AIDS Fund and a Drug Addicts Support Fund, and we are now trying to create an organization for women's education. Other organizations, however, do not participate in AIDS prevention measures, with the exception of the Catholic organization Caritas.

Knowledge and attitudes

The people of Lithuania have been informed about AIDS and the risks of infection, but this level of knowledge is insufficient. Fear of casual infection, for instance through eating utensils or other non-sexual domestic contact, still remains. Almost 14 per cent of medical workers believe that this route of infection is possible. This figure is based on the results of two AIDS Centre surveys: the first was conducted in 1990 and involved 1,056 doctors nationwide; the second, in 1993, involved 1,600 doctors and nurses. Genito-urinary physicians and infectious disease experts have the best knowledge and are most interested in this problem. The worst levels of knowledge have been found in district physicians

(family doctors). Almost 57 per cent of medical workers would not want to care for an AIDS patient. However, the general population's feeling of hate is changing increasingly to one of tolerance and sympathy. More medical workers are aware that it is not necessary to isolate HIV-infected people: in 1990 some 47 per cent of medical workers in answering our questionnaire favoured proposals to isolate HIV-positive people but in 1993 the figure had fallen to 30 per cent.

Sexually transmitted diseases

The actual prevalence of STDs in Lithuania is unclear: only statistics on syphilis and gonorrhoea have been formally compiled. There are still no reliable and generally available diagnostic systems for chlamydial and other infections. Prevention of STDs was based on compulsion, the main task being to test as many people as possible on a mandatory basis (all in-patients, pregnant women, people arrested by the police, etc.). Confidentiality for STD patients was often not kept. STD patients who avoid treatment, or who consciously expose other people to the risk of infection with an STD, can still face legal action for failing to disclose sexual contacts and for consciously exposing another person to HIV. These articles in the Penal Code are not used in practice at present, and the new Penal Code foresees only a legal responsibility for wilful infection with HIV. The previous requirements transformed a doctor into some kind of policeman, and people were afraid to come forward for medical help to medical institutions. Instead, they looked for other possible, usually illegal, methods of treatment. For some medical workers this system earned them a fortune and they are looking now for arguments to justify its continued existence.

Anonymous testing

Since 1987 anonymous testing for HIV and other STDs has been available. In 1991 55 per cent of persons diagnosed with gonor-rhoea and 71 per cent of others found to have urinary and genital inflammations refused to undergo treatment because they would have to register for it. The AIDS Centre has proposed anonymous treat-ment. All persons who have applied to anonymous testing sites have agreed to undergo anonymous treatment there. In 1991–93 testing detected two persons with HIV, 22 with syphilis and 224 with gonor-rhoea. As the anonymous treatment of STDs has justified itself, on October 1993 the Ministry of Health officially sanctioned its implementation in the whole Republic. However, the idea of anonymous treatment has divided venereologists into two camps.

National prevention programme

As a unified strategy for prevention of STDs does not yet exist, the Ministry of Health has obliged the AIDS Centre and all venereologists of the Republic to prepare the unified programme of STDs prevention in 1994. We have been working on the pro-gramme for the observation, care and treat-ment of all AIDS patients and HIV-infected persons. Lithuania uses the AIDS case defi-nition adopted in Europe, sends standard-ized data on AIDS to the World Health Organization (WHO) Collaborating Centre on AIDS near Paris and the quality of tests performed in the AIDS Reference Labora-tory is checked constantly by the WHO.

Blood screening for HIV

At the end of 1987 on the basis of an order from the former Minister of Health in the USSR the screening of donated blood began, and gradually this became mass HIV screening. For this purpose the Russ-ian HIV antibody test systems have been used. The testing is done by fifteen labora-tories: the results are reported and the quality of the laboratories' work checked by the Reference Laboratory of the AIDS Centre. Mass screening for HIV is not jus-tified either in economic, ethical or epi-demiological terms. At present, on the

basis of WHO recommendations, we have a prepared programme and introduced sentinel HIV observation instead of mass screening. In 1993 all donated blood was being tested by the Abbott HIV antibody test system only. In 1994 we have reduced the amount of testing by selecting STD patients and persons from other 'risk' groups. All these blood tests will be per-formed with the same test kits.

Finance

The financing of the AIDS Centre derives from the state budget through the Min-istry of Health and covers the mainte-nance of the Centre and the partial implementation of its programmes. This money (the total requested budget was not allotted) was transferred irregularly and in small amounts into the account of the AIDS Centre (sometimes as often as four to five times a month). This system has hindered much of the work of the lab-oratory and delivery of care.

In 1991 a sum of 230,000 Litas (then about US$61,000) was allocated for the mainte-nance of the AIDS Centre and partial implementation of the National AIDS Pre-vention Programme. In 1992 the sum remained the same but in 1993 the sum was increased to 690,000 Litas (then about $177,000), including 30,000 Litas for medi-cine and diagnostic test systems. Private and commercial institutions, non-govern-mental organizations, local authorities in towns and regions have not received any additional resources for medical care and scientific research.

Costs

In 1993 general costs for one person infected with HIV amounted to US$8,850 (nearly 40 times less than analogous expenses in Switzerland). Direct expenses for one AIDS patient were about twenty times less than in Switzerland.

Conclusion

The AIDS Centre still does not have its own premises and its different departments are housed in rented accommodation at five different sites in Vilnius, far from one another. With each change of Minister of Health the attitudes towards the AIDS Centre, its role in the whole system of public health care and its need for proper accommodation have also changed. It was established on the basis of the orders and directives of a former Minister of Health of the USSR. During its first years, it established links with WHO and colleagues from Western countries. This made our staff aware that the Soviet concept of prevention of AIDS was radically different from that of the WHO; its successors still maintain this difference in approach. In all countries, treating AIDS as a social problem has and will demand considerable social changes.

With help from colleagues in the West and within Lithuania who hold the same view as we do, we have been made aware of the importance of AIDS and have been able to use it as an activator of social changes. Thus, we have started new activities, often at considerable personal risk professionally, which sometimes conflicted with Lithuanian laws and prevalent moral standards.

At the beginning of the AIDS era, it was not customary to speak about sexual life and drugs openly. Myths were propagated that in socialist states neither homosexuality nor prostitution existed and there was no drug abuse because the social conditions for these evils of the capitalist world did not exist. Our first task was to start open discussions about these problems, STDs and preventive measures – something which we have succeeded in doing despite financial insecurity and frequently without government backing.

1 DAY TOP is an American system and stands for Drug Addicts Youth Treatment on Probation. It is a rehabilitation programme based on the 12 Steps of Alcoholics Anonymous. The aim of the programme is two-fold and complementary: first, to deal with the addiction and second, to help the individual concerned to readapt to society. Group therapy, therefore, plays a major part in the programme.

HIV/AIDS in Poland: Prevention Activities and Costs

Professor Wladysława Zielińska and Dr Anna Korczak-Rogoń

Diagnostic/Clinical HIV/AIDS Centre, Gdańsk, Poland

The Republic of Poland (area 312,683 km^2 and estimated population of 38,418,000) is divided for administrative purposes into 49 *voivodships* (provinces). When HIV/AIDS emerged, several large cities, voivodship capitals and academic centres (Gdańsk being one of them) attempted to create a comprehensive system that would help to solve the problem. First, obligatory HIV testing was introduced in 1985 for blood donors and both organ and tissue donors and recipients. At the same time, voluntary testing was encouraged among those 'at risk' – mainly injecting drug users, prostitutes, sailors and other people travelling abroad. By the end of 1993, HIV tests (ELISA) were available in 93 laboratories all over the country. Six laboratories at selected medical schools (in Warsaw, Gdańsk, Łódź Wrocław, Katowice and Cracow) can also do confirmatory tests (Western Blot). Since the beginning of HIV screening in 1985, to the end of 1993, HIV infection has been confirmed in 2,864 people, of whom at least 2,011 (70.2 per cent) were injecting drug users. The actual number of people infected is certainly higher, as is well recognized. Voluntary HIV testing has not been widely accepted, especially among those people at 'high risk' and, inexplicably and worryingly, shows a downward trend. Some 167 AIDS cases have been reported, of which nine were fatal.

Situated in the centre of Europe, Poland lies at the junction of major trade routes – including those for illicit drugs. Drug abuse was a problem here long before HIV and AIDS were recognized. Because of the particular distribution of HIV infection in the Polish population, the measures taken to fight the epidemic cannot be simple and must consider all social ramifications. Close collaboration is needed between healthcare providers, social workers, school authorities, educators and law enforcement agencies. Three HIV/AIDS centres in Poland have been set up in the infectious diseases clinics of teaching hospitals in Warsaw, Gdańsk and Katowice and a fourth one is being established in Cracow. These centres have developed comprehensive responses, with particular regard to the problems unique to the regions they serve. In this chapter we shall describe the main structural and functional principles, together with some of the economic aspects, of the policy created and implemented by the Diagnostic/Clinical HIV/AIDS Centre for the Gdańsk voivodship. Their programme is the most advanced in the country.

The Diagnostic/Clinical HIV/AIDS Centre in Gdańsk was established in December 1988, and is based in the Clinic for Infectious Diseases at Gdańsk School of Medicine. The

Clinic serves as the Voivodship Hospital for Infectious Diseases and also provides the laboratory and diagnostic facilities of the HIV/AIDS Centre. Since 1988, the Centre has been consistently developed according to the plan shown in Figure 1 in order to meet all the possible health and social needs resulting from the spread of HIV in the population. The Centre provides comprehensive healthcare for the inhabitants of ten voivodships (Figure 2).

HIV/AIDS facilities at the Clinic for Infectious Diseases

Sixteen two-bed rooms (total: 32 beds) have been assigned to HIV-infected and AIDS patients. The number of beds currently occupied varies according to actual need, the remainder serving patients with other infectious diseases. Since December 1988, 148 patients have been admitted to hospital, some several times, with a total of 230 admissions. Some 54 patients (87 admissions) were treated in 1993 (Table 1).

Reasons for admission are varied and include: post-injection abscesses and phleg-mon, traumas, bone fractures, thrombophlebitis, lymphangitis, drug overdosage, infectious diseases (tuberculosis, septicaemia, endocarditis, pneumonia and pleuritis, pulmonary abscesses, bronchitis, sinusitis, herpes zoster, viral hepatitis), taeniasis, neoplasms, fever of unknown origin, social reasons and symptomatic HIV disease including AIDS. To date, fifteen AIDS patients have been admitted to the Clinic (nine of these in 1993) (Table 2). Nine patients have since died (three in 1993). In four cases this was due to diseases indicative of AIDS (cerebral toxoplasmosis, *Pneumocystis carinii* pneumonia, digestive tract candidiasis). And in four other cases this was due to other diseases that might have developed in connection with AIDS (bacterial pneumonia, enterococcal sepsis, staphylococcal septicopyaemia and endocarditis, and pituitary tumour). In one case, death was caused by drug overdosage – probably suicidal. One HIV-infected homosexual patient died in the pre-AIDS stage of the infection, owing to pleural mesothelioma. In 106 HIV-positive cases, CD4 cell counts were measured by flow cytometry. The results are alarming: only in 31 patients (29.2 per cent) were the CD4 cell counts higher than

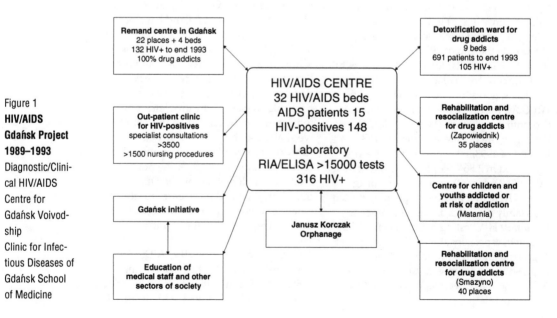

Figure 1
HIV/AIDS
Gdańsk Project
1989–1993
Diagnostic/Clinical HIV/AIDS Centre for Gdańsk Voivodship Clinic for Infectious Diseases of Gdańsk School of Medicine

Figure 2
Confirmatory test centres
(Western Blot)
Location of centres and areas of coverage

500/mm³. In 60 patients, counts between 200 and 500 CD4 cells/mm³ were found, and in fifteen the numbers were lower than 200/mm³. The medical and economic consequences of this fact are obvious: the Clinic is about to experience a rapid increase in the number of AIDS cases.

Laboratory and diagnostic services of the Centre

As mentioned above, the laboratory and diagnostic services of the HIV/AIDS Centre are provided by the Voivodship Hospital for Infectious Diseases. The policy of centralizing diagnostic procedures within this hospital has two aspects: epidemiological (the results are readily accessible and comparable) and economic. The basic diagnostic equipment of an institution conducting HIV/AIDS diagnosis and treatment is shown in Table 3. Since 1985, 15,175 HIV ELISAs have been performed in the Centre, 316 of which were positive (confirmed by Western Blot) (Table 4). PCR technique has been introduced recently and implemented in 26 cases in which Western Blot results were indeterminate (including three seropositive children born from HIV-infected mothers).

Outreach activities

The HIV/AIDS Centre also works in close co-operation with the following units and organizations:

Transmission group	Patients hospitalized in 1993		All hospitalized patients 1988–1993
	overall[a]	once	
IDUs	37	11	122
Homosexual men	2	1	6
Bisexual men			1
Heterosexuals	9	1	9
Blood-product recipients	1	0	4
Children of HIV+ mothers	3	2	2
Unknown[b]	2	0	4
Total	54	15	148

[a] Repeated admissions to hospital were predominantly of IDUs
[b] Heterosexual contacts? IDU?

HIV/AIDS out-patients clinic

This clinic was established in 1985 and is based in the Voivodship STD Out-patients Clinic in Gdańsk. It provides general specialist care for HIV-infected patients 24 hours a day and in certain cases staff make home visits. Free HIV testing is provided on demand. The team of consultants include specialists in: internal medicine, paediatrics, surgery, dermatology, neurology and psychiatry, dentistry and nursing. Over the period 1985–93 the number of specialist consultations exceeded 3,500 and that of nursing procedures, 1,500. In 1993 there were more than 500 medical consultations, 347 dental consultations and 242 nursing procedures carried out.

Detoxification ward for drug addicts

The above is part of the Voivodship Neurological and Psychiatric Hospital, Sre-brzysko, in Gdańsk. An existing ward was rebuilt and renovated as a nine-bed ward and was brought into use in 1990. By the end of 1993, 691 drug addicts had been treated there, of whom 105 were HIV-infected. During 1993, 176 patients were admitted to the ward. The recommended full detoxification course is fourteen days but the average stay lasts ten to eleven days. For all patients analytical and bio-chemical tests are performed in the laboratories of the HIV/AIDS Centre, including liver and kidney function tests, hepatitis B virus and hepatitis C virus screening, toxicological tests and chest X-radiography. Detoxification treatment is supplemented with individual psychotherapy aimed at encouraging further rehabilitation and resocialization in one of the specialist centres all over the country. This is successful in about 10–20 per cent of cases.

Table 2
AIDS patients in the HIV/AIDS clinical ward December 1988 – December 1993

Year	Age (years)	Transmission group	AIDS diagnosis	CD4 (CDC criteria)	CD4/CD8	Time count (months) from diagnosis of infection to admission		Treatment	Deceased
						HIV	AIDS		
1988	35	homosexual	Cerebral toxoplasmosis	X	X	8 days	12	Acyclovir, AZT	+
1989	40	homosexual	*Pneumocystis carinii* pneumonia	0	0.33	11 days	11	AZT, Co-trimoxazole, Anti-TB	+
	31	bisexual	Progressive multifocal encephalopathy (papovavirus)	few	0.1	7	1	Penicillin, AZT	+
1992	33	IDU	Cerebral toxoplasmosis	X	X	12	3	Decadron, Mannitol	+
	33	IDU	*Pneumocystis carinii* pneumonia	X	X	18	?	Cefradine	+
	54	homosexual	*Pneumocystis carinii* pneumonia, digestive tract candidiasis, pulmonary tuberculosis	66	0.06	1	10	Pentamidine, Co-trimoxazole, Cefradine	+

× not done
* infectious mononucleosis (?) 4 years ago
? lost to follow-up

Table 2
continued

Year	Age (years)	Transmission group	AIDS diagnosis	CD4 (CDC criteria)	CD4/CD8	Time count (months) from diagnosis of infection to admission		Treatment	Deceased
						HIV	AIDS		
1993	39	heterosexual	Polyneuropathy, digestive tract candidiasis pulmonary tuberculosis	60	0.06	11	6	Anti-TB, Interferon , Co-trimoxazole, AZT, Ketoconazole	
	29	heterosexual	Digestive tract candidiasis	9	0.015	30	1	Ketoconazole, Interferon, Co-trimoxazole	?
	35	homosexual	Digestive tract candidiasis	39	0.03	48*	1	Ketoconazole, Interferon, Co-trimoxazole	
	33	IDU	AIDS dementia, digestive tract candidiasis	53	0.15	24	2	Cefradine, Ketoconazole, Interferon, Co-trimoxazole	
	22 mnths	HIV + mother's child	Mesenteral liposarcoma	215	0.25	26?	5	Interferon, Chemotherapy	
	33	IDU	*Pneumocystis carinii* pneumonia, digestive tract candidiasis	80	0.13	36	1	Cefradine, Ketoconazole, Interferon, Co-trimoxazole	+
	32	unknown	Digestive tract candidiasis	40	0.025	3	4	Interferon, AZT	+
	29	heterosexual	Pulmonary tuberculosis	180	0.26	1	8	Anti-TB	
	38	heterosexual	Digestive tract candidiasis	11		9	12	Ketoconazole	

HIV/AIDS section of the Gdańsk Remand Centre

The HIV/AIDS section was separated from the rest of the remand centre in 1990 and consists of 22 places and four hospital beds for those in custody who need hospital treatment. General and dental surgery as well as a special day-room used for psychotherapy are available. Laboratory tests are performed in the laboratories of the HIV/AIDS Centre and specialist medical care with regard to HIV infection is provided by physicians from the Clinic for Infectious Diseases. Appropriate treatment (zidovudine, interferon) is given under supervision of the medical staff of the prison. In order to encourage voluntary HIV testing, those who are found to be HIV-infected are offered better than average living conditions and a high-calory diet supplemented with vitamins. To date, all residents of this section have been injecting drug users.

Rehabilitation and resocialization centres for drug addicts

Two voivodship centres, in Smażyno and Zapowiednik (providing 75 places for drug addicts), have closely co-operated with the Diagnostic/Clinical HIV/AIDS Centre since it was created. For the past two years the provision of medical care by the staff of the Centre has been expanded to the MONAR centre for children and youths addicted or at risk of addiction in Matarnia. All diagnostic tests, as well as other medical procedures, are performed in the laboratory of the Diagnostic/Clinical HIV/AIDS Centre and in the collaborating clinics of Gdańsk School of Medicine. The results of HIV antibody tests are presented to people in charge of the centres (psychologists) who disclose them to the individuals concerned after counselling. It is up to the infected person whether he or she decides to reveal the fact of their infection to other residents. For epidemiological reasons, all the residents are instructed to behave as if all might be infected. In most cases in the centres, detailed liver function tests are required, owing to the particularly frequent infection among drug users with the hepatitis viruses, hepatitis C (90 per cent) and hepatitis B (70 per cent, compared with 40 per cent of HIV infection), as well as the hepatotoxic action of drugs.

Janusz Korczak Orphanage

This orphanage was rebuilt and adapted in 1992–93 for the admission of children (orphans and abandoned children) – some of whom are or may be infected with hepatitis B, hepatitis C or HIV – with a special concern for the prevention of cross-infection. The number of staff employed in the orphanage (nursemaids, nurses, teachers and psychologists) must ensure that not more than three to four children remain under supervision of one staff member at a time. The orphanage will admit children aged 0–7 years – after an initial three- to four-day observation period at the Clinic for Infectious Diseases in order to maintain confidentiality. Medical documentation from that observation will be handed over to the pediatrician in charge of the orphanage. All further diagnostic and therapeutic procedures will also be performed at the Clinic for Infectious Diseases. Several problems, including the elaboration of formal and legal adoption procedures concerning the HIV-infected children, remain to be solved.

'Gdańsk Initiative'

For the past two years a group from the Gay and Lesbian Community (LAMBDA) has been involved in the medical and educational activities of the Centre. This joint effort is known as the 'Gdańsk Initiative'.

Costs

The overall cost of the HIV antibody tests done in 1993 has been calculated at $44,139 (926,915,800 złotys).[1] Materials (films, paper, contrast media) used for the X-rays per-

Table 3

Cost of basic diagnostic equipment of an institution conducting HIV/AIDS diagnosis and treatment

Equipment	Approximate cost (in złotys)	Status of equipment at Gdańsk centre
Imaging		
X-Ray	5,000,000,000	Due to be replaced
USG with doppler	3,600,000,000	present
ECG with defibrillator	200,000,000	present
EEG	500,000,000	absent
Endoscopy		
Gastroscope	500,000,000	present
Duodenoscope	550,000,000	present
Colonoscope	500,000,000	present
Sigmoidoscope	400,000,000	present
Fibre optic bronchoscope	150,000,000	absent

formed in 1993 on the HIV-infected patients admitted to the Centre amounted to $786 (16,500,000 złotys); for electrocardiograms the sum was $67 (1,400,000 złotys); for electroencephalograms, $50 (1,040,000 złotys); and for abdominal ultrasound examinations, $157 (3,300,000 złotys) (Table 5). Costs of single basic diagnostic procedures, according to the HIV infection and the classification of the patient, are shown in Table 6. The numbers are highly illustrative of the scale of economic impact of the HIV/AIDS epidemic. As far as the Voivodship Hospital for Infectious Diseases is concerned, the cost for HIV/AIDS patients (excluding the costs of equipment and salaries) accounted for 8.8 per cent of its

Table 3
continued

Equipment	Approximate cost (in zlotys)	Status of equipment at Gdańsk centre
Intensive care unit		
Respirator	642,000,000	present
Cardiomonitor	290,000,000	present
Laboratory equipment (in addition to standard equipment: centrifuges, refrigerators, microscopes, photometers, etc.)		
Biochemical and base-acid balance analysers	1,400,000,000	present
Haematological and coagulation analysers, flow cytometer	2,000,000,000	present
Serological analyser (COBAS EIA)	350,000,000	present
OTHER (IF microscope, autoclave)	270,000,000	present
Total	**16,352,000,000**	**Equipped in 66%**

(PZ 21,000 = US$1 in 1994)

annual budget. Assessing very roughly the actual need in Poland for six HIV/AIDS centres like Gdańsk, one must think in terms of an annual budget of about $1,428,571 (30,000 million złotys) – 0.05 per cent of the annual budget of the Ministry of Health and Social Welfare. And this is just the beginning of the HIV/AIDS epidemic in Poland.

Informative and educational activities in the Centre

To finish on a somewhat more optimistic note, there are cheap and effective methods of fighting the spread of the HIV/AIDS epidemic. Here we are talking about prevention – which may be

Table 4

Results of serological HIV testing (ELISA confirmed by Western Blot) at the Diagnostic Clinical HIV/AIDS Centre at the Clinic for Infectious Diseases, Gdańsk School of Medicine

Group (number)

Year/Period	Prostitutes F +	Prostitutes F T	Homosexuals M +	Homosexuals M T	Sexual Contacts F +	Sexual Contacts F T	Sexual Contacts M +	Sexual Contacts M T	IDU F +	IDU F T	IDU M +	IDU M T	Prisoners[a] F +	Prisoners[a] F T	Prisoners[a] M +	Prisoners[a] M T	Medical staff F +	Medical staff F T	Medical staff M +	Medical staff M T	Dialysis patients F +	Dialysis patients F T	Dialysis patients M +	Dialysis patients M T	HIV+ mothers' children F +	HIV+ mothers' children F T	HIV+ mothers' children M +	HIV+ mothers' children M T	Others[b] F +	Others[b] F T	Others[b] M +	Others[b] M T	Total F +	Total F T	Total M +	Total M T
1985 to 30 April 1989	3	560	0	55	–	–	–	–	–	–	55	184	–	–	–	–	–	–	–	–	–	–	–	–	–	–	–	–	0	250	5	905	3	810	60	1144
1989 (from 1 May)	–	–	–	–	–	–	–	–	4	4	14	14	–	–	–	–	0	21	0	2	–	–	–	–	–	–	–	–	0	32	0	70	4	57	14	86
1990	0	94	1	54	–	–	–	–	13	69	58	191	0	43	8	999	0	75	0	8	0	75	0	121	0	21	0	23	0	498	8	899	13	875	75	2295
1991	0	78	1	19	1	65	3	172	13	83	50	241	0	14	7	1242	0	86	0	35	1	105	2	107	2	27	0	32	0	284	3	724	17	742	66	2572
1992	1	100	2	18	2	79	1	151	4	93	20	209	–	–	3	7[c]	0	57	0	19	3	61	0	46	0	21	1	22	3	705	3	1033	13	1116	30	1505
1993	0	32	0	21	0	73	0	184	2	85	7	203	0	10	4	2024	0	31	0	14	0	87	0	106	0	5	0	16	1	274	7	808	3	597	18	3376
Total	4	864	4	167	3	217	4	507	36	334	204	1042	0	67	22	4272	0	270	0	78	4	328	2	380	2	74	1	93	4	2043	26	4439	53	4197	263	10978

Overall (HIV-positive / number tested):

Prostitutes	Homosexuals	Sexual Contacts	IDU	Prisoners	Medical staff	Dialysis patients	HIV+ mothers' children	Others	Total
4/864	4/167	7/724	240/1,376	22/4,339	0/348	6/708	3/167[d]	30/6,482	316/15,175

F - female, M - male, T - number tested, + - HIV-positive

a newly diagnosed cases only
b including Tuberculosis Outpatients Clinic patients
c shortage of diagnostic kits
d including older children of some mothers, born before introduction of HIV screening
e tests performed in IMMiT (Institute of Maritime and Tropical Medicine, Gdynia)

COMMENT:

17% of injecting drug users found HIV-infected, which accounts for 61.1% of the HIV-positives in population
1.2% of homosexual men found HIV-infected, which accounts for 1.2% of the HIV-positives in population (sexual contacts – 2.2% of the HIV positives)

achieved at a relatively low cost. Since it started, the Centre has run several different educational courses for various professional groups and sectors of society. First, the staff of all the institutions collaborating within the Centre were trained both to deal with the main problems resulting from the HIV/AIDS epidemic and to teach others. That required numerous meetings with physicians and nurses, psychologists, teachers, prison warders, policemen, etc. – all of whom, owing to the character of their job and their position in the Centre, must be particularly aware of and well educated about HIV/AIDS epidemiology and prevention. The members of the above-mentioned Gdańsk Initiative have been included in that basic educational programme. In return, they have developed an extensive educational and informative policy, based on the professional help and consultations with the Centre's qualified staff and on their own wide contacts with corresponding organizations abroad, which extend far beyond the homosexual environment. The members of this community take part in the training activities of the Centre, edit and publish appropriate informative leaflets and posters addressed to other groups in society, and also use for educational purposes their own contacts with the press, radio and TV. All these forms of training and education are conducted by volunteers and are free of charge.

Another part of the Centre's educational activities is its involvement with the national postgraduate study system, coordinated by the Centre for Medical Postgraduate Training (Centrum Medycznego Kształcenia Podyplomowego, CMKP) in Warsaw. The CMKP commissions the Gdańsk Centre to run specialist one- to two-week courses on HIV/AIDS each year for physicians in charge of hospital wards in internal medicine, paediatrics and infectious diseases all over the country. The courses are financed by the Ministry of Health and Social Welfare. The courses include visits to the Centre.

Both the authorities and the staff of the Centre are greatly aware that they are not fighting the HIV/AIDS epidemic alone. Given the modest budget of the Polish Ministry of Health and Social Welfare, financial help from various sources is indispensable to keep the whole thing running. Equally, if not more, important, however, is practical and professional assistance from colleagues with more and longer experience of the epidemic. The Centre has established a close co-operation with two bodies abroad: Yale University and the 'Pompidou Group' (Co-operation Group to Combat Drug Abuse and Illicit Trafficking in Drugs, affiliated to the Council of Europe).

The Adult Health Division of Yale University in the USA has received a grant from the World AIDS Foundation to help to train the trainers. During our two-year co-operation, two conferences were organized: these aimed to inform and recruit volunteers from among healthcare providers and students from the psychology, sociology and pedagogic faculties of Gdańsk University with a view to further preventive and educational outreach work within society. They were followed by more specialized and detailed courses for future educators, mainly physicians and nurses, but also for psychologists, teachers and headmasters of secondary and vocational schools in the Gdańsk conurbation (Gdańsk, Sopot, Gdynia). This collaboration is very promising. Our American colleagues were surprised to find the organization of the Centre so consistent and, in some aspects, worth copying. Further consolidation of the divisions of the Centre, as well as expansion of its educational, preventive and epidemiological activities, has become possible since autumn 1992 thanks to the co-operation with the Pompidou Group.

The Pompidou Group has been involved in creating an information system for collecting data on drug abuse and drug trafficking from European institutions such as

Table 5
Cost of imaging, treatment and HIV/AIDS prophylaxis (HIV/AIDS patients of the Clinic for Infectious diseases, 1993)

Procedure	Cost (złotys)
Radiology, (chest, digestive tract, sinus, vertebral column x-rays, urography) – films and contrast media; 550 examinations	16,500,000
ECG – paper; 140 examinations	1,400,000
EEG – paper; 52 examinations	1,040,000
USG – gel, paper; 220 examinations	3,300,000
Treatment	1,500,000,000
Disposable equipment, scourers and detergents	175,300,000
Total	**1,697,540,000**

Test	Cost of the test (złotys)	HIV+ Patient		
		Routine procedure	IDU	AIDS Symptoms
ALAT	12,000	+	+	+
AspAT	12,000	+	+	+
Alkaline Phosphatase	12,000	+	+	+
GGTP	12,000	+	+	+
Diastase	12,000	+	+	+
Bilirubin (total)	21,000	+	+	+
Thymol	12,000	+	+	+
Urea	12,000	+	+	+
Creatinine	12,000	+	+	+
Creatinine clearance	13,000		+	+
Cholesterol	12,000	+	+	+
Triglyceride	13,000	+	+	+
Lipid electrophoresis	26,000	+	+	+
Total protein	12,000	+	+	+
Protein Electrophoresis	20,000	+	+	+
Glucose	12,000	+	+	+
Sodium	9,000	+	+	+
Potassium	9,000	+	+	+
Iron	12,000	+	+	+

Test	Cost of the test (złotys)	HIV+ Patient		
		Routine procedure	IDU	AIDS Symptoms
Base-acid balance	34,000			+
IgG	40,000	+	+	+
IgM	40,000	+	+	+
IgA	40,000	+	+	+
C3c	40,000			+
C4	40,000			+
C-reactive protein	40,000			+
Apo A-1	41,000			+
Apo B	41,000			+
Transferrin	40,000			+
Fibronectin	37,000			+
Haptoglobin	52,000			+
RBC	19,000	+	+	+
Haemogram	11,000	+	+	+
ESR	11,000	+	+	+
Reticulocytes	7,000			+
CD4/CD8	300,000	+	+	+
IMK+	520,000		+	+
Prothrombin time	27,000	+	+	+

Table 6 (left and right) **Cost of diagnostic (biochemical, analytical and serological) procedures performed at the Diagnostic Clinical HIV/AIDS Centre for Gdańsk Voivodship (First examination, 1993)**

Test	Cost of the test (złotys)	HIV+ Patient		
		Routine procedure	IDU	AIDS Symptoms
Bleeding time	8,000			+
Recalcination time	12,000			+
Fibrinogen	122,000			+
Blood group, Rh	23,000	+	+	+
CSF - general	13,000			+
CSF - cell count	4,000			+
HBsAg	30,000	+	+	+
HbeAg	140,000	+	+	+
anti-HBc	110,000	+	+	+
anti-HBc IgM	132,000	+	+	+
anti-HBe	139,000	+	+	+
anti-HBs	65,000	+	+	+
anti-HCV	104,000	+	+	+
anti-HDV	136,000		+	+
anti-CMV IgG	181,000	+	+	+
anti-CMV IgM	360,000	+	+	+
anti-TOXO IgG	150,000	+	+	+
anti-TOXO IgM	320,000	+	+	+
anti-HIV (EIA)	30,000	+	+	+
anti-HIV (WB)	1,100,000	+	+	+

Table 6 **continued**

Test	Cost of the test (zlotys)	HIV+ Patient		
		Routine procedure	IDU	AIDS Symptoms
HIV (PCR)	2,100,000		+	+
Urine culture	12,000	+	+	+
Stool culture	12,000	+	+	+
Throat swab culture	12,000	+	+	+
Sputum culture	12,000	+	+	+
Blood culture	31,000			+
CSF culture	12,000			+
Pus culture	12,000			+
Other culture	12,000			+
Culture - fungi	12,000			+
Culture-anaerobes	81,000			+
Biochemical identification	12,000		+	+
Serological identification - Salmonella	26,000		+	+
Serological identification - Shigella	27,000		+	+

Table 6 **continued**

Test	Cost of the test (złotys)	HIV+ Patient		
		Routine procedure	IDU	AIDS Symptoms
Serological identification - E. coli	77,000		+	+
Identification - fungi	9,000			+
Antibiogram	60,000			+
Antimycogram	36,000			+
Antistreptolysin-O	17,000			+
Paul-Bunnel-Davidson	11,000			+
Vidal	143,000			+
Candida-Ab (IF)	221,000		+	+
P. carinii-Ab (IF)	116,000		+	+
Stool - general	15,000			+
Stool - parasites	10,000			+
Urine - general	10,000	+	+	+
Urine - morphine	110,000		+	+
Urine - barbiturates	110,000		+	+
Urine - amphetamine	110,000		+	+
Urine - marijuana	110,000		+	+
Urine - cocaine	110,000		+	+
Total		**3,672,000**	**7,592,000**	**8,491,000**

Table 6 **continued**

hospitals, out-patient clinics, schools, remand centres, police stations, etc. The inclusion of Gdańsk in the WHO's 'Multi-city network' resulted in the creation of the Gdańsk–Pompidou Group Collaborating Centre, consisting of representatives from divisions of the Diagnostic/Clinical HIV/AIDS Centre, as well as from other institutions in Poland (e.g. the Voivodship Superintendent's Office). This system is aimed at getting a more precise and detailed picture of the extent and structure of the HIV/AIDS epidemic, based on the extent and pattern of risk behaviours (drug abuse, delinquency, etc.). In the strong belief that either party can benefit from professional and educational co-operation, the Diagnostic/Clinical HIV/AIDS Centre welcomes proposals for collaboration from other institutions fighting HIV/AIDS.

Conclusion

Owing to its delay in reaching Poland, in comparison with other European coun-tries and the USA, the spread of the HIV/AIDS epidemic in our country seems relatively slow. (In 1991, by commission of WHO, 1,113 randomly chosen, anony-mous people were screened in our region, of whom two (0.18 per cent) were found to be HIV-positive.) However, what is now needed are well-planned, anonymous, epidemiological surveys to estimate the real range of infection.

The most affected environment in Polish society is that of injecting drug users (IDUs). However, little is known about the HIV prevalence among prostitutes and homosexual men who, discouraged by the common lack of tolerance and social approbation, rarely report to have their blood tested.

After more than five years' experience, we feel that only a comprehensive pro-gramme which links hospital and ambulatory medical care with social and psy-chological support rendered to those at risk (i.e. mainly IDUs) might be successful in fighting and preventing HIV/AIDS. Such a programme requires the close co-operation of hospitals, out-patient clinics, detoxification wards, rehabilitation and resocialization centres for drug addicts, HIV divisions of remand centres, and orphanages with one specialized multi-potential institution. An extensive educa-tion programme (preferably propagated by volunteers, to lower the costs) con-cerning not only professionals, but all members of society – children, youths and adults – is the basis for the effective prevention of any further spread of the infec-tion. Sexual education should be stressed, as it is the sexual route which is pre-dicted to play a major role in HIV transmission in the near future.

There is, however, one basic disadvantage of such a comprehensive pro-gramme, even though it has proven effective in our region. Namely, it costs more than our country in its present economical situation can afford. But the question is, whether our country will be able to afford the costs of treatment of all those infected if the programme is not realized.

---

1 US$1= 21,000 złotys in 1994 (2.10 new złotys in 1995)

AIDS in Post-communist Central Europe: Education of the General Population as a Priority Prevention Strategy

Dr Vlastimil Mayer

Coordinator of the AIDS Prevention Programme, Slovak Academy of Sciencies, Slovak Republic

The Central European countries that were part of the so-called 'Soviet Bloc' for more than 40 years have, for several years following the overthrow of the communist regimes, been undergoing fundamental political, social and economic changes and transitions which challenge all sectors of society. Among these countries – in particular, the Czech Republic, Hungary, Poland and the Slovak Republic – the situation in the latter regarding the spread and prevention of HIV/AIDS may be taken as a typical.

Background

Slovakia is a landlocked country of almost 43,000 km², bordered by the Czech Republic, Poland, Ukraine, Hungary and Austria, and has 5.4 million inhabitants. Before independence on 1 January 1993 Slovakia was the eastern, poorer part of the former Czech and Slovak Federal Republic.

The emerging democracies in Central Europe are inadequately equipped to deal with the challenges raised by the HIV/AIDS epidemic in western and southern parts of Europe. The political restraints of the 'Iron Curtain' placed on the popula-

tions by their totalitarian regimes (for Slovakia this continued until 1989) considerably delayed the penetration and slowed the spread of HIV in Central Europe.

In Western Europe, as a whole, the increase in the number of AIDS cases has been steady rather than exponential (as, for instance, initially in the USA) – most probably because of the impact of prevention efforts in numerous countries. At the end of March 1994, the number of AIDS patients in Europe exceeded 109,000 cases[1] and is expected to continue to rise for many years to come. Together, Western countries cumulatively reported 106,364 cases of AIDS, whereas those of Central and Eastern Europe reported only 3,581 – 3.36 per cent that of Western Europe. The 'Iron Curtain effect' is also expressed in the (best) estimates of numbers of cases of HIV infection in the Western and Central–Eastern part of Europe, both of which have similar populations of about 400 million.[2] By the end of February 1994 the number of HIV-infected persons in Central and Eastern Europe was estimated as 16,900 or more, whereas in Western Europe it is 514,850 or more (97.7 per cent of the total).

Nevertheless, HIV continues to spread in all areas of the world already affected and increasingly affects countries or regions that until now showed little evidence of HIV infection. In spite of preventive measures in Europe, the estimate of newly occurring cases of HIV infection was about 75,000 for the year 1991 alone.[3]

These estimates need to be considered cautiously but are of great value in determining the trends of the HIV/AIDS epidemic. It is also necessary to mention that extrapolations based on data from countries with well-established HIV/AIDS monitoring programmes are not necessarily adequate for populations where surveillance is not yet fully established. Thus the number of known cases of HIV infection does not reflect the real number of infected people.

HIV/AIDS in Slovakia

As of 15 April 1994, a cumulative total of seven cases of AIDS and 46 cases of HIV-infection had been reported in Slovakia, and the best estimate for the number of HIV-infected persons is 160. Neighbouring states report from 6.7 to 25 times (or more) greater cumulative numbers of AIDS cases, except Austria, where the reported cumulative number of AIDS cases is as high as 1,122.

Similarly, the best estimates for the numbers of HIV-infected persons in neighbouring former socialist countries are nine to eighteen times higher than in Slovakia. In Austria – not part of the former 'socialist bloc' – the estimate is 10,000 or more persons. Thus the population of Slovakia has been relatively spared from the spread of HIV.

It is most unlikely that the low prevalence of HIV infection and AIDS in the Slovak Republic is due to under-reporting before 1991–92, because there had been systematic national surveillance of the infection since the autumn of 1986. The blood supply from more than 938,000 donors, 'vulnerable groups' (843 female prostitutes, 228 illicit drug users, 30,313 sexually transmitted disease clinic clients), 311,000 pregnant women and 113,000 other individuals has been tested. Even so, the figures cited above may not reflect the true prevalence, for the detection of HIV-positive persons in the April 1993/94 period has been relatively more frequent than hitherto.

Better information and easy access to free anonymous testing may play a role here, but besides a suspicion that some persons may have avoided blood testing in the past, an increase in the underlying spread of HIV cannot be excluded.

The relatively frequent occurrence in people known to be infected with HIV of another sexually transmitted disease or diseases, and the homosexual orientation of most of the infected people suggests that sexual contact is the primary mode of transmission.

The above, seemingly impressive, figures illustrating the extensive large-scale screening (although mass screening of pregnant women was discontinued from 1992) do not represent epidemiologically valuable results, as would be obtained from deliberate and systematic sentinel surveillance studies and/or monitoring. They were done on an exceptional basis during the years of the totalitarian regime and have not been repeated since. Design of investigations in 'vulnerable groups' (including sex workers, their clients and some ethnic minorities such as gypsies), as well as in adolescents, was not effective enough to yield useful information.

The overall picture of HIV/AIDS in the Slovak Republic, as seen from the angle of a new different social situation, warrants massive efforts now in order to maintain the low risk of HIV infection as the spread of HIV in Europe and globally continues.[4] Central Europe is still one of the few areas in the world where the HIV/AIDS incidence is relatively low, but it is also greatly endangered by numerous unfavourable factors inherent in European civilization at the end of the twentieth century.[5] We shall discuss these further, in particular contacts through tourism and trade.

The Communist legacy and aftermath

Before World War II the former Czechoslovakia had a strong history of industrial and economic success (seventh largest gross domestic product in the world at that time), but productivity deteriorated markedly during the 41 years of Communist economic policy. This has continued in Slovakia during the past five years owing to the political, social and economic upheaval since the 'Velvet Revolution' in 1989. This situation has been aggravated by the division of the Czech and Slovak Federal Republic and the resulting need to create the administrative structures of a new sovereign state under conditions of striking changes to the social order.

The national economy is changing towards a free-market system. The move to democracy is complicated by the legacy of more than 40 years of dictatorship by one political party, and some structures of democratic life need to be improved. The existence of some political and economic instability is therefore not surprising. The situation is also affected by the economic crisis in Western Europe, which also influences moves towards integration into European political and economic structures.

During the totalitarian regime expenditure on healthcare was limited to about 4.2 per cent of the gross domestic product. Low salaries in the health sector were associated with severe, persistent shortages in medical technology and drugs. A similarly unfavourable situation also pertained in medical research, precluding much-needed sustainable progress.

With the recent liberalization of prices, several devaluations of the currency (which is still not convertible), together with the consequences of dismantling the Eastern Trading Bloc, the health sector – faced with increasing costs, shrinking purchasing power and a serious brain drain – is under threat (as of April 1994) of having to work under crisis management.

The overall state of health and the environment in Slovakia, as in other former socialist countries, lags behind that of Western Europe and is considered one of the worst heritages of totalitarianism.

Lack of concern or of appropriate education towards teaching individuals to be responsible for their own health (health problems were formerly declared to be tasks of the state) led to an insufficient degree of preventive behaviour and of low awareness of factors that might damage health, including high consumption of tobacco, alcohol and unhealthy dietary habits. Inadequate family planning programmes are clearly connected to the persisting high abortion rates, illustrating the pattern of unsafe sex.

Private voluntary organizations and organized self-help programmes (i.e. those of non-governmental organizations, NGOs) were not allowed under the socialist regime and the development of a sense of personal responsibility was not encouraged. Environmental initiatives were also considered as unacceptable by the repressive socialist regime. For decades the general public remained almost passive in the face of growing health problems, since they were without vitally relevant information. In this setting, even after the revolutionary events, the newly emerging NGOs and grass-roots private initiatives need consultancy and managerial help in order to increase their ability to set appropriate targets and skills for fundraising. This latter is particularly difficult to develop in a post-communist society and economy, not familiar with citizens' initiatives and with appropriate legislation still under development.

Last, but not least, not all the newly appointed staff in the health sector since 1989 or the political changes of 1993 are experienced public health or hospital administrators. Some served earlier as clinicians or worked in the Slovak Academy of Sciences and need time to gain the necessary skills to manage disease control programmes at the highest level.

Initial attempts to deal with HIV

Dealing with the challenges raised by HIV/AIDS before 1989 – after recognition of the introduction and initial spread of HIV in Slovakia in 1984–85 – was set back by two events. The first was the 'Programme of the Fight against AIDS', created in 1986. As a product of its time but also of a rigid bureaucracy, this programme was, unfortunately, oriented mainly to extensive screening, which was in some respects mandatory. It was without measures deliberately targeted to slow the spread of HIV effectively. It neglected entirely the psychosocial problems associated with HIV disease. Nevertheless, one may observe that at this time the global strategy for HIV/AIDS prevention also lacked many of those progressive elements characteristic of current efforts.

Health and HIV/AIDS education at the time also suffered from approaches that would now be considered conservative. Most disseminated information was based on messages of fear, thus not fulfilling the psychological criteria now stressed as being more appropriate to induce change in risk behaviour. Moreover, the relevant information was sporadic and frequently just 'more of the same'. It was unidirectional and its impact was not professionally evaluated.

The programme was not modernized or reshaped. Its laboratory base, the National

Reference Laboratory for AIDS, was established in 1984 at the Institute of Virology of the Slovak Academy of Sciences to aid the health sector, but lacked the necessary professional staff. Its functioning, essential for primary and secondary prevention, was supported by the health sector only partially and temporarily. This laboratory, serving as the conceptual, methodological and epidemiological forerunner as well as an expert centre for HIV/AIDS in Slovakia, was finally closed as superfluous in 1991. The public health service then deliberately relied on the central laboratory in the capital of the former Federation, Prague. Medical and other professional staff, critical for the implementation of the programme, were not sufficiently trained and their skills were not improved. New, young co-workers were not appointed. Laboratory equipment for HIV testing was not of a satisfactory quality and not purposefully distributed to laboratories across the country.

In February 1991 a short-term programme of prevention and control for the former Czech and Slovak Federal Republic was prepared with the help of the WHO Regional Office for Europe. Unfortunately, the part of it planned for Slovakia was not implemented.

Management was uncommitted and ineffective and this resulted in limited financial resources being allocated to public health. The consequences were unfortunate. On the eve of independence, the country lacked an effectively functioning HIV/AIDS prevention programme and a reference laboratory for AIDS. Besides their indispensable functions at local levels, both were essential for the development of a fruitful partnership and co-operation with the Global Programme on AIDS of the World Health Organization (WHO).

Last but not least, owing to the asymmetry in the Czechoslovak federation, Slovakia has not satisfactorily developed international working contacts in the field of HIV/AIDS prevention. As a result, the national programme was not integrated into internationally coordinated and supported preventive actions. The lack of links with WHO, European Union Programmes or any bilateral co-operation in HIV/AIDS prevention represented serious obstacles to the development of effective projects either in the immediate or in the more distant future. And because of the political and economic isolation from the Western World in the years 1948–89 both the transfer of research technology and international scientific collaboration – important for preventive programmes and, for example, clinical research – have been limited. Moreover, the present complicated transition from the 'planned' economy towards a free-market system, overshadowed by pressing social issues, may temporarily result in a decrease in funding of HIV/AIDS prevention programmes.

Meeting the challenge

In the light of HIV/AIDS prevention undertaken up to 1993, the warnings from WHO's Global Programme on AIDS, in particular its Regional Office for Europe (GPA/EURO), appear extremely pertinent. According to GPA/EURO, the HIV epidemic in Central Europe could be worse than in Western Europe because the health system structures in every Central European country are involved in complicated transformations and are working under numerous pressures. Owing to the region's economic difficulties they cannot afford the burden of the epidemic.[6]

In the five years since the democratic overthrow of socialism one important change is the free contact that now exists with other parts of the world, resulting in a sharp increase in mobility: for example in tourism, commercial exchange and external migration. Social upheaval has led to growth in the import of illicit drugs, an increase in male and female prostitution as well as 'sex tourism' from Western countries. All these realities are associated

with inherently greater risk of HIV infection, as is the expected higher rate of unemployment and growing number of poor and homeless people. It seems as important to note that with the liberalization of social conventions and laws, together with 'imported' Western habits, and the simultaneous creation of new opportunities for social contacts (discos, newspaper personal columns, sex shops, etc.) an overall increase in sexual liberality is going on. These phenomena together may negatively influence the HIV/AIDS and STD prevention efforts. Nevertheless, the views on such an impact differ, especially when seen in the long term.

According to the WHO's Global Programme on AIDS in Copenhagen[7] all the transmission patterns and behaviours enabling HIV infection are in place in the Central European region, together with a marked increase in sexually transmitted diseases such as gonorrhoea and syphilis: evidence of more intensive unprotected sexual promiscuity.[8] Slovakia is no exception in this respect. The situation is considered potentially explosive and only concerted complex prevention measures may (hopefully) be successful.[9]

There is certainly still a chance to slow considerably or even prevent a significant spread of HIV in the Central European region, where the development of the HIV/AIDS epidemic still lags five to eight years behind that of Western Europe. In this respect, it should be underlined that even when the countries of this region, recognizing the imminent threat of the spread of HIV/AIDS have the political will, qualified staff will be needed to implement prevention measures and manage them effectively. Some realities must be recognized, however, if Western countries are to be addressed as donors of financial assistance.

In spite of the unfavourable epidemiological situation, it seems that in Western countries, after the crisis situation five to seven years ago, the general interest shown earlier in AIDS has decreased markedly, not only among the general public but also among target groups.[10] Generally, their national programmes claim that either at present, or in the foreseeable future, the financial resources for preventive campaigns will stagnate or even be reduced. All this necessitates restructuring of the established programmes and a search for new solutions in order to give clear directions for coping with the worsening epidemic situation.

In other words, the obstacles and shortcomings in countries with established AIDS prevention structures show that the conditions for collaborative, mass prevention campaigns in Central Europe, which undoubtedly needs assistance, are essentially less favourable than they were during the comparable epidemiological situation in Western Europe.

At present (April 1994) the danger of becoming infected and the danger of a greater spread of the virus in Slovakia still appears low in the short term. Nevertheless, this assumption is based on the results of unsystematic HIV-postive epidemiological surveillance studies, lacking targeted investigations or anonymous sentinel studies. Surveillance studies were done in a limited way and incompletely in the past years and do not necessarily describe the present situation. The relatively higher number of HIV cases diagnosed during the first quarter of 1994, compared to the same time period of 1993, may support the above doubts.

At this time, continuing changes in the current political and economic situation in Central European countries results in unstable and uncertain development. It is therefore not too surprising that other anxieties and cares of immediate concern have assumed a higher relevance in the general public's mind than AIDS, which is perceived to be a problem of 'others'. The campaigns can no longer count on the particular *élan* and creativity of organizers and sponsors observed in the earlier years after the initial 'AIDS shock'. It is not easy to recruit and motivate dedicated volunteers for non-governmental organizations in order to keep the latter socially active. The lack of financial resources, undermining such community-based activities that are a valuable adjunct to the professional healthcare and government prevention programmes, appears to be typical in postcommunist societies at the present stage of their transformation.

As a matter of fact, some of the initial assistance and supporting measures begun by various Western organizations were inadequate, usually of short duration and not well-orientated. Only in the most recent years has it become clearer that the simple transfer of programmes and interventions from Western to Central and Eastern European countries does not meet expectations of an immediate build-up of effective prevention structures. This was stated explicitly at the Vth European Consultation on Public Education and AIDS Prevention (1991).[11] What is transferable is more the philosophy of the prevention work, including the standards of programme development and management,[12] which then need to be implemented in the specific contexts of individual countries; in other words, prevention work may draw on the experience of others, but must also respect the political structure, cultural background and social development of the country at hand.

Plans and tools for action

In the next few years, it is unlikely that any new scientific achievement, for example an effective vaccine, will emerge to change our understanding of how best to control the spread of HIV.[13] The presently expanding pandemic of incurable and fatal HIV disease is expected to remain a major public health issue for many years to come.

The new Government, in an attempt to modernize and reshape the HIV/AIDS prevention programme, realized that an aggressive, complex education and prevention programme must be implemented and that its cost-effectiveness must be maximized. For the present, public information and the promotion of behavioural change remain the only immediately available strategies for a new programme. To achieve these aims, co-operation with nations with advanced AIDS programmes, along with appropriate use of research and new forms of education strategies, will be critically important in slowing the spread of HIV infection in Slovakia.

Four new elements incorporated into this programme were:

- a psychosocial dimension, including counselling (completely lacking in the past);
- a special concern to address appropriately the ethnic and linguistic minorities living in the Slovak Republic, particularly the Gypsies;
- research relevant to the local situation as an integral driving force of the modernized programme;
- the need for prevention programmes *not* to be seen as separate from human rights issues and the activities of self-help groups, organized as non-governmental organizations. The efforts of the latter need to be supported by the official government preventive programme.

The programme's conceptualization and implementation has been positively influenced by three factors:

First were the conclusions of 'Investment in Health', a meeting of Ministers of Health and Finance on HIV/AIDS in the countries of Central and Eastern Europe, held in Riga (Latvia) on 1–2 April 1993. These were summarized as 'The Riga Initiative: A Call for Action'. This plan responds to the risk of exponential growth of HIV infection in these countries, stress-ing the necessary investment in the health of Central and Eastern European countries as a long-term, cost-effective strategy for Europe as a whole. The spread of HIV/AIDS may result in an enormous future social and economic burden, if not reduced by a concerted action before a full-scale epidemic develops.

Secondly, the Riga Initiative created a favourable environment for working out the technical assistance of GPA/EURO WHO to the Slovak Republic's new National AIDS Programme for the period 1994–95. With this assistance an integration of the Slovak preventive programme in the context of the Global Programme on AIDS' strategy will be realized. It is expected that the successfully implemented short-term and the subsequent medium-term prevention programmes could initiate, as well as support, complementary local resources in order to sustain the national programme activity in the next years. It is thus hoped to keep the HIV prevalence in Slovakia as low as possible. Well-coordinated co-operation with neighbouring states is considered a prerequisite.

Finally, owing to the assistance of the Swiss government, a long-term education campaign has been implemented. It addresses the general population in order to achieve a consistent and sustained level of public awareness, interest and concern about HIV/AIDS. This maintenance of concern should result in a large-scale and permanent modification of personal behaviour in order to reduce or eliminate the risk of HIV transmission. Behavioural change, where it has occurred, is parallelled by the existence of strong community structures, peer education and the development of safer sex as a community norm.[14]

Moreover, education is expected to empower a sense of tolerance and reduce discrimination in society and among those who may eventually have to treat people with HIV.[15] The Swiss help in this respect cannot be overestimated. It allows the realization of the campaign through modern advertising and marketing methods, using a multi-media approach. The campaign is managed in closest co-operation with local AIDS experts (Ministry of Health, Slovak Republic; Slovak Academy of Sciences; National Programme on HIV/AIDS Prevention; NGOs) as well as with the experts from the Swiss 'STOP AIDS' campaign. In this way the impact of the campaign is assured in a country-specific context whilst incorporating the exten-sive experience of the successful Swiss AIDS prevention strategy.[16]

In January 1994 the National AIDS Policy Consensus Conference was held under the title 'Complex Programme of HIV/AIDS Prevention in the Slovak Republic'. This consensus meeting was and will be followed by other specifically targeted activities in the education area, by the establishment of the Slovak AIDS Prevention Centre, a reference laboratory for AIDS and the creation of training opportunities for young health professionals.

Conclusion

The low incidence of HIV infection reported until 1994 in Slovakia appears to have resulted mainly from political isolation. From the situation described in this chapter it is clear that Slovakia should be considered highly vulnerable to an increase in HIV prevalence, situated as it is on the western edge of the Central European region. However, the knowledge and experience accumulated during more than a decade of prevention efforts in Western European countries and worldwide makes it possible to choose the most effective and appropriate preventative measures to slow the spread of the virus.

Slovakia appears to be a typical example of a post-communist country striving to confront many problems to ensure future stabilization and prosperity. The HIV/AIDS prevention programme it is developing may well serve as an example of a fruitful international co-operative partnership.

1 European Centre for the Epidemiological Monitoring of AIDS, Paris, *Quarterly Report*, 41, 1994.

2 J. Hallauer, European Regional Coordinator, Global Programme on AIDS, World Health Organization, personal communication, 1994.

3 J. Mann, 'AIDS – The second decade: a global perspective', *Journal of Infectious Diseases*, 165, pp. 245–250, 1992.

4 V. Mayer, G. Shor-Posner, M. Baum, 'Czech and Slovak Federal Republic: not too late to slow HIV-1 spread', *Lancet*, i, 339, p. 1162, 1993.

5 M. Balter, 'East Europe: a chance to stop HIV', *Science*, 262, pp. 1964–65, 1993.

6 J. Hallauer, *HIV/AIDS in Countries of Central and Eastern Europe: Epidemiological and Social Aspects*, from 'Investment in Health', a meeting of Ministers of Health and Finance on prevention of HIV/AIDS in countries of Central and Eastern Europe, Riga, 1–2 April 1993.

M. Balter, 'East Europe: a chance to stop HIV', *Science*, 262, pp. 1964–65, 1993.

7 J. Hallauer, European Regional Coordinator, Global Programme on AIDS, World Health Organization, personal communication, 1994.

8 Federal Centre for Health Education, Germany. Materials from the 5th European Consultation on Public Education and AIDS Prevention 'State of the Art and Perspectives in

an Integrating Europe', Cologne, 17–19 November 1991.

M. Balter, 'East Europe: a chance to stop HIV', *Science*, 262, pp. 1964–65, 1993.

9 J. Hallauer, *HIV/AIDS in Countries of Central and Eastern Europe: Epidemiological and Social Aspects*, from 'Investment in Health', a meeting of Ministers of Health and Finance on prevention of HIV/AIDS in countries of Central and Eastern Europe, Riga, 1–2 April 1993.

10 N. Gilmore and P. Aggleton, 'AIDS – 92/93. Social, cultural and political aspects', *AIDS 92/93, A Year in Review, Supplement 1*, pp. 241–242, 1993.

Federal Centre for Health Education, Germany. Materials from the 5th European Consultation on Public Education and AIDS Prevention 'State of the Art and Perspectives in an Integrating Europe', Cologne, 17–19 November 1991.

11 Federal Centre for Health Education, Germany. Materials from the 5th European Consultation on Public Education and AIDS Prevention 'State of the Art and Perspectives in an Integrating Europe', Cologne, 17–19 November 1991.

12 *Ibid.*

13 M. Potts, R. Anderson, M-C. Boily, 'Slowing the spread of human immunodeficiency virus in developing countries', *Lancet*, ii, 338, pp. 608–613, 1991.

14 N. Gilmore and P. Aggleton, 'AIDS – 92/93. Social, cultural and political aspects', *AIDS 92/93, A Year in Review, Supplement 1'*, pp. 241–242, 1993.

15 Federal Office of Public Health, The National AIDS Commission, Switzerland, *HIV Prevention in Switzerland. Targets, Strategies, Interventions*, 1993.

16 *Ibid.*

HIV-related Risk Behaviour among International Travellers: an Overview

Dr Michael Bloor

School of Social and Administrative Studies, University of Wales, Cardiff

The epidemiological role of international travel is seen most clearly in the early stages of epidemics when a high proportion of those infected in a given locality will be returned travellers or migrants from other areas. In South Korea in 1990, for example, there were a mere 52 known cases of HIV infection but half of these were Korean nationals who had returned from overseas job assignments.[1] This pre-eminent early epidemiological role for international travel then diminishes in relative importance once infection is introduced into local social circles of sexual partners and syringe-sharers. It diminishes but it does not disappear: where there remain substantial differences in HIV prevalence between different countries, then an important fraction of new cases of infection in low prevalence countries will be persons who contracted their infection by risk behaviour in high prevalence countries. For example, there were a total of 490 known cases of HIV by heterosexual exposure in England and Wales up to the end of March 1993, excluding HIV-positive migrants and cases still under investigation,[2] but there were seventeen known cases which were the result of heterosexual exposure among UK travellers to just one destination in 1991 and 1992, namely Thailand.[3] In countries where total numbers of heterosexual infections are low, then 'sex tourism' to Third World countries may become an important component in such infections.

The topic of international travel and HIV infection is one which has generated more heat than light. Many governments have attempted to deny entry to their countries to HIV-positive persons but have shown little interest in funding research on the risk behaviour of travellers. While massive demonstrations were staged *outside* the International AIDS Conference in San Francisco in 1990 over the US government's travel restrictions on HIV-positive people, *inside* the conference there were only two scientific papers, among the many hundreds in total, which addressed the empirical issue of risk behaviour among travellers. As with so many other aspects of the epidemic, entrenched political positions have been taken up without reference to scientific enquiry. And xenophobia, like homophobia, is a latent feature of many discourses on HIV and AIDS.

In view of the passions aroused by the issue of international travel and HIV infection, it is advisable at the outset to be clear about what topics will and will not be addressed in this chapter. I shall be concerned solely with HIV-related risk behaviour (sexual risk behaviour and syringe-sharing) among international travellers; I shall not be concerned with governmental policies on travel restriction for HIV-positive persons (for an overview of such policies see Gilmore et al.[4]). Moreover, Haour-Knipe and her colleagues in an EC Concerted Action study [5] found it advisable to distinguish between travellers and migrants (concentrating their attention on the latter) since they found the main issues in respect of HIV to be very different between the two groups; I shall make the same distinction and concentrate my attention on travellers, rather than migrants. Among travellers I include both tourists and business travellers; within the latter I include expatriate workers while recognizing that some expatriate workers may approximate more to long-term migrants than short-term business travellers. The chapter reviews current evidence on HIV risk behaviour among travellers under four headings: non-commercial sexual risk behaviour (that is, with private partners), sex tourism (commercial sexual risk behaviour), risk behaviour among travel, transport and tourism workers (such as seamen, lorry drivers and cabin crew) and syringe-sharing by travellers.

Non-commercial sexual risk behaviour

It is widely believed that people are more prone to engage in non-commercial sexual encounters when travelling than when at home. Holidays have what anthropologists term a 'liminal' character, where conventional norms of behaviour are relaxed or disregarded. Advertising of holidays makes much of their associations with 'romance' and many holiday organizations cater specifically for single people in mixed sex groupings. Tourists, business travellers and expatriate workers may find themselves lonely and separated from their regular partners for long periods. For a variety of reasons then, travellers are thought to have an increased propensity to meet new sexual partners.

Such assumptions about the association between travel and partner change are not always born out by research findings. The UK's NATSSAL (National Survey of Sexual Attitudes and Lifestyles) study found that those male respondents whose work led them to stay overnight away from home were *not* more likely to report more heterosexual partners.[6] However, if male respondents are split into the monogamous, those who report serial partners, and those who report concurrent partners, then those with concurrent partners are more likely to have work which takes them away from home than those who are monogamous or have serial partners. Moreover, although women were much less likely than men to have jobs which took them away from home, those who did have such jobs were more likely to report more partners than other women. The picture is a complex one and the NATSSAL authors are careful to point out that no causal relationship can be assumed: for example, persons with heavy domestic responsibilities are both more likely to be monogamous and less likely to opt for jobs which involve overnight absence. However, one interpretation might be that the liminal effect of travel is more influential for women than for men, women finding their sexual behaviour subject to greater social constraint than men in their usual 'home' environment.

It remains possible that, while overnight absence itself may be only weakly associated with partner change, certain types of travel experience are associated with partner change much more closely. It may be, for example, that holiday-makers are more likely to find new partners than business travellers, or vice versa. It may be that longer-term business absences are more closely associated with partner change than short trips. The instance of the returned Korean expatriate workers has already been mentioned and Dutch and Belgian studies of returning ex-patriates confirm the view that such workers may be at particular risk of infection. A study of nearly 2,000 Dutch expatriate workers returning from work in sub-Saharan Africa reported high levels of risk behaviour and five cases of HIV infection.[7] The Belgian study was of nearly 6,000 advisors and expatriates who had spent at least six months in Africa in the previous five years; 56 persons were HIV-positive and risk factors for infection included sexual contact with local partners and commercial sexual contacts.[8]

The only national sex survey to ask specifically about partner change while on holiday was a Swiss telephone survey conducted in 1990. Among 1,220 men aged 17–45, 66 per cent had holidayed abroad in the first nine months of 1990 and 7 per cent of the sample reported that they had sexual relations with a person in the holiday country in that year.[9] The only broadly similar study to the Swiss telephone survey is an anonymous postal survey of a sample of 1,030 men and women aged 16–40, drawn from a Family Practice register in Nottingham in the UK.[10] Some 65 per cent of respondents had travelled abroad during 1988 or 1989; 8.5 per cent of these travellers (12 per cent of the men, 6 per cent of the women) had a 'romantic or sexual relationship' with a new partner on their last trip; 4.8 per cent of travellers (8 per cent of the men, 2 per cent of the women) had sexual intercourse with a new partner on their last trip; and men, single people and younger people were significantly more likely than others to report a new sexual relationship. Information was not sought on numbers of new partners outside travel episodes, so it is not possible to say whether travel is directly associated with partner change.

These Swiss and UK data on travel related partner change are not strictly comparable. The Swiss data concerned men only and reported on all trips in the previous nine months, while the Nottingham data only sought data on the last trip and did not distinguish between holiday sexual partners from the UK and those from the

host country or elsewhere. Moreover, the Nottingham data may be an under-report because of response rate bias: while the overall response rate (56 per cent) was comparable with that in many postal surveys, younger men (21 to 25 years) were both the group most likely to report a new sexual partner and the group least likely to respond to the questionnaire.

Although it is a matter of importance to collect data on partner change, these data need to be supplemented by further information, most notably on condom use and on partners' nationalities. The Nottingham study found that 71 per cent of those reporting a new sexual partner did not use a condom on all occasions,[11] but the total number of reports (seventeen respondents with new partners) is small. Studies of clinic attenders, although not representative of the travelling public, present larger numbers of reports of risk behaviour for analysis. Hawkes *et al.* report on the results of an anonymous questionnaire completed by 757 attenders at the Hospital for Tropical Diseases in London, almost all of whom had travelled to tropical or sub-tropical countries in the previous year;[12] these out-patients were also anonymously urine tested for HIV: 2.2 per cent were HIV positive. More than half those out-patients (54 per cent) reporting new partner(s) abroad (141 respondents) never used condoms with those new partners. Surprisingly, while travel may have a liminal or disinhibiting effect in the sense of increasing the traveller's propensity to encounter new sexual partners (as in the NATSSAL study), there was no evidence in the London out-patients study for this disinhibiting effect to extend to an increased disinclination to use condoms. While 54 per cent of respondents never used condoms with new partners during their last trip, 59 per cent of respondents reported never using condoms with new partners before their last trip.[13] Among the London out-patients, in contrast to the Nottingham findings, age and gender were not associated with reporting a new sexual partner while abroad. Instead, reporting a new partner was associated with having travelled on an overland tour, having paid for sex in the past five years and having been treated for a sexually transmitted disease in the past five years.[14]

Sexual mixing patterns among travellers are not random and most epidemiological interest attaches to sexual partnerships between persons from different countries. However, it seems that a substantial proportion of new sexual partnerships are formed between travellers from the same country. A study of Swedish male travellers aged 19–21 years found a three-way split in the countries of origin of their casual sexual partners: a third were Swedish female tourists, a third were tourists from other countries and a third were women in the 'host' country.[15] In the London out-patients study, respondents were grouped into those from so-called 'WHO Pattern I' countries (i.e. Western Europe, North America and Australasia), sub-Saharan Africa, Asia and the Rest of the World (only six respondents fell into the two latter categories). Of the new partners of Pattern I respondents, 56 per cent were themselves from Pattern I countries; 73 per cent of the partners of respondents from sub-Saharan Africa were also from sub-Saharan Africa.[16]

Men who have sex with men are thought to be relatively frequent travellers: they have fewer children and are more likely to be in social classes I and II, with consequently greater disposable income.[17] However, studies of travellers' risk practices in clinic samples report too few men who have sex with men to allow separate analysis.[18] And purposive samples drawn from gay organizations, gay publications or gay bars do not normally distinguish in their analyses between sexual risk behaviour conducted locally and that conducted abroad.[19] Among a sample of Colombian men reporting receptive anal intercourse, international travel was weakly associated with HIV infection, but sexual contact with foreign visitors to Colombia was much more strongly associated with HIV infection[20] – a

necessary reminder of the Janus-faced nature of international travel, one country's traveller being another country's visitor.

Commercial sexual risk behaviour

Recourse to commercial sexual partners is a relatively uncommon activity. In the NATSSAL survey 6.8 per cent of male respondents reported that they had paid for sex with a woman at some point in their lives and only 1.8 per cent reported that they had done so within the past five years.[21] However, paying for sex was relatively more common among those men whose work took them away from home.[22] In the Swiss telephone survey 1.2 per cent of the men had paid for sex abroad in the previous nine months.[23] Thus, although paying for sex is a minority practice, it is relatively more common among persons travelling abroad.

Prostitution is an international industry and 'sex tourism' is an important phenomenon. It is perceived in visitor countries and host countries alike as a significant route of HIV infection. In the Dominican Republic, a well-known sex tourism destination for North Americans, reporting sex with a tourist was the best predictor of HIV-positivity in a case control study of Dominican women seeking HIV testing.[24] The term 'sex tourist' is convenient but inaccurate in that it implies that the persons concerned are exclusively holiday-makers. In fact, the provision of prostitute partners is sometimes an aspect of corporate hospitality, particularly among Japanese firms.[25] Sex tourism is overwhelmingly a male activity, The Gambia being the only notable sex tourism destination for female visitors.

Companion studies of German-speaking heterosexual and homosexual sex tourists in Thailand present somewhat different patterns of risk.[26] In their first study of 152 heterosexual respondents 46 per cent never wore condoms in their contacts with Thai women, a much higher level of commercial sexual risk behaviour than is reported in prostitution contacts in Germany. While this may be partially attributable to the power relationship between sex tourists and Third World prostitutes which makes the women less able than First World prostitutes to insist on condom use, the authors suggest that a further reason lies in the reluctance of many men to see the relationship as a commercial one. Many men viewed the relationship as a 'holiday romance', two-thirds of the respondents spending several days with their Thai 'date'. The women unintentionally collude in this fiction, since it is regarded as shameful not to show any affection towards their clients.[27] In Urry's phrase, there is a 'tourist gaze' which organizes and constructs the traveller's experiences, sexual experiences included, in particular ways.[28]

In contrast, the gay sex tourists in Bangkok reported less penetrative sex (less than 50 per cent reported insertive anal intercourse and 25 per cent reported receptive anal intercourse) and more consistent condom use in penetrative sexual encounters. However, they also reported more sex partners during their stay than the heterosexual sex tourists.[29]

Prostitutes as well as clients may be geographically mobile. Some of these women are free agents (see, for example, the description by Pickering et al.[30] of the movements of prostitute women from Senegal and Guinea-Bissau working in The Gambia), while others appear to have been constrained and lured into highly exploitative prostitution.[31] This traffic occurs between Third World countries (e.g. the sending of Burmese women into Thai brothels), between Third World and First World countries, and (most recently) between East and West Europe.[32] About half the female prostitutes in Holland are believed to be of foreign origin.[33] Many male street prostitutes in Amsterdam, Berlin, Hamburg and Vienna are from Eastern Europe.[34] Many of the transvestite prostitutes in Milan and other Italian cities are from Brazil.[35]

Risk behaviour among travel, transport and tourism workers

Travel, transport and tourism workers can play an important role in HIV spread by providing links between local networks of sexual contacts. Early on in the HIV epidemic it was noticed that infection rates were highest in those districts of East and Central Africa which abutted major highways. It has been suggested that lorry drivers and their assistants may have played an important unwitting role in transmitting the virus between different local prostitute populations along the highways. This is the 'core groups' hypothesis,[36] a modern version of an old story: 'If a man be burnt with a harlot, and do meddle with another woman…he shall burn the woman that he shall meddle withal' (Andrew Boord, 1547).[37] Levels of HIV infection among East African lorry drivers and their assistants are certainly high – 35 per cent among those passing through a transport depot in Uganda.[38] However, this core transmitter group role may be of locally variable importance: in The Gambia Pickering and her colleagues found that prostitute women were themselves highly geographically mobile, making lorry drivers unnecessary as a linking population;[39] a third local pattern was found in a study of prostitution at the isolated commercial fishing stations along Lake Kariba in Zimbabwe, where prostitute women from the towns would visit the fishing stations but would often pay for their lorry or boat transport with sexual services.[40]

Lorry drivers are by no means the only transport workers to be singled out for attention. Studies of seafarers show them to be between five and twenty times more likely than other males to contract gonorrhoea;[41] 42 per cent of the known AIDS cases in Bulgaria in 1991 were international seafarers.[42] And the vilification of a deceased Air Canada steward as the 'Patient Zero' of the American HIV/AIDS epidemic is one of the less attractive features of Shilts' gripping social history of the epidemic.[43]

Persons working in tourist industries, such as bar and hotel staff, also report high levels of risk behaviour with tourist partners. A survey of 386 migrant tourist industry workers in the UK resort of Torbay reported that only 7 per cent of tourist workers had not engaged in intercourse in the past year; nearly half the male workers had engaged in intercourse with four or more tourists. Levels of condom use were low with only 40 per cent using a condom during their last intercourse; levels of condom use were lower still among those respondents reporting the most partners.[44]

Syringe-sharing by travellers

Although there have been a few reports of travellers acquiring HIV infection through medical treatment (contaminated injecting equipment or blood supplies), it should be emphasized that international travellers are currently at very low risk of such infection.[45] It is syringe-sharing by travelling injecting drug users (IDUs) that is much the more epidemiologically important phenomenon. Several studies of local samples of IDUs have established that respondents are highly mobile and that many have injected drugs abroad; interviews with 919 Glaswegian IDUs in 1990 and 1991 revealed that 6 per cent had shared needles and syringes outside Glasgow in the previous two years.[46]

HIV infection among drug users is by no means a problem confined to the developed world. Every developing country that is on a drug trafficking route, from Nagaland to Nigeria, has its own indigenous population of IDUs: HIV infection has followed those drug trafficking routes. The characteristic pattern of the HIV epidemic among IDUs has been one of sudden explosions of infection, followed by near stabilization of HIV prevalence.[47] The Edinburgh epidemic was an early example, but there have been better documented instances in more recent years. In Manipur, the Indian state that borders the 'Golden Triangle' of opium cultivation in Burma, Laos and Thailand, the prevalence of HIV among local injectors rose from nothing in September 1989 to 54 per cent in June 1990; the researchers believe that the appearance of the virus is associated with heroin smuggling from Burma.[48] The similar epidemic among Thai IDUs in 1987 proved to be the precursor to a general heterosexual epidemic, as a consequence of the ties between drug injection and prostitution.[49]

Injecting drug users clearly may travel for a wide range of reasons that have nothing to do with drug trafficking. They may travel as holiday-makers, for business reasons, or as transport workers: another recent Indian study reports that 2.4 per cent of a large sample of lorry drivers along the National Highway of the North-Eastern States were heroin injectors.[50] Whatever the reasons they may have for travelling, they will be reluctant to carry injecting equipment through border check-points for fear of being identified as a drugs trafficker; the fear of carrying their own injecting equipment may make them more vulnerable to syringe-sharing.

It is also clear that certain cities, most notably Amsterdam, attract large numbers of non-nationals seeking to obtain and consume drugs, a phenomenon sometimes called 'drugs tourism'. Arnhem, a Dutch border town of around 100,000 inhabitants, attracts repeated visits (an average of eight visits per year) from large numbers (500–800) of German drug users.[51] HIV-infected drug users may also be attracted to certain cities by locally superior drugs services. This is said to be a factor in attracting Irish IDUs to London.

Conclusion

Information currently available on travellers' HIV-related risk practices is fragmentary. Much more information is needed, both on general samples of travellers, and on purposive samples of particular small but important subgroups of the travelling population. Among the latter, concerns about sex tourists, drugs tourists, transport workers and tourism workers have already been noted. Discussions at the UK's Medical Research Council's 1993 AIDS Programme Workshop also highlighted the lack of information on possible risk behaviour by members of ethnic minority communities visiting relatives and/or business colleagues in developing countries.

Information already gathered suggests that there is indeed a liminal or disinhibiting effect of travel which may result in greater rates of partner change among travellers. However, this liminal effect may be proportionately greater for women than for men. And although it may result in greater partner change, it does not result in a greater propensity to engage in unprotected sex with those new partners. Moreover, sexual mixing patterns among travellers are skewed and new partners are likely to be recruited disproportionately from among travellers' fellow nationals. Demographic data on those travellers most likely to report new partners show differences between different studies, but are largely predictable: men are more likely to report new partners than women; single persons (and unaccompanied travellers) are more likely to report new partners than those with a steady partner; younger persons are more likely to report a new partner than older persons; persons who have recently paid for sex and/or had a recent sexually transmitted disease are also more likely to report a new partner.

Concern in the developed world about travellers' risk practices often centres, implicitly or explicitly, upon the 'importation' of infection. This is epidemiologically naive as well as ethnocentric. All countries should be equally concerned with the exportation as well as the importation of infection. In combating a global epidemic with ten million casualties that has rolled silently through every frontier, xenophobic policies, practices and pronouncements have no place.

1 K. Choi, M. Kim, J. Catania et al. 'First HIV seroprevalence survey in South Korea', [abstract M.C. 3235], VII International Conference on AIDS, Florence, 1991.

2 Public Health Laboratory Service, 'The incidence and prevalence of AIDS and other severe HIV disease in England and Wales for 1992–97: projections using data to the end of June 1992.

Report of a working group convened by the Director of the Public Health Laboratory Service (Revised Day Report)', Communicable Disease Report, 3, Supplement 1, 1993.

3 A. Noone, N. MacDonald, B. Evans, J. Heptonstall, 'HIV transmission, travel and Thailand', letter, Lancet, 305: 892, 1992.

4 N. Gilmore, A. Orkin, M. Duckett, S. Grover, 'International travel and AIDS', *AIDS*, 3, Supplement 1: S225–S230, 1989.

5 M. Haour-Knipe, *Migrants and Travellers Group: Final Report* (Assessing AIDS Prevention. EC Concerted Action on Assessment of HIV/AIDS Preventive Strategies). Institut universitaire de médecine sociale et préventive, Lausanne, 1991.

6 A. Johnson *et al. Sexual Attitudes and Lifestyles*. Blackwell, Oxford, 1993.

7 H. Houweling, R. Coutinho, 'Risk of HIV infection among Dutch expatriates in sub-Saharan Africa', *International Journal of STD and AIDS*, 2: 252–257, 1991.

8 L. Bonneux, P. van der Stuyft, H. Taelman *et al.* 'Risk factors for infection with human immunodeficiency virus among European expatriates in Africa', *British Medical Journal*, 297: 581–584, 1988.

9 D. Hausser, E. Zimmerman, F. Dubois-Arber, F. Paccaud, *Evaluation of the AIDS Prevention Strategy in Switzerland: Third Assessment Report, 1989–1990*. Institut universitaire de médecine sociale et préventive, Lausanne, 1991.

10 P. Gillies, R. Slack, N. Stoddart, S. Conway, 'HIV-related risk behaviour in UK holidaymakers', *AIDS*, 6: 339–342, 1992.

S. Conway, P. Gillies, R. Slack, *The Health of Travellers*. Department of Public Health and Epidemiology, University of Nottingham, 1990.

11 S. Conway, P. Gillies, R. Slack, *The Health of Travellers*, p. 41.

12 S. Hawkes, G. Hart, A. Johnson *et al.* 'Risk behaviour and HIV prevalence in international travellers', *AIDS*, 8: 247–252, 1994.

13 S. Hawkes, 'International travellers and mixing', paper presented to MRC AIDS Directed Programme Workshop, University of Sussex, Brighton, 1993.

14 S. Hawkes, G. Hart, A. Johnson *et al.* 'Risk behaviour and HIV prevalence in international travellers', *AIDS*, 8: 247–252, 1994.

15 P. Maardh, I. Kallings, 'Tourism has a great impact on the epidemiology of sexually transmitted diseases: emphasis on a European perspective', *Tourist Health* (ed. W. Pasini). WHO Collaborating Centre for Tourist Health and Medicine, Rimini, 1990. Cited in Hendriks, note (31).

16 S. Hawkes, G. Hart, A. Johnson *et al.* 'Risk behaviour and HIV prevalence in international travellers', *AIDS*, 8: 247–252, 1994.

17 A. Johnson *et al. Sexual Attitudes and Lifestyles*. Blackwell, Oxford, 1993.

18 S. Hawkes, G. Hart, A. Johnson *et al.* 'Risk behaviour and HIV prevalence in international travellers', *AIDS*, 8: 247–252, 1994.

19 P. Davies, F. Hickson, P. Weatherburn, A. Hunt, *Sex, Gay Men and AIDS*. Falmer, Brighton, 1993.

20 N. Merino, R. Sanchez, A. Munoz *et al.* 'HIV-1, sexual practices and contact with foreigners in homosexual men in Colombia, South America', *Journal of Acquired Immune Deficiency Syndromes*, 3: 330–334, 1990.

21 A. Johnson *et al. Sexual Attitudes and Lifestyles*. Blackwell, Oxford, 1993.

22 *Ibid.*

23 D. Hausser, E. Zimmerman, F. Dubois-Arber, F. Paccaud, *Evaluation of the AIDS Prevention Strategy in Switzerland: Third Assessment Report, 1989–1990*. Institut universitaire de médecine sociale et préventive, Lausanne, 1991.

24 M. Espinal, E. Koenig, M. Lavandera, 'Sex tourism and HIV: a hazardous association in the Dominican Republic', [abstract PO-D10-3675], *IX International Conference on AIDS*, Berlin, 1993.

25 S. Vorakitphokatorn, R. Cash, 'Factors that determine condom use among traditionally high drug users: Japanese and commercial sex workers in Bangkok, Thailand', [abstract PoD 5237], *VIII International Conference on AIDS*, Amsterdam, 1992.

26 M. Wilke, D. Kleiber, 'AIDS and sex tourism', [abstract WC 3361], *VII International Conference on AIDS*, Florence, 1991.

M. Wilke, D. Kleiber, 'Sexual behaviour of gay German sex-tourists in Thailand', [abstract PoD

5239], *VIII International Conference on AIDS*, Amsterdam, 1992.

27 M. Wilke, D. Kleiber, 'AIDS and sex tourism', [abstract WC 3361], *VII International Conference on AIDS*, Florence, 1991.

28 J. Urry, *The Tourist Gaze: Leisure and Travel in Contemporary Societies*. Sage, London, 1990.

29 M. Wilke, D. Kleiber, 'Sexual behaviour of gay German sex-tourists in Thailand', [abstract PoD 5239], *VIII International Conference on AIDS*, Amsterdam, 1992.

30 H. Pickering, J. Todd, D. Dunn *et al*. 'Prostitutes and their clients: a Gambian survey', *Social Science and Medicine*, 34: 75–88, 1992.

31 A. Hendriks, *AIDS and Mobility: The Impact of International Mobility on the Spread of HIV and the Need and Possibility for AIDS/HIV Prevention Programmes*. EUR/HFA Target 4, Copenhagen: WHO, 1991.

32 *Ibid*.

33 S. Biersteker, *Internationally Working Prostitutes from Developing Countries*, Report of the Expert Meeting on AIDS and Mobility, Amsterdam, 1–2 March, 1991. Cited in Hendriks (31).

34 A. Hendriks, *AIDS and Mobility: The Impact of International Mobility on the Spread of HIV and the Need and Possibility for AIDS/HIV Prevention Programmes*. EUR/HFA Target 4, Copenhagen: WHO, 1991.

35 M. Galli, S. Antinori, R. Esposito *et al*. 'Seroprevalence of HIV-1 among South American and Italian transvestites active in prostitution in Milan', [abstract F.C.549], *VI International Conference on AIDS*, San Francisco, 1990.

36 F. Plummer, N. Nagelkerke, S. Moses *et al*. 'The importance of core groups in the epidemiology and control of HIV-1 infection', *AIDS*, 5: 327–335, 1991.

37 A. Boord, *Breviary of Helthe*, 1547. Cited in M. Waugh, editorial, *Journal of the Royal Society of Medicine*, 82: 319–320, 1989.

38 J. Carswell, G. Lloyd, J. Howells, 'Prevalence of HIV-1 in East African lorry drivers', *AIDS*, 3: 759–761, 1989.

39 H. Pickering, J. Todd, D. Dunn *et al*. 'Prostitutes and their clients: a Gambian survey', *Social Science and Medicine*, 34: 75–88, 1992.

40 D. Wilson, D. Mavesere, R. Katuria, 'Ethnographic and quantitative research to design a community-based intervention among commercial fishermen on Lake Kariba, Zimbabwe', [abstract W.D.4042], *VII International Conference on AIDS*, Florence, 1991.

41 P. Vuksanovic, A. Low, 'Venereal diseases and AIDS among seafarers', *Travel Medicine*, 9: 121–123, 1991.

42 E. Kabakchieva, 'AIDS and travellers in Bulgaria', *Abstract Book on AIDS and Mobility*. National Committee on AIDS Control, Amsterdam, 1991. Cited in Hendriks (31).

43 R. Shilts, *And the Band Played On*. Penguin, Harmondsworth, 1987.

44 N. Ford, 'Safer sex in tourist resorts', *World Health Forum*, 13: 77–80, 1992.

45 J. Chin, 'HIV and international travel', *Global Iimpact of AIDS* (eds. A. Fleming *et al*.). Alan Liss, New York, 1988.

46 D. Goldberg, M Frischer, A. Taylor *et al*. 'Mobility of Scottish drug users and risk of HIV infection', *European Journal of Epidemiology*, in press.

47 M. Bloor, M. Frischer, A. Taylor *et al*. 'Tideline and turn? Possible reasons for the continuing low HIV prevalence among Glasgow's injecting drug users', *Sociological Review*, in press.

48 T. Naik, S. Sarkar, H. Singh *et al*. 'Intravenous drug users – a new high risk group for HIV infection in India', *AIDS*, 5: 117–118, 1991.

49 N. Ford, S. Koetsawang, 'The socio-cultural context of the transmission of HIV in Thailand', *Social Science and Medicine*, 33: 1–10, 1991.

50 S. Ahmed, 'Truck drivers as a vulnerable group in N.E. India', [abstract PO-C08-2773], *IX International Conference on AIDS*, Berlin, 1993.

51 M. Grapendaal, R. Aidala, *Duitse drugsverslaafden in Arnhem*. Ministerie van Justitie, The Hague, 1991. Cited in Hendriks (31). [Nl]

People who Move: Developing HIV/AIDS Prevention Programmes in Multicultural Settings

Mary Haour-Knipe

Institut universitaire de médecine sociale et préventive, Lausanne, Switzerland

That Europe's migration situation is undergoing rapid change is beyond question. This chapter discusses some of the major principles emerging from a survey of HIV/AIDS prevention programmes for migrants and ethnic minorities in European countries.[1] The premise is that these same principles can be applied to major employment settings, where personnel at any given site may include people from many different cultures, and where employees are sent abroad for sojourns in which they, themselves, in turn become 'foreigners'. After briefly discussing who the migrants are in today's Europe, we present some of the main problems arising when it comes to HIV/AIDS prevention in multicultural situations, and some ways of sidestepping the problems.[2]

First, however, it is essential to spell out the reasoning behind the programmes, or just why 'migrants', or 'ethnic minorities', are of concern for HIV/AIDS prevention.

Programme planners occasionally describe 'migrants' (or 'ethnic minorities', or a given ethnic group), globally, to be at particularly elevated risk of transmission of HIV. The parallel is sometimes made to sexually transmitted diseases, where it is sometimes argued that rates may be higher for foreign than for host populations. For reasons that will be a main theme of this chapter, this particular line of argument has been rejected. However, there are several other reasons why migrants are of concern for AIDS prevention:

Worldwide differences in HIV patterns and knowledge levels: migrants move from one country to another, and thus are particularly affected by worldwide differences in both HIV patterns and prevention efforts. Being in a high incidence country (Switzerland, France, or the United States, for example) with a low level of prevention knowledge can be dangerous.

Social inequalities: social inequalities in health persist, and the spread of HIV and AIDS is very much related to them. In developed countries migrants often tend to live in economic, sanitary, and housing situations less adequate than that of the host population. They may be more subject to unemployment and to poverty, and also to racism. Migrant health often falls between gaps of programmes, especially where prevention is concerned, and some migrants may not even have access to adequate healthcare.

Potential risk situation: the situation of some migrants or members of ethnic minorities may lead to potential exposure to risk, for example because of:

- lack of access to information and to healthcare;
- linguistic and cultural difficulties in comprehending prevention messages (for example because of profoundly different approaches to, and attitudes concerning, sexuality in its various permutations);
- particularities in living situation (for example because of legal restrictions on family reunification);
- social and economic difficulties which could lead to high-risk behaviours.

Who are Europe's migrants today?

Migration patterns mirror both world economic development and world political events. They reflect, in yesterday's Europe, the sequels of wars and of colonialism and the waves of labour migration that occurred during the 1970s' economic expansion. In today's Europe they are reflected in people seeking asylum, as well as being influenced by the radical changes in Central and Eastern European countries.

The result of many different migration patterns, under the label 'migrants', 'foreigners' or 'ethnic minorities' in European countries are people of extremely diverse origins, who live in equally diverse situations in their host countries: it would be difficult to buy food in England or in France outside usual hours if it were not for the Pakistani or the Algerian small shop owner. The Italian who went to Switzerland as a labourer in the early 1970s may now be trying to decide whether to retire in his village as he had always intended, or near the grandchildren beginning to arrive to his children, who are now Swiss. The former Hungar-ian, Czech, Chilean, or Vietnamese refugee may also have faced a dilemma around the dream of going back.

The migrant arriving in Europe today is most likely coming to join a loved one, or may be a Northern European teacher retiring in Spain. He may be a Portuguese youth hoping to earn enough money to start his own business, coming with his girlfriend to work in a hotel. She may be from the Philippines, cleaning peoples' houses and without a work permit, or her boss, trying to cope with both young children and a career as an executive or a diplomat. The would-be immigrant might be a qualified mechanic from Poland, or computer programmer from the United States, both ignoring advice that it will be impossible to find a job once they arrive. The African in Portugal, in France, or in Belgium could be a scholarship student from a former colony, or someone with minimal, or no, education in precarious underpaid employment. The asylum seeker may be fleeing from war in Bosnia or Kosovo, Afghanistan or Angola, or may be a desperate 'mule', intestines stuffed with bags of drugs.

Reactions from the host countries are similarly varied. Although attempts are being made to harmonize official migration policies in view of the development of a common Europe, these still vary widely from country to country, as do policies concerning assimilation and according citizenship. If twin brothers, for example, had moved together from Turkey fifteen years ago, the brother who moved to Germany would still be a foreign 'guest worker' while his twin in Sweden would likely be Swedish by now. On a less official level we find both signs of growing integration, such as an increasing rate of mixed marriages, and alarmingly increasing incidents of racism and xenophobia.

It is this latter note, fear of foreigners, that brings us to the theme of stigma.

A major problem: stigma and the fear of stigma

A major problem found to concern HIV/AIDS prevention among ethnic minorities in all countries was that of targeting prevention efforts without simultaneously stigmatizing a group which may already be marginalized. People in host countries may have subliminal fears of 'disease-bringing foreigners', whilst people in minority communities may, in turn, feel unfairly singled out and threatened when they are mentioned in even remote conjunction with a stigmatized disease such as AIDS.

Certain diseases have always carried stigma, classically defined as: 'an attribute that is deeply discrediting, something that reduces the person in front of us from a whole and usual person to a tainted, discounted one.'[3] Epilepsy, haemophilia, cancer, alcoholism, and most mental illnesses are classical examples of stigmatized diseases. In its most primitive form, stigmatization is a way of categorizing persons, establishing the boundaries of the good through the identification of the wicked, the boundaries of the normal by the abnormal.[4]

Stigmatization is also a feature of epidemic diseases, for example plague, cholera, leprosy, syphilis, tuberculosis, and later AIDS, as discussed elsewhere in this book. Epidemics of communicable disease create uncertainty, and tend to be accompanied by epidemics of fear and suspicion, focusing not only on individuals affected by the disease, but also on those belonging to groups suspected of being vectors of it.

It is here that foreigners and aliens become vulnerable: since they are already 'other', aliens need not be split off in order to be blamed for bringing disease. Plague and cholera, thus, came from elsewhere, brought by soldiers, seamen, merchants.

Discussions of quarantine and of border controls often occur in relation to epidemics of contagious diseases. During mediaeval epidemics, for example that of bubonic plague which struck Europe in the fourteenth and fifteenth century, deaths were in many instances attributed to the sole physical presence of aliens, setting off waves of persecution of communities of those thought to have introduced and spread the disease.

Comparisons are particularly instructive with diseases seen as revealing and punishing moral laxity or turpitude. Syphilis, particularly, has throughout the ages been systematically attributed to the country next door: the French disease for the English, the Italian disease for the French, the Spanish disease for the Italians, the Polish disease for the Russians, and the Chinese disease for the Japanese. A social history of venereal disease in the United States offers striking examples concerning a disease which 'had become, preeminently, a disease of the "other", be it the other race, the other class, the other ethnic group'.[5] Over a period of ten years around the turn of the century more than two-thirds of a million Europeans crossed the Atlantic, the massive influx eventually stimulating fear that 'degenerate racial stocks' would pollute the gene pool of those already settled, or outnumber the respectable middle class. The 1891 Immigration Act excluding 'persons suffering from a loathsome or dangerous contagious disease' codified the part of the fear crystallized around venereal disease.

In arguments curiously presaging things said about HIV today, some experts singled out immigrant populations as particularly prone to infection: some suggested that poor urban conditions contributed to immorality and the spread of venereal diseases. The number of immigrants actually found to be infected remained low, but those who did not want to be convinced were not: critics suggested that the low number of such diseases found among immigrants revealed only that they had not been examined adequately. It was feared that venereal disease would spread to the local middle class via foreign-born prostitutes.

Today, if 'the war against AIDS' has, by definition, to be fought against an enemy, it is, of course, far easier that an enemy be foreign. Communities and governments have tended to first deny, then to blame someone else: homosexuals, drug users, Haitians, Africans, US seamen, Filipino prostitutes, Europeans, foreigners, depending on where one is sitting. In Africa, AIDS was for years often called the 'European' or the 'American' disease, whilst in Europe and in the United States lively popular and scientific debates attempted to place the origins of the epidemic in Africa. Studies of discussion groups in the United Kingdom, for example, have explored peoples' tendency to see the continent next door as a generalized non-differentiated mass, without specific cultures or different AIDS epidemics.

In sum, foreigners, migrants, or ethnic minorities, are particularly liable to stigmatization where HIV and AIDS are concerned. What repercussion has this potential for stigmatization had on prevention programmes? In 1988, seven years after the start of the epidemic and some three years after the first general population information campaigns in Europe, prevention programmes for migrants were just beginning. Two contradictory (or perhaps complementary) processes are at work.

First, migrants, as 'other', or 'not us', are usually marginalized in the countries in which they are living, and foreign or migrant populations are not usually a priority for country public health programmes. Migrants are thus ignored.

The root of the second process has less to do with the migrants themselves, than with the people working with them. Those who might be responsible for pro-grammes or for policies may be afraid of stigmatization. In many instances fear of stigmatization has caused delay in establishment of programmes for migrants. Not knowing how to tackle the problem, being afraid of damaging the target group, they do nothing. Migrants are thus overprotected.

Towards overcoming the problems

Although they began several years after those for host country residents, most Western European countries now have HIV/AIDS prevention programmes for migrants.

Generally speaking programmes are of three types: government-sponsored, those of non-governmental organizations, and what can best be described as informal *ad hoc*. The latter category includes some of the most interesting and creative work being done, although often on the simple basis that it needs to be done, and with very little or no funding.

As for more official government-sponsored programmes for migrants, the first had already begun in 1986, a discreet programme in Brussels, assessing knowledge and attitudes before starting to work with the African community. The first larger national programmes for ethnic minorities were established in 1988 in The Netherlands and the United Kingdom, followed during 1989 and 1990 by programmes developed in at least seven other Western European countries, including Germany, France, Norway, Sweden, and Switzerland.

Definition of the target group and bases of programmes

As for stigmatization, if stigmatizing means cutting off, separating, making 'others' different from oneself, the opposite is to stress solidarity. Some national HIV/AIDS prevention campaigns, in the United Kingdom, The Netherlands, and Sweden for example, have approached the problems of racism and xenophobia by putting a multicultural accent on messages addressed to the general population. Posters, for example, might show people obviously of many different races and cultures.

Another level of stigmatization is found in the very definition of the target group. It is much easier to marginalize 'others' if they are part of an undifferentiated mass. Subtle distinctions which recognize cultural and other differences, and for which specific images and messages have been carefully chosen and tested, have a better chance of getting the appropriate message through. Such distinctions also have a vastly better chance of rendering the programme acceptable as they imply respect for the target group. Thus, instead of addressing 'ethnic minorities', or 'migrants' or 'foreign workers' as though such were a homogeneous group, programmes in France, Denmark, Sweden, Switzerland, Italy, or the United Kingdom, for example, may specifically address newly arriving asylum seekers, language teachers, commercial sex workers, middle level managers, adolescents, gays or hospital cleaning staff from Brazil, Spain, Pakistan, Turkey, Zaire, Bosnia…

An important corollary concerns the very basis of a prevention programme for migrants. Many national HIV/AIDS prevention programmes have eliminated the notion of 'risk group' as potentially stigmatizing, focusing as it does on categories of individuals rather than on the real target of interventions, risky behaviours. Along the same lines, and as mentioned in the introduction, an HIV/AIDS prevention programme for foreign or migrant populations justified on the basis of a presumption of 'high risk' runs great risk of offending the very people it is trying to reach. In other words, although it may be epidemiologically correct to justify a programme for people from a specific country on the basis of an elevated incidence of HIV in that country, such a programme runs the risk of being perceived as stigmatizing: the message will be perceived as 'people from your country are diseased' which can quickly turn to: 'people from your country are morally inferior'. Whatever its other merits, a programme perceived in this way is hardly likely to be other than offensive, and rejected.

Reframing, redefining the programme on the non-stigmatizing basis of a universal right to information neatly sidesteps the problem. In other words, a programme is based on the idea that migrants, just as anyone else, have the right to know, and, moreover, to be informed in the terms of their own language and culture. Calculations of relative risk do not enter into the equation since the programme is based on the idea that we are all potentially at risk.

Paradoxically, approached this way, the very people the 'high risk' strategy was trying to reach may well then become the most engaged. Certainly we now know that communities affected have mobilized among the most effectively: people best hear HIV/AIDS prevention messages when they have been personally touched. As for migrants, experience in several countries would seem to indicate that people from high incidence countries are not only receptive listeners to non-stigmatizing prevention messages in European host country prevention programmes, they may also be among the first volunteers to become 'mediators', to receive training to educate others.

Working with the community

A second basic set of principles for establishing HIV/AIDS prevention programmes for migrants, infinitely easier to state than to manage on a daily basis, involves working with the community, in synergy between 'top–down' and 'bottom–up' community-based programmes.

As those readers who have been sojourned abroad as expatriates will know, migrant, or foreign, populations tend to live in an 'us'–'them' world with the local society. What happens in the local society is very often perceived as having nothing to do with 'us.' Whether he is a restaurant worker, a grocery shop owner, or a businessman, many a foreigner will not bother to read the HIV prevention information from national programmes that appears in his mail box, and may not even perceive the posters from the host country: information that concerns 'them' is simply not pertinent. What he will be more likely to hear are messages coming from the employer, or from his own community in the host country.

HIV/AIDS prevention work requires frank discussion of intimacy and relations between the sexes; about sex, not in general but in detail, from acknowledging the possibility that sex partners may not be entirely faithful, to demonstrating how to unroll a condom, to talking about vaginal fluids and anal intercourse. It requires talking about injecting drugs, thereby implying one might do so, or that one's children might do so. It requires talking about risk taking, about responsibility for others, about illness and dying.

That such discussions can occur between people of different cultures is beyond doubt, but it is hardly likely that adequate dialogue can be established if those who are trying to do the informing are perceived as an alien 'them'. Programmes for migrants or for ethnic minorities thus require working with and through community or target groups at all phases, from determination of needs to evaluation. Gradually expanding networks and relations of confidence are keys.

At the same time there are now several international networks of people and projects working with various ethnic minority or immigrant populations, starting with the AIDS and Mobility Project in Amsterdam.

Among others is a network of Turkish expatriates active throughout several countries, an important migrants and ethnic minorities component to the EuroCASO council of AIDS service organizations, and the NAZ Project working with South Asian, Turkish, Iranian, and Arab communities out of London, throughout Europe and to the home countries.

Such organizations assure that interventions with their target communities are culturally appropriate, and that needs are defined and integrated into the programme from within the community itself. Some highly sensitive subjects, also, are much easier to approach from within than from without. One example specific to migrants is the delicate problem of people becoming infected during visits to their home countries of high HIV prevalence. The NAZ Project information on travelling abroad,[6] developed by people from Southern Asia and exposing problems of availability of condoms and risks from untested blood 'in many of our home countries', will undoubtedly be better received than the same information prepared by the host country, which may be perceived as implying, at best, that 'your country is dangerous'.

Some unanswered questions

Substantial progress has been made in establishing HIV/AIDS prevention programmes for migrants and ethnic minority communities in European countries in the past five years, but, if there is some room for some satisfaction, there is none at all for complacency. Many programmes were established on the basis of urgent need, and even the best established programmes are currently under-funded, and of precarious future. Not all programmes were properly thought out or grounded in the communities they were meant to serve: some disappear rapidly, leaving behind a climate of resentment and distrust, or having exhausted committed workers. There is need for both rigorous programme evaluation and supportive collaboration and co-operation. Links must also be forged between workers and programmes in host countries and those in countries of origin since there is much reason to think that knowledge could flow in both directions.

Migration is hardly likely to cease, and several issues yet need addressing: new populations will bring new challenges. Several dilemmas and questions have appeared, and need working out, such as the need for a link between HIV/AIDS prevention and care where migrants are concerned, and the ethical conundrums that are raised.

Conclusions

Whilst catastrophic predictions concerning an approaching epidemic are perhaps useful as a tool to alert those who should be responsible for establishing programmes, they have a pernicious element, implying that hope is useless. It is not. Research has shown that AIDS prevention campaigns do work, but under certain conditions.

The fact that HIV is transmissible long before it is clinically evident means that protection must be voluntary, and in addition that individuals be convinced enough so that they change some of their most intimate behaviours. Coercive measures have been shown to be singularly ineffective, leading to resistance, to rejection, and also to a false sense of security among those who believe that they need thus not take precautions, as discussed elsewhere in this volume. Effective prevention thus requires the co-operation of individuals, and people are willing to make the behavioural changes required if they:

1. feel personally affected;

2. feel solidarity.

In this article I have focused on a main theme in HIV/AIDS prevention for migrants or ethnic minorities – stigmatization. There are several points of comparison between HIV/AIDS prevention for migrants and that in business community employee programmes, starting with the fact that multinational companies, by definition, and at all levels of labour and management, both employ people who are of a culture different from that of the country in which they are living, and send employees to work as foreigners abroad.

Stigmatizing leads to resistance, and to rejection. An HIV/AIDS prevention programme in a multicultural setting must thus be formulated so that it does not single out any particular group as especially 'at risk'. Rather than being based on any notion of increased risk, a programme should be based on a universal right to know. In other words the programme must be grounded in respect, in the conviction that members of the target group are capable of responsible choices, or ultimately, in an 'obstinate faith in ultimate human decency'.[7]

A second basic principle for AIDS prevention in a multicultural setting was also formulated, that of working in true collaboration with people from the target group at all levels of the programme, from planning to evaluation. Taking this a step further, we have also stressed the necessity for building bridges between people working with similar populations, across national, and programme boundaries.

Finally, I have shown how stigmatization of foreigners in relation to HIV and to AIDS falls on a fertile terrain of unease concerning foreigners and diseases in general. The nineteenth-century American fear of disease-bringing foreigners was the crystallization of a more general fear of being invaded by immigrants. It is at least possible that today's fears of HIV-positive foreigners also reflects a more generalized fear of being invaded by Third World refugees. Whether or not we are able to do something about the world social inequities that cause massive population movements, what we can do is to 'start in our own back garden'. Just as they now deal with drugs, alcohol, and smoking, firms have a vital role to play in establishing effective programmes to address the people who work for them, of whatever culture, about HIV and AIDS, making it impossible, for pragmatic if not for ethical reasons, for people to feel: 'it's not my problem'.

Further reading

Frankenberg, R. 'The other who is the same: epidemics in space and time', conference paper, *Youth and AIDS*, 1988.

Haour-Knipe, M. *Migrants and Travellers Group: Final Report*, European Community Concerted Action on Assessment of AIDS/HIV Preventive Strategies, Doc. 72, Institut universitaire de médecine sociale et préventive, Lausanne, 1991.

Haour-Knipe, M. 'AIDS prevention, stigma and migrant status', *Medical Sociology Research on Chronic Illness* (eds. T. Abel, S. Geyer, U. Gerhardt, W. van den Heuvel, J. Siegrist). Informationszentrum Sozialwissenschaften, Bonn, 1993.

Haour-Knipe, M. 'AIDS prevention, stigma and migrant status', *Innovation in Social Science Research*, 6 (1), pp. 19–35, 1993.

Haour-Knipe, M. and Dubois-Arber, F. 'Minorities, immigrants and HIV/AIDS epidemiology: concerns about the use and quality of data', *European Journal of Public Health*, 3, pp. 259–63, 1993.

Kitzinger, J. and Miller, D. 'African AIDS: the media and audience beliefs', *AIDS: Rights, Risk and Reason* (eds. P. Aggleton, P. Davies, G. Hart), pp. 28–52. Falmer, London, 1992.

Organization for Economic Co-Operation and Development, *Trends in International Migration (SOPEMI), 1988 and 1989*. Paris, 1989 and 1990.

Packard, R. and Epstein, P. 'Epidemiologists, social scientists, and the structure of medical research on AIDS in Africa', *Social Science and Medicine*, 33 (7), pp. 771–94, 1991.

Panos Institute, The Third Epidemic: Repercussions of the Fear of AIDS. Panos, London, 1990.

Sabatier, R. *Blaming Others: Prejudice, Race and Worldwide AIDS*. The Panos Institute, London, 1988.

Sontag, S. *AIDS and its Metaphors*. Penguin, London, 1989.

1 The reflections in this article are drawn from a 1989–91 European Community concerted action monitoring AIDS prevention activities among four population groups: general populations, men having sex with men, injecting drug users, and migrants. The author coordinated the migrants group, for which individuals responsible for prevention programmes in their countries described HIV/AIDS prevention activities for migrants in: Belgium, France, Germany, Greece, Italy, The Netherlands, Norway, Portugal, Spain, Sweden, Switzerland, and the United Kingdom.

2 Much of the content of this chapter has been published in a slightly different form in the articles listed.

3 E. Goffman, *Stigma: Notes on the Management of Spoiled Identity*. Prentice-Hall, Englewood Cliffs, New Jersey, 1963.

4 P. Strong, 'Epidemic psychology: a model', *Sociology of Health and Illness*, 12 (3), pp. 249–59, 1990.

5 A. Brandt, *No Magic Bullet: A Social History of Venereal Disease in the United States Since 1880*. Oxford University Press, Oxford, 1985.

6 NAZ Project, HIV/AIDS Information Pack, 241 King St., London W6 9LP, United Kingdom.

7 A. Schlessinger, 'Eulogy of Willy Brandt', *Reflections*. United Nations Society of Writers, 8 December 1992.

Testing a Policy Decision: What Can Happen When You Screen for HIV

Dr Ronny A. Shtarkshall

Braun School of Public Health and Community Medicine, The Hebrew University and Hadassah, Jerusalem Chairman, Israeli Family Planning Association

Yael Davidson

National Public Health Nursing Supervisor, Ministry of Health, Jerusalem, Israel

In this chapter we examine one major policy decision regarding HIV/AIDS and the consequences it has had for the Ethiopian community in Israel. The decision was to screen all incoming 1991 immigrants from Ethiopia 'inside the gate' for various infectious diseases, including HIV. We also examine some of the conditions that led to this decision, how it was pursued and also where it backfired. We believe that the study of this one policy decision, albeit in a small country such as Israel, has some general value because similar flaws in basic assumptions and procedures can happen anywhere; equally, our proposals for their remedy can be generally applied.

Political background

Over one weekend in May 1991, about 14,500 Ethiopian Jews were airlifted from Addis Ababa to Israel in what became known as 'Operation Solomon'. A further 4,500 immigrants arrived that same year, bringing the total to 19,000 for 1991.[1] Previous waves of immigration had occurred in the early and mid 1980s but were characterized by two main differences. First, the prevalence of HIV in Ethiopia was still very low at the time and, second, the first-wave immigrants had trekked over the rural areas where they originally lived, across the Sudanese borders and from there had reached Israel by various means.

In contrast, the 1991 immigrants were concentrated for about a year in Addis Ababa as they awaited permission to emigrate. This was dictated by the independent action of various philanthropic organizations and the political circumstances of a long civil war in which the ruling regime, which opposed their departure, was losing its grip. As the only way to get out of Ethiopia at that time was through Addis Ababa airport, it was reasonable to concentrate the Jews near it in the hope that a breakthrough in negotiations would allow them to leave. This also made sense in terms of relief work.

The move was oppportune. In the twilight of the Marxist regime, permission to emigrate was granted and the airlift took place over one weekend when Addis Ababa airport was in neutral territory. Had the Jews been dispersed in the rural Gondar region, where the majority of them came from, or even in regional centres, it would have been impossible to bring all of them out.

Social climate

Most of the Jews had lived in Addis Ababa for nine to twelve months. Although conditions were dire, in many ways they were superior to those of the population around them. These new living conditions, together with the traditional machismo of the men and the breakdown of the usual social constraints in force in their isolated rural environments, may have facilitated the introduction of HIV into the community.

In 1990–91, the prevalence of HIV in Addis Ababa, mainly among bar girls and prostitutes, reached very high proportions.[2] Men at the 'age of fire' – one of the stages of life in the Ethiopian world view when macho and unbridled emotions are heightened (generally up to the age of 40) – were suddenly free to indulge themselves and also had the opportunity, the economic means (under the relief effort) and the time to associate with bar girls and prostitutes.[3]

Given the high prevalence of HIV in the area, another possible source of infection could have been street-corner injections of vitamins and antibiotics, and traditional medicine practices involving lacerations and surgery.[4]

The decision to screen for HIV

The debate about the ethics, desirability, effectiveness and cost-effectiveness of screening 'high risk' groups for HIV and the social and political implications

involved is long and tortuous.[5] Generally, it evolves around situations in which screening has in some way been used to exclude those who are found to be HIV-positive. It is important to point out where the situation we are discussing is unique.

The experience with the previous wave of immigration from Ethiopia and information from the camp at Addis Ababa indicated that there was risk of a high prevalence of various serious infectious diseases (malaria, tuberculosis, schistosomiasis and hepatitis B, to name just a few). The Israeli decision not to turn anybody away 'at the gate' created a dilemma: major infectious diseases that had been highly prevalent in Israel in the past – but were eradicated for all practical purposes – had all the environmental conditions for redistribution, including the vectors (e.g. mosquitos, snails) where these were needed for transmission. And they were about to be reintroduced to the country.[6]

As we have no access to written or verbal evidence for the rationale behind the decision to screen the population, we can only conjecture from the facts. The lack of a specific policy on what to do with the data collected, and of plans to deal with the social consequences, would suggest that the decision to screen for HIV was a reflex reaction, the traditional medical and public health approach to infectious disease: that detection leads to control. It was not an unreasonable response and was appropriate, for example, in the case of hepatitis B. Changes in vaccine availability and decreasing cost, the very high prevalence of hepatitis B among the immigrant community and the role of both sexual practice and traditional medicine in spreading the virus influenced the decision to vaccinate all Ethiopian immigrants over the age of nine years against hepatitis B, as well as all newborn babies in the Ethiopian community. A year later this policy was made universal to include all babies born in Israel.

Detection may be an essential step in the efforts to control many infectious diseases but it is only a first step. Once infected individuals and risk groups are identified, the deciding factor is what you do next. For detection to help in stemming an epidemic, there must be a well thought-out policy and plan of action on how to apply the information gathered for the benefit of all concerned. And this has to be properly implemented.

As viruses go, HIV poses a more complex problem than most. No vaccine exists and only temporary symptomatic treatment is available. Sexual practice is one of the main routes of transmission and, labelled as an epidemic, it gives many people the false impression that it is easily caught. In short, it is perceived as 'highly contagious, immediate, acute and lethal'. It induces shame and sometimes the feeling of being stigmatized; may create isolation or harassment; and can impose feelings of despair that sometimes lead to depression. All of these are barriers to preventive efforts.[7]

The reaction in Israel

Israel was and is still defined as a country with a low prevalence of HIV infection.[8] For this reason, perhaps, no preconceived policy or plan of action appears to have been in place before the screening of Ethiopian immigrants in 1991 to deal with a situation in which prevalence in a community was found to be much higher. We can only conjecture – from this, and the way in which the results of the screening were handled – that the decision-makers assumed that those people found to be HIV-positive would be treated in the same manner as the general Israeli population.

However, several very important differences were not taken into account. First, most of the general Israeli population was not screened. The only groups screened were injecting drug users (IDUs) entering treatment, prison inmates among whom

the percentage of IDUs is very high and people with haemophilia who received contaminated blood derived factor VIII. These groups were either under supervision of the authorities or in contact with medical institutions for reasons other than HIV infection. Other people voluntarily tested for HIV at one of the eight AIDS centres located in hospitals around the country and returned in person to the testing site to receive the results.

In the case of the immigrants, all of them, male and female, from nine years of age were screened without their prior knowledge. The health authorities then notified those people who tested HIV-positive, and thus increased the likelihood of their HIV status being exposed to other members of their community.

Secondly, several unique factors relating to the tested population aggravated the situation. On arriving in Israel, the immigrants were not given permanent national ID numbers, only temporary ones, because of technical difficulties; in many cases, names which were difficult to pronounce or meaningless to the Hebrew-speaking clerks were misspelled or changed for Hebrew ones. When the temporary ID numbers were changed to permanent ones and names were corrected, this only added to the confusion and to the difficulty of locating people.

When it came to the HIV test, no counselling was provided. This was not seen as important enough to merit funding or the preparation of appropriately trained personnel. As a result, many of those found to be HIV-positive only heard about the disease and the concepts surrounding it when they were notified of their condition. And most of the immigrants – including those found to be HIV-positive – were unfamiliar with the biomedical model of disease.

All the immigrants were concentrated in assimilation centres or in temporary assimilation centres created in large hotels for a period of nine to twelve months. This created physical conditions in which it was very difficult to keep discretion and rumours would spread very fast. Furthermore, none of the immigrants could speak Hebrew and every communication between individuals and health professionals had to pass through translators. As very few long-established Israeli citizens could speak Amharic, most of the translators were immigrants from the previous wave of the 1980s, many of whom had relatives among the new immigrant population. For the most part, they were not health professionals and were only temporarily employed as translators. Thus, they could not be expected to adhere strictly to the idea of confidentiality, and were also torn between loyalty to their temporary employer and to their family members in what to them might seem a life-threatening situation.

Another problem was the difficulty of explaining HIV/AIDS through translators when the attending physicians or nurses did not understand the culture of the new immigrants, their perceptions of disease, its transmission, relations between the sexes and even the ways in which they react to authority. Also, many of the *translators* did not fully comprehend the biomedical model of infectious disease and especially the issues of carriers and of specific modes of transmission.

Thus the assimilation, health and welfare systems were not prepared for what ensued, and may even have contributed to events, mainly by omission.

Some consequences of screening an immigrant population for HIV

Several news items and articles have described some of the facts which we detail below.[9] However, most of the information presented in this chapter has been gathered from working directly with the Ethiopian community, from supervising professionals who were doing care and educational work within the community, from university colleagues, and from being members of committees and teams which have had to decide on policies and implement programmes in the midst of events.

We believe that what follows is the first comprehensive description to be published of the chain of events that took place as a result of screening a whole immigrant population for HIV infection.

Several reactions occurred – either in sequence or in parallel – at individual, family and community level, within the immediate social environment of the community and within society at large.

At an individual level, the inability to communicate properly reduced the level of counselling and support available to a point of inadequacy, thus adding to mental suffering, despondency and depression.

This was aggravated either by actual or anticipated negative reactions from within the family. There were several cases in which family members who were found to be HIV-positive were expelled from the family unit. In some cases, the intervention of care professionals allowed that member to return, but the damage of exposure had already been done. In other cases alternative living arrangements had to be made, sometimes away from the assimilation centre.

One of the most distressing reactions to both individuals and their families was the shunning of people rumoured or known to be HIV-positive by their own community. Though surprising to the care professionals involved, this was traditional Ethiopian practice: people, or even families and villages with specific infectious diseases like tuberculosis, were habitually shunned. It meant that the support of the community, which is extremely important to an Ethiopian, was withdrawn from the individual and his family, thus aggravating feelings of loss and despair as well as increasing the hardship of existence.

The situation was also aggravated by several cases of less than the strictest concern for confidentiality. This stemmed either from the pressures under which the AIDS centres were operating in locating all the individuals found to be HIV-positive, or from some stereotypical view of the immigrants which contributed to their feelings of being stigmatized. Equally insensitive was the procedure of bussing people from the assimilation centres to the AIDS clinics. While it was necessary to provide transport for people living far away, with no financial resources and the ability to travel by themselves, it exposed some of the HIV-positive individuals to the community at large. With some forethought these arrangements could have been made differently. In many cases people who were infected with HIV severed their contacts with the AIDS centres; they perceived the procedures and the behaviour of staff as improper and responsible for much of their environmental suffering. Consequently, they received no follow-up examinations and treatment.

On the level of immediate care for the immigrants, the welfare, education and health staff and the staff at the assimilation centres were not prepared to deal with the issues of HIV. Fears were aroused and rumours (general and specific) spread very fast. The reactions were sometimes distressing. In several cases, community health workers, social workers and even teachers demanded the names of people who were HIV-positive. In several cases, workers going into living quarters refused invitations to drink coffee or water, thus insulting the residents. There were reported cases of care professionals avoiding all physical contact, including handshaking. This was deeply wounding to a people whose traditional greetings include four-hand-shaking, shoulder hugging and cheek kissing.

Attempts to improve the situation encountered many objective difficulties. The education level of the care professionals ranged from MDs and PhDs through lower academic level and high school education to barely elementary education, so that any attempt at educating staff had to be adjusted to meet different educational levels *and* made specific to various professional activities. Another difficulty was the geographical spread of the assimilation centres all over the country.

Reactions in widening circles of the surrounding population have been similar, only more extreme. These have been fanned by media reports, some of which are simply false, others misinformed and stigmatizing. The last wave of reports, as recent as August 1994,[10] provoked adverse reactions in the general population, and elicited feelings of pain and anger among the Ethiopian community. Several attempts to counter the situation through media response have appeared and their effect is as yet unclear. Further general educational efforts could have an adverse effect, as they will keep the issue high on the public agenda and increase the degree of association between the Ethiopian community and HIV infection.

Thus we find adverse reactions at every level, from the individual and the family unit through the immigrants' community to the surrounding environment and caregiving system. This is hardly surprising: the screening programme for the Ethiopian population managed to fall into every possible trap,[11] and then create a few more.

The institutional response

The main public health issue was how to lower the incidence of HIV infection in a community with a higher HIV prevalence than the general population, also a community with distinct cultural features and one in which individuals choose sexual partners mainly from among their own people. The issue was further complicated by the adverse effects of the screening programme which made prevention efforts that much more difficult.

Several organizations and professionals responded on different levels. An interdisciplinary group of professionals, organized under the auspices of the Braun School of Public Health and Community Medicine of the Hebrew University and Hadassah (BSPH group), proposed a plan to deal with the situation. The Israeli Joint Distribution Committee (JDC), which had done relief work with the community in Ethiopia and continued to do so within Israel, organized consultations with the National AIDS Steering Committee and the public health branch of the Ministry of Health. Other organizations – the Ministry of Immigration and Assimilation, the Histadrut Sick Fund and the Jewish Agency – were also party to the attempts to create a coordinated response.

In consultation with the other organizations, the JDC and the National AIDS Steering Committee selected the proposal submitted by the BSPH group, and this formed the basis of a policy toward the Ethiopian community and the methods and strategy to implement it.

The two main policy decisions were:

1. To focus culturally appropriate preventive efforts at this specific community.
2. To alleviate some of the fears and reduce the stigma associated with HIV/AIDS among professionals in contact with the community of immigrants from Ethiopia.

The main effort (1) was devised as a combined strategy. It was to be based on the development of a culturally sensitive prevention programme, using appropriate educational materials, and on the training of professionals from within the community to implement it. The trainees were also to serve as community representa-

tives and as a source of insight in developing both the educational messages and educational materials.

The preventive effort was then to be delivered at two levels: first, to the general adult population of Operation Solomon; and second, to those people already identified as HIV-positive, together with their sexual partners. This is where trained professionals from within the Ethiopian community would be able to act as cultural mediators, helping other professionals deliver the biomedical, psychosocial and behavioural messages in ways acceptable and comprehensible to the immigrant community. It would also help the care professionals understand and interpret the messages directed at them by the immigrants.

An interorganizational steering committee was formed from the above-mentioned organizations. In December 1991, five months after Operation Solomon took place, it contracted the BSPH team to develop an educational programme and educational materials to train professionals from among the longer-standing immigrants of the Ethiopian community, and to implement a public information and education campaign with the general population of the Ethiopian immigrants of 1991.

As an immediate effort, full-day training sessions for the various professionals caring for the community were carried out around the country. Feedback from these sessions indicates that they served to counteract some of the stigmatizing effects of the screening programme by combining information about HIV and AIDS with teaching about the cultural background, beliefs and behaviour of the immigrant community; they also dealt with processing fears and appropriate behaviour. The publication of Be Gobez [12] provided important background material on the beliefs of the community with relevance to AIDS, as well as culturally specific materials for explaining prevention messages. The material collected in this publication was also used in the preventive efforts within the community.

As far as the main preventive effort is concerned, a full description of what was implemented can be found in papers by Chemtob et al., Shtarkshall et al. and Soskolne et al.[13] But this consisted mainly of the following:

- The development of a culturally sensitive, multi-channel educational programme for the general population and its component educational materials. The programme included face-to-face lectures/discussion groups within the regular and temporary assimilation centres and a set of posters highlighting the main messages; a booklet depicting the same messages as the set of posters, to be used in individual counselling; an audio-cassette with nine programmes that delivered the preventive messages using proverbs, fables and Ethiopian music; a weekly radio programme which was broadcast live in co-operation with the trained professionals from within the community and which reiterated the preventive messages; and pamphlets in Amharic, delivering preventive messages and other messages related to the disease.
- The training of professionals. A group of professionals was trained in the dual role of educators and cultural mediators. The training was done in an initial three-day workshop followed by a series of full-day weekly, bi-weekly and monthly sessions. The latter served several purposes: to continue training; to develop and test educational messages and educational materials; to reinforce teaching skills; to supervise the trainees in their teaching/facilitating work within the community (which started after the second of these follow-up sessions) and for trouble shooting.
- Delivery of the educational messages by the trained facilitators in all the assimilation centres to groups of immigrants consisting of 25–30 people and in all boarding schools that had concentrations of immigrant students. Distribution of the audio-tapes in the centres (one per family) with permission to copy them as needed. More than 75 per cent of the adult population in the centres was covered by this effort.
- Evaluation of the training programme and its impact on the trainees was carried out using various methods (questionnaires, observations of the training sessions and the facilitation work and interviews), as well as evaluation of the primary preventive efforts within the general population.

The prevention programme, educational materials and training procedures used were based on the literature available about Ethiopian culture and beliefs on health, and on the experience of team members in working with HIV/AIDS issues and with immigrants from Ethiopia.[14] The educational messages were adapted accordingly, tested first with the trainee facilitators and then with the general population.

The means to deliver the messages were also developed according to the conditions in the assimilation centres and within the community. Thus, instead of slides or overheads we used posters: these did not need any technical means of delivery and on the back of them we could print the main points contained in the visual message in both Amharic and simple Hebrew. When we learned that many of the immigrants use tape recorders and cassettes to listen to Ethiopian music we developed the audio-cassette programmes.

These educational materials carried the main message of the programme. They were tailored to meet the specific needs and conditions within the community, some of which were aggravated by the screening and subsequent policies. The messages were:

- HIV/AIDS is a great but controllable menace. Each person must be responsible for protecting himself/herself against infection. This was embodied in the message, 'Your life is in your own hands' – which was also the name of our poster series – as well as in the idea 'Be Gobez', which refers to being victorious over one's enemies, including HIV.

- 'It is better to do things when you can prevent them than to cry when you are already suffering and there is nothing you can do' – a well-known Amharic proverb.

- Each and every member of the community can protect himself, his family, the Ethiopian Jewish community (Beta Israel) and all the people of Israel. This message was planned to tap their solidarity as a group on the one hand and as an integral part of Israeli society on the other.

- 'There is hope' – people who are infected with HIV should not despair and perceive death as their immediate fate. The development of the disease can be postponed and the quality of life of infected persons can be improved through early detection and proper, continuous care.

- 'There is no need to know who is infected' – protection lies in behaving as if everybody may be infected. This is, of course, a message to the general Israeli public. An exception to the situation is being a sexual partner of a carrier. This should be dealt with in counselling and not in educational interventions.

- 'There is no need to shun or ostracize people with HIV or people with AIDS.' One can do the right and honourable thing: befriend them and help them in a dire situation, while taking the necessary precautions.

These messages appeared repeatedly in the visual and audio materials and the facilitators were instructed to utilize them whenever appropriate.

It is unrealistic to hope that that part of the programme which was implemented –

mainly informational and partly educational – will affect behaviour. Additional interventions are needed: some, like the 'Sexual Health Sexual Responsibility' campaign, a comprehensive educational programme for immigrant youths from Ethiopia, are in the process of being carried out. Additional extensive and intensive educational efforts are still needed within the community at large.

Mistakes nonetheless

When the BSPH proposal was selected for implementation, only the development of a preventive educational programme for the general immigrant population and the training of Ethiopian professionals to carry it out were actually commissioned. The adoption of the second level preventive effort – to specifically addresss those people found to be HIV-positive and their sexual partners – was postponed to a later date. At the time, this was not viewed as critical by the BSPH team in charge: the immediate concern was to get the general preventive programme off the ground; when this was in place, the authorities could be then be approached to commission the other component.

This would prove to be a mistake.

In May and August 1992, an additional plan to deal with this situation was submitted. It proposed to involve the cultural mediators already in place in the care of people with HIV and their sexual partners.[15] The proposal was later amended and submitted to the National AIDS Steering Committee in an effort to introduce the concept of case managers to the Israeli system.[16] These case managers were to combine the task of caring for the person with HIV and his partner/family with cultural mediation and ensuring early access to medical treatments.

Unfortunately, despite efforts by several groups within the healthcare system and outside it, as of August 1994 very little has been implemented in the way of cultural mediation and appropriate psychosocial and behavioural work among those who are HIV-positive and their sexual partners. We consider this to be very problematic and, in a way, wasting one of the very few benefits that could have been gained from screening the immigrant population in the first place.

Discussion and recommendations

The initial decision to concentrate the Ethiopian Jews in Addis Ababa was beyond the control of the decision-makers in Israel; the decision to bring all of them out – despite knowledge of the infection – was ideological, based on the existence of a culturally identifiable group with an obvious connection to the Israeli population. We believe that the decision to screen all the immigrants 'inside the gate' was not only the reflex reaction of public health procedures but also inevitable in a political culture that favours action above inaction.

This was a unique situation: no amount of discussion can really establish whether other decisions could have been taken to better effect. The main purpose of this analysis is not to examine the the validity of screening in itself – properly handled, it *can* be a highly decisive tool in helping prevent the spread of disease in a humane and supportive way.[17] The issue is this: what could or should have been done differently in this particular case? While no two situations are the same, careful analysis of the decisions taken here, and the way they were implemented, can help identify where the process went wrong and help us not to make the same mistakes again.

We do not wish to imply that what happened to the Israeli community of Ethiopian Jews was the result of malice or deliberate neglect. However, most of our evidence is negative, indicating a lack of appropriate action – a lack, even, of plans for action.

In retrospect, which is an uncomfortable place to start from, three points are clear: first, the implications of mass screening an identifiable subpopulation and the consequences thereof were not considered in depth before making the decision to screen the immigrants from Ethiopia in 1991. Had they been considered, we believe that the decision to screen would have remained the same, but the way it was implemented might have been quite different.

Second, once the decision was made to screen these immigrants for HIV, a special plan of action and implementation strategy should have been formulated to deal with the consequences of that policy and its implementation. It was unrealistic to assume that the ordinary structures, procedures and processes, designed mainly for people who test voluntarily, would suffice to deal with this totally different situation and with a culturally different population.

Third, once the screening had been carried out, comprehensive and effective measures should have been taken *immediately* to help those people found to be HIV-positive, as well as their partners, families and friends. To date, little has been done.

Guidelines for the future

The fact that many people object to the use of screening on various grounds, reasons of public health included, does not preclude the need to formulate guidelines for the implementation of such a policy where it is made. *Appropriate* guidelines and their careful implementation may make the difference between good care and unnecessary, aggravated suffering. In many situations, professionals are faced with the results of decisions they had no influence on; nevertheless, they still have to deal with the consequences.

On the basis of what we have described above, we suggest that the following factors be considered *before* the implementation of any screening policy. These points relate mainly to dealing with immigrants or with socially or culturally distinct populations – a situation which could arise in many countries. Some of our suggestions will also be salient to other minority groups.

These points can be used as a checklist and can be elaborated upon and customized to suit specific situations; other items can be added as appropriate.

Individuals found to be HIV-positive

When dealing with people who do not contact the testing or treatment site voluntarily, and who would not come back of their own volition to receive the results, bear in mind the following:

- means of notification (this relates to confidentiality);
- counselling the individuals who are found to be seropositive and their sexual partners;
- dealing with the reaction of immediate families;
- confidentiality (issues like translation: Who will translate in the case of language differences? What are the loyalties?).

The community subpopulation in which screening is carried out

- spreading of rumours within neighbourhoods in which the community is concentrated;
- dealing with shame, denial and anger at community level;
- being stigmatized and dealing with the stigma in a constructive way;
- preparation of tailored and targeted, culturally sensitive preventive interventions and implementing them with the general population of that subgroup, and with 'higher risk' groups within it (e.g. unmarried young adults).

Professionals/carers working with the community

- dealing with fears and the resulting callous or stigmatizing behaviour towards individuals in their care;
- the ability to communicate in a constructive manner with individuals who may have difficulty in accepting premises of the biomedical model and directives embedded in it.

The general population within which the screened group live

- openness or secrecy;
- counteracting stigmatizing behaviour.

Conclusion

We suggest that any system that decides to screen populations or subgroups within it should take responsibility for dealing properly with the information, the people and the community at all levels, even at very high costs. As the process of screening and its sequels shapes a new reality, it is up to those who bring it about to deal with the repercussions.

1 H. Rosen, A. Rubinstein, 'The demography of the Ethiopian Community in Israel', *Israel Journal of Medical Sciences*, 29 (6–7): 333, 1993.

2 Ethiopian Ministry of Health, *AIDS Control and Prevention Activities: Annual Report*. Report to WHO/GPA, Government Press Office, Addis Ababa, 1989.

Ethiopian Ministry of Health, *The AIDS Situation in Ethiopia*, July 1990.

3 H. Rosen, 'Adolescence and maturation', *Questions and Answers Regarding Ethiopian Jews*, 4. Hadassah Council, Jerusalem, 1986. In Hebrew.

4 R.A. Shtarkshall, 'Comment on Pollack', *Israel Journal of Medical Sciences*, 29 (10), 1993.

5 L. Liskin, 'AIDS – a public health crisis', *Population Reports*, Series L(6). Population Foundation, New York, 1986.

D. Altman, 'The politics of AIDS', *AIDS: Public Policy Perspectives* (ed. J. Briggs), pp. 23–33. United Hospital Fund, New York, 1987.

R.C. Johnston, 'AIDS and "otherness"', *AIDS: Public Policy Perspectives* (ed. J. Briggs), pp. 77–82. United Hospital Fund, New York, 1987.

6 A. Rubinstein (ed.), 'Medical and epidemiological aspects of the Ethiopian immigration to Israel', *Israel Journal of Medical Sciences*, 27 (5): special edition, 1991.

A. Rubinstein (ed.), 'The Ethiopian immigration to Israel – medical, epidemiological and health aspects', *Israel Journal of Medical Sciences*, 29 (6–7) 1993.

7 D. Altman, The Politics of AIDS, *AIDS: Public Policy Perspectives* (ed. J. Briggs), pp. 23–33. United Hospital Fund, New York, 1987.

M. Krim, 'Introduction', *AIDS: Public Policy Perspectives* (ed. J. Briggs), pp. XV–XXXIV. United Hospital Fund, New York, 1987.

8 Department of Epidemiology, Israeli Ministry of Health, *AIDS and HIV in Israel, mid 1994*, monthly epidemiological record, weeks 18–22, May 1994.

9 N. Worgraft, N. Drory-Wilf, 'The failure of silence' [Keshel Hashtikah], *Kol Ha'Ir*, Jerusalem, 14 August 1992. In Hebrew.

A. Zilberman, 'All those present in the emergency room heard the announcement, "The Ethiopian child has AIDS"', *Kol Haifa*, 25 December 1992. In Hebrew.

10 I. Baum, '50 infected with AIDS found at Neveh Carmel', *Yediot Aharonot*, 8 August 1994. In Hebrew.

Sa'ar, 'Half the Ethiopian immigrants living in caravan sites carry TB', *Ha'Aretz*, 15 August 1994. In Hebrew.

H. Yavin, R. Noyman, '350 cases of AIDS among the Ethiopian community', *Mabat* (Evening news programme of the National Television Authority), 9 August 1994. In Hebrew.

11 J. Rennie, 'Grading the gene tests', *Scientific American*, 270 (6): 66–74, 1994.

12 D. Chemtob, H. Rosen, *'Be Gobez' For the Sake of your Health*. Multi-agency Committee for Education and Information on HIV Infection and Related Diseases, Jerusalem, 1992.

13 D. Chemtob, H. Rosen, R. Shtarkshall, V. Soskolne, 'The development of a culturally specific educational programme to reduce the risk of HIV and HBV transmission among Ethiopian immigrants: a preliminary report on training veteran immigrants as health educators', *Israel Journal of Medical Sciences*, 29 (6–7): 437–442, 1993.

R.A. Shtarkshall, V. Soskolne, D. Chemtob, H. Rosen, 'The development of a culturally specific educational programme to reduce the risk of HIV and HBV transmission among Ethiopian Immigrants II: evaluating the effect of the training programme on trainees who were veteran immigrants from Ethiopia', *Israel Journal of Medical Sciences*, 29 (10): 48–54, 1993.

V. Soskolne, R.A. Shtarkshall, D. Chemtob, H. Rosen, 'The development of a culturally specific educational programme to reduce the risk of HIV and HBV transmission among Ethiopian Immigrants III: evaluating the impact of the educational effort within the general population of Ethiopian immigrants'. In preparation, 1994.

14 D. Chemtob, H. Rosen, *'Be Gobez' For the Sake of your Health*. Multi-agency Committee for Education and Information on HIV Infection and Related Diseases, Jerusalem, 1992.

D. Chemtob, H. Rosen, R. Shtarkshall, V. Soskolne, 'The development of a culturally specific educational programme to reduce the risk of HIV and HBV transmission among Ethiopian immigrants: a preliminary report on training veteran immigrants as health educators', *Israel Journal of Medical Sciences*, 29 (6–7): 437–442, 1993.

R. A. Shtarkshall, V. Soskolne, D. Chemtob, H. Rosen, 'The development of a culturally specific educational programme to reduce the risk of HIV and HBV transmission among Ethiopian Immigrants II: evaluating the effect of the training programme on trainees who were veteran immigrants from Ethiopia', *Israel Journal of Medical Sciences*, 29 (10): 48–54, 1993.

V. Soskolne, R.A. Shtarkshall, D. Chemtob, H. Rosen, 'The development of a culturally specific educational programme to reduce the risk of HIV and HBV transmission among Ethiopian Immigrants III: evaluating the impact of the educational effort within the general population of Ethiopian immigrants'. In preparation, 1994.

15 R.A. Shtarkshall, V. Soskolne, letter to Professor A. Morag, Chairman of the subcommittee for information and education, National AIDS Steering Committee, May 1992. In Hebrew.

R.A. Shtarkshall, V. Soskolne, D. Chemtob and H. Rosen, 'The continuation of development and implementation of intervention programmes to reduce the risk of HIV transmission among the immigrants from Ethiopia', document submitted to the National AIDS Steering Committee, August 1992. In Hebrew.

16 Shtarkshall, Soskolne, Bentwiz, Davidson and Zamir-Levine, 'The role of case managers in the care of people who are HIV-positive and their partners among the population of immigrants from Ethiopia and in preventing the spread of HIV within it', document submitted to the National AIDS Steering Committee, Ministry of Health, March 1994. In Hebrew.

17 J. Rennie, 'Grading the gene tests', *Scientific American*, 270 (6): 66–74, 1994.

Public Awareness of AIDS: Discrimination and the Effects of Mistrust

Dr Jacques Marquet, Dr Michel Hubert
and Dr Luc Van Campenhoudt

Centre d'études sociologiques, Facultés universitaires Saint-Louis, Brussels, Belgium

This chapter covers the state of a general population's knowledge about how HIV is transmitted and means of protection. We try to interpret the meanings of the alleged 'misinformation' of the population about AIDS. First, we present the current state of adults' knowledge of these issues in Belgium and in some other European countries. We then show to what extent knowledge of the virus's transmission and protective measures is affected by the feelings of mistrust that many people have *vis-à-vis* others, especially specialists. After that, we study the links between knowledge and discrimination towards HIV-positive individuals. In focusing on these last two points we show how complex the process of acquiring knowledge about so ticklish a problem as AIDS is. It is not merely a matter of having access to supposedly correct information. Lastly, we discuss the importance of this issue when considering the socio-economic impact of AIDS.

As Schütz says, 'All our knowledge of the world, in common-sense as well as in scientific thinking, involves constructs, i.e. a set of abstractions, generalizations, formalizations, idealizations specific to the respective level of thought organization. Strictly speaking, there are no such things as facts, pure and simple. All facts are...always interpreted facts...'[1] In other words, it is impossible to isolate knowledge about a specific problem (such as knowing how HIV is or is not transmitted) from the more complex process of apprehension (in a philosophical sense) of this problem. Moreover, knowledge is part of a larger set of representations that includes complex cognitive, emotional and cultural components and fulfils psychological and social functions (reassurance, need to belong to a group, etc.) that are vital for the individual.[2] Consequently, knowledge does not result from a purely rational approach and individuals do not necessarily accept the explanations given by the most authoritative specialists (in this case, doctors), especially if the explanations run counter to the convictions upon which they have organized their lives and behaviour. Information is filtered; its acceptance may obey types of logic that are far removed from that of prevention officers. So, we cannot be satisfied with the explanation that knowledge is inadequate because of the lack of information.

If one wants to change the population's images of AIDS, it clearly is not enough to identify the 'poorly-informed' or 'under-informed' groups and increase the number of messages containing what specialists and officials consider to be 'correct' information. One must explore the whys and meanings of such misconceptions. This is the focus of this text.

The results presented are based mainly on the findings of the Belgian national survey on sexual behaviour and attitudes towards HIV risk that was carried out by the Brussels-based sociological research centre, Centre d'études sociologiques of the Facultés universitaires Saint-Louis, and the Antwerp-based university department, Departement Politieke en Sociale Wetenschap of the Universitaire Instelling Antwerpen (UIA), from 31 March 1990 to 30 June 1993.[3] This was a telephone survey of 3,733 respondents from a sample of the Belgian resident population (both nationals and foreigners) between the ages of 15 and 59.[4]

Knowledge of the virus's transmission and means of protection

We start by examining the state of the adult population's knowledge of how the virus is transmitted and means of protection. Particular attention is paid to the importance and significance of the representations of risk that turn a blind eye to prevention messages and are considered by specialists to fall short of current medical knowledge.

Knowledge of the virus's modes of transmission

The questions on the degree of knowledge of the virus's modes of transmission all have the following structure: 'In your opinion, is transmission of the AIDS virus possible in each of the following circumstances?

• by sitting on a toilet seat?

• by drinking from someone's glass?'

and so on.

The respondents were asked to answer either 'yes' or 'no'. However, some of the respondents who were especially wary of the expert's messages did not identify with either of the two possibilities that were offered and spontaneously expressed their feelings of mistrust. Their replies were placed in a third category, 'they say it is not possible, but I'm not sure'.

The bulk of the population is aware of the fact that HIV is transmitted by sexual relations and contaminated needles shared by injecting drug users (Table 1). However, some people fear alleged modes of transmission despite the reassurances of specialists and prevention officers. Blood transfusions and donations are clearly the focus of the greatest fears. While we can understand that doubts about the safety of blood transfusions persist, the fact that 33.4 per cent answered that one can be infected with HIV by giving blood is frankly astonishing, given the total absence of such a risk in Belgium.

Still, the positive rates for the other supposed modes of transmission are not low. If the 'yes' and spontaneously volunteered 'sceptical' answers are combined, between 10 and 15 per cent of the respondents think that it is possible to be infected by kissing someone on the mouth, by a mosquito bite, by sitting on a toilet or by drinking from someone else's glass. To this we must still add the 'don't know' answers, which are not negligible (especially for transmission through mosquito bites), although this category was not proposed explicitly by the interviewers but emerged spontaneously.

The risk of HIV transmission by sexual relations or by sharing contaminated needles is widely recognized in the other recent European surveys:[5] for example, the figures are respectively 99 per cent and 97 per cent in the 'analysis of sexual behaviour in France'.[6] Strictly speaking, it is difficult to compare the answers to our two questions about receiving blood or

In your opinion, is transmission of the AIDS virus[a] possible in each of the following circumstances?	%				
	Yes	No	('They say it's not possible but I'm not sure')[b]	(Do not know)	(No answer)
during sexual intercourse	98.1	1.5	–	0.4	0.0
by injecting drugs (with a contaminated needle as well)	98.0	1.4	–	0.6	0.0
by getting blood in Belgium today	53.8	36.6	7.6	2.0	0.0
by giving blood in Belgium today	33.4	61.8	2.8	2.0	0.0
by kissing someone on the mouth	13.4	83.9	1.4	1.3	0.0
via a mosquito bite	12.4	80.6	1.7	5.3	0.0
by sitting on a toilet seat	11.2	85.5	1.3	1.9	0.0
by drinking from someone's glass	9.1	88.4	1.4	1.2	0.0

[a] We used the term 'AIDS virus' instead of HIV, as the latter is not yet familiar to the French public.

[b] The brackets mean that these items were not explicitly proposed when the question was first formulated. They came up in the HIV respondents' comments and hesitations.

Table 1
Knowledge of HIV transmission (N = 3732)

giving blood because of the reference to 'Belgium today'. Moreover, many surveys investigate only whether transmission of HIV is possible, in principle, by receiving or by giving blood. Nevertheless, the fear of blood transfusion[7] and blood donation[8] is reported in many studies. Robertson *et al.* sought responses to a very specific question related to this fear: 'In your opinion, can people become infected with the AIDS virus by giving blood, for example, at a Blood Donor Centre?', to which 17.3 per cent answered 'yes' and 7.4 per cent 'I don't know'.[9] For the last four lines of the table, a comparison with the French

Knowledge, Attitudes, Beliefs and Practices (KABP) survey of 1992 shows that the positive rates for these supposed modes of transmission are far lower in the Belgian survey than in the French one, where they are respectively 32.7 per cent (saliva), 25.9 per cent (mosquito), 27.1 per cent (toilet) and 16.6 per cent (glass).[10] In the Dutch survey the positive rates are intermediate, but closer to the Belgian ones for the last two questions (toilet and glass).[11] In the Scottish survey 23.1 per cent of the respondents reported that one could become infected with HIV by kissing with exchange of saliva and 2.5 per

Table 2
Knowledge of means of protection against HIV (n = 3732)

Means of protection against HIV	%				
	totally effective	rather effective	rather ineffective	totally ineffective	(don't know)
Is coitus interruptus (withdrawal before ejaculation/before the end of intercourse)...	6.2	8.5	18.9	64.6	1.7
Is washing after sex...	6.2	6.9	13.3	72.4	1.1
Is choosing partners who appear to be in good health...	11.0	14.3	20.3	53.4	0.8
Is using the pill...	3.2	3.1	5.5	87.2	0.9
Is using a condom...	57.2	37.9	3.4	1.3	0.4
Is having one's partner take a screening test and waiting for the results before having sex...	61.0	27.2	6.2	5.1	0.4
Is being faithful to a partner who is faithful, too...	61.4	28.2	6.0	3.9	0.4

To simplify the presentation, the 'no answer' column is not shown here cent by using public toilets.[12] These two questions were also characterized by a high number of 'I don't know' answers (respectively 19.5 per cent and 4.3 per cent). Overall, all the recent European surveys show substantial rates of misconceptions. The Belgian rates seem to be equal to or even lower than those in other European countries.

Knowledge of means of protection against the risk

The results displayed in Table 2 show that most of the adult population has good knowledge of the means of protection against HIV infection. Still, close to 15 per cent of the respondents think that coitus interruptus is a good protective measure, while close to 13 per cent believe that washing oneself after sex is a relatively effective way of eliminating the risk of infection. One out of four considers that choosing partners who appear to be in good health is an effective means of protection from HIV. In a way, these figures temper somewhat the optimism that might follow the fact that 98.1 per cent of the population know that the virus can be transmitted through sexual intercourse. Another figure (not given in this table) that helps gauge the extent of this knowledge is that 13.6 per cent of the respondents believe that sex is dangerous in terms of HIV risk only if it involves two men. For prevention purposes the key question is whether these people do or do not expose themselves to the risk of HIV infection. We shall come back to this later.

There is another question (not shown in these tables) that further points to the danger of interpreting an indicator in isolation, namely, 'As a rule, for the AIDS screening test to be possible (effective), how long is one supposed to wait after possible contamination before taking the test?' More than half of the respondents (52.6 per cent) were unable to answer this question. More than one out of five (22.2

per cent) answered less than six weeks, which is too short a period for current screening tests. Yet 88.2 per cent of the respondents feel that an effective way of protecting themselves from HIV is to have their partners take an antibody test and wait for the outcome before having sex.

Here, an international comparison of the results is very difficult because of the precision of our categories. For example, only the Belgian survey mentions the idea of waiting for the screening test results before having sex; few surveys speak about *mutual* fidelity; and only the Belgian survey refers to partners 'who appear to be in good health' when investigating the choice of partners. Moreover, the response scales vary from one survey to the other. Consequently, the comparison is limited. In *Les Comportements sexuels en France* 22 per cent of the men and 25 per cent of the women think that coitus interruptus is a good protective measure and 35 per cent of the men and 32 per cent of the women believe that washing oneself after sex is a relatively effective way of eliminating the risk of infection.[13] With regard to the effectiveness of condoms, Spira *et al.* and van Zessen *et al.* find the same level of positive answers (around 90 per cent) as in the Belgian survey.[14]

Areas of ignorance

A considerable fraction of the population has a very poor, even false understanding about AIDS, its means of transmission, and means of protection, if we consider what the specialists in the field commonly hold to be true. If we consider only the people who have at least partly incorrect knowledge of the means of protection,[15] that is, 40.2 per cent (1502 out of 3733) of the respondents, 15.1 per cent of them (226 out of 1502) actually did expose themselves to the risk of infection in their sexual practices.[16] This figure cannot be discounted. In fact the risk-exposure rate for the respondents who at the time of the survey had knowledge of the means of protection in line with preventive medicine's messages is similar, even slightly higher (430 out of 2,231, or 19.3 per cent).[17] This clearly confirms, as many authors have already shown, that knowledge about AIDS is not a good predictor of behaviour change and that other factors must be considered.[18] However, the two groups unquestionably pose different problems for prevention and call for different types of intervention.

Ignorance and misconceptions about transmission modes and means of protection overlap only partly. So, for example,

29 per cent of the individuals who asserted that coitus interruptus was completely ineffective as a means of protecting oneself from HIV nevertheless believe that there is a risk of transmission when giving blood, 13.9 per cent by kissing someone on the mouth, 11.8 per cent from a mosquito bite, 9.5 per cent by sitting on a toilet seat, and 8.1 per cent by drinking from someone else's glass. These figures are not very different from those given in the first column in Table 1. This means that we do not have a large majority of the population that has correct knowledge of the problem versus a minority holding all the misconceptions about the risk, but

Table 3
Frequency of adults' representations of HIV transmission versus highest level of instruction completed[a]

In your opinion, is transmission of the AIDS virus possible in each of the following circumstances?	Level of instruction (%)	
	Primary	University
by getting blood in Belgium today: yes	63.7	36.0
by giving blood in Belgium today: yes	48.7	13.8
by kissing someone on the mouth: yes	19.0	12.9
via a mosquito bite: yes	17.1	6.6
by sitting on a toilet seat: yes	20.9	4.6
by drinking from someone's glass: yes	15.7	5.6
by injecting drugs (with a contaminated needle as well): no	3.0	0.5
during sexual intercourse: no	5.3	0.0
Total (n)	274	314

[a] These tables are obviously simplistic, since they present only the extreme levels of education and thus overlook a substantial part of the population. This presentation is nevertheless justified by the fact that the groups representing the extremes of the educational spectrum also proved to have opposite profiles in terms of the correctness or incorrectness of their representations. Secondary-school and non-university higher education appeared to occupy a middle position that was relatively close to that of primary school graduates in the case of lower secondary-school graduates, and close to that of university graduates in the case of non-university higher education graduates.

rather a fairly large segment of the population that is partly mistaken. This rather broad dissemination of misconceptions poses a problem for prevention and doubtless means that information targeting the entire population is still necessary.

Generally speaking, the frequency of misconceptions correlates with the level of instruction. This applies to knowledge about both transmission and protection, as Tables 3 and 4 show this clearly. The patterns we discern in adults who have completed their schooling or university education are also found among teenagers and young adults who are still at school.

The factor involved here is the level of education and all that it encompasses, that is, the cultural environment in which one is immersed, access to reliable information, discernment, a critical attitude towards prejudices, distance from or proximity to scientific discourse, etc. The specific role of the school itself is a component of this much broader context of influences. The school's role nevertheless may continue to be decisive, especially for certain categories of young people for whom it is one of the only sources of transmission of reliable knowledge. By default this raises the crucial problem of information for individuals who drop out of school very early and young people who barely attend school or are not receptive to its influence.

This leads to the question of whether AIDS is likely to become (or is already becoming) a disease of the socially weak and culturally and economically marginalized in Belgium and elsewhere. This would call for an important turnaround in prevention policies, for who would think

Means of protection against HIV	Level of instruction (%)	
	Primary	University
Is coitus interruptus (withdrawal before ejaculation/before the end of intercourse): totally effective[a]	13.6	1.3
Is washing after sex: totally effective	18.7	0.5
Is choosing partners who appear to be in good health: totally effective	2.9	2.8
Is using the pill: totally effective	7.4	0.0
Is using a condom: totally ineffective	4.5	0.0
Is having one's partner take a screening test and waiting for the results before having sex: totally ineffective	5.0	8.4
Is being faithful to a partner who is faithful too: totally ineffective	9.3	0.2
TOTAL (n)	274	314

Table 4
Frequency of adults' representation of means of protection against HIV varsus highest level of instruction completed

[a]The full set of questions asked was as follows: To protect oneself against HIV is (...) totally effective, rather effective, rather ineffective or totally ineffective? The percentages given here are for those who responded 'totally effective'/'totally ineffective'.

that messages, means of information, approaches, etc., that are generally designed to reach an educated population could be applied, unchanged, to a culturally underprivileged audience?

The frequency of representations that are considered incorrect also depends on age. First, the quality of the information is systematically poorer among the 15 to 19-year-olds than among the 20 to 24-year-olds. Secondly, at the other end of the scale, the oldest age groups likewise have less correct knowledge of the risk than the other adult age groups. The fact that poorer knowledge is to be found in the youngest and oldest age groups tends to show that age is above all an indicator of a position in the life cycle that is marked by concern about sexual matters and prevention. In our sample, 37.7 per cent of the 15 to 19-year-olds had already had sex versus 85.3 per cent of the 20 to 24-year-olds. In a way, the youngest respondents thus joined the oldest respondents, whose sex lives are often stabilized or diminished. We might also add that the body of prevention messages dispensed during the years of schooling is capitalized upon most of all by the 20 to 24-year-old age group.

Knowledge and mistrust

Although information remains crucial, some data show that knowledge acquisition is not limited to having access to information that is considered correct. The fact that a considerable fraction of the population has incorrect ideas about HIV risk results, at least in part, from complex phenomena that we must try to elucidate. With regard to blood transfusions, for example, 7.6 per cent of the respondents (besides the 53.8 per cent who felt that the transmission of the virus was possible in such a circumstance) spontaneously declared that they were wary, despite the specialists' reassuring statements. All in all, 12.8 per cent of the respondents professed such scepticism

with regard to at least one of the six questions concerning the virus's transmission (see Table 1). In addition, if we isolate the respondents who agreed totally with the proposition 'you can't trust anyone these days' (649 subjects), we see that the rate of medically incorrect answers regarding prevention is clearly above average in this group (see Table 5).

We can deduce from this breakdown that if some people are not receptive to prevention messages, it may be in part because they are wary of other groups, including specialists and prevention agencies and their reassuring statements. The result for prevention is that the work of prevention agencies must not consist in merely sending out yet another prevention message. Here, the scientifically incorrect representations reflect mistrust rather than a lack of information.

Still, we cannot confine ourselves to this sole explanation. There do seem to be two different types of mistrust. The mistrust that is expressed by the statement 'they say it isn't possible, but I'm not sure' is voiced by a clearly smaller number of people than the ordinary mistrust of others, which is measured in this study by total agreement with the statement 'you can't trust anyone these days'. It is tempting to explain this quantitative difference by the fact that the range of answers was proposed explicitly in the second case, whereas in the first case the interviewees themselves transcended the proposed categories to impose their own responses. More thorough analysis, however, shows that this hypothesis falls short of the mark, for our two indices of mistrust appear to be totally independent of each other.

This independence is reflected indirectly in the following findings. Only 44.8 per cent of the respondents who said they 'agreed totally' with the statement 'you can't trust anyone these days' had correct knowledge of protective measures compared with 62.9 per cent for the rest of the

In your opinion, is transmission of the AIDS virus possible in each of the following circumstances?	Percentage of respondents	
	In total agreement with expression of mistrust	Rest of the population
	(n = 649)	(n = 3051)
by getting blood in Belgium today: yes	70.0	50.2
by giving blood in Belgium today: yes	50.1	29.9
by kissing someone on the mouth: yes	21.8	11.6
via a mosquito bite: yes	17.8	11.2
by sitting on a toilet seat: yes	20.4	9.2
by drinking from someone's glass: yes	13.9	7.9

Table 5
Knowledge of HIV transmission versus level of agreement with the proposition 'you can't trust anyone these days'

respondents.[19] We thus find a negative correlation between the degree of ordinary mistrust and the degree of knowledge of protective measures. In contrast, the mistrust that is expressed by 'they say it isn't possible, but I'm not sure' correlates positively with the degree of knowledge of protective measures (71.1 per cent of the 'sceptics' held correct views on the subject). So, everything seems to point to the existence of a sort of 'distant mistrust' that seems to increase the chasm between the sceptics and prevention messages (unless it is the chasm that explains the mistrust), on the one hand, and the 'vigilant mistrust' that makes the individual even more prudent vis-à-vis prevention messages.

If we perform a cross analysis of 'distant mistrust' and 'vigilant mistrust' versus the two factors that appeared to be linked to the degree of knowledge, namely, age and level of education, we get contrasting results. The two types of mistrust seem to be linked to age as follows: 'distant mistrust' is expressed by 11.7 per cent of the 15 to 19-year-olds and 29.0 per cent of the 55 to 59-year-olds whereas 'vigilant mistrust' is expressed by 3.9 per cent of the former and 20.5 per cent of the latter. In both cases, the extreme age classes hold the extreme positions. The situation is completely different with respect to the level of education. Here, 'distant mistrust' is inversely correlated with the level of education. It is shared by 39.1 per cent of the adults who have completed primary school, 26.8 per cent of the adults who have completed lower secondary school, 20.3 per cent of the adults who have completed upper secondary school, and 7.2 per cent of the graduates of higher education and 11.7 per cent of lower secondary school students, 11.6 per cent of upper secondary school students, and 7.6 per cent of the students in higher education. 'Vigilant mistrust', for its part, appears to be largely independent of the level of education, for the various groups do not differ by more than 4 percentage points, adults and students alike. It appears to be less correlated with any given social group. 'Distant mistrust', in contrast, appears to be mainly a reaction of culturally underprivileged individuals who, we may hypothesize, are not attuned to the way political, scientific and other 'leaders' approach reality. It seems to be wariness of experts and their world. 'Vigilant mistrust' appears more to be a lack of trust in prevention messages, although this attitude does not rule out a certain ability to grasp the meaning of medical terms.

Both ignorance and mistrust reach their apogees when it comes to blood-borne transmission. The majority of respondents (53.8 per cent) do not believe the reassuring statements about blood transfusions. Quite unexpectedly, a large proportion of the respondents (33.4 per cent) also believe there is a risk of being contaminated attached to giving blood. The recent scandals concerning blood transfusions and the images associated with blood have led to regrettable confusions in this area. In addition, whereas the number of people who believe that there is a risk of contamination in both giving and receiving blood is clearly higher in less educated groups of the population, this does not hold true for those who fear transfusions only, for the proportions are about the same at all levels of education. This second group's characteristics approach those of the 'vigilantly mistrustful' subpopulation. Perhaps it is merely another manifestation of the same state of mind.

The influences of level of education, age, and 'distant mistrust' on the one hand versus age and 'vigilant mistrust' on the other hand overlap partially but do not cancel each other out. Analysis of these factors (which we cannot give here) showed that each factor or, more correctly, what it covers, exerts its own influence over how the risk and ways to protect oneself from it is seen. The only reservation we can make in this regard is that, for identical levels of education, the differences in knowledge of HIV transmission in the 15 to 19-year-old and 20 to 24-year-old groups disappears. To sum up, education, age, 'distant mistrust' and 'vigilant mistrust' do indeed affect knowledge of the virus's transmission and ways to protect oneself from HIV infection. Each of these effects is specific, but they strengthen each other when they are combined.

Knowledge and discrimination

Besides the HIV epidemic *per se*, prevention officials often speak of the 'social epidemic', that is, discriminatory attitudes towards HIV-positive people and groups that have rightly or wrongly been identified as the main carriers of the virus. The question they ask themselves is then whether such discriminatory attitudes are or are not correlated with ignorance of the disease and if unjustified fears of the virus's transmission do or do not elicit an attitude of rejection intended to ward off all risks of contamination.

The questions concerning attitudes to be taken with regard to HIV-positive people are presented in Table 6.

In the French investigation, *Les Comportements sexuels en France*, 86 per cent of the men and 87 per cent of the women would agree to work in the company of an HIV-positive person and 59 per cent of the men and 60 per cent of the women would leave their children or grandchildren in the company of an HIV-positive person.[20] These figures are very close to our findings which are respectively 87.9 per cent and 90.2 per cent for the first question, 59.9 per cent and 62.6 per cent for the second one. In the KABP French survey 9.2 per cent of the respondents would agree ('totally' or 'more or less') to the isolation of people with AIDS from the rest of the population, 6.5 per cent would agree to the sacking of a person who had AIDS and 89.8 per cent would agree to have an AIDS-patient centre open next door (82.1 per cent in the Belgian survey).[21] In the Greek survey 9.3 per cent of the respondents to an open question aimed at discovering what they thought could be done to prevent AIDS patients or those with HIV transmitting the virus suggested isolation of HIV-infected individuals and AIDS patients.[22]

The discrimination issue is very complex. On the one hand, the answers to segregation-related questions, that is, the first six questions in Table 6, show little correlation with questions concerning the conditions of the antibody test's applicability (the last two questions of Table 6), for example. On the other hand, a favourable attitude towards the need to get the patient's consent before conducting a screening test is not necessarily accompanied by rejection of all authoritarian attitudes towards HIV-positive people, for example prosecuting people with HIV if they fail to inform their partners of their condition, allowing the medical authorities to inform their partners, etc.

However, in most cases the respondents who tended to discriminate more against HIV-positive people had poorer knowledge of how the virus is transmitted and means of protection. For example, Table 7 shows the knowledge of modes of transmission of the respondents who would refuse to work with an HIV-positive person.

The differences between the two columns point systematically to greater ignorance in the group that exhibits a discriminatory attitude. This group also knows less about ways of protecting oneself from infection by HIV.

	Percentage of respondents
People with AIDS must be isolated from the rest of the population: 'agree totally' and 'agree more or less'	6.1
An employer must be able to sack a person who has AIDS: 'agree totally' and 'agree more or less'	8.2
Would you agree to work or study in the company of an HIV-positive person? 'no'	10.2
Medical staff must be able to refuse to take care of people with AIDS: 'agree totally' and 'agree more or less'	15.9
Would you agree to have an AIDS patient centre open next door to you? 'no'	17.4
Would you leave your children or grandchildren in the company of an HIV-positive person? 'no'	36.0
To avoid being rejected, an HIV-positive person has the right to keep his or her diagnosis a secret: 'disagree more or less' and 'disagree totally'	65.4
People who know that they are HIV-positive and have unprotected sex without warning their partners should be prosecuted: 'agree totally' and 'agree more or less'	81.2
If your partner were HIV-positive, you should be informed even without his or her consent: 'agree totally' and 'agree more or less'	88.2
Getting the person's consent before performing a screening test should be mandatory: 'disagree more or less' and 'disagree totally'	32.2
It is normal for doctors and hospitals to conduct AIDS tests without informing the individuals first: 'agree totally' and 'agree more or less'	44.5

Table 6
Attitude taken with regard to HIV-positive people

In your opinion, is transmission of the AIDS virus possible in each of the following circumstances?	Would you agree to work or study in the company of an HIV-positive person?	
	Yes (would work/study)	No (wouldn't)
by getting blood in Belgium: yes	52.5	69.7
by giving blood in Belgium today: yes	32.6	46.6
by kissing someone on the mouth: yes	11.9	22.2
via a mosquito bite: yes	11.8	19.4
by sitting on a toilet seat: yes	10.8	23.3
by drinking from someone's glass: yes	7.1	17.3
TOTAL (n)	1695	195

To simplify the presentation, the 'don't know' and 'no answer' column is not shown here. Only a sample (50% of the whole population) had to answer this question.

Table 7
Knowledge of modes of transmission and segregation

How should we interpret this correspondence between what we can consider to be incorrect ideas in the light of current medical discourse and discriminatory attitudes? We might think that these discriminatory attitudes are explained to a great extent by ignorance. However, this interpretation is not enough. We know, for example, that a common way to construct one's identity and strive to fit in with one's entourage is to create 'out groups', that is, claim a distance between oneself and other groups. Such a strategy, in which people with HIV and the whole problem of AIDS are lumped together, may be at work here.

If we focus on the individuals who express segregationist attitudes, we find that they are over-represented in the over-50 age bracket as well as among the less educated segments of the population. The proportion of respondents between the ages of 15 and 45 who refuse radically all segregationist talk is systematically equal to or greater than 42 per cent in all age groups, with peaks at 50 per cent for certain age groups. The figure falls to 35.9

per cent for the 50 to 54-year-olds and plummets to 29.6 per cent for the 55 to 59-year-olds. A third (32 per cent) of the adults who only completed primary school rejected all forms of segregation versus 51.8 per cent of college graduates and their ilk. The same pattern is discerned among young people who are still in school: radically antisegregationist views are held by 42.5 per cent of those who are in lower secondary schools versus 57.2 per cent of non-university higher education and university students. Finally, whereas segregationist sentiments are totally independent of 'vigilant mistrust', they do appear connected to the attitude of 'distant mistrust'. Indeed, whereas 34.8 per cent of the respondents who subscribed totally to the statement 'you can't trust anyone these days' refused all forms of segregation in the strictest manner, this attitude was exhibited by 57.7 per cent of the respondents who rejected the statement outright.

When all these elements are taken together, they seem to lend strength to the theory of personal and social structuring based on a 'distancing–repulsion' logic. We can indeed isolate a group that may be said to consist of 'social sideliners' on various scores (older, less educated population that believes it is useful to beware of others) who are both less knowledgeable about the virus's transmission and protective measures, and hold segregationist attitudes towards people with HIV. In other words, everything points to a situation in which standing back and excluding others from the group seem to function as this group's general characteristics. If we pursue this logic, its members' segregationist attitudes towards people with HIV would appear to be less the consequence of specific ignorance of the disease, AIDS, than the sign of a way of building one's identity and trying to fit in with one's entourage that consists in establishing a distance between oneself and others. Given certain characteristics of this group (older, less educated, etc.), we might also wonder if it is not also plagued by a vague feeling of insecurity and fear of everything that upsets the usual social boundaries.

In a word, the ideas about AIDS that are circulating in society are socially and culturally charged. They do not stem from the absence or availability of information or the quality of information alone.

Conclusion

Our conclusion is that knowledge about HIV/AIDS (modes of HIV transmission, means of protection, etc.) and discriminatory attitudes towards people with HIV do not stem from a purely rational approach. Rather, they are part of a larger set of representations that includes complex cognitive, emotional and cultural components and fulfils psychological and social functions.

In the case of our analyses, some of our respondents' answers to our survey questions reflect a degree of trust or mistrust of specialists. For these respondents it is less a matter of knowing (only specialists truly 'know', and only within the limits of their knowledge) than of believing in the correctness of the knowledge produced by specialists and in the professional standards of those in charge of healthcare, especially blood bank managers. For us, these respondents express what we have called 'vigilant mistrust'. We have also been able to isolate a group that may be said to consist of 'social sideliners' who are both less knowledgeable about the virus's transmission and protective measures and hold segregationist attitudes towards HIV-positive people. These attitudes express what we would call 'distant mistrust'.

These first findings show that representations take place within social interaction processes and more complex communication models should be used to allow better for interactions between groups that could be in conflict on some issue about AIDS. This is particularly true when considering the issue of discrimination that some communities and companies are facing. We should thus wonder about the content and the form of the information that is given to the population. Since discriminatory attitudes do not seem to be dispelled merely by the better circulation of information about the disease, specific interventions aimed at countering discrimination should be set up.

1 A. Schütz, *Collected papers*, 1, p. 5. Martinus Nijhoff, The Hague, 1982 (first edition 1962).

2 S. Moscovici, 'The phenomenon of social representations', *Social Representations* (eds. R.M. Farr and S. Moscovici). Cambridge University Press, Cambridge, 1983.

3 For the first research report see: M. Hubert and J. Marquet (Coordinators), J.-P. Delchambre, D. Peto, C. Schaut and L. Van Campenhoudt, *Comportements sexuels et réactions au risque du sida en Belgique*. Centre d'études sociologiques, Facultés universitaires Saint-Louis, Brussels, 15 November 1993.

The success of the national survey was made possible by the help of the following institutions: Belgium's medical research fund, FRSM, in the framework of the National AIDS Research Programme; Belgium's national scientific research fund, FNRS; the Commission of the European Communities (DGV); and the Brussels-Capital Region. In addition, the Belgian Institute of Hygiene and Epidemiology (IHE) and AIDS Prevention Agency (APS) helped to pre-test the survey in November and December 1992.

4 This sample was taken randomly from the national registry, which is the most complete and up-to-date list of residents in the country.

Only French- and Dutch-speaking respondents were invited to participate in the survey.

5 A. Spira, N. Bajos et le groupe ACSF, *Les Comportements sexuels en France*. La Documentation Française, Collection de rapports officiels, Paris, 1993.

G. van Zessen, T. Sandfort, *Seksualiteit in Nederland; seksueel gedrag, risico en preventie van aids*. Swets & Zeitlinger, Amsterdam/Lisse, 1991.

6 A. Spira, N. Bajos et le groupe ACSF, *Les Comportements sexuels en France*, p.205. La Documentation Française, Collection de rapports officiels, Paris, 1993.

7 D. Agrafiotis *et al. Knowledge, Attitudes, Beliefs and Practices in Relation to HIV Infection and AIDS: The Case of the City of Athens (Greece)*. Athens School of Public Health, Department of Sociology, 1990.

J.-P. Moatti, W. Dab, M. Pollak, 'Les Français et le SIDA', *La Recherche*, no. 247, vol. 23, pp. 1202–1211, October 1992.

G. van Zessen, T. Sandfort, *Seksualiteit in Nederland; seksueel gedrag, risico en preventie van aids*. Swets & Zeitlinger, Amsterdam/Lisse, 1991.

8 J.-P. Moatti, W. Dab, M. Pollak, 'Les Français et le SIDA', *La Recherche*, no. 247, vol. 23, pp. 1202–1211, October 1992.

G. van Zessen, T. Sandfort, *Seksualiteit in Nederland; seksueel gedrag, risico en preventie van aids*. Swets & Zeitlinger, Amsterdam/Lisse, 1991.

B.J. Robertson, D.V. McQueen, L. Nisbet *et al. AIDS-Related Behaviours, Knowledge and Attitudes; Provisional Data from the RUHBC Cati Survey*, data update no. 32, June–December 1992. Research Unit in Health and Behavioural Change (RUHBC), Edinburgh, Scotland, 1992.

9 B.J. Robertson, D.V. McQueen, L. Nisbet *et al. AIDS-Related Behaviours, Knowledge and Attitudes; Provisional Data from the RUHBC Cati Survey*, data update no. 32, June–December 1992. Research Unit in Health and Behavioural Change (RUHBC), Edinburgh, Scotland, 1992.

10 J.-P. Moatti, W. Dab, M. Pollak, 'Les Français et le SIDA', *La Recherche*, no. 247, vol. 23, pp. 1202–1211, October 1992.

11 G. van Zessen, T. Sandfort, *Seksualiteit in Nederland; seksueel gedrag, risico en preventie van aids*. Swets & Zeitlinger, Amsterdam/Lisse, 1991.

12 B.J. Robertson, D.V. McQueen, L. Nisbet *et al. AIDS-Related Behaviours, Knowledge and Attitudes; Provisional Data from the RUHBC Cati Survey*, data update no. 32, June–December 1992.

Research Unit in Health and Behavioural Change (RUHBC), Edinburgh, Scotland, 1992.

13 A. Spira, N. Bajos et le groupe ACSF, *Les Comportements sexuels en France*, p. 208. La Documentation Française, Collection de rapports officiels, Paris, 1993.

14 A. Spira, N. Bajos et le groupe ACSF, *Les Comportements sexuels en France*, p. 208. La Documentation Française, Collection de rapports officiels, Paris, 1993.

G. van Zessen, T. Sandfort, *Seksualiteit in Nederland; seksueel gedrag, risico en preventie van aids*. Swets & Zeitlinger, Amsterdam/Lisse, 1991.

15 That is to say, those who subscribed to one of the following answers: 'withdrawing the penis before ejaculation – coitus interruptus (totally effective, rather effective or don't know); washing after sex (totally effective, rather effective or don't know); choosing partners who appear to be in good health (totally effective, rather effective or don't know); using the pill (totally effective, rather effective or don't know); you can be vaccinated against AIDS (yes or don't know).

16 We considered that persons who were unsure of their partner or partners' faithfulness and did not use condoms, had had several partners over the past five years and had never had a screening test or used a condom, did not take any precautions the first time they had sex with a new partner, stated that they had had an STD over the past five years, had stopped using condoms with the partner without having any additional information about the partner's serological status, or a combination of the above exposed themselves to the risk of HIV infection.

The total of 226 people nevertheless seems to be a minimum, given that the survey protocol was designed to collect specific information only with regard to the last three partners and did not allow investigation of relationships that had ended more than twelve months prior to the survey. So, 171 individuals with partially incorrect knowledge did not take any risks in the relationships that were investigated but

may have had other partners over the past five years about whom we cannot say anything.

17 The two groups have fairly different social and sexual profiles. We must also point out that nothing enables us to ascertain whether the level of information manifested by the second group at the time of the survey had already been acquired at the time of risk taking. It is not uncommon for requests for information to be made after a supposed risk has been taken.

Some 310 individuals did not present any risks for the relationships being investigated but had had other partners over the past five years.

18 M. Becker, J. Joseph, 'AIDS and behavioural change to reduce risk: a review', *American Journal of Public Health*, 778 (4), 394–410, 1988.

J.A. Kelly, J.S. St Lawrence, *The AIDS Health Crisis: Psychological and Social Interventions*. Plenum Press, New York and London, 1988.

M. Pollak, J.-P. Moatti, 'HIV risk perception and determinants of sexual behaviour', *Sexual Behaviour and Risks of HIV Infection. Proceedings of an International Workshop Supported by the European Communities* (ed. M. Hubert). Publications des Facultés universitaires Saint-Louis, Brussels, 1990.

19 We have defined people with correct knowledge as those who did not consider any of the largely ineffective means of protection to have some efficacy.

20 A. Spira, N. Bajos et le groupe ACSF, *Les Comportements sexuels en France*, p. 270. La Documentation Française, Collection de rapports officiels, Paris, 1993.

21 J.-P. Moatti, W. Dab, M. Pollak, Les Français et le SIDA, *La Recherche*, no. 247, vol. 23, p. 1206, October 1992.

22 D. Agrafiotis *et al. Knowledge, Attitudes, Beliefs and Practices in Relation to HIV Infection and AIDS: The Case of the City of Athens (Greece)*, p. 77. Athens School of Public Health, Department of Sociology, 1990.

Public Health and Human Rights: Finding a Balance in HIV Prevention[1]

Jonathan Glasson

Consultant, UK Forum on HIV and Human Rights, London, England

Protection against epidemics is one of any government's main tasks arising from the human right to health. The International Covenant on Economic, Social and Cultural Rights includes 'the prevention, treatment and control of epidemic...diseases' among the measures that States Parties should undertake towards the full realization of the right to health.

However, much discrimination has been justified on the grounds of 'public health'. The question of what is a justifiable public health response to HIV is therefore critical. Denial of human rights and discrimination against people with impaired health is part of the public health heritage. Furthermore, international human rights law accepts that human rights may be limited on the grounds of public health if such limitations satisfy criteria of legitimacy, legality and proportionality and, most importantly, if they are imposed without discrimination.[2]

In respect of HIV there have been two fundamentally different public health approaches. One, based on a traditional public health rationale, invokes restrictive and coercive measures. The other has emphasized changes in individual behaviour, education and anti-discrimination.

The first approach has encompassed policies such as travel restrictions, quarantine and the compulsory notification of partners of people diagnosed with HIV. An analysis of these measures by human rights criteria established that many of them were incompatible with international human rights requirements.[3]

The second approach to public health has focused on community-based preventive work and removing stigma and discrimination. This approach pays particular attention to the fine balance between protecting the public from avoidable exposure to potentially serious infections and also protecting the individual's right to privacy, liberty and security of person. Commentators have emphasized that legal controls which interfere with these or other basic human rights can only be justified if they are necessary and proportionate for the protection of the public health or some other specified legitimate interest.

Many commentators have stressed that the protection of human rights must be a cornerstone of public health approaches to HIV. Dr Jonathan Mann, the first director of the World Health Organization's (WHO) Global Programme on AIDS, has argued forcefully that 'discrimination may endanger public health; stigmatization may itself represent a threat to public health...protecting the human rights and dignity of HIV-infected people, including people with AIDS, and members of population groups, is not a luxury – it is a necessity. It is not a question of "the rights of the many" against the "rights of the few": the protection of the uninfected majority depends upon and is inextricably bound with the protection of the rights and dignity of the infected persons.' [4]

Indeed, research conducted by the McGill Centre for Medicine, Ethics and Law in Montreal has shown that public health interventions and protection of human rights are compatible and mutually reinforcing. Public health interventions and human rights efforts were analysed in relation to the availability of explicit information, peer education, and risk-reducing equipment (e.g. condoms, needles, gloves); access to and quality of treatment; breaches of privacy or confidentiality; and discrimination. The research concluded that coercive or repressive public health interventions often threaten or abuse human rights, are counterproductive, and jeopardize public health goals. On the other hand, public health interventions which increase people's autonomy and decrease their vulnerability reinforce respect for human rights and are compatible with efforts to promote and protect those rights.[5]

It is of key importance that these conclusions be recognized in interpreting how the 'public health' is served, for public health has often been cited as a legitimate ground for limiting human rights in international human rights law, as well as in invoking the defence of 'public interest' in domestic law.

Indeed the International Covenant on Civil and Political Rights (ICCPR) acknowledges: 'In time of public emergency which threatens the life of the nation and the existence of which is officially proclaimed, the States Parties to the present Covenant may take measures derogating from their obligations under the Present Covenant to the extent strictly required by the exigencies of the situation, provided that such measures are not inconsistent with their other obligations under international law' (Article 4(1)). However, another paragraph of the same Article always excepts from this provision a number of the rights guaranteed by the instrument, in particular: the right to life; the freedom from cruel, inhuman or degrading treatment or punishment; and the freedom from slavery.

The human rights lawyer Paul Sieghart considered whether the prevalence of AIDS within a country could ever be so high as to amount to 'a public emergency threatening the life of the nation', entitling the government of that country to suspend the human rights of its inhabitants. He concluded that 'it is difficult to see how even the most drastic measures could help to prevent the further spread of a disease with such limited infectivity and such a long incubation period, and so justify derogations on the ground of a public emergency.' It is submitted therefore that there are no grounds for arguing that in violating the ICCPR with regard to HIV the UK government has any justification for such derogations from the Covenant.[6] But despite its apparent commitment to preventing the spread of HIV and to developing treatment for people with HIV, UK legislation and policy reveal deep conflicts within the Government's approach.[7] While it has emphasized the avoidance of discrimination in many of its international statements, the Government has done nothing to provide legal protection against such discrimination within the UK. Moreover, it has failed to repeal legislation, as discussed below, which significantly hampers effective HIV prevention. Where it has introduced protective guidelines and allocated specific funding for HIV, neither the implementation of such guidelines nor the use of such funds have been monitored adequately.[8]

The Government has highlighted HIV as one of the key topic areas in its White Paper on health, *The Health of the Nation*, and has acknowledged HIV to be 'arguably the greatest new threat to public health this century'.[9] Furthermore, it has allocated significant financial resources to health authorities to develop preventive work. Despite this, it has singularly failed to target resources effectively or to monitor adequately the use of these funds.[10]

The history of its policy and practice shows a government with conflicting aims which has failed to repeal the legislation which inhibits effective prevention or to direct preventive work with confidence. Access to information is a universally recognized human right whose application in the context of AIDS requires a careful balance of the rights and responsibilities of those directly involved.

The risk of contracting HIV infection because of ignorance means explicit information is important, but because the main mode of transmission of HIV is through sexual intercourse this approach has caused conflict. However, as Tomasevski has argued: 'Human sexuality is by definition controversial, but recognizing this should not be the end of the debate, but its beginning.' [11]

Young people and children

This contradictory approach to HIV prevention is demonstrated in the history of the government's policy on HIV education for young people.

The need for effective, properly resourced programmes which enable young people to make informed choices about personal relationships has been widely advocated. For instance, the Royal College of Obstetricians and Gynaecologists' report into

Unplanned pregnancy (1991) identified improvements to sex education as the most important factor in affecting the current levels of unplanned pregnancy.

Similarly, the government has set targets for reducing the incidence of HIV and other sexually transmitted diseases and unwanted pregnancies and recommends the formation of 'healthy alliances' between health, education and other sectors to achieve these targets. However, a recent survey found that 50 health education coordinator posts were to be lost immediately with further cuts expected in the near future.[12]

Most importantly the Education Act 1993 will allow parents to withdraw their children from sex education at school, while information on HIV and other sexually transmitted diseases and sexual behaviour will disappear altogether from the science curriculum. The parental right of withdrawal means that parents can withdraw children from these lessons without giving any reason, even when the children are over the age of consent or sexually active.[13] This seems to conflict directly with the spirit of the Children Act 1989 which cites the welfare of the child as the paramount consideration in determining all questions relating to a child's welfare.[14] That parents may withdraw their children gives cause for concern: the withdrawal may be prompted by pressure from local social or religious communities, and the National Society for the Prevention of Cruelty to Children has suggested the fear of disclosure of sexual abuse as a reason for withdrawal.[15]

Some have seen the 1993 Education Act's requirement that schools keep a written statement of their policy on sex education as a progressive step, but in fact schools already had to have a policy under the Education (No. 2) Act 1986. Furthermore, a school's policy on sex education could be not to provide sex education. It has been shown that even before the 1993 Act was passed, over a quarter of governing bodies had still not fulfilled their statutory obligations.[16]

The ICCPR recognizes the 'liberty of parents to ensure the religious and moral education of their children in conformity with their own convictions'.[17] This freedom has sometimes been exercized by parents to prevent their children from being educated about the transmission of HIV. However, the UN Convention on the Rights of the Child stresses that the guiding principle is the best interests of the child, not the parents. The Convention reaffirms the freedom of the child to seek and receive information and, moreover, in defining the contents of the right to health, it obliges states to ensure that children have access to education. Article 24 of the Convention, dealing with the right to health, obliges states to take appropriate measures 'to ensure that all segments of society, in particular parents and children, are informed, have access to education, and are supported in the use of basic knowledge'.[18]

The European Convention on Human Rights affirms 'the right to…receive information' (Article 10) and asserts that 'no person shall be denied the right to education' (Article 2). By allowing parents to withdraw their child from sex education the government is arguably breaching these rights under the Convention. It may point to the qualifying provisions in both Articles as justification for such a breach: either 'for the protection of morals' or 'for the protection of the rights of others' the Articles may be suspended. However, given that children's health can only be protected if they are given information about the transmission of HIV or the dangers of unwanted pregnancy it has been argued that these exceptions do not apply. Indeed, the European Court of Human Rights has rejected an application of some Danish parents who sought to withdraw their children from sex education on similar grounds.[19]

Gay men and HIV prevention

The government shows itself it to be peculiarly double-handed with regard to this area of work. Guidance to health authorities has emphasized the need to work with gay men and *The Health of the Nation* lists gay men among the priority groups for prevention.

However, it has enacted legislation which has been widely interpreted (albeit wrongly) as prohibiting HIV work with young people which includes reference to homosexuality. It has failed to enact legislation to bring a parity in the ages of consent for gay and heterosexual sex and has failed to monitor the work of health authorities in the area of gay men and HIV prevention. The result is that HIV transmissions among gay men seem now to be increasing, while recent HIV transmissions appear to affect younger gay men disproportionately.[20]

Parliament decriminalized homosexuality only partially in 1967. The age of consent for consensual acts between men in private was, until 1994, 21 while the age of consent for lesbians and heterosexuals is 16. In February 1994 the House of Commons voted for an amendment to the Criminal Justice Bill which reduced the age of consent for gay sex from 21 to 18, and this came into effect later that year. Thus gay men continue to be discriminated against. Many HIV workers have voiced their anxiety about HIV education which requires open discussion about sexual behaviour because of this disparity.

This anxiety is further complicated by Section 28 of the Local Government Act 1988 which forbids a local authority to:

'a) intentionally promote homosexuality or publish material with the intention of promoting homosexuality;

b) promote the teaching in any maintained

school of the acceptability of homosexuality as a pretended family relationship.'

The Section goes on to say that this shall not prohibit 'the doing of anything for the purpose of treating or preventing the spread of disease' and this has been accepted to exclude any HIV-related work:

> 'Thus activities in the counselling, healthcare and health education fields undertaken for the purpose of treating or preventing the spread of disease, including AIDS, will not be prohibited. This includes activities concerned exclusively with the needs of homosexuals.' [21]

Section 28 only applies to local authorities and local education authorities. Head teachers and governors, who are responsible for sex education, are excepted from the provisions of the Act. However, many reports have suggested that the effects of Section 28, together with the law relating to the age of consent, significantly prevent work with young people[22] and with gay men.[23]

A recent survey has indicated that out of 190 NHS agencies with an HIV prevention remit, 24 HIV-specific voluntary sector agencies and twelve local government agencies, only 34 per cent had undertaken specific work with gay or bisexual men, while only 3.5 percent were undertaking substantial work in this area.[24] Reasons given for the absence of such work veered from 'we've no homosexual community here, you might try district X - they have a theatre' to 'we cannot target gay men specifically because of the legal situation'.

And yet in 1992 gay and bisexual men constituted approximately 80 percent of all reported cases of AIDS, while they represent just under 70 percent of all new HIV transmissions.

The obscenity laws

The main piece of legislation in this area is the Obscene Publications Act 1959. This prohibits the publication of an 'obscene article' which is defined in Section 1 of the Act. This states that the effect of the article in question taken as a whole must be to 'tend to deprave and corrupt [a significant proportion of] persons who are likely…to read, see or hear the matter contained' in the article. Judicial interpretations of this definition have shifted in the last 30 years.[25] Other relevant pieces of legislation are the Video Recordings Act 1984; the Customs and Excise Management Act 1959; Post Office Act 1953; Unsolicited Goods and Services Act 1971; Indecent Displays (Control) Act 1981 and the Public Order Act 1986.

The confusion over the interpretation of the effect of these laws has made many statutory and voluntary agencies cautious about developing sexually explicit material on HIV prevention. Until 1993 there had been no prosecutions in this country of safer sex materials. However, the organizers of an AIDS information service (Supportlink) were threatened with prosecution in September 1993 for displaying a poster produced by the Terrence Higgins Trust. The prosecution was threatened under Section 5 of the Public Order Act 1986: the organizers were alleged to have displayed a threatening, abusive or insulting sign within the sight of a person likely to be caused harassment, alarm or distress thereby.[26]

Prostitution and sex work

Most of the activities surrounding prostitution are unlawful although prostitution itself is not illegal. Soliciting, pimping, managing a brothel and kerb crawling are all criminal offences. This has significant implications for HIV prevention initiatives such as counselling and outreach to prostitutes and sex workers. Moreover, the criminalization of prostitution-related activities prevents prostitutes from negotiating the terms of the sexual encounter.[27]

While the fact that someone is carrying condoms is, by itself, not sufficient to establish one of the criminal offences mentioned above, the carrying of condoms has been used by the police as corroborative evidence to support an allegation that an individual is working as a prostitute. In police prosecutions of brothels and saunas, the presence and availability of quantities of condoms on the premises has been used as evidence to indicate that unlawful sexual acts and/or prostitution have taken place there.

The effect of such prosecution policies is to increase the likelihood of prostitutes agreeing to unsafe penetrative sexual intercourse, and of brothel keepers restricting the availability of condoms on their premises.

Once again the government's policies are contradictory. On the one hand it encourages health authorities to provide condoms and other HIV prevention services to prostitutes and sex workers and on the other hand the police are permitted to use the presence of condoms as evidence that criminal offences have been committed.

Drugs

A similar conflict is seen in the government's policy towards drugs. It has acknowledged that 'HIV is a greater threat to public and individual health than drug use'.[28] As a result many needle and syringe schemes have been introduced and a policy of harm minimization is now followed by most health authorities. Despite this, the possession of proscribed drugs (classes A and B) for personal consumption remains illegal even though the experience of other countries (such as Holland) shows that liberal drug laws for personal consumption can reduce the incidence of HIV transmission through drug use.

Conclusion

In 1991 the UK Government endorsed the recommendations of the Pan-European Consultation on HIV in the Context of Public Health and Human Rights ('The Prague Statement'), which called for member states to 'ensure that all laws, policies and practices which directly or indirectly affect HIV/AIDS prevention or control, or could inhibit the legal emancipation and empowerment of women and vulnerable population groups, take full account of those [human rights] principles... In this respect special attention should be paid to the needs and rights of men who have sex with men, drug users, sex workers, prisoners, migrants, refugees and ethnic minorities.'

It states that:

'Member states should strive to ensure that policies and practices in the public domain do not discriminate against people solely on the grounds of their HIV status, and study the appropriateness...of introducing protective legislation to provide individuals with legal protection against...discrimination, whether by public authorities, private bodies or individuals, relating to HIV/AIDS status in the enjoyment of such rights as the right to work, education, access to social and health care and other resources of society.'

'Since obligations under international legal instruments on human rights include the obligation of states to ensure protection against arbitrary interference with the enjoyment of the right to privacy, Member States should examine present law and practice with a view to ensuring that adequate safeguards are in place to protect confidentiality at all levels of health care and social welfare services.'

It is clear that in many respects the UK has failed to heed the recommendations of the Prague Statement. In tackling the HIV crisis, it is vital to ensure that everyone in the UK enjoys the right to accurate and effective HIV prevention. As the Hon Justice Michael Kirby, President of the Court of Appeal of New South Wales and Chairman of the International Committee of Jurists has pointed out:

'The punitive model will not work. There is not enough barbed wire nor funds enough for the model of quarantine. We are without a cure. No mass vaccine is immediately in prospect. We must depend, very largely, upon behaviour modification to contain this epidemic. To win behaviour change, always so difficult as every lawyer will tell, we must gain the confidence and respect of those most at risk and those already infected. By protecting them we protect everyone... In the face of this global enormity which threatens our species, we should be prepared to act boldly. We should do this because it is the pragmatic thing to do and...it is meet and right so to do. It is our bounden duty to promote and respect human rights. In the struggle against AIDS, it is a happy coincidence that the protection of human rights is also the best strategy for containing the epidemic.' [29]

1 This paper is based on' HIV and Civil and Political Liberties', a report commissioned by the UK Forum on HIV and Human Rights in the summer of 1993. The report was designed to inform the Forum's submission to the United Nations Human Rights Committee on the United Kingdom's observance of the International Covenant on Civil and Political Rights.

2 The Siracusa principles on the limitation and derogation provisions in the International Covenant on Civil and Political Rights, Annex to UN Doc E/CN.4/1985/4, 28 September 1984.

3 P. Sieghart, AIDS and Human Rights : A UK Perspective. BMA Foundation for AIDS, London, 1989.

4 Dr Jonathan Mann, Director, Global Programme on AIDS, WHO, 'AIDS discrimination and public health', address to the IV International Conference on AIDS, 1988.

5 N. Gilmore, WS-D22-6, International Conference on AIDS, Berlin, 1993.

6 P. Sieghart, AIDS and Human Rights : A UK Perspective. BMA Foundation for AIDS, London, 1989.

7 All legislation referred to in this article is that of England and Wales.

8 National Audit Office, HIV and AIDS Related Health Services, report by the Comptroller and Auditor General. HMSO, 1991.

9 The Health of the Nation : A Strategy for Health in England. HMSO, 1992.

10 National Audit Office, HIV and AIDS Related Health Services, report by the Comptroller and Auditor General. HMSO, 1991.

11 K. Tomasevski, The AIDS Pandemic and Human Rights, collected courses of the Academy of European Law, vol. II, book 2, 99–150.

12 'Health Education Coordinators – LGDF survey results', unpublished, Association of County Councils, 1993. For further information contact: Rachel Thomson, Sex Education Forum, Family Planning Association, London.

'Patten announces education grant programme', Department of Education press
release, 20 July 1992.

13 Confirmed in correspondence between
Baroness Blatch, Minister of State at the Department for Education, and Baroness Jay following
the debate on the Third Reading of the Act in
the House of Lords on 6 July. Blatch wrote that
'I believe that certain parents might find it difficult to understand why the law regarded them
as the best judges of their children's maturity
up to the age of sixteen, but deprived them of
the right thereafter.'

14 Children Act 1989, C. 41, Section 1.

15 'Bill may help sex abusers', *Times Educational
Supplement*, 16 July 1993.

16 R. Thomson, L. Scott, *An Enquiry into Sex
Education: Report of a Survey into Local Education
Authority Support and Monitoring of School Sex
Education*. Sex Education Forum, 1992.

17 International Covenant on Civil and Political Rights, annex to General Assembly Resolution 2200 A (XXI) of 16 December 1966, Article
18(4).

18 Convention on the Rights of the Child,
annex to General Assembly Resolution 44/25
of 20 November 1989.

19 *Kjeldesen, Busk and Pederson* v. *Denmark*, 1976.

20 Barry Evans, 'Sexually transmitted diseases
and HIV-1 infection among homosexual men in
England and Wales', *British Medical Journal*, 306:
426–8, 1993.

21 Circular 12/88, Department of the Environment.

22 *The National AIDS Trust Youth Initiative: Liv-
ing for Tomorrow*, National AIDS Trust, 1991.
Evaluation of Action AIDS, Oxford Regional
Health Authority, 1991.

23 M. Rooney, *Gay Men: Sustaining Safer Sex?*
North West Thames HIV Project, 1991.

24 E. King, M. Rooney, P. Scott, 'HIV preven-
tion for gay men: a survey of initiatives in the
UK'. National AIDS Manual, North West
Thames Regional Health Authority HIV Pro-
ject, The Terrence Higgins Trust and Gay Men
Fighting AIDS, 1992.

25 'HIV prevention and the law', *National AIDS
Manual* (Spring 1993 edition): chapter 7 for a
detailed discussions of the cases concerned.

26 Angus Hamilton, 'Messing with the safer
sex message', *Gay Times*, November 1993.

27 'The violation of prostitutes' human rights is
a major risk factor for HIV', International Committee for Prostitutes Rights, International
AIDS Conference, Berlin, 1993.

28 Advisory Council on the Misuse of Drugs,
AIDS and Drug Misuse. HMSO, 1988.

29 The Hon. Justice Michael Kirby, 'AIDS and
the Law', the Doughty Street Lecture, 29
November 1993.

Living with HIV/AIDS in Switzerland: Exclusion or Solidarity

Jacqueline De Puy

IPSO Research Centre, Geneva, Switzerland

The contents of this chapter are based on a study carried out by the IPSO Research Centre[1] to evaluate tendencies in Swiss society to stigmatize people living with HIV or AIDS. We have defined 'stigmatization' as holding distorted attitudes towards an individual who deviates from the norm; this is not just limited to rejection and exclusion, but can also be expressed in the form of excessive compassion.[2]

The focus of the study was on attitudes of individuals in certain social situations rather than in the population as a whole. We chose to look specifically into interactions with professionals playing a direct and essential part in the everyday life of people with HIV or AIDS.

The empiric material of our study was collected through simulated testing of real-life situations. This experimental phase was preceded by exploratory research in order to obtain general background information on attitudes and measures affecting people with HIV or AIDS.

In this chapter I briefly present our main findings, with emphasis on the impact of stigmatization in the workplace and the socio-economic costs of such behaviour and attitudes.

I have based the analysis on three perspectives:

- public opinion and institutional policies regarding people with HIV or AIDS in Switzerland; testimonies of people with HIV or AIDS about concrete situations they faced in connection with their serological status;
- scenarios involving imaginary people with HIV or AIDS.

Public opinion and institutional policies

Since 1986, the Federal Office for Public Health has been involved in a vast information campaign about AIDS ('STOP SIDA'). The primary aims were to prevent new infections and to ensure assistance to those people already infected. As of 1988 the campaign has included a call for solidarity with people with AIDS or HIV. And solidarity would imply not only the absence of discrimination, but also the promotion of justice and equality for all.

This effort has certainly contributed to the fact that public opinion in Switzerland appears to be quite tolerant towards people with HIV or AIDS. As much as 92.9 per cent of the population support non-discriminatory policies as far as medical care is concerned. 41.5 per cent suggest welfare measures, such as the creation of nursing homes or special housing, as well as financial assistance with the high medical costs involved in treating the disease.[3] And 40 per cent are in favour of non-discrimination in sectors such as employment and housing. Few people are openly in favour of discrimination.

While there is a clear desire to support people with HIV or AIDS, this is on certain terms: that responsibility be delegated to hospitals, social welfare agencies and the state. People are more reserved when it comes to getting personally involved. Hence, more than three-quarters of 17 to 45-year-olds consider people with AIDS to be rejected in our society, and many still believe that AIDS is some kind of punishment.[4]

fact, since 1987 the Swiss Medical Association has actually classified HIV infection as a disease. Consequently, insurance companies have been turning away HIV-positive applicants. The situation is similar in the case of a number of pension funds. With the exception of state-related pension funds and those offered in large companies,[5] admission is conditional upon a negative reply to the question: 'Have you had an HIV test with a positive result?' If the answer is yes, you cannot join the pension scheme, and under these circumstances it is practically impossible to get a job.

Outside these sectors, professional associations (employers and trade unions), political parties and churches have issued statements and guidelines that are generally in favour of the integration and acceptance of people with HIV or AIDS.

Institutional policies

A set of statements published between April 1988 and March 1990 (Figure 1) suggested that most discrimination against people with HIV or AIDS occurs within the healthcare and insurance sectors. In

Testimonies

A total of 85 direct and indirect testimonies were collected. Thirty-one were obtained directly, in the form of letters or telephone interviews. To source respondents, we contacted eleven medical doc-

Figure 1
Institutional statements on HIV/AIDS
(N = 58)

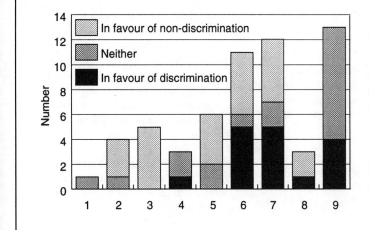

1. international organizations
2. employees' associations
3. employers' associations
4. insurers
5. health services
6. physicians, associations of physicians
7. state institutions / political parties
8. churches
9. others

tors and 46 associations likely to be of help and asked them to distribute a press release explaining the purpose of our study. We also set up a hotline: it was clear from the response that there was tremendous need for people with HIV or AIDS to share their feelings (conversations often exceeded an hour), although it was difficult to break the initial silence. The anonymity of the telephone encouraged people to call, but many had hesitated a great deal before doing so.

The remaining testimonies were published in the press and scientific studies between 1988 and 1990.

These various testimonies resulted in descriptions of 177 different situations involving:

• overt stigmatization (76 cases);
• fear of rejection (52 cases);
• shows of solidarity (49 cases).

Of these cases, 128 involved stigmatization of some kind (actual rejection or fear thereof), and took place in the following contexts – by decreasing order of frequency:

• family and friends
• the workplace
• medical care
• insurance
• public administration
• social care
• school and education

Relationships in the workplace or with family and friends make up 80 of these negative experiences, resulting in withdrawal and the isolation of those concerned.

More specifically, stigmatization at work resulted in a significant number of dismissals and pressure to resign or retire, and was motivated by fear of contamination:

'My boss yielded to the pressure and asked me to keep away from the company in order to avoid internal problems.... The fact that I was HIV-positive frightened my colleagues who no longer wanted to work with me.' [6]

Fear of stigmatization in the workplace meant that HIV-positive employees lived in a climate of insecurity and stress, under threat of being dismissed or not hired should their status be discovered. Others feared that relationships with their colleagues would suffer:

'Nobody knows [that I am HIV-positive] where I work. I am scared I might lose my job. I am a schoolteacher in a rural community.' [7]

Reactions of solidarity at work were only experienced by those already established in employment. (This is hardly surprising since pension fund policies[8] are a serious obstacle to non-discrimination of job applicants with HIV.) Some people mentioned that they had benefitted from a climate of understanding, support and tolerance from their management and colleagues. Even in cases of people with full-blown AIDS, employers had agreed to keep them in the company and to change their schedules if necessary:

'In my company, I experienced a lot of understanding and support. They adapt to my capacities. Right now I am working part-time.... My boss arranged for me to stay in [a convalescent home] and agreed to cover extra costs involved. I have the feeling my situation has allowed me to become closer to my colleagues. Many of them come into my office and talk to me about their personal affairs; it was not the case before.' [9]

We agree with Sontag that people with HIV or AIDS should not be condemned to social death because of beliefs associated with this infection.[10]

Testing attitudes

Test scenarios were established on the basis of the most common situations described in the testimonies. These were designed to comply with the criteria of scientific experimentation so as to permit valid comparisons.

Requests for employment, childcare, dental care, private sector housing, social services and participation in sports clubs were made by imaginary people with HIV or AIDS. In order to appraise the influence of the independent variable (HIV or AIDS), control simulations were also enacted, involving no other handicap (e.g. hepatitis, tuberculosis, Alzheimer's disease).

Other factors of influence were controlled by making requests under otherwise favourable circumstances. For example, requests for employment concerned imaginary people with good qualifications.

The purpose of the tests was to study initial reactions to letters or telephone enquiries. Managing the tests was a complex task. We were careful to maintain a balance between requests made by men and women in each sector, and between people with HIV or AIDS. We chose to over-represent the requests made by people with HIV or AIDS, compared to those made in the controls, in order to study the HIV/AIDS cases more in detail. In the control situations, we merely wanted to observe tendencies.

The geographical location and the number of cases in each simulated test and control were dictated by criteria of feasibility and so as to permit comparison. For instance, to test kindergartens, we selected six small towns with about the same population, because we knew that *these* had vacancies, whereas those in large cities do not.

For the tests carried out in the employment sector, two major Swiss cities were selected, and advertisements, published in the press, were answered on behalf of imaginary candidates with qualifications in high demand.

This resulted in the distribution of tests shown in table 1.

The forms of stigmatization we could observe as a result of the tests were quite different according to the context in which they took place.

In the context of childcare, sports clubs, social services and dental care, these imaginary people were usually seen as 'victims' (especially the children and teenagers).

	HIV	AIDS	Other disability	No disability	TOTAL
Employment	37	–	–	38	75
Housing	–	28	10	–	38
Social Services	–	13	5	–	18
Childcare	2	–	2	2	6
Dental Care	34	–	–	–	34
Sports Club	23	–	5	–	28
Total	96	41	22	40	199

Table 1
Number and type of request made

This did not, however, prevent exclusion – in a compassionate way – of HIV-positive teenagers from sportsclubs, and was motivated by fear of contamination.

Stigmatization was also identified in some requests with a favourable outcome, taking the form of exaggerated attention and precautions. For example, one child would only be admitted to a kindergarten on condition that she be attended first by one of two doctors designated by the kindergarten director. No inquiry was made as to whether the child was *already* being attended by a doctor. There was also a dentist who only agreed to treat a patient with HIV in the evening ('so that the instruments can be soaked in disinfectant the whole night').

Others, more commonly in the process of looking for a job or joining a sports club, were stigmatized in the form of long delays in receiving a reply and by refusals. At best, a distant compassion was expressed ('Good luck and courage for the future').

No brutal, aggressive stigmatization was registered. This was, of course, a consequence of the method used: initial contact by letter or telephone tends to be rather formal, and our precise purpose was to detect forms of ordinary, indirect stigmatization.

A general pattern could be identified in terms of type of stigmatization. Relatively long delays in replies to requests from peo-

Figure 2
Summary of replies

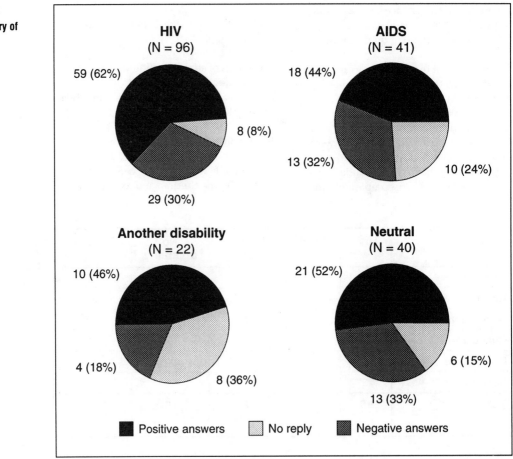

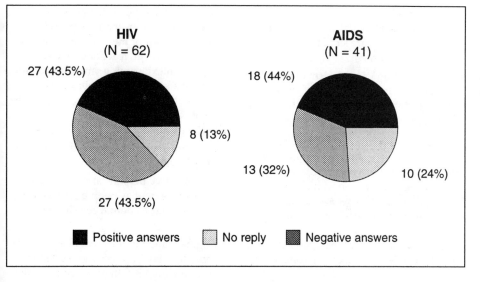

Figure 3
Summary of replies to people with HIV or AIDS (excluding dental care)

ple with HIV or AIDS (as compared to control groups) revealed the reluctance of recipients to deal with them. The longest delays came from sports clubs: 20–26 days on average for letters from HIV-positive teenagers – twice as long as delays for teenagers with hepatitis B (thirteen days on average). Requests for employment made by people with HIV also met relatively long delays (thirteen days on average), compared to an average delay of eight days for people with no disability at all.

A number of positive (mostly childcare and sports clubs) as well as negative responses (mainly employment and housing) were indicative of overprotection on the one hand, and exclusion on the other.

Figure 2 summarizes the positive and negative replies, as well as absence of reply, according to whether the imaginary people in the scenarios are identified as HIV-positive, having AIDS, with no handicap or with another handicap.

The following comments can be made:

• Requests by people with HIV and, to a lesser extent, with AIDS are more often replied to (negatively or positively) than requests made by people with other handicaps, who are more often treated with indifference and get no response at all.

• The rate of positive replies to people with HIV is high if we include the simulations involving dental care.[11] If these are excluded, the rate of positive replies (e.g. to requests for employment[12] and membership of sports clubs) drops from 62 to 43.5 per cent, and the rate of nega-

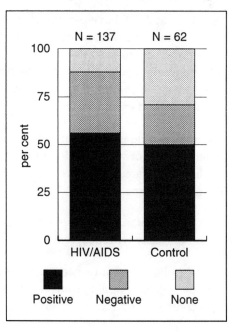

Figure 4 **Comparison of replies** HIV/AIDS against control group

tive replies increases from 29 to 43.5 per cent. Excluding dental care, rates for the HIV simulations are similar to those for AIDS (see Figure 3).

- Discrimination – in the form of negative replies – is clear in the case of employment and sports club membership as far as people with HIV are concerned.

When comparing HIV and AIDS variables with the control variables (see Figure 4), a clear discrepancy was obtained: one out of three requests by a person with HIV or AIDS is rejected, whereas the refusal rate is only one out of five for others (control groups).

Based on the findings of these test cases, we would formulate the following conclusions:

- People who identify themselves as HIV-positive or with AIDS are more likely to receive a negative reply to various everyday requests than people who do not mention it or mention another disability. However, reactions vary according to context: gaining employment and joining a sports club *is* subject to discrimination, whereas dental care, for the most part, is not.

- People with handicaps other than AIDS are more likely to be ignored than people with AIDS.

- HIV-positive persons are rejected to the same extent as people with AIDS, except as far as dental care is concerned.

- Stigmatization in the form of absence of reply to a letter applies more often to people with AIDS than to people with HIV.

Conclusions and recommendations

Stigmatization of people with AIDS, especially in the workplace, results in a waste of human potential (and may even open the door to other forms of discrimination, such as racism). The main task of decision-makers – if they are to combat the socio-economic costs incurred – will be to *foster solidarity*.

People with AIDS have periods of remission, which are increasing as medical knowledge and treatment evolve. During these times, professional activity can be of great benefit to someone with AIDS who can then feel useful, active and integrated. From an employer's perspective, an attitude of solidarity is not merely a act of charity: it is clearly in a company's interests to make the most of its experienced employees.

As far as people with HIV are concerned, there is no reason for them to be considered unfit for work. By definition, they are in good health, and fortunately some of them are able to live many years without developing the immunodeficiency syndrome.

On the basis of our study, we would suggest the following measures to promote solidarity with people living with AIDS or HIV:

- Public information campaigns should be directed at the general population as well as at target groups who have a key role in stimulating solidarity and combatting discrimination – business managers; human resource managers; professionals in the field of social and medical care, of sports and leisure; teachers and educators – in order to sensitize them about the need for solidarity. To this end, testimonies of people with HIV or AIDS should be disseminated, giving examples of daily experiences of exclusion and solidarity. Moreover, practical problems in this respect should be addressed (fears, prejudices, obstacles, limits).

• There should be legislation against all forms of discrimination, including discrimination against people with HIV and AIDS. (This is particularly important in view of the practice of insurance companies.)

• Issues raised by the AIDS epidemic in the field of public health should be considered in a global perspective, and not separated artificially from those of other life-threatening diseases.

• Concrete initiatives should be encouraged, aimed at developing solidarity with and between people with HIV or AIDS, such as support and self-help groups and associations for the defence of their rights.

Exclusion of people with HIV or AIDS from society, and in particular from the labour market, is not only unacceptable from an ethical point of view but also because it has proven counter-productive as a preventive measure in the fight against HIV/AIDS (desocialized, marginalized individuals are certainly not open to public health campaigns).

Solidarity is an important principle in Swiss society, and is commonly referred to in political debates (solidarity with the elderly, between the different linguistic regions, rich and poor *cantons*, men and women…). As mentioned above, it implies both absence of discrimination and promotion of justice and equality for all. However, the daily behaviour of individuals and the action of decision-makers do not necessarily live up to principle. In our opinion, positive action in the case of HIV and AIDS has been insufficient in recent years. One only has to look at the practice of insurance companies to see where solidarity can break down.

According to the most optimistic projections, the number of people with HIV or AIDS will continue to increase considerably in the years to come. Under these circumstances, solidarity, nominal or otherwise, is likely to be seriously undermined unless active measures such as those outlined above are taken for the benefit of society as a whole.

1 IPSO is a private Swiss research institution based in Zurich and Geneva. It has carried out various research projects and surveys on social issues. Among others, it has produced regular evaluations of the Swiss AIDS Prevention Campaign ('STOP SIDA') on behalf of the Swiss Federal Office for Health.

This study was carried out with a team from the IPSO centre in Geneva. The project was part of National Program 26c on Psycho-Social and Cultural Aspects of AIDS, sponsored by the Swiss National Science Foundation. (See D. Gros *et al.* note (6) below; also D. Gros and J. De Puy, *Piégés par le virus: sida et discrimination dans la vie quotidienne*, Stämpfli et Cie, Berne, 1993.)

2 E. Goffmann, *Stigma: Notes on the Management of Spoiled Identity*. Prentice Hall, Englewood Cliff, New Jersey, 1963.

3 There is no national health service in Switzerland. Healthcare is paid for through private insurance schemes. In addition to the premium, one also has to pay approximately 10 per cent of medical costs incurred. In the case of HIV and AIDS, this can amount to extremely high sums of money. For people without health insurance, the situation is obviously graver still.

4 IPSO, *Solidarität mit AIDS-Kranken und HIV-Positiven zur aktuellen Situation*. Zurich 1991.

5 Probably as a result of efforts to prevent discrimination, state-related pension funds and those of large companies do not, for the moment, practise 'filtering' of HIV-positive applicants. (Findings of the 1994 report by Dialogai, the official antenna of the Swiss AIDS Prevention Association.)

6 D. Gros, M. Vuille, P. Zeugin, J. De Puy, R. Radeff, *Sida et discriminations: évaluation de la stigmatisation des personnes concernées par le sida en Suisse*, p. V: 88, 1991. (Travail éxécuté dans le cadre du programme national de recherche no. 26 du fonds national suisse de la recherche scientifique 'Homme, santé, environnement', requête no. 4026-026870, Geneva, IPSO.)

7 *Ibid.* p. V: 93.

8 In Switzerland, social security for retirement is partly financed through a state programme, partly through contributions to private pension funds. The law obliges employers and employees to subscribe to both. In fact, most companies provide a pension plan beyond the minimum legal standards, and this is where discrimination can come in.

9 D. Gros, M. Vuille, P. Zeugin, J. De Puy, R. Radeff, *Sida et discriminations: évaluation de la stigmatisation des personnes concernées par le sida en Suisse*, p. V: 92, 1991.

10 S. Sontag, *Le SIDA et ses métaphores*. Christian Bourgois, Paris, 1989.

11 The degree of knowledge that dentists' assistants had in response to telephone enquiries from people with AIDS shows that treatment of such patients has become routine. This is most certainly a result of 'STOP SIDA', which directed a specific campaign at the dental profession.

12 A positive reply to request for employment would mean that the individual has been selected as a suitable candidate, i.e. that the employer is usually calling him for an interview. Positive replies vary considerably according to the skills involved and the market situation. In the particular cases we studied, the 'normal' situation was assessed through the control scenarios. For example, we simulated applications on behalf of people with commercial skills (e.g. multilingual secretary, accountant) at a time when these were in high demand.

Processes of Stigmatization and their Impact on the Employment of People with HIV

Dr Gill Green

Medical Research Council, Medical Sociology Unit, Glasgow, Scotland

Attempts to reduce discrimination in the workplace against people with HIV have tended to concentrate upon the attitudes of employers and their staff.[1] The rationale is that legislation to end discrimination against people with HIV, and appropriate interventions to combat hostile attitudes towards them in the workplace, will provide equal opportunities for people with HIV at work.

People with HIV may be covered by international declarations of rights which suggest that an applicant for a job cannot be legitimately refused employment, nor can an employee be dismissed, solely on the grounds that he or she is HIV-positive.[2] It has also been declared that screening for HIV as part of the assessment of fitness to work is unnecessary and should not be required; nor is an employee obliged to inform the employer regarding his or her HIV/AIDS status as there is no risk to colleagues from routine social contact in the workplace.[3] These are endorsed by the European Social Charter, yet many employers pay only lip service to such declarations of rights, and may contravene them. In Britain, the Sex Discrimination Act 1975 and the Race Relations Act 1976 check discrimination related to gender or race and thus protect people in certain 'high risk' categories. However, an attempt to add a clause to the Employment Bill, which would have made discrimination on the grounds of a person having HIV illegal, was defeated in the House of Commons in February 1989, and some large companies routinely screen prospective employees despite the Government's Chief Medical Officer's recommendation that anyone who is asked by an employer about his or her HIV status 'should tell the employer to mind his own business'.[4] Legislation has thus only succeeded in offering limited protection to people with HIV in the workplace.

Problems with HIV at work fall into three broad categories: employers who do not wish to employ someone who is HIV-positive; workers who do not wish to work with anyone who is infected; and individuals with HIV who fear discrimination or rejection by their employers and colleagues. Few studies have examined the perceptions about, and experiences of people with HIV in the workplace to examine the relative impact of each of these stigmatizing processes.

The aim of this chapter is to examine the processes of stigmatization with reference to whether people with HIV have an accurate assessment of public attitudes, and the impact that this has upon their employment histories following diagnosis. To what extent have they experienced overt discrimination either from employers or colleagues in the workplace? Have they stopped working or stopped looking for work because they are fearful of discrimination being enacted against them? How do they perceive attitudes of 'generalized others', that is, of people who may be their colleagues or their employers towards people with HIV, and does this have an impact upon their employment? In order to contextualize the environment in which people with HIV work or seek employment, the first part of this chapter examines whether people with HIV feel stigmatized by their condition. The second part examines the impact of stigma upon the work histories of people with HIV, and it is argued that the perceptions of people with HIV may have more impact on their employment than active discrimination against them. Thus, one may have to look beyond legislation to offer people with HIV a work environment in which they do not feel stigmatized.

There have been a huge number of studies about attitudes towards people with HIV, which, in the main, show that although the majority of the general population supports the rights of people with HIV,[5] at least a minority of the population worldwide (from Europe and the United States to the Indian subcontinent) holds extremely repressive attitudes towards people with HIV.[6] In general, hostile attitudes are more prevalent among people who are older, non-white, less well educated, and politically to the right.[7]

There are a number of examples of outright discrimination in the workplace. King reported that almost one-quarter of a sample of people with HIV (mostly gay men) had received a negative or discriminatory response from at least one person to whom they had disclosed their HIV status, and employers were more likely than family, friends or colleagues to respond unsympathetically.[8] It has been noted that people with AIDS may 'pass' or conceal their HIV status in the workplace, or devise a 'cover' (such as a less discrediting illness) to disguise symptoms of the illness,[9] and that many HIV-positive men choose not to inform their boss or co-workers of their status, fearing they will either lose their jobs or have their work opportunities restricted or make their co-workers uncomfortable because of unfounded concerns about transmission through casual contact.[10] A number of healthcare workers have been forced to resign after it became known that they were HIV-positive.[11]

Processes of stigma among people with HIV

In this analysis, a distinction is made between 'enacted stigma' (active discrimination) and 'felt stigma' (fear of discrimination), as this distinction has provided useful insights into the nature of stigma associated with epilepsy.[12] 'Enacted stigma' refers to sanctions actually being individually or collectively applied to people with the stigmatized condition, and 'felt stigma' relates to feelings of shame and an oppressive fear of 'enacted stigma'. Both may have severe social consequences for people with HIV or AIDS in terms of their rights, freedom, self-identity and social interactions. In Scambler and Hopkins' study of epilepsy,[13] 'felt stigma' was far more prevalent than 'enacted stigma', a finding that has recently been supported by Jacoby, who reported that only five per cent of a sample of 600 people with epilepsy in remission recalled any active discrimination in the workplace in the previous two years, whereas 32 per cent felt that their epilepsy made it more difficult for them to get a job.[14]

Measuring 'felt stigma' is problematic as it is rather an intangible concept. In a study recently conducted in Scotland,[15] two measures were used to test the hypothesis that people with HIV felt stigmatized. The first was a measure of whether people with HIV have very different perceptions of themselves to the general public. Differences in this respect would suggest that people with HIV have a 'special view of the world', which has been identified as an indicator of 'felt stigma'.[16] Another measure compared attitudes of people with HIV to what people with HIV perceive public attitudes to be. An over-estimation of the hostility of public attitudes would indicate 'felt stigma' among people with HIV.

To test these hypotheses, a street survey was conducted to collect data on *reported attitudes* in two cities in Scotland – Glasgow, where HIV prevalence rates are low, and Edinburgh, where prevalence is high and concentrated among drug users.[17] A quota sample of 300 adults stratified by gender, age, housing tenure (as an indicator of socio-economic status) and location were asked to rate their views on fifteen items about people with HIV on a scale from 'strongly agree' to 'strongly disagree'.

The questionnaire was designed after extensive in-depth interviews with a sample of men and women with HIV. It aimed to include three domains which people with HIV reported as elements of the stigmatizing process: cognitive aspects, that is, what people with HIV are like; 'victim-blaming', i.e. whether they should be blamed for being HIV-positive; and treatment from society, that is, whether they should be discriminated against or their behaviour circumscribed. All the items deliberately avoided mention of any specific category of people with HIV, such as gay men, drug users or haemophiliacs. The scale was also completed by 42 men and women with HIV who are being followed up annually to assess the psychosocial impact of HIV. This sample was a theoretical sample representing a full range of 'risk groups' recruited from hospital clinics, voluntary organizations, self-help groups and prisons. The sample of people with HIV was also asked to complete the questionnaire imagining that they were 'a typical member of the public'. The data from the two samples were grouped into three data sets:

1. Attitudes of people in the street survey (**SS**).
2. Attitudes of people with HIV (**HIV**).
3. People with HIV's perception of 'generalized others' (**HIV-O**).

Table 1 shows the proportions in each group who expressed an 'illiberal' attitude to each item.

Overall, the general public (**SS**) have a relatively liberal view of people with HIV although over one-third indicated that some restrictions should be placed upon people with HIV in the workplace, in that people with HIV should not work with children. This illiberal tendency was particularly marked if there was a risk of passing the virus on to others and almost three-quarters indicated that people with HIV should not have a child. People with HIV (**HIV**) were often broadly in agreement with the general public, but tended to express more liberal attitudes. On all items, people with HIV thought the public had very much more illiberal views than they themselves held (**HIV-O** compared with **HIV**), and there was a clear trend for people with HIV to attribute to the public much more illiberal views than the public reported that they held (**HIV-O** compared with **SS**). There was, however, some consensus between **HIV-O** and **SS** with regard to which items were associated with most illiberal views, indicating that people with HIV have an accurate assessment that it is their behaviour, particularly that which puts others at risk of HIV infection, which elicits maximum public opprobrium.

The individual items were designed to be used as a scale and were combined to form a total attitude score ranging from -30 to +30 (a positive score representing a liberal attitude and a negative score representing an illiberal attitude).

		What the general public think (SS)	What people with HIV think (HIV)	What people with HIV think the general public think (HIV-O)
		n=300	n=42	n=41[a]
1.	People with HIV are dirty (agree)	6.7	4.8	63.4
2.	People with HIV are as intelligent as anybody else (disagree)	2.3	4.8	39
3.	People with HIV are not to be trusted (agree)	7	2.4	53.7
4.	Being HIV-positive says nothing about who you are (disagree)	9.3	4.8	53.7
5.	People with HIV are no different from anybody else (disagree)	25.7	33.3	75.6
6.	You can't tell by looking if someone has HIV (disagree)	16.3	9.5	26.8
7.	Nobody deserves to be HIV-positive (disagree)	10.3	9.5	41.5
8.	People with HIV should be ashamed of themselves (agree)	9	0	70.7
9.	People with HIV have nothing to be feel guilty about (disagree)	28.7	4.8	63.4
10.	Most people become HIV-positive by being weak-willed or foolish (agree)	42.7	23.8	82.9
11.	Needs of people with HIV should be given top priority (disagree)	39.7	35.7	78
12.	Prisoners with HIV should be segregated (agree)	47	9.5	73.2
13.	It is safe for people with HIV to work with children (disagree)	33.7	0	82.9
14.	People with HIV must expect some restrictions on their freedom (agree)	64.7	31	87.8
15.	People with HIV should not have a child (agree)	73.3	54.8	92.7

[a]One respondent in the HIV sample said she was unable to complete HIV-O.

Table 1
Percentage of respondents expressing an 'illiberal' attitude towards-people with HIV'

Figure 1 compares the median score and range of all three data sets and confirms the trends noted above for the individual items. People with HIV have a higher score indicating more liberal attitudes than the general public (**HIV** median score 20: **SS** median score 8). An ANOVA model including both the **SS** and **HIV** samples confirmed that, controlling for age, gender and tenure, HIV status has a significant independent effect on the total score.[18] Figure 1 also clearly shows that the general public has a higher score than people with HIV perceive them to have (**SS** median score 8: **HIV-O** median score -9), and this difference is also statistically significant.

These results provide evidence of 'felt stigma' among people with HIV. People with HIV have more liberal attitudes about people with HIV than the general population, but have an exaggerated view of the hostility of the opinions of 'generalized others'. People with HIV clearly feel 'marked out', and their expectations of public scorn (even though these may be exaggerated) may lead them to conceal their HIV status and/or isolate themselves from society. The following section of this chapter examines the extent to which HIV status in general, and stigma in particular, may affect the employment of people with HIV.

Work experiences of people with HIV following diagnosis

Data on which this analysis is based were collected from 66 people with HIV who were interviewed in 1991; 40 of them were interviewed again in 1992. Respondents were asked as part of an in-depth interview about the interpersonal impact of HIV, whether their HIV status had affected their employment. Those who answered in the affirmative were asked to give further details about how they had been affected. Table 2 gives details of this sample.

It includes both men and women from all 'risk groups' and over 50 per cent are or were drug users, reflecting the epidemiology of HIV in Scotland. Although thirteen were in prison at the time of interview, they are included in this analysis as the majority were only serving short sentences for minor drug-related offences. Over one-half of the sample had last been employed in manual work in factories, building sites or in the service sector, and many had worked in the informal sector, for example working as labourers, bar workers, prostitutes, 'fences' (people who deal in stolen goods) or drug dealers. About one-quarter had been, or were currently, employed in non-manual work, half of them in professional occupations.

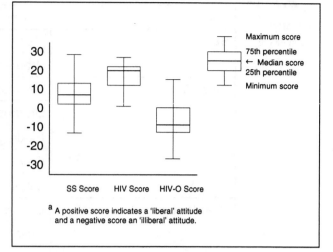

a A positive score indicates a 'liberal' attitude and a negative score an 'illiberal' attitude.

Figure 1
Summary scores of attitudes for all three groups

Only a small minority of the sample were working at time of interview although this figure excludes those who were doing temporary voluntary work or very occasional casual work. A variety of reasons were given for lack of employment, some of which were unrelated to HIV. Before diagnosis, for example, many respondents were in receipt of welfare benefit and some had been designated as 'not economically active' or not available for work, usually on account either of their drug use or haemophilia. For these people an HIV-positive diagnosis had no impact upon their employment; they had not worked for a long time before their diagnosis and five respondents had never worked.

A comparison between the HIV sample and a control group of people who were HIV-negative (matched for gender, age and 'risk group'), clearly shows that an HIV diagnosis affects employment. Both groups had similar qualifications, but a far higher proportion of the HIV-negatives were currently working (40 per cent compared to 12 per cent of the HIV-positive group) and far fewer defined themselves as not economically active (12 per cent compared to 55 per cent of the HIV-positive group).

Table 2
Details of the
HIV sample

Total		66
Sex	Men	54
	Women	12
'Risk Group'	Haemophiliac	10
	Drug user	28
	Ex-drug user	5
	Gay	14
	Other	9
Residence	Community	47
	Prison	13
	Hospital/rehabilitation centre	5
Qualifications	University or technical	21
	Highers or O grades	11
	None	34
Social (occupational) class	Professional (I or II)	9
	Clerical (IIINM)	9
	Manual	43
	Never worked	5
Current employment status	Employed	8
	Unemployed	10
	Not economically active	36
	Institutionalized	12

The physical and emotional impact of HIV has a large impact upon employment. Some of those interviewed had given up work as they became too ill, or lacked sufficient energy to work. Others were restricted by their health status, such as the engineer who had previously worked in the Third World but felt to return to work there would be too dangerous for his health and he was concerned lest he fall ill when there. Another felt restricted to part-time and flexible work in order to take time off for hospital visits.

Stress of work was also seen to be potentially detrimental to health, and one clerical worker gave up working the day he was diagnosed as he felt it was a low priority and he had more important things he wanted to do. Another left his job as his psychological state was so disturbed after being diagnosed that he could not perform his work effectively. Respondents were often encouraged by professional care workers to give up employment and helped to apply for the wide range of welfare payments in Britain that are available for some people with HIV, particularly those experiencing poor health. Others who had continued working noted that they had become less ambitious. As one haemophiliac said: 'Yes, I'm less ambitious. You tend to put work into more perspective. Why should I bust a gut when in six months' time I could be in a box', and another had given up a promising career in scientific research as he felt he was spending too much time thinking about HIV to devote sufficient energy to his research.

Many respondents, however, felt that their employment had been affected by the stigma associated with HIV (see Table 3).

Six reported that they had been the victims of overt discrimination ('enacted stigma') although they realized that this would be almost impossible to prove. These cases are listed below:

1. A haemophiliac went for two interviews and reported that the atmosphere changed immediately after he mentioned HIV and he was not offered either job:

R20: We had a little talk about medical matters and then I was in between whether to tell them I had HIV or not to tell them and I thought well I'll try it and see what happens...it got a very cold reception, very cold.

GG: In what way did they become cold?

R20: Their attitude changed. It was a kind of rolling interview and going along quite well and then all of a sudden it became broken, staccatoed kind of thing, humming and hawing and saying 'oh, well, eh', that kind of thing but I mean they were very nice but they always are, you know, when they are about to say no anyway.

In the second interview, he disclosed he was a haemophiliac:

R20: And we talked about it for a few minutes and it was fine, you know. He then says 'wasn't there something to do with haemophiliacs being HIV?' So I took it that he was interested in the subject and he would be quite sympa-

Enacted stigma (n=6)
Not given job, new contract or promotion
Husband's career ruined
Forced to leave country in which job based
Sacked because of reaction of colleagues
Felt stigma (n=12)
Non-disclosure for fear of losing job
Non-disclosure for fear of colleagues' reaction
Not 'fit' for work because of risk associated with nature of work
Not seeking work for fear of reaction to voluntary or involuntary disclosure
'Covering' by disclosing a less discrediting condition

Table 3
Employment-related stigma

thetic towards it you know and asked whether HIV is a question they ask when hiring in the company or something like that. Of course as soon as I opened my mouth I knew I'd done the wrong thing. He looked at me as though I'd hit him with a brick.

GG: Did he actually ask you 'are you HIV'?

R20: No but he had made the link and that was it, it was gone. From that point it had gone.

2. An engineer working on a short-term contract in the Third World was unable to keep his diagnosis confidential. His employers refused to renew his contract when it expired, although previous renewals of contract had been straightforward.

3. A young teacher who had informed his employer of his HIV status failed to be promoted although he felt he was the most qualified applicant for the job.

4. An army wife reported that her husband's career was ruined following her diagnosis, although he tested HIV-negative. He was confined to working in a restricted number of countries and his opportunities for advancement were severely restricted. He left the army a few months later.

5. A health professional was told by his European employers to leave after being diagnosed with HIV, as the country he was working in did not permit HIV-positive foreigners to reside there.

6. A sex worker was sacked when her colleagues found out she was HIV-positive and refused to work with her.

It is, however, worth noting that one or two respondents who had disclosed their HIV-status claimed to have suffered no discrimination in the workplace either from their colleagues or their employers. Most of these were involved in voluntary work for HIV-related agencies, but also included are a hairdresser who claimed his colleagues were a major source of sup-

port to him, a gay man who was offered a place on an acting course at one of the most prestigious drama schools in the country, and a TV programme operator who received many supportive letters from his colleagues when he was eventually forced to retire because of ill health.

The majority of respondents who had worked since their diagnosis, however, 'felt stigmatized' in the workplace, and in general had not disclosed their HIV status to their employers or colleagues. As one male heterosexual said: 'Nobody at work knows. Our company is a kind of hire and fire company and would sack us on the spot...There is no unions.' Another woman was not sure whether she would lose her job if she disclosed but feared the reaction of her colleagues:

GG: Would you consider mentioning that you are HIV-positive?

R55: Oh no!

GG: Do you think you'd lose your job if you did?

R55: I don't know. I wouldn't mention it. Just because there's so much stigma about it that people are frightened.

Concern abut colleagues or clients being frightened if they found out about their co-worker being HIV-positive was voiced by several respondents, and was often the main reason for them not looking for work. A barmaid, for example, said she was not prepared to work again as it would involve getting to know a lot of new people and she feared the reactions should they 'find out' about her HIV status. Another preferred not to work rather than 'living a lie' at work by not disclosing, as 'some days you are going to be very down...It would be like playing a game. I don't think I could.'

Some people felt restricted because of the nature of their trade which they felt could potentially put other people at risk. The WHO clearly states that there are no grounds for restricting the involvement of those who are HIV-positive in the preparation and distribution of food,[19] yet one man who had given up work owing to ill health said, 'if I had told my employers about the virus I would have been sacked straight away. I was handling food.'

And a gay man who had worked as an assistant chef elected to stop working:

R5: I would be very nervous of starting again. As a chef I had great flair for knife control…I'm very fast with a blade and sometimes you just nick yourself and because the blade's that sharp you don't notice until half the food is ruined. You can't walk into a restaurant, cut your finger and throw the whole tray out or say I cannae work tonight, I've got a wee scratch on my finger. Most chefs would just put a plaster on and get on with it. With me I'd have to stop work.

Some felt compelled to disclose their HIV status to any potential employer either because of the potential risk of transmission or the social risk lest it be discovered. Some felt that this would automatically make them unsuitable employees, or at least less suitable than another applicant who was not HIV-positive. A haemophiliac in a professional occupation in the private sector, for example, said he was restricted from advancing his career as he could not change jobs because of the medical which would inevitably accompany a change of employment. He felt he would have to disclose at the medical as they would be taking a blood sample, and that even if a potential employer had liberal attitudes towards people with HIV, they would be unlikely to give him the job because of the possible reactions of the people he would work with. Another man said he would compromise a little and tell potential employers that he had cancer. The compulsion to disclose is perhaps best illustrated by a young female respondent who was doing a crèche course to gain qualifications to work in a nursery. Her supervisor had to fill in a form to comply with the Children's Act to confirm 'that this person is fit to look after children'. Neither HIV nor AIDS were specifically mentioned on the form, but her supervisor, to whom she had disclosed, was unsure whether to sign her as fit or not and she sympathized with his dilemma:

GG: In what sense would anyone argue that you are unfit?

R10: Well, no as far as my supervisor is concerned I am fit. But it's just that for some reason if it got out that I was HIV-positive, well you can imagine how parents would feel. You know they'd be terrified and I can understand…So he's got to see various people about that before he actually signs the forms to keep himself in the right and also to keep me in the right.

GG: So do you think his behaviour is quite reasonable?

R10: Well yeah, I wouldn't want him to put himself in jeopardy. Em, but as far as he thinks, he'll be signing it anyway.

Out of the 66 respondents, 29 mentioned that HIV had had some impact upon their employment, and the great majority of those not affected had not worked for many years prior to their diagnosis. For most of these 29, the principal impact of HIV upon their employment was caused by a deterioration in their physical or mental health. Six reported incidents of discrimination in the workplace and, in the main, these would be difficult to prove in a court of law. A larger number (twelve in total) mentioned 'felt stigma' as affecting their employment. This took the form of non-disclosure to employers (fearing the sack) or to colleagues or clients, fearing hostile, or at least, horrified reactions. In many cases fear of discrimination or rejection prevented them from seeking work.

Conclusion

This study found that many people with HIV are not affected by stigma in the workplace. This may reflect the fact that over half the sample are drug users or people with haemophilia, many of whom did not have a career prior to diagnosis. Those who are working, however, are more likely to be affected by deteriorating health than stigmatisation. In this sample, those who have experienced stigma are more likely to report 'felt stigma' than 'enacted stigma', although this is less marked than in studies of people with epilepsy.[20]

Although overt discrimination in the workplace affected only a minority of people in this study, it is a very real threat to people with HIV. One has to question, however, the potential efficacy of anti-discriminatory practices in the workplace in the light of the evidence presented here. The recent blockbuster Hollywood film *Philadelphia* demonstrates (albeit with more than a touch of sensationalism) the difficulty of proving discrimination against people with AIDS in the workplace in a court of law, even for a highly paid articulate professional with a brilliant track record, supportive family and good-looking lawyer. Such difficulties would be magnified for less socially advantaged people with HIV, and none of the six reported here who had experienced 'enacted stigma' in the workplace even considered suing their employer. Further legislation would only have limited impact on reducing the stigma for most people with HIV in the workplace, and is unlikely to have assisted the employment or to have alleviated the workplace stigmatisation of this sample of people with HIV.

Most people with HIV, however, experience 'felt stigma' and expect hostile reactions from the majority of the general public and, for some, this has a direct effect on their employment in that it may prevent them seeking work or disclosing their HIV status to employers or colleagues. Legislation to protect rights in the workplace will have no effect upon 'felt stigma' as it is rooted in the personal perceptions of people with HIV. Thus I would argue that reducing discrimination in the workplace should perhaps focus upon the attitudes of employers and employees towards people with HIV, and aim to foster an environment of positive discrimination in which people with HIV can overcome the fears of rejection generated by 'felt stigma'.

The mass media and Health Education Authority could assist in this process to alleviate discrimination against people with HIV. Despite the fact that attitude surveys in Britain consistently show that the majority of the general population reports broadly liberal, sympathetic attitudes towards people with HIV, all publicity tends to concentrate on the negative, illiberal minority.[21] This gives an impression that the hostile minority voice is pervasive and in the ascendancy. Perhaps it is time for the media to focus upon the *lack* of discrimination or hostile reactions towards people with HIV which, although less sensational, represents the attitude of the majority. The Confederation of British Industry or Health Education Authority could run campaigns to let employers know that attitudes towards people with HIV are, in the main, fairly liberal and by no means universally hostile. This would go some way towards alleviating the 'felt stigma' associated with HIV. Without such assistance and encouragement people with HIV will not have equal opportunities in the workplace.

Acknowledgements
This research was carried out at the MRC Medical Sociology Unit at Glasgow University and funded by the Medical Research Council of Great Britain. Thanks are due to Steve Platt who played a major role in the overall design of the study and conducted almost half of the interviews. I am also extremely grateful to the respondents, and to Steve Green, Miriam Guthrie, Helen Mien and Anne Pinkman for their assistance with recruitment. Thanks also to Sally Macintyre for her comments on an earlier draft.

1 M.B. King, 'Prejudice and AIDS: the views and experiences of people with HIV infection', *AIDS Care*, 1 (2), pp. 137–143, 1989.

P. Sieghart, *AIDS and Human Rights: A UK Perspective*. British Medical Foundation for AIDS, London, 1989.

Health Education Authority, *HIV/AIDS in Employment* (eds. M. Kapila, D. Williams), London, 1990.

J.B. Pryor, G.D. Reeder, J.A. McManus, 'Fear and loathing in the workplace: reactions to AIDS-infected co-workers', *Personality and Social Psychology Bulletin*, 17 (2), pp. 133–139, 1991.

2 P. Sieghart, *AIDS and Human Rights: A UK Perspective*. British Medical Foundation for AIDS, London, 1989.

3 WHO (in association with ILO), *Statement from the Consultation on AIDS and the Workplace*, WHO, Geneva, 1988.

4 Health Education Authority, *HIV/AIDS in Employment* (eds. M. Kapila, D. Williams), London, 1990.

5 L. Brook, 'The public's response to AIDS', *British Social Attitudes: The 5th Report* (eds. R. Jowell, S. Witherspoon, L. Brook), pp. 71–91. Gower Publishing Company, Aldershot.

K. Wellings, J. Wadsworth, 'Aids and the moral climate', *British Social Attitudes, the 7th Report* (eds. R. Jowell, S. Witherspoon, L. Brook), vol. 1990/91, pp. 109–126. Gower Publishing Company, Aldershot, 1990.

6 S.M. Kegeles, T.J. Coates, T.A. Christopher, J.L. Lazarus, 'Perceptions of AIDS: the continuing saga of AIDS-related stigma', *AIDS*, 3 (Suppl. 1), S253–S258, 1989.

S.B. Porter, 'Public knowledge and attitudes about AIDS among adults in Calcutta, India', *AIDS Care*, 5 (2), 169–176, 1993.

M. Nisbet, D. McQueen, 'Anti-permissive attitudes to lifestyles associated with AIDS', *Social Science and Medicine*, 36 (7), pp. 893–901, 1993.

7 A. Peruga, D.D. Celentano, 'Correlates of AIDS knowledge in samples of the general population', *Social Science and Medicine*, 36 (4), pp. 509–524, 1993.

8 M.B. King, 'Prejudice and AIDS: the views and experiences of people with HIV infection', *AIDS Care*, 1 (2), pp. 137–143, 1989.

9 K.L. Sandstrom, 'Confronting the deadly disease: the drama of identity construction among gay men with AIDS', *Journal of Contemporary Ethnography*, 19 (3), pp. 271–294, 1990.

10 K. Siegel, B.J. Krauss, 'Living with HIV infection: adaptive tasks of seropositive gay men', *Journal of Health and Social Behaviour*, 32, pp. 17–32, 1991.

11 N. Daniels, 'HIV-infected professionals, patient rights, and the 'switching dilemma', *Journal of the American Medical Association*, 267 (10), pp. 1368–1371, 1992.

12 G. Scambler, A. Hopkins, 'Being epileptic: coming to terms with stigma', *Sociology of Health and Illness*, 8, pp. 26–43, 1986.

13 *Ibid.*

14 A. Jacoby, 'Felt versus enacted stigma: a concept revisited', *Social Science and Medicine*, 38 (2), pp. 269–274, 1993.

15 G. Green, 'Attitudes towards people with HIV: are they as stigmatizing as people with HIV perceive them to be?', submitted for publication to *Social Science and Medicine*, 1994.

16 G. Scambler, A. Hopkins, 'Being epileptic: coming to terms with stigma', *Sociology of Health and Illness*, 8, pp. 26–43, 1986.

17 D.M. Tappin, R.W.A. Girdwood, E.A.C. Follett, R. Kennedy, A.J. Brown, F. Cockburn, 'Prevalence of maternal HIV infection in Scotland based on unlinked anonymous testing of newborn babies', *Lancet*, 337, 1565–1567, 1991.

18 In this model, 'attitude to people with HIV' was the dependent variable and the independent variables were HIV status, age, gender and tenure. This enabled a calculation of the significance of the variance of 'attitude to people with HIV' by HIV status, while controlling for the effects of age, gender and tenure.

19 WHO, *Social Aspects of AIDS Prevention and Control Programmes*, WHO, Geneva, 1987.

20 A. Jacoby, 'Felt versus enacted stigma: a concept revisited', *Social Science and Medicine*, 38 (2), 269–274, 1993.

G. Scambler, A. Hopkins, 'Being epileptic: coming to terms with stigma', *Sociology of Health and Illness*, 8, pp. 26–43, 1986.

21 G. Green, 'Attitudes towards people with HIV: are they as stigmatizing as people with HIV perceive them to be?', submitted for publication to *Social Science and Medicine*, 1994.

HIV and Homelessness: Intervention and Backlash in Local Authority Policy

David Cowan

Lecturer in Law, Centre for Legal Studies, University of Sussex, England

Very little attention has been paid to the way the concepts in the homelessness legislation have been interpreted by local authority housing officers in relation to HIV.[1] An examination of the ways in which homeless people with HIV are guided through the process of making a homelessness application through to its conclusion tells us much about the homelessness legislation in itself, as well as about the administrative process of policy formulation and practice. Furthermore, it also shows the effectiveness of a cohesive group or groups in lobbying both from inside the system, as well as without.

The homelessness legislation gives local authorities' homeless persons units much discretion in applying its key concepts: homelessness, priority need, intentionality, and local connection. These concepts are much criticized both because of their political antecedents as well as their practical implications.[2] I found that the more specific concerns for people with HIV surround the definition of homelessness (broadly, whether it is reasonable for a person to continue to occupy accommodation), as well as the definition of priority need. The key, though, is priority need. Single people with HIV must fit into the category of priority need that relates to vulnerability due to 'mental illness or handicap or physical disability or other special reason'.

This chapter first outlines why people with HIV might be homeless; secondly, the methods used in this research; thirdly, the effect of lobbying; and finally, the application of the homelessness legislation to people with HIV is appraised.

The relationship between HIV and homelessness

In this section, I argue that homelessness is, in many cases, a consequence of being diagnosed HIV-positive. I consider the relationship between homelessness itself and the worsening of HIV disease. The former can, to a large extent, be proved just by reference to the number of people seeking help from homeless persons units. In one London borough where the hospitals have excellence in the treatment of HIV, over the most recent period of a year 235 applications were received from people with HIV from a community estimated to be between 2,436 and 5,220 strong (4.5–10 per cent). These figures are comparable with those of at least two other London boroughs. A housing advice centre operating in two London boroughs has also noticed an increase in people with HIV seeking their assistance with a homelessness application (in the last year, about 5.4 per cent).

The reasons for homelessness among this client group are broadly the same as other client groups: rent arrears; problems with social security benefits; harassment (sexual or racial); discrimination; poor-quality housing, as well as housing that is not sufficiently adapted to their needs. The mistake that was often made in the past was therefore to treat this client group similarly to others (in some cases also actually acting prejudicially owing to an outmoded conception of the way in which people become infected). As Jonathan Montgomery has written: '…a flawed framework will force upon those with HIV a set of burdens which is both undesirable and undeserved. To categorize those with the virus using principles developed to deal with other conditions is to associate them with those conditions.' [3]

The reality is that the housing by-product of a diagnosis of HIV infection exacerbates either a currently poor housing situation or the correlation between housing and employment status in the community. Take an example that is commonplace: a person lives on the sixth floor of a block of flats with a lift that rarely works. One might consider it reasonable for that person to carry on living there but an HIV-positive diagnosis may well change that because it is likely that at some point, if not then, respiratory problems will become apparent. Of course, if the client is 'street homeless' then the significance may be greater because, for example, of prostitution. Equally, access to healthcare for homeless people generally can prove difficult particularly in the market-oriented approach of the 1990s.[4]

The most important impact of poor quality accommodation or street homelessness on a person with HIV is the stress that it causes. HIV acts as an immunosuppressant and the stress of homelessness may compound this.

Raynsford and Morris, for example, in their report quote a doctor from St Stephen's Hospital (now the Chelsea and Westminster Hospital) as saying:

'there is a strong belief among doctors that if a patient is very depressed and in poor circumstances then the disease might move faster. And if you have someone living in bad housing, they are more likely to be depressed. Depression is an immunosuppressant, and on top of the infection [homelessness] acts as a second dose of immunosuppressant and can make things worse. You can't quote a paper to support this and evidence would be difficult to find, but most doctors would support this.' [5]

These factors clearly mark out HIV from other illnesses. Stress is an inevitable consequence of homelessness generally, but the relationship between it and HIV makes it crucial to take into the balance.

Methodology

I wrote to each homeless persons unit in London asking about their policies on priority need. As a comparator, I made the same inquiry of local authorities in Devon. This was followed up with in-depth taped interviews of five local authorities in London as well as legal advice centres in each area where they existed. A wider scale postal survey had been done in 1990 by the AIDS and Housing Project but this had only achieved thirteen responses from London boroughs.

The reason for this only fair response rate was partly, it was thought, the fact that the survey named the local authorities concerned. If local authorities have benign policies sometimes they do not want them publicized because of the possibility of a flood of applicants. Consequently, all of the current research was conducted under a strict banner of anonymity. The written inquiry and follow-up research generated twenty responses from London boroughs (61 per cent) and six from local authorities in Devon (60 per cent). The results of this survey will be considered later but for present purposes are as follows:

London

- Seven authorities (35 per cent of respondents) treated a person with asymptomatic HIV infection as being in priority need – presumably a person who had symptomatic HIV disease would also be treated by these authorities as in priority need.

- Five authorities (25 per cent) treated a person as being in priority need only if the viral infection had reached a symptomatic stage.

- Five authorities (25 per cent) only regarded a person with HIV as having a priority need on the recommendation of their medical officer.

- Two authorities (10 per cent) accepted people with HIV as having priority need only if it was in conjunction with other unrelated or 'quite minor illnesses'.[6]

- One authority (5 per cent) accepted a person with HIV as having a priority need if 'they faced particular difficulties in securing housing and whether homelessness would place them in an especially difficult position'.

Devon

- Four authorities (67 per cent) accepted a person with HIV as having a priority need, whether asymptomatic or symptomatic.

- Two authorities (33 per cent) were more circumspect. One said that no automatic assumption would exist but discussions would take place between the community physician and the applicant's General Practitioner (subject to the applicant's consent): 'As AIDS develops beyond the HIV-positive stage it is increasingly likely that an applicant would be considered vulnerable but only on the basis that the applicant was at risk due to a medical condition and not automatically because that condition was AIDS-related.'

The other authority again said that there was no automatic assumption of priority need and the cases would be assessed on the individual's circumstances.

The impact of lobbying

The interest of these figures lies partly in the change in policy since only 1990. The AIDS and Housing Project survey of all local authorities nationwide found that out of 184 responses only 27 per cent considered HIV to be sufficient to fall within the priority need category, while 39 per cent did not. There are many reasons for this dramatic change in policy: greater public understanding of HIV and AIDS; fear that if something is not done when the virus is first contracted, they might be under greater obligations once the virus advances; and fear of opprobrium within an unsympathetic community. That so many local government officers have been involved in training programmes on HIV and AIDS issues conducted internally and/or externally would not have happened without concerted lobbying to bring it about.

One consideration that might be expected to weigh heavily on local authorities would be fear of challenge through the courts or the Local Government Ombudsman. However, it became apparent when interviewing those offering legal advice to homeless people generally that advisers took a cynical view of this type of challenge: they felt that local authorities perceived such a threat as being very rare because a person with HIV would not wish to go through the long, drawn-out process of judicial review (as well as risk losing confidentiality) because at the end of the day it may be too late; the Local Government Ombudsman was clearly viewed in the same light (if it had been considered at all). Consequently, some advisers felt that local authorities were using this to their own advantage by coming to 'outrageous decisions'.

Perhaps the main reason for the change in policy, though, is the impact of lobbying. External groups such as the AIDS and Housing Project, the National AIDS Trust, Terrence Higgins Trust and The Landmark have had a significant impact in publicizing the issues, training, as well as acting as, advocates. Their effect will be examined after what this chapter throughout refers to as internal lobbying.

Internal lobbying

The role of the HIV liaison officer

Many local authorities now have an HIV liaison officer. Their job is primarily to liaise between the different departments of their authority, negotiating a joint response to the issues thrown up by HIV and drawing up policies on HIV for comment. Some local authorities (particularly outside London) also use such officers in a proactive role by making them act as advocates for the person with HIV when they make a homelessness application. This development, generally encouraged by the homeless persons unit, means that before any application is made, the person with HIV either goes straight to this person or is sent by officers at the unit who put together the relevant material, including doctors' reports, and liaise with only one senior homeless persons officer at all times.

These two roles of the HIV liaison officer have undoubtedly had a significant effect on homelessness policy and practice in this area. Taking the second role first: it does require a sympathetic homelessness officer but the important thing, as far as the latter is concerned, is that the relevant documentation is before them. Also, if a good relationship develops between the

two this can have beneficial results for the client. For example, one officer said that he had worked on a few cases where the homelessness officer was considering making an adverse finding and telephoned him with this news, and he had been able to change that person's mind. Indeed in this authority, which receives about twelve applications every year from homeless people with HIV, there had never been an adverse finding on an application.

Perhaps more important though is their policy-making role. This is often used to inform members of the homeless persons unit as to the issues of HIV, suggesting policy changes that might ameliorate some of the difficulties faced by a person with HIV in making a homelessness application. A good example of this concerns confidentiality: one internal document suggests that officers should refer to the person as 'having a life-threatening illness'. Generally, though, the major influence is in changing policies in relation to the key concepts of the Act. One officer, barely six months in the post, had managed to persuade the homeless persons officers and relevant councillors to change the policy on priority need to include all people with HIV, whether symptomatic or not. Another officer who had just taken up his post was on the verge of writing a paper to the same effect.

Finally, these officers are aware of the views and opinions of those in the homeless persons unit. Consequently, they can shield potential applicants from those with an unsympathetic attitude, as well as give advice on advocates outside the authority whom the person with HIV should see.

Homeless persons officers

It should not be forgotten that homeless persons officers can also effect a change in policy. In two authorities visited, the officers dealing with HIV also spent some evenings working at HIV drop-in and advice centres. Consequently, they were in a better position than most to handle applications from persons with HIV. This was because they were more aware of the issues affecting this client group, the various stages of illness, and how this might affect their interpretation of the legislation. They also showed themselves as being extremely sympathetic to applicants from this client group.

External lobbying

Research organisations

There is now a significant body of campaigning literature on the enabling role of local authorities in relation to homelessness[7] as well as the type of accommodation required by a person with HIV.[8] Although most of this material will not filter down to ground level, it is often referred to in internal documents emanating from the HIV liaison officer and provides a useful example of how such literature can be used to benefit the applicant.

Peer pressure

One of the motivations behind one local authority's change in practice was the fact that they had recently been obliged to accept a referral from a neighbouring authority even though that person did not fulfil their criteria for acceptance under the Act. This acted as a spur to them partly because they believed that their current policy might be too harsh and partly because they did not believe that it would have any great effect on their housing stock.

External advocates

People with HIV have access to specialist services that are unavailable to many other client groups. Specialists in the homelessness legislation are often the first stop for many potential applicants often

before they make the application itself. Such people advise on what information to take to the homeless persons unit, which officer to see, and, importantly, what information should and should not be given to the officer. For applicants not versed in legislative interpretation or case law, such assistance is invaluable and operates as a buffer between themselves and the administrative process.

Equally important is the converse role of helping the homelessness officer through the mire of terminology involved with HIV, explaining graphically, for example, the effects of homelessness on a person with HIV.

Lobbying: success or failure?

This heading may seem strange given the above, but two new aspects must now be added to the equation. The first is political; the second might perhaps be best described as a backlash. In any event, the two are closely related.

The qualification used above that the HIV liaison officer needs a sympathetic audience must be related to the political reality. Local authorities generally, but especially in London and whatever their political complexion, are coming under increasing pressure in relation to their housing stock. Consequently, they look to ways in which they can reduce that pressure. In much the same way as the Government has aimed to reduce the public sector borrowing requirement, local authorities seek to contract what are seen to be 'generous policies'. While nothing can be done to reduce their duty to make a priority need finding against families, much can be done to reduce the numbers and scope of single people in priority need. One authority, bucking the current trend, has recently reversed its policy. The change was away from accepting a person with HIV as having a priority need to only granting this if the applicant is symptomatic HIV. In the process of this change of heart, the HIV liaison officer was bypassed. Homelessness officers in another authority were expecting their generous policies on homelessness and intentionality to be changed shortly. They had found that if a single person was rehoused by them, the local community would automatically assume (because single people are so rarely housed in this authority) that that person had HIV/AIDS, and that person consequently experienced some harassment. This prevailing political wind obviously has an impact on the day-to-day running of homeless persons units generally, as well as more specifically in relation to HIV.

The backlash referred to above really arises because of the battery of support workers that exists for people with HIV that does not exist for people with other illnesses, such as multiple sclerosis. Almost as a reflex action, many HIV liaison officers spoken to in the course of this research automatically justified the policies so that they would not be considered 'generous'; some also found it necessary to justify their own position. Indeed, while obviously helping a person with HIV, it also marginalizes that person not only to themselves but also within society. The Body Positive campaign and the current trend tends to run contrary to this veritable armoury. Jonathan Montgomery argues:

> 'This general background encourages us to see those with HIV as a type of victim. They are in need of rescue from a disease, and are therefore placed in the hands of the emergency services. This image is debilitating... The person with HIV is therefore forced to adopt a role which oppresses them.' [9]

It can, of course, be argued first that many of these lobbying mechanisms are open to other groups, albeit not in such proliferation; secondly, that information imparted to local authorities generally on the issue of HIV/AIDS is crucial so that they can act in a prophylactic role in the community;

and thirdly, that the potential relationship between HIV/AIDS and homelessness is such that it merits special consideration (because HIV is an immunosuppressant and the stress of being homeless may well worsen its impact). The ostensible success of these various lobbying methods are 'the proof of the pudding' and should consequently continue.

However, it can certainly be argued that these arguments are a double-edged sword. Local authority homeless persons units cannot afford to adopt a prophylactic approach to their housing units because they are so limited. In any event, a prophylactic approach begs the question: why stop with people with HIV? After all, if depression is an immunosuppressant, people suffering from depression should fit in here. Going one further step also exposes this policy: if the threat of someone's condition worsening is enough for them to have priority need, then all people who are street homeless and likely to contract HIV should also have a priority need. Such an idealistic policy consequently is frail in the light of reduced housing stock. Such arguments are powerful and give further scope to those who want to grant priority need only to people who have symptomatic HIV disease. As we shall see, such policies are also frail because HIV does not fit neatly into such categories.

HIV and the homelessness legislation: policy and practice

This section delineates the areas of homelessness legislation which represent the major obstacles for people with HIV in relation to the policy and practice of local authorities in interpreting the homelessness legislation.

Homelessness

If a person is not found to be homeless, then no duty to that person will arise and they will not appear in the local authority's official statistics of homeless persons. It is this key concept which local authorities have traditionally been keen to define rigorously. It appears also that generally these standards are becoming ever more rigorous; falling homelessness statistics reported so avidly in the popular press do not necessarily imply that there are less homeless people; it is far more likely that local authorities are interpreting the term illiberally.

There are two issues of importance in relation to people with HIV:

(1) When is it unreasonable to continue to occupy a property? (One definition of homelessness.)
(2) When will it be possible for a partner or carer to be treated as a member of the 'family' so that that person is able to be joined into the application?

Whether reasonable to continue to occupy

Local authorities visited appeared aware that there was a link between poor quality accommodation and the worsening of HIV disease. Consequently, they did accept many people with HIV as homeless who would not normally have met their criteria. Nevertheless, they also accepted that this was becoming ever more difficult because their remaining free units of accommodation – both temporary and permanent – were becoming ever more scarce and this was bound to influence who they accepted as homeless. As became apparent through interviewing advice centres, some bizarre decision-making is occurring. For example, a homelessness finding was not forthcoming where a person with HIV was not physically able to live in his property because there were walls and floorboards missing and major works going on at the time.

On the other hand, local authorities were generally far more liberal on the question of violence/harassment and injunctions. They all realized that injunctions had little positive effect on the person causing the harassment/violence and they did not require them even if there was a possibility that it might cause it to stop. However, there are still some authorities that require possession proceedings to be fought if there is a chance that the applicant might win, even though the inevitable result would be that, eventually, a successful court eviction would be effected by the landlord.

Who is a member of the family?

A local authority comes under a duty to house not only an applicant but also any member of his family who normally resides with him and any other person with whom it is reasonable to expect the applicant to reside. As the stock of two-bedroom properties diminishes, so the interpretation of this clause becomes more strict. Furthermore, the accommodation needs of a person with HIV are such that they need to be housed as close to a hospital/care centre as possible. One authority reported that they had no such two-bedroom accommodation and their stock of one-bedroom accommodation had almost been extinguished.

The practical reality deriving from this backdrop is that few two-bedroom properties are provided to people with HIV. Usually, a partner/carer who lived full time with the applicant would be treated as being able either to share the same bed with the applicant or to sleep on the sofa. This occurred even when the partner/carer also had HIV as well as when the person with HIV was exhibiting such side-effects as incontinence or diarrhoea. When it was suggested that this in itself might render the 'family' homeless once again, the argument in response was that this was the best accommodation that the council could provide. The final reality was that two-bedroomed accommodation would only be provided when the illness had reached an advanced stage.

Priority need

For most people with HIV, priority need is the key that unlocks the door to the Act and places the full housing duty on local authorities (i.e. the provision of permanent accommodation). From the results of the survey (*see above*), there is a broad distinction between five different categories. As each category is considered, it becomes apparent that while the first category may well appear unlawful, it is nevertheless the best approach.

'All people with HIV have priority need'

The local authorities within this category recognized that this was the most humanitarian response to the problem of homelessness and HIV. When these proposals were formulated, some were careful also to point out its financial benefits. The approach was seen as prophylactic, that is, preventive. It was their perception of HIV that there is a link between poor quality accommodation and the worsening of HIV illness. Consequently, they realized that if they did not formulate an appropriate response, their duties would become greater as the virus progressed.

Be that as it may, such departments also expressed some major concerns. Of particular importance was the 'floodgate' argument: if their policy became known in the community, this might lead to a vast increase in applicants who might have applied elsewhere but for a higher standard there. In an internal document, one HIV liaison officer attempted to allay such fears by arguing that the actual numbers of applicants who were asymptomatic was *de minimis*. Yet it was clear that this is a major concern to authorities with such policies and this argument, in that officer's view, had not persuaded everybody.

Another argument that has some currency is that no group should be treated differently and if one accepts all people with HIV who, to all intents and purposes, appear well then one should be accepting everybody as in priority need. This argument is really aimed at the prophylactic nature of the authority's approach and finds some currency in legal definitions of vulnerability. This type of argument derives some support from the current ideological perspective of personal responsibility and self-sufficiency – forget the 'nanny state'. It is also one which finds itself – perhaps not stated in such terminology – given currency in some homeless persons units which operate this policy.

'Only those exhibiting symptoms'

One local authority in this category honestly admitted that the reasoning behind this policy was resource based, even though this was possibly unlawful. There is no doubt legalistically that this reasoning is unlawful as at this stage the authority should only concern itself with the nature of the illness and whether a person with HIV is 'vulnerable' because of 'some other special reason'. Resource issues are only relevant when dealing with homelessness and intentionality. Nevertheless, this is an interesting perspective: recognizing that intentionality is a minefield of legalism, they preferred to rest their decision here. Other reasoning based itself on the main arguments against an all-embracing policy on HIV, particularly the floodgates argument. They reported that few people who were asymptomatic HIV actually made an application to them, believing this to be because such people made applications to other authorities (even though no referral under the local connection provisions had been made to them).

The real problem with this category though is that a person with HIV might have symptoms or appear unwell one day and the opposite the next. Consequently, this category, although commonly used by the medical profession, ill-fits the circumstance. For example, if a person with HIV presents as homeless but does not exhibit any illness, local authorities in this category might not consider the person as symptomatic. Threshold, writing about seroconversion, describes it as 'the point at which antibodies to HIV are produced by the body. There has been exposure to HIV and it can be passed on to others. Seroconversion may be accompanied by a short flu-like illness.'[10] If a person arrives at the local authority during the period of this illness, that may be enough to fall within the symptomatic HIV category (even though it should not strictly be treated as exhibiting symptoms), whereas just after it stops they might not.

'Chief Medical Officer's recommendation'

Local authorities in this section relied on the recommendation of their Chief Medical Officer (CMO) as to whether or not a person with HIV is vulnerable. This type of policy has been held unlawful because the decision must not be delegated to another person or body (R. v. *London Borough of Lambeth ex parte Carroll*). Nevertheless, one might expect that the CMO is in the best position to judge whether a person with HIV should be considered vulnerable, taking into account the individual circumstances of the applicant, and the current medical diagnosis and prognosis within the context of the Act.

However, there was much scepticism about this type of policy not only from advisers but also from within the homeless persons unit. First, the CMO does not actually see the applicant but merely judges on the basis of the papers before him, mostly including the opinion of the applicant's General Practitioner; secondly, the CMO generally has a heavy workload and the experience of one was that 'he makes his decisions in the car when stopped at traffic lights'; thirdly, much depended on the way the request for assistance was worded by the homelessness officer in charge of the case. For example, if asked for a prognosis, this would usually be hedged as the CMO was not prepared to make such value judgments. Fourthly, and crucially, often the advice would contain medical terms which the homelessness officer is not briefed to understand let alone appreciate and this could work adversely. Often also, if the officer does not agree with the advice, they will accept the person. Finally, the documentation provided by the applicant's GP may not be sufficient to enable the CMO to draw any conclusions from the specific legislative concepts, the GP not having any appreciation of them.

'Only when accompanied by other minor illnesses'

In retrospect, this category of authorities operates a policy that falls within the 'only those exhibiting symptoms' category, although the authority referred to in endnote (6) may well be somewhat harsher. Similar considerations apply as outlined in that category. The acceptance that there must be serious social factors as well is a reference to the *Carroll* decision.

'Only when problems in seeking accommodation elsewhere'

This authority did not have any policy on HIV/AIDS and consequently restated the legal test for vulnerability, albeit colloquially. It is difficult to draw any conclusions from this.

Intentionality

The local authorities visited tended to shirk away from considering intentionality. Consequently, a standard question was formulated to decipher some future practice. The question supposed that a person, living in a secure tenancy, is diagnosed as HIV-positive. That person gives up his tenancy to go travelling and during their travels they may become unwell or develop symptoms or remain asymptomatic. On return, they present themselves as homeless. All authorities argued that, even though the initial act of giving up the tenancy was a deliberate act, if the person developed symptoms or became unwell, that would operate as a intervening act and consequently they would seek to circumvent the intentionality provision in this way. The more difficult question, therefore, occurred if the applicant remained well. At this point, none would admit that they would find this person intentionally homeless (although it was clear that at least 50 per cent would) but all said they would treat the application 'with sympathy'.

Local connection

People with HIV gravitate towards areas where there is a good standard of treatment or organizations that provide care and assistance. A question that arises is whether this is sufficient to meet the criteria of local connection due to special circumstances. For some time, the local authorities visited had operated generous policies and accepted all such people. However, this had rapidly changed in the preceding months because of a steady

realization that little accommodation in their area was available. In these cases, officers would look to the *National AIDS Manual* to see if a reasonable level of service could be provided in the area with which the applicant had a local connection, even if it did not meet the standard of service provision in their own area – although they would take into account any relationship already developed with the service providers in their own area. If the applicant could receive a reasonable standard of care in the other area, a referral would automatically be made.

Some horror stories have arisen as a result of this general tendency. One authority was in the process of referring a black person with HIV back to an area where his status may have been known and there was a risk of harassment/violence in the future in that area. It became known that a third authority was willing to accept the applicant in their area. The first authority required this in writing, which the third authority refused to do, and the referral was made. The refusal to put this in writing was based on the fact that the third authority was afraid of creating a precedent and, therefore, opening the floodgates.

Conclusion

The aim of this chapter has been to provide an insight into policy-making and its practical application which provides pitfalls for the unwary applicant with HIV. It has shown how the homelessness legislation, when applied in these circumstances, has many defects, particularly because it was drawn up at a time when HIV had not been diagnosed and because the Code of Guidance studiously ignores the issue. Whatever the predictions of numbers of people susceptible to contracting the HIV virus, the issue is not one that can carefully be swept under the carpet until a later time when more people will be affected.

There must be some scepticism about whether people with HIV should automatically be in priority need but the alternative is to allow untrained people to pass judgments which have their basis in that person's moral judgment.[11] There is widespread concern among the local authorities which operate generous policies that these will be unsustainable. It is here that the force of the essentially political judgment concerning housing stock becomes crucial. Throughout this chapter, I have referred to the concern that less housing stock will equal harsher interpretation of the Act. Yet, if the overriding need of the applicant is for accommodation, it seems unjustifiable to deny that need because of limited housing stock. This argument, however, must bow to the legislation which gives local authorities the power to take this into consideration.

I believe that the future requires an interdepartmental coordinated approach. It has become clearer during the passage of time since the Housing (Homeless Persons) Act 1977 (the forerunner to the Housing Act 1985, Part III) that it is equally narrow to consider homelessness as a pure housing issue. This has been recognized, at the least, by the Children Act and community care legislation. Homelessness must, it is submitted, be treated as an issue involving all agencies: social services, housing, probation officers, to name but three. The treatment of those with HIV is the apotheosis; other examples can be used, such as the treatment of victims of abuse or violence, or homeless ex-offenders.

Such co-operation is, at present, somewhat difficult to achieve for a number of reasons: first, each department has duties to its own applicants which must be satisfied before seeking to provide for a demand from other departments; secondly, the duties of the housing department are essentially those of the fire-fighter, in that they have no duties to plan for the future and have limited duties to prevent homelessness, whereas social services must produce plans in respect of their future requirements and consequently have fire prevention duties; thirdly, contradictory guidance from Central Government Departments exacerbates the conflict between local authority departments.[12] Housing is only one need; other needs equally require to be satisfied.

Acknowledgements
The author is indebted to everybody who made this chapter possible. In particular, I should like to thank Dr Julia Fionda, Jonathon Montgomery and David Carson who read and commented on earlier drafts of this paper. All remaining errors remain those of the author.

1 From an adviser's point of view, however, see G. O'Brien, J. Carrier and D. Ward, 'Housing law and people with HIV infection', *AIDS: A Guide to the Law* (eds. D. Harris and R. Haigh), Routledge, London, 1990.

2 D. Hoath, 'Homelessness law: first aid in need of intensive care', *Critical Issues in Welfare Law* (ed. Freeman). Stevens & Sons, London, 1990.

I. Loveland, 'Legal rights and political realities: governmental responses to homelessness in Britain', *Law and Social Inquiry*, 16, 249, 1991.

3 J. Montgomery, 'Victims or threats? – the framing of HIV', *Liverpool Law Review*, 25, 1990.

4 K. Fisher and J. Collins, *Homelessness, Health Care and Welfare Provision*. Routledge, London, 1993.

5 N. Raynsford and C. Morris, *Housing Is an AIDS Issue*, p. 7. National AIDS Trust, London, 1989.

6 One authority in this category gave the following examples: 'a combination of serious social problems – drug/alcohol dependency,

unsettled lifestyle, mental health problems, etc.' The other gave no such examples.

7 Threshold HIV Project/Resource Information Centre, *Road Home – Housing Advice for People with HIV*. Resource Information Centre, London, 1993.

AIDS and Housing Project, *Building for Immunity*. AIDS and Housing Project, London, 1989.

AIDS and Housing Project, *Survey of Local Authority Housing Department Policy and Provision for People with HIV and AIDS*. Local Authority Association, London, 1991.

AIDS and Housing Project, *Survey of Planned and Existing Specialist Housing Provision for People with HIV and AIDS*. AIDS and Housing Project, London, 1992.

L. Moroney and J. Goodwin, *Homelessness: A Good Practice Guide*. Shelter, London, 1993.

8 N. Raynsford and C. Morris, *Housing is an AIDS Issue* . National AIDS Trust, London, 1989. AIDS and Housing Project, *People with HIV and AIDS*. AIDS and Housing Project, London, 1992.

9 J. Montgomery, 'Victims or Threats? – The Framing of HIV', *Liverpool Law Review*, 25, 1990.

10 Threshold HIV Project/Resource Information Centre, *Roads Home – Housing Advice for People with HIV*, p. 18. Resource Information Centre, London, 1993.

11 See, similarly, in terms of offenders, D. Cowan and J. Fionda, 'Meeting the need: the response of local authorities to the housing of homeless ex-offenders', *British Journal of Criminology*, forthcoming, 1994.

12 Department of Environment Circular 10/92, *Housing and Community Care*, para 15.

Department of Health, *Community Care in the Next Decade and Beyond*, paras 1.1 and 1.12. HMSO, 1990.

Department of Health Local Authority Circular 93 (10).

HIV: A Special Housing Need?

Peter Molyneux

Director, AIDS and Housing Project, London, England

There is a long tradition in Britain of using housing to promote public health. From the Public Health Acts of the 1850s to the Housing Acts of the 1980s, authorities have routinely intervened to house those whose ability to operate in the housing market is undermined by poor health. However, within the tradition of meeting the housing needs of sick people there are contrasting approaches of disease prevention and health promotion on the one hand, and containment and control on the other. The declining significance of public sector housing in recent years has had implications for the effectiveness of mainstream housing provision to meet medical needs. Two consequences have been the development of special needs housing and, more recently, increasing levels of people who are ill among the homeless population.

These two traditions are reflected in the responses that have been developed to meet the housing needs of people with HIV. Even in the de-institutionalizing environment of the late 1980s with the development of community care, those of us who believed in the importance of housing had to show 'benefit' either in terms of preventing the spread of disease, or in terms of providing a place to which

services could be delivered supposedly more cost-effectively. Those of us who were advocating self-contained housing were told that we were being irresponsible wanting to isolate people, or profligate because of the perceived increased costs of supporting a dispersed population.

At a Department of Health Conference ('Caring for AIDS in the Community') in 1985 one professor of genito-urinary medicine said, 'what we need is hostels for people with AIDS', the argument being that it would make it easier to deliver medical services.[1] Two neighbouring health authorities argued strongly that people with HIV needed to be clustered so that medical equipment could be stored and community nursing services could cluster visits, while others argued that there would be no benefit as people did not all fall ill at the same time.

In this chapter I want to look at the housing needs of people with HIV: their experience of housing services, and the way in which they could best be enabled to operate as equals in the housing market and maintain their independence for as long as possible.

HIV: a special housing need?

There have been no particular principled reasons for developing 'special housing' for people with HIV. However, people with HIV were, and still are, experiencing problems accessing parts of the housing market – both private and public.

Access to mortgages was, and continues to be, problematic as so many mortgage products are dependent on life assurance for which people with HIV are, of course, ineligible. Unemployed or economically inactive, whether forced through discrimination, or as a result of sickness or choice, individuals may be unable to sustain mortgage payments.

Social housing access systems were not designed for 'single people' aged 30–45 as most (though not all) people with HIV were in the early stages of the epidemic in Britain. In addition some housing providers refused to take people with HIV where their status was known.

Housing assessors often misunderstood medical terminology and falsely applied it to limit the number of people they accepted. In addition, many people with HIV were worried about revealing their status to housing services, though they needed to do this to access them. Many felt that there was little understanding of confidentiality and that they were often passed from pillar to post.

In this context two strategies were developed by campaigners in the late 1980s:

(1) to develop new initiatives as models of good practice and (2) to effect change in mainstream housing organizations. The primary principle we needed to establish was that people with HIV should have access to self-contained housing, where they could control their environment, maintain their support and friendship networks, and live independently. AIDS and Housing Project (AHP) was established as part of this process.[2]

Models of good practice

From four surveys conducted between 1990 and 1994, it is possible to establish the housing experience of people with HIV. Although based on relatively small samples they provide a consistent picture of the needs as expressed by people with HIV. They revealed that in Lambeth and Southwark,[3] Kensington and Chelsea,[4] London, Portsmouth and Manchester,[5] and Newham[6] there is a high level of demand (82 per cent, 54 per cent, 80 per cent and 99 per cent respectively) for self-contained accommodation but with supportive or HIV-educated housing management. A number of their requests were not dissimilar to those expressed by other chronically sick people or frail older people.

HIV disease is characterized by a wide range of symptoms often occurring concurrently. However, it is possible to group them under a number of general headings and identify the impact they have on the design and management of housing stock. Table 1 outlines some of the needs that might arise for someone living with HIV.

From these it is then possible to draw out a list of design requirements:

- *Internal features* – Bedroom large enough for equipment storage; kitchen large enough for food preparation and cooking whilst seated; shower; easy- to-use handles and ironmongery; bathroom large enough for chair, walking frame and assistance; second bedroom for carer or partner (during disturbed nights); layout which facilitates easy movement from one room to another; dry central heating; good sound and heat insulation; double glazing.

- *Accessibility* – Located near shops, transport and support networks; level access or well lifted; car park nearby; no internal steps; stairs suitable for chair-lift.

- *Security* – well-lit approach; entry phone; spy hole; adequate safeguards

Breathing difficulties	Common illnesses, including *Pneumocystis carinii* pneumonia, will often result in shortness of breath and associated difficulties with mobility. Properties with internal stairs will present mobility difficulties. Access can be improved by ramping stairs, providing stair lifts and grab rails. If a flat is above the ground floor in a block with a lift, lift maintenance and the speed of repairs is important. Damp housing conditions will also aggravate these symptoms.
Persistent diarrhoea and night sweats	These may be experienced by those who have not had a diagnosis of AIDS as well as by some of those who have. Easy access to a toilet has proved essential so that when designing new provision, locating a toilet next to the bedroom should be considered. Shower facilities have proved to be the most commonly requested adaptation, and again should be considered when designing new stock. Persistent diarrhoea may leave someone feeling extremely weak and there are consequently mobility considerations too. People with HIV who have night sweats often have to make regular changes of bedding and so find that laundry and drying facilities are important.
Impaired eyesight	HIV infection in the brain and nervous system can affect eyesight. For example, CMV retinitis can cause severely impaired vision and bilateral blindness. This means that straightforward controls on heating systems, cookers, etc, will make life easier for them. For someone with failing eyesight the familiarity of the home and the locality is important – moving to a new home may make for more difficulties. Sometimes the current home is so unsuitable that a move is unavoidable but we have found that early assessment of other future needs (particularly mobility) when allocating housing can add considerably to quality of life.
Memory loss, confusion and dementia	There is a considerable range of neurological manifestations of AIDS. HIV is thought to attack certain cells in the brain and nervous system. As many as 75 per cent of those dying from AIDS-related illnesses have symptoms associated with disease in the central nervous system. HIV infection in the brain can cause meningitis with severe headaches and fevers. It can also cause impairment of thinking and memory. When severe it is often referred to as AIDS dementia and is likely to be more common in the later stages of illness and in people who have had AIDS for a long time. In this situation a person may become bedridden and incontinent. Homes need to be made as safe as possible with safety catches on kettles, gas that cannot be left on, etc. In some cases people have to move to supported accommodation as continuing in the home may not be possible and a move is the only solution available.
General frailty, weakness and fatigue	Many of the HIV-related illnesses, including *Pneumocystis carinii* pneumonia and Kaposi's sarcoma, will lead to general symptoms of weakness and exhaustion. These are also general symptoms of anyone in the later stages of a terminal illness. Difficulties with mobility are inevitable and can be reduced by appropriate allocation of accommodation at earlier stages and by the kind of adaptations mentioned above. In addition, a person will need to be warm, implying the need for central heating they can control.

Table 1 **Symptoms associated with HIV disease which have an impact on housing needs**

against break-in, for example window locks, laminated glass, self-extinguishing letter boxes; private, safe, secure outside space; link to central alarm.

In the current cost-cutting environment there are some design needs that can seem like a wish list or for which we have to fight particularly hard. For example, good sound insulation becomes even more important when you are very ill, bed- or housebound. This requirement was in part to counteract noise from neighbours, but people were also concerned that they could not use toilets or laundry facilities during the night because of disturbing others. This is often the first thing to go when developers are looking to cut avoidable costs but is really very important.

Cost cutting is not the only motive influencing building design. One approach I come across all the time is what I call 'the science of the small bathroom'. People with HIV often need to sit down in the bathroom or they need to have help to bathe, etc. However, architects and developers often try and save space in kitchens and bathrooms, priding themselves on the way they have squeezed all the equipment in! Most people with HIV we talk to would willing give up a little living space for a bigger kitchen and bathroom.

Fear of discrimination or harassment can also add to the list of demands in a way that may need explaining. In a survey commissioned from AHP by the Joseph Rowntree Foundation,[7] many respondents with HIV said they wanted a garden so that, as one person stated, they:

'...can face the world without really having to face it.'

In all the surveys there was a high level of harassment experienced by the respondents, with testimonies such as the following:

'I had a letter through the door saying you're gay...twice the door was burnt in the shape of a cross upside down.'

In the recent Newham Survey 79 per cent of the sample had been forced to move by neighbours, friends, or family.[8] And 34 per cent had experienced harassment from landlords or fear of discrimination, as is well illustrated by this example:

'The harassment started after the ambulance came one day. Everyone put two and two together and since then it's been hell. Kids shout abuse and put excrement through the letter box. The landlord said he wanted us out as he'd had complaints from the other residents of the block.'

Developing housing to meet these needs

These surveys revealed that moving into housing association stock was at least perceived as an option that created more security. Although it does not remove the risk of harassment, at least a sympathetic ear – in the form of housing professionals – would be available.

By April 1994, 400 units of 'specialist' accommodation had been developed in the UK to meet these needs, mainly through the Housing Corporation's development programme.[9] Whilst this represents a significant achievement, it is not a solution. Mainstream providers of housing still have an enormously important role to play.

Effecting change in mainstream provision

The reality is that many people with HIV are already housed by housing associations and local authority housing departments or indeed are home owners using mortgage lenders, often without reference to or knowledge of their HIV status. To respond to this, organizations such as the Local Authorities Associations and the National Federation of Housing Associations (together with the AIDS and Housing Project) have produced guidance for their members. These were designed not only to encourage good practice, as defined within this chapter, but also to maintain the health of those with HIV. That is, they were to encourage housing organizations to take on a wider role in creating environments in which healthy living could take place, for example through training staff to be supportive.

Private sector

Mortgage lenders have been chary of issuing such guidance preferring to leave lending decisions and renegotiation decisions to branch managers. This has often felt problematic to people with HIV as they are unsure of the reaction they will receive when, for example, they might need to renegotiate repayments because of a change in financial circumstances.

Public sector

Under community care housing authorities have the duty to identify housing needs in their area and to develop a strategy for meeting those needs. The annual housing strategy statement covers all housing in the area, not just the authority's own housing. However, although housing authorities must develop this strategy to meet housing needs, they do not have a duty to provide housing themselves. They are required by law to consult with a range of other agencies in the field of housing and health as well as social care in developing their community care strategy. Under the National Health Service and Community Care Act 1990, social services authorities also have the duty to identify social care needs in their area and to develop a strategy for meeting those needs to be published in their annual community care plan.

Each year when the housing authority submits its housing strategy to the Government (Department of Environment), it is also submits its bid for permission to spend capital on housing. This bid is called the Housing Investment Programme (HIP).

Very few new council homes are now being built. Housing associations now provide the main increase in housing outside the private sector. Associations get the capital finance for new housing partly from public sources, usually through the Housing Corporation but sometimes through local government, and partly from borrowing in the private sector. The Housing Corporation will not fund new housing association developments unless they fit in with the housing strategy of the housing authority in that area.

These different requirements show that:

- if new public housing is needed to meet the needs of people with HIV, this must be included in these annual housing strategies or it is very unlikely to get funded;
- definitions of the housing needs of people with HIV need to be linked to definitions of their social and healthcare (i.e. community care) needs;
- if different social or healthcare provision is needed as a result of the impact of their housing situation on people with HIV, those needs should be included in the community care plan;
- the community care plan and the HIP need to complement each other, with a consistent approach to the community care needs and the housing needs of people with HIV.

Some housing needs can be met by changes in policies or procedures, for example in relation to privacy in interviewing or prioritization of repairs. These changes can be effected quickly. But others require investment in housing, whether new stock or the adaptation of existing stock. It takes years to get from the planning stage to the first letting of a new housing scheme. Housing authorities may not see assessment of local HIV-related housing need as a priority when they are facing major challenges such as stock transfer (the transfer of local authority housing stock to a housing association or private company) and compulsive competitive tendering. It will be less of a priority where HIV incidence is low – or appears to be low, because it has never been assessed.

Accessible housing

There will never be enough special housing. Need is inevitably going to exceed the resources made available, leading to competition between groups for a share in a diminishing programme. Although much has been achieved by mainstream providers they too are working within resource constraints and need to ensure that they are allocating their resources to people most in need. In addition, as HIV becomes more prevalent among the more disadvantaged sections of society, the option of home ownership will become increasingly unlikely.

There is a third way – that all housing should be built to basic accessibility criteria so that it is usable, easily adaptable and accessible by all the population whatever their age, health or family circumstances. There will still, of course, be special needs to be met, particularly in terms of support and personal care resulting in the necessary specialist accommodation. However, if all domestic property was built to accessible standards, fewer people would have to (1) move into other accommodation or into care, (2) adapt their home, often at great expense to themselves or the state, or (3) be sentenced to living or just getting by in totally unsuitable accommodation.

As well as being more cost-effective, avoiding the need for very costly adaptation work, accessible housing would greatly enhance the quality of life of millions of people. Of course, in the foreseeable future most of us will not be living in new accommodation and will have to put up with the shortcomings of existing homes, but we have to start somewhere and there is no justification for delaying this change any longer.

A fit able-bodied person aged 18–40 of average height, right-handed, with good sight and good hearing can congratulate themselves on being part of the 18 per cent of the population for whom British houses are designed. For people not in this category – parents with pushchairs, pregnant women or someone with a sports injury – getting into and around most homes may be at best inconvenient and at worst impossible. All these people can be counted into the 1 in 10 adults who have some kind of mobility impairment. Recent surveys reveal that as many as 1 in 4 households may contain at least one person who has a disability.

What is accessible housing?

The main features of accessible housing are:[10]

- wherever the lie of the land allows, entrances should have a level or gently sloped approach;
- easy access to parking space;
- lifts to upper storey flats should be wheelchair accessible;
- sufficient door widths, and circulation space in the hall, to allow easy passage for disabled people;
- in houses with more than one storey, an entrance level toilet and a staircase designed to allow for possible future installation of a stair-lift.

The Government has announced a review of Part M of the Building Regulations (i.e. the part that deals with accessibility) and has commissioned research from Black Horse Agencies, a leading estate agency, to look at the impact on the housing market of accessibility criteria. The Building

Regulations Advisory Committee will advise the minister responsible on what change, if any, to make after a period of consultation in 1994.

Such regulation would have many advantages. It would ensure built-in flexibility and anticipate the varied demands made on a house or flat over a long period of time. A national access standard could stimulate demand for new construction projects, ensuring that they are cheap and readily available. Developers will all be subject to the same regulations, putting none at a disadvantage in competitive terms. And finally, as accessible housing becomes the norm rather than the exception, it will become affordable housing. Older and disabled purchasers, currently disadvantaged by a dearth of accessible housing, will be able to enter the housing market on equal terms.

Problems

Change is urgent. The percentage of the population over 75 years is on the increase. As long-stay hospitals and residential institutions close, more and more older people, people with chronic illnesses and people with disabilities will be living in ordinary housing. However, the push towards value for money has meant that the number of homes being built to an accessible standard has actually reduced. Also, the current trend towards two-storey houses has led to one-storey accommodation or properties with lifts becoming an increasingly scarce resource.

Most new homes today are built for sale by private developers or for rent by housing associations. Whilst a few developers have made efforts to build to an accessible standard, most developers are reluctant to take on accessible housing. They are concerned that people will not buy houses that look different and that contractors will not be able to adapt. They are loathe to take on or pass on the minimal extra costs that accessible housing will create until the new size fittings become 'standard'.

It is difficult to estimate the additional costs of including accessibility criteria in new schemes since it is difficult to know exactly whether you are comparing like with like. However, assessments by the Joseph Rowntree Foundation suggest that on a volume-build project with an average unit cost of £44,000 the additional cost would be £600, compared to a cost of £4,000 if you were to adapt later.[11]

Some housing associations have also made efforts in this direction. The Housing Corporation, for example, has included some of the modifications in its Design Performance Criteria. However, noise insulation, space standards, straight staircases, for example, are the first to go in an attempt to get a project under cost limits set by the Housing Corporation. Value for money may not necessarily mean that the housing is of any less quality or that the slums of the future are being produced, but it does make for housing that is completely unsuitable for the vast majority of the population.

The National House Builders Federation have produced their own criteria which fall short of those being demanded by the Access Committee and disabled peoples' organizations. Their main concerns are that (1) any increase in price will affect salability, (2) level thresholds will lead to water ingress (the flow or leakage of water into the dwelling), (3) they will not be able to use standard parts, and (4) that the houses will look different and be difficult to sell. In fact the increase in price would be removed if these parts became standard; water ingress is not a problem for shops so it is hard to see how it could be different for domestic property and most people would not notice the difference.

Conclusion

Housing is the foundation of community care. Yet for people with HIV who want to lead independent lives, achieving good quality housing, appropriate to their needs and at an affordable price, is one of their greatest challenges. People with HIV do not need 'special' housing. However, because of discrimination and because social housing systems are not geared to younger groups they have had to become a special case.

The irony is that if all housing was built to minimum standards of accessibility, there would be much less emphasis of 'special housing' for a whole range of groups, as well as easier use by people with sporting injuries or small children. However, as a result of the insensitive design, common in mainstream housing, there has been an emphasis on specialist provision.

So long as prejudice and discrimination are part of the picture for people with HIV there will always be special needs associated with it. But with the right attitude all parts of the housing market could play their part to makes things easier so that those living with HIV or AIDS could operate as equals and live with dignity.

1 S. Smith, 'AIDS, housing and health', *British Medical Journal*, 1990.

2 AIDS and Housing Project encourages the development and management of good quality housing for people with HIV. AHP provides advice, training, consultancy to housing organizations and undertakes research to further these aims.

3 M. Drake, *HIV and Housing in South London*, The Landmark/AIDS and Housing Project, 1990.

4 Royal Borough of Kensington and Chelsea, *Housing for People with HIV*, 1990.

5 R. Pendlebury, *Survey into Levels of Satisfaction among Tenants Housed Because of HIV Infection*, Josepth Rowntree Foundation, 1991.

6 L. Firth and P. Molyneux, *HIV/AIDS and*

Housing Services, London Borough of Newham, 1994.

7 *Assessing Local Housing Need for People With HIV. Housing and Individual Needs Assessments. Housing and Community Care Joint Planning*, AIDS and Housing Project, 1993.

8 L. Firth and P. Molyneux, *HIV/AIDS and Housing Services*, London Borough of Newham, 1994.

9 The Housing Corporation provides finance and monitors the performance of housing associations in the United Kingdom.

10 Full details in *Building Homes for Successive Generations*, The Access Committee for England, House of Commons, 1992.

11 *Lifetime Homes*, Joseph Rowntree Foundation, 1993.

AIDS and Insurance: Some Very British Questions

Peter Roth

Chairman of the Insurance Working Party, Terrence Higgins Trust, 1989–1994*

Insurance involves sharing by the many of risks that will eventuate only for the few. Therefore, those taking out insurance pay moderate premiums calculated to enable the accumulation of sufficient funds by the insurer to cover those risks. An insurer has to estimate the total reserves of funds required for this purpose and it seeks, by underwriting, to assess those asking for cover to ascertain whether they present a significantly greater than average risk. For a group scheme, that may be done in aggregate, but for an individual applicant particular underwriting of the individual will be carried out. Heavy smokers are charged higher premiums for health and life insurance than non-smokers; and someone whose hobby is hang-gliding may have to pay more for accident insurance than another whose pastime is bridge. If there is a high probability that the circumstances for which insurance is requested will materialize, the insurer may decline to cover that risk altogether. The very old or the very ill may not get health or life insurance.

Before 1982, AIDS was unknown in Britain. During the previous twenty years,

actuaries had predicted falling mortality rates for the general population and those assumptions were taken into account in setting the level of premiums. By the mid 1980s, as the significance of AIDS became appreciated as a new disease for which there was no cure, insurers grew considerably alarmed. There were disturbing forecasts of the possible spread of the disease. In 1987, the Institute of Actuaries AIDS Working Party estimated that by the end of 1994 there would be between 139,000 and 464,000 HIV-positive males in the United Kingdom and between 8,500 and 19,000 AIDS-related deaths during 1994 alone.[1] Moreover, AIDS appeared to be affecting largely the younger population, many of whom would otherwise be considered good insurance risks.

The impact of AIDS for insurers fell in particular in the fields of health and life insurance. Because of the free availability of medical treatment of high quality under the National Health Service (NHS), medical expenses insurance and AIDS/HIV has not been an issue in Britain, in sharp contrast to the position in the United States. With the state as the

---

* The views expressed are not necessarily those of the Trust.

primary provider of medical care funded out of taxation, independent health insurance brings only additional benefits such as a private hospital room and greater choice of specialist. All the leading British doctors in the AIDS field treat patients under the NHS. Life insurance, however, plays an important role in contemporary Britain. It is significant as a means of savings, encouraged by the tax incentives given for this form of investment; and it is fundamental to house purchases, through endowment mortgages and other forms of mortgage-linked policies.[2] Spending on life insurance in the United Kingdom is by far the most per head of all countries in the European Union. Around 66 per cent of British households have the protection afforded by some kind of life insurance. At the start of 1994 there were almost 84 million individual life policies.[3]

The funds involved are enormous: total UK premium income for life insurance (i.e. excluding pensions) in 1993 was £21.8 billion.[4] Life insurance and pension funds together account for 52 per cent of the total financial assets of the personal sector, over four times as much as the deposits held either in banks or in building societies.[5]

In consequence, the supply of life insurance in Britain is a service of major social and economic implications provided by the commercial market. Assessment of the impact of the British life insurers' approach to AIDS and HIV prompts a number of issues of policy. The British insurance industry is largely self-regulating, with statutory control concentrated on solvency margins and accounting.[6] Insurance is exempt from the anti-cartel provisions of the Restrictive Trade Practices Act 1976 and the control on unreasonable exclusion clauses in the Unfair Contract Terms Act 1977.[7] The overwhelming majority of companies belong to the Association of British Insurers (ABI), through which they are able to coordinate their conduct. The British insurers have presented a largely uniform response to AIDS, particularly relating to the questions that they ask with regard to AIDS/HIV risk. Although the insurance companies set up the Insurance Ombudsman's Bureau, an independent body that effectively upholds 'good insurance practice', the Ombudsman essentially judges a complaint against an insurer according to the codes of conduct established by the industry itself; he is cautious about any determination that the prevailing standard is inadequate.[8]

In Britain, AIDS has been largely associated with certain sections of the population, and in particular homosexuals who in any event meet with prejudice and discrimination, although there are signs that new infection with HIV is spreading faster among heterosexuals. Insurance underwriting traditionally uses classification by broad categories. But to what extent should insurers have unlimited freedom to ask for and use information about membership in such a group? Insurers point out that the underwriting process is about discrimination, that is, the differential determination of premiums, for the reasons set out above. Ideally, every individual applicant would be assessed on a detailed investigation of his or her particular circumstances, and it is of course individual behaviour and not sexual orientation that creates the risk of catching HIV. However, such investigation may be impractical either because it involves questions of an intimate nature that would be viewed as offensive and the answers to which would be unreliable, or because it imposes unacceptable costs. Some forms of discrimination are viewed by society as so repugnant that even if they may be justifiable in actuarial terms, insurers are not permitted to adopt them. Use of racial criteria in determining premiums is forbidden by law.[9] Another approach is to permit insurers to use the criteria only insofar as it is actuarially justified. That is the position in the United Kingdom regarding differential premiums for men and women.[10] Alternatively, insurers can be left to apply 'group' criteria as they feel appropriate, free from any constraint.

The insurers' approach to AIDS/HIV

The insurance companies' reaction in the United Kingdom to the 'arrival' of AIDS was to impose a general increase in premiums by up to some 150 per cent for single males. This was seen both as provision for new risks and to cover the potential effect on their funds of claims in respect of the many people already insured who might contract the disease. AIDS exclusion clauses were introduced in medical expenses and permanent health policies, but such exclusions have never been favoured in Britain for life insurance both because of the difficulty of ascertaining at the time of a claim whether a death was due to AIDS (this will often not appear on the death certificate) and because such a policy would not be acceptable as security by mortgage lenders. Instead, insurers introduced a series of measures in an effort to ensure that insurance was not newly granted to someone who was HIV-positive or whom they considered was at significant risk of becoming HIV-positive in the future.

Insurers started to request applicants (referred to as 'proposers') for life cover in substantial amounts to take an HIV antibody test. Following advice issued by the ABI in 1986, insurance companies introduced onto all proposal forms questions that asked whether the proposer had ever had either an 'AIDS test' or counselling about AIDS. A supplementary questionnaire was produced, and sent to proposers according to sex, marital status and the amount of cover sought (the ABI recommended that it should be sent on any proposal for £75,000 for single males and £150,000 for married males) that asks whether the proposer falls within any of the following 'AIDS high risk groups':

'(a) homosexual men
(b) bisexual men
(c) intravenous drug users
(d) haemophiliacs
(e) sexual partners of the above'.

And insurers began to ask the proposers' General Practitioners (GPs) not only whether his or her patient had taken an HIV test but also whether the patient was homosexual or even, in some cases, whether there was 'anything about the patient's lifestyle' that makes it likely that they would get a sexually transmitted disease.

Anyone who tested HIV-positive was automatically refused life cover. Many homosexuals also found that their proposals were declined, or accepted only at such greatly increased rates as to make insurance unattractive. A 200 per cent increase over normal terms was not uncommon. And a proposer who disclosed that he had previously taken an HIV test, although with a negative result, was treated with considerable suspicion. The fact of having had a test was in itself viewed as indicator of an 'at risk' lifestyle, which could lead to declining of the proposal or acceptance only on 'special' (i.e. much higher) terms.

Criticism – and the response

Predictably, some of these measures provoked considerable criticism, which intensified as the early forecasts about an 'AIDS epidemic' in the United Kingdom fortunately proved greatly exaggerated. Although someone seeking life cover can 'shop around' between different insurance companies, any difficulties are compounded by the effect of one insurer's judgment upon another. Every proposal form asks whether the proposer has been declined or had special terms imposed on a previous insurance (and if so for details). Moreover, there were cases where the imposition of such special terms because of homosexuality led the proposer's name to be added to a shared database used by most insurers (ominously called 'the Impaired Lives Registry') as a person who 'on health grounds' was of lower than normal life expectancy. Such an entry should be removed once a complaint was made, but most people were wholly unaware of the Registry's existence.[11]

For an insurer to send a proposer for an HIV test may not be unreasonable, as other medical tests may also be required in connection with life insurance. However, the sensitivity surrounding HIV means that particular care is needed to ensure confidentiality of results from insurance broker or banker (e.g. in the case of a bank-arranged mortgage) and consent to such a test must be preceded by proper counselling so that the proposer is truly prepared to accept the risk of a positive result. But insurance-requested HIV tests are usually performed by doctors under contract to the insurance company and not at specialist clinics, and there have been indications that the pre-test counselling may be perfunctory at best.[12] General Practitioners strongly resented being asked to speculate on their patient's lifestyle.[13] The substantial loading of premiums on homosexuals, if their proposals were accepted at all, did not reflect the individual risk and ignored, for example, the fact that the proposer might be in a stable relationship and much more alert to the danger of HIV infection than a promiscuous heterosexual.

The strongest criticism was directed at the insurers' demand to know about prior negative HIV tests. In 1989, the All-Party House of Commons Social Services Committee recommended that the Government should seek the agreement of insurance companies that questions about prior HIV tests should not be asked in connection with applications for life insurance.[14] The leading AIDS charity, the Terrence Higgins Trust, commenced a

campaign to persuade insurers that they should cease to ask about prior *negative* tests or counselling and substitute the question: 'Have you tested positive for AIDS/HIV?' Following extensive discussions between the Government and the ABI, an independent, national survey was commissioned to consider whether the form of insurance questions was indeed deterring individuals from coming forward for HIV tests, as the Terrence Higgins Trust and others had claimed. The report, published in July 1991, clearly found that the questions indeed had this effect. Although it was cautious in estimating the numbers involved, the report considered that 'it would certainly be in the thousands, possibly in the tens of thousands'.[15] The then Minister of Health, Mrs Virginia Bottomley, observed that these figures '…include some of the people we would most want to encourage to come for a test.' And she stated: 'We must remove unnecessary barriers [to testing] in the interests of public health.'[16]

At the same time, the projections for HIV infection in the United Kingdom were being significantly reduced. In March 1991, the Institute of Actuaries issued its *AIDS Bulletin No.5* which duly recorded that the spread of AIDS had been nothing like as extensive as it initially forecast, and put forward much lower projections. For example, for 1994 it estimated under 56,000 HIV-positive males by the end of the year and under 2000 AIDS-related deaths during that year.[17]

Why was the influence of the insurance questions on HIV testing so important? The decision for an individual whether or not to have an HIV test is often an anxious one. There is no cure for infection with HIV; the knowledge that one has HIV can cause immense emotional stress although the individual may remain asymptomatic for many years; and the stigma that sadly continues to surround AIDS creates anxiety about disclosure to employers and even family and friends. Nonetheless, there is a substantial body of medical opinion that favours early diagnosis as assisting treatment; and for many who are most unlikely to have contracted HIV verification of this can relieve lingering anxiety. Furthermore, early in a new relationship for both partners to be reassured on their HIV status may be a very responsible step. These are difficult issues, beyond the scope of this chapter, but they highlight one very relevant aspect. Concerns about a future life insurance proposal or the ability to obtain a mortgage should play no part in the individual's decision whether or not to have an HIV test.

Moreover, from the public health perspective, the British programme of voluntary, self-referred and confidential HIV testing plays a major role in combating the spread of AIDS/HIV. Not only do test results provide important epidemiological information about the prevalence of the virus, but it is generally believed that discovery by an individual that he or she is HIV-positive in most cases encourages behaviour to avoid transmission. Indeed, the very process of having an HIV test at a specialist clinic is part of the educational process, irrespective of the result. Such a test is always accompanied by full professional counselling, both before and on returning to receive the result even when it is negative. It is not surprising that the Government's strategy for HIV and AIDS, issued in June 1993 on the establishment of the Communicable Diseases branch of the Department of Health, identified as a key policy for the future:

'[to] continue to make HIV testing facilities more widely known and more readily available through primary health care and other local sources.'

Balanced against these considerations, from the insurers' own perspective the information elicited by these questions was of doubtful value. There are a multitude of reasons why individuals seek a test and the numbers having a test rise markedly at the time of increased media publicity over AIDS, without any corresponding increase in the proportion testing positive.[18] A study in 1993 found that a large proportion of those having HIV tests are women, who have a very low incidence of HIV infection in Britain.[19] Moreover, it was widely acknowledged that many of those who have had a previous test lie in answer to the insurance question, relying on the fact that information held by a hospital clinic is strictly confidential. So long as the information is not passed to the proposer's GP, an insurer may be unlikely to discover the truth.

Nonetheless, the British insurance industry persisted in retaining the questions about prior negative tests. The insurers' response was to emphasize a distinction between 'routine' and 'non-routine' tests. Under strong pressure from the Department of Health, the ABI agreed to make clear that a test taken as part of antenatal screening would be ignored. Shortly before publication of the results of the 1991 survey and in the knowledge of its contents,[20] the ABI produced a Statement of Practice which declared:

'Having had a negative HIV test will not, of itself, prevent someone from obtaining life insurance or even affect the cost, provided there are no adverse risk factors present. Consequently having a test for routine purposes such as giving blood, pre-natal screening or employment creates no problem regarding life insurance.'

However, this failed to resolve the problem because insurers specifically required disclosure of *the reason* why the individual had a test, and that reason could be the basis for an adverse underwriting decision. The question on the proposal form remained;[21] and for the individual who had sought a test on their own initiative, nothing had changed.[22] The public felt no reassurance, and at one leading London genito-urinary clinic, 28 per cent of patients said that they would still not disclose the fact of having an HIV test to an insurance company.[23] GPs remained unclear as to the way insurers used the information which they were asked to provide and some did not insert the fact of HIV testing on patients' medical records.[24]

The Institute of Actuaries' Working Party in its 1991 *AIDS Bulletin* explained that the much lower homosexual spread than originally anticipated was probably the result of behavioural changes among homosexuals in the mid 1980s. It noted the need for insurers to take account of heterosexual spread of HIV, often the result of infection abroad. Depending on the assumptions made, heterosexual spread could readily account for one third of the total AIDS cases by the late 1990s, and possibly more. The Working Party recommended greater emphasis on HIV testing, as a more objective means of assessment of risk, and a switch of emphasis in insurers' 'lifestyle' questionnaires from sexual orientation to sexual behaviour: 'Increasingly it is the latter which is the determinant of the risk of infection.'[25]

In response, the insurers' general approach was to *add* further questions to supplementary questionnaires but not to reconsider fundamentally the logic that led to the formulation of the insurers response to the threat of AIDS as perceived in 1986. In 1992, some companies started to ask proposers whether they have received blood products abroad, or even if they have had a sexual relationship with anyone resident abroad (and if so, when and where).[26] Homosexual proposers may be asked whether they are in a stable relationship (and if so, for how long this has been the case), and about the number of their sexual partners over the past two years[27] – although reassuring answers (in insurance terms) to such questions do not necessarily avoid a significant 'homosexual' loading on the terms offered. The intrusiveness of some of the questions

serves to highlight the lack of any effective law of privacy in the United Kingdom, although there may be doubt regarding the compatibility of this situation with the European Convention on Human Rights.[28]

The position elsewhere

In following the above approach, the British insurance companies were out of step with the insurance industry elsewhere in western Europe. In France and Belgium, insurers do ask about previous HIV tests, but only to ascertain if a proposer has tested positive. No information is sought about why the test is taken, and French insurers regarded the suggestion that taking a test may indicate a 'high risk' lifestyle as an extraordinary concept.[29] An agreement concluded in 1991 between the French government and the four main insurance associations in France prohibits signatories from asking questions of a sexually intimate nature concerning the private life of the applicant and, in particular, concerning sexual orientation.[30] A committee was established to monitor compliance with the agreement. In Germany, the Association of Life Insurers recommends that its members ask about HIV tests only whether it has been established that the proposer either is HIV-positive or has AIDS. In the Netherlands, although Dutch life insurers had asked about HIV blood tests in general, the practice was changed following a Code of Conduct agreed with the Dutch government in February 1993.[31] The Code specifies the questions that may be asked and the circumstances in which the insurers may request the proposer to take an HIV test. Seeking information about previous negative tests or the proposer's sexuality is not permitted.

In the rest of Europe, however, homosexual spread of HIV infection is not significant. But it has of course been a prominent feature of the epidemic in North America. Nonetheless, as early as

1987 the Canadian Life and Health Insurance Association adopted guidelines which state: 'No question should be directed towards determining, directly or indirectly, the proposed insured's sexual orientation.'[32] In the United States, the National Association of Insurance Commissioners, the state insurance regulators, issued comprehensive guidelines which proscribe any attempt to ascertain the proposer's sexual orientation or to use this in the underwriting process.[33] They also provide alternative options whereby a state may permit insurers to ask about previous positive test results or prohibit any question about previous HIV testing; questions about prior negative tests are in any event impermissible. Legislation on this pattern has been introduced in some American states, and the guidelines have in any event been endorsed by the two trade associations whose members account for the overwhelming proportion of life and health insurance sold in the United States, the American Council of Life Insurance and the Health Insurance Association of America.

In Australia and New Zealand, the incidence of AIDS has so far been predominantly among the homosexual community. But in these countries, with a similar legal heritage to the United Kingdom, legislation has been introduced that provides some of the most comprehensive protection regarding insurance and HIV/AIDS. The New Zealand Human Rights Act 1993 prohibits discrimination in insurance on grounds that include infection with HIV or sexual orientation except where differential treatment is reasonably based on actuarial data or (if that is not available) reputable medical or actuarial opinion.[34] In Australia, the Disability Discrimination Act 1992 permits discrimination in the field of insurance on the grounds of existing or past disability or disability 'that may arise in the future' or which 'is imputed to a person' (e.g. a belief that someone will become HIV-positive in the future) only on similar grounds of statistical/actuarial data or reasonableness.[35] In addition, some of the Australian states have enacted extensive statutory provisions that cover also discrimination on the grounds of sexual orientation; however, as regards specifically life (but not health) insurance, those enactments have not yet taken effect for constitutional reasons.[36]

Progress under pressure – remaining problems

By late 1993 it had become clear that the practice of the British insurance industry would not change without the threat of legislation. The industry was confident that the Conservative Government, committed to self-regulation, would not introduce any further statutory control. Accordingly, the Terrence Higgins Trust decided to seek to have introduced a statute in Parliament as a Private Member's Bill. To command the widest acceptance, the scope of the proposed legislation was restricted to the issue of previous negative HIV tests. A short Bill was drafted that would prohibit insurers, directly or indirectly, from seeking this information while allowing questions about a positive HIV test. In co-operation with the officers of the All-Party Parliamentary Group on AIDS, the Trust set about soliciting support for the Bill, which was to be introduced in the House of Lords. At about the same time, the Government Actuary informed insurance companies that because projections of the number of AIDS cases had proved too pessimistic, they could reduce the reserves set aside to cover potential claims.[37]

In the first part of 1994, support for the Bill gathered apace across all political parties.[38] It received the formal endorsement of the British Medical Association, the Royal College of General Practitioners and the Royal College of Nursing. The target date for the Bill was 30 November 1994, the eve of World AIDS Day. But the extent of backing which the Bill attracted brought additional pressure to bear on the British insurance industry. On 26 July 1994, the last day of the House of Lords sitting before the parliamentary recess, the ABI announced the withdrawal of its recommended question in insurance proposal forms on HIV testing. A new Statement of Practice was issued that states that insurance companies will no longer ask about previous negative results to HIV tests or counselling.[39] The ABI recommended a new form of question:

'Have you tested positive for HIV/AIDS or Hepatitis B or C, or have you been tested/treated for other sexually transmitted diseases or are you awaiting the result of such a test?'

The ABI explained this change on the basis that life insurance payouts for AIDS deaths had been much lower than first envisaged and that HIV testing had become more commonplace.

Adherence to the Statement of Practice can be enforced by the Insurance Ombudsman[40] and the Bill was accordingly not proceeded with. Should there be widespread non-compliance, the Bill can still be introduced, but this seems unlikely.

Conclusion

It is to be hoped that the 1994 Statement of Practice may inaugurate a more responsible approach by the British life insurance companies to questions about HIV/AIDS risk. The history, however, does not give grounds for optimism. Insurers continue to use homosexuality as an underwriting criterion. Although in one respect an issue of 'gay rights', this provokes a more general concern about stereotyping used against a section of the community that has frequently been the target of discrimination. Issues of privacy are raised by some of the questions now employed. In group superannuation and pension schemes, where no individual underwriting takes place, there are sometimes problems over blanket AIDS exclusion clauses.[41]

For those with HIV, insurance cover is not a feasible option in Britain on the commercial insurance market. But as for others with a serious medical condition who are nonetheless able to live and work for many years, there is no safety net to provide them with the insurance that may be necessary to assist in purchasing a home.

The insurers in the United Kingdom, despite the number of companies competing in the market, operate as regards the questions that they ask as oligopolistic suppliers of fundamental services. The issues raised by underwriting in respect of AIDS and HIV have highlighted the social implications of insurers' conduct, and recent developments have demonstrated how outside regulation, or at least such a threat, may be necessary to protect the public interest. This is not the only area where such a public interest and the subjective commercial viewpoint of insurers may conflict. Genetic screening looms on the horizon as an approaching problem. How great a sense of social responsibility and what degree of accountability will insurers show in the future? Those are the real AIDS questions that now face the British insurance industry.

---

1 *AIDS Bulletin No.1*. The range of figures reflect differing assumptions, but all were based on a model of only homosexual spread among the male population.

2 62 per cent of all first mortgages advanced by Building Societies in 1993 were endowment mortgages (source: Building Societies Association) and a significant proportion of the remainder would have required the borrower to effect life cover, for example a mortgage protection policy.

3 Association of British Insurers, *Insurance Review Statistics 1989–93*.

4 *Ibid.*

5 CSO, *Financial Statistics*, Aug. 1994, Table 9.1J.

6 Insurance Companies Act 1982, Part II. In addition, under the European Community Directives, companies authorized to transact insurance business in other member states of the European Community may now sell directly in the United Kingdom: see for life insurance, Council Directive 92/96/EEC of 10 November 1992, OJ No. L360/1 (1992).

7 Restrictive Trade Practices (Services) Order 1976, Schedule, para. 8; Unfair Contract Terms Act 1977, Schedule 1, para. 1(a).

8 L. Slade, 'AIDS – insurance practice in the making', *Journal of the Society of Fellows* of the Chartered Insurance Institute, 6: 9, 1992.

9 Race Relations Act 1976, Sect. 20(2)(c).

10 Sex Discrimination Act 1975, Sects. 29(1), (2)(c) and 45.

11 See the case reported in *Which?* September 1990, pp. 522–23. A person has a statutory right under the Data Protection Act 1984 to obtain a copy information about himself held on the Registry. Following representations from the Terrence Higgins Trust, the Data Protection Registrar is now requiring insurers to disclose the existence of the Registry on insurance proposal forms.

12 D. Morgan, 'AIDS stigma in insurance market', *British Medical Journal*, 299: 1536, 1989.

13 O. Samuel, 'Our patients' lifestyle is their business', *British Medical Journal*, 298: 59, 1989.

14 Social Services Committee, 7th Report (1988–89), *AIDS*, HC 202.

15 Department of Health, *AIDS and Life Insurance*, pp. 35–36, 1991.

16 Department of Health Press Release, 25 July 1991.

17 Institute of Actuaries, *AIDS Bulletin No.5*, Report from the AIDS Working Party, March 1991, Appendices 2.1, 2.5; cp. at note 1 above.

18 Beck *et al.* 'An Update on HIV-testing at a London Sexually Transmitted Diseases Clinic: long-term impact of the AIDS media campaigns', *Genitourinary Medicine*, 66: 142, 1990.

19 Public Health Laboratory Service, *AIDS/HIV Quarterly Surveillance Tables*, No.20, June 1993, Table 24.

20 *Supra*, n.15. As co-sponsor of the survey, the ABI was given a copy of the draft report.

21 In 1993, the ABI recommended the addition of a rider that specifically points out that the proposer should indicate if the test was for 'routine screening' or 'for other reasons'.

22 See S. Barton and P. Roth, 'Life insurance and HIV antibody testing: One more hurdle to clear', *British Medical Journal*, 305: 902, 1992.

23 N. Hulme, S. Smith and S. Barton, 'Insurance and HIV antibody testing', *Lancet*, 39: i: 682, 1992.

24 F. Keane and S. Young, 'GPs, STDs and Life Insurance', *International Journal of STD & AIDS*, 5: 318, 1994.

25 *Supra*, n.17 at pp. 20–22. The Working Party's views on homosexual spread were echoed by the Government Actuary in his letter of 30 September 1993: *infra* n. 37.

26 E.g. Legal & General Assurance, 'Additional Information Form'.

27 E.g. Commercial Union Life 'Supplementary Lifestyle Questionnaire'.

28 See Article 8: right to respect for private and family life.

29 Research carried out by J. Simor for the Terrence Higgins Trust.

30 Convention sur l'assurabilité des personnes séropositives et sur les règles de confidentialité du traitement des informations médicales par l'assurance, 3 Sept. 1991.

31 Ministry of Justice, Dept. of Civil Law Legislation, Ref. 307430/93/6.

32 Guidelines with Respect to AIDS for the Sale and Underwriting of Life and Health Insurance, November 1987, para. 4(b). The Guidelines also state that no underwriting decision should be based on 'previous consultation or testing for HIV exposure with a negative or unknown result'.

33 NAIC Model Regulation Service, 'Medical/Lifestyle Questions on Applications and Underwriting Guidelines Affecting AIDS and ARC', 1988.

34 Sects. 21(1)(h)(vii), (m) and 44, 48. Compliance is monitored by the Human Rights Commission.

35 Sects. 4, 24, 46.

36 E.g. New South Wales, Anti-Discrimination Act 1977, sects. 49ZG, 49ZP. Such state insurance provisions have been held to be precluded by the Commonwealth Life Insurance Act 1945 that prevails under the Australian Constitution: *AMP v. Goulden* (1986) 160 CLR 330. See generally the excellent discussion by M. Neave, 'Anti-discrimination Laws and Insurance: the Problem of AIDS', *Insurance Law Journal* [Austr.], 1: 10, 1988.

37 Circular letter dated 30 September 1993 from C.D. Daykin, the Government Actuary (unpublished).

38 The Bill was to be introduced by Baroness Gardner of Parkes, the Chair of the Royal Free Hospital NHS Trust. Among its leading supporters were two former Health Ministers, Lords Ennals (Labour) and Hayhoe (Conservative) and two senior medical Peers, Lords McColl and Walton.

39 ABI Statement of Practice – Underwriting Life Insurance for HIV/AIDS, 25 July 1994.

40 Supra at n.8.

41 This has been a problem in Australia where a report commissioned by the Commonwealth Department of Health, Housing & Community Services found no evidence that adverse selection, the justification for such exclusions, was greater for AIDS than for other causes: Trowbridge Consulting, 'HIV/AIDS, Superannuation and Insurance', Oct. 1993.

HIV and Life Insurance: Costs and Ethics of Non-Discrimination

Per Sandberg

UNIGEN, Centre for Molecular Biology, University of Trondheim
Centre for Medical Ethics, University of Oslo, Norway

In Norway, all applicants for individual life assurance must confirm that they have not undergone a blood test which shows that they are HIV-positive. People living with HIV are routinely refused such insurance coverage. Similar practices are followed in other European countries. These practices are criticized as deterring people from testing for HIV, and there is hence reason to look for alternative policies. Using Norway as a case-study, this chapter explores the economical and ethical implications of one such alternative – the 'no-question' policy – under which insurers are forbidden to ask about applicants' HIV status for small sums assured, but allowed to do so when the cover sought is above a certain limit. I will begin by outlining the basic principles of European life assurance, and then calculate the economic consequences of introducing the no-question policy in Norway. Finally, I will discuss the ethical and practical implications – particularly the feasibility – of introducing the policy Europe wide.

European Life Assurance

All member states of the European Union finance essential health services through their social security system or through other forms of public spending.[1] The same is also true for the members of the European Economic Area. In these states, it is mandatory to contribute to the health and social security systems through payment of taxes, and the benefits are distributed on the basis of objective criteria of need. This is an example of community-rated insurance, in which all people in a given community pay comparable rates, irrespective of individual risks, although on a sliding scale according to tax liability.

A foundation of voluntary private life insurance on the other hand is risk-rating, where premiums and other terms of policies for groups and individuals are set according to the age, sex, occupation, health status and health risks of applicants. Risk, in this context, means the hazard that something will happen which will effect payment according to the insurance terms.[2] Insurers normally obtain risk information through the insurance application form. Those applying for large insurance sums must often provide a physician's statement or be examined by the insurance company's doctor, and are sometimes tested for certain risk factors (e.g. HIV). Insurers have various direct and indirect ways to use the information obtained: they can charge a higher premium; write exclusion clauses; deny coverage altogether; exclude entire industries or groups; introduce waiting periods; or use other indirect ways to discriminate according to their assessment of the risks involved.[3]

Insurance is based on the complementary principles of solidarity and equity. Solidarity means that the population as a whole, or in broad groups, shares the responsibility and the benefits in terms of costs; equity, in the context of insurance, means that each individual's contribution should be roughly in line with his or her known level of risk.[4] Insurance markets exist because people are more willing to pay modest premiums on a regular basis rather than risk great losses at unpredictable times.[5] But they only exist under certain conditions. There is some maximum price above which the individual will decide not to purchase insurance. There is also some minimum premium that the insurer must receive in order to be willing to supply insurance. As long as these prices overlap, an insurance market will exist.[6]

In order to capture what function European life insurance serves, it might be useful to distinguish between three types of goods:

Primary social goods are goods that everyone needs for leading a life under decent material conditions. Well-ordered societies normally guarantee all their members access to these goods.

Commodities are goods that are sold on the 'normal' free market, for example cars and clothes.

Non-primary social goods fall between these types. They are not serving basic human needs, but neither are they just commodities. They serve a social function, but are usually not considered so important that access to them must be guaranteed to all members of a society.

I believe that it is reasonable to see European life insurance not as a primary social good but more as an optional good: that is, as a non-primary social good. It is an instrument for rational agents to secure a certain economic standard of living – above the publicly guaranteed minimum floor – for their dependants in the event that they die. But dependants of Europeans who are unable to receive private life insurance will nonetheless be guaranteed a minimum standard of living, thereby securing access to primary goods. European life insurance is, however, more than just a commodity as it serves valuable social functions. And if we accept that, European life insurance should be regarded as a non-primary social good. We can then argue that European life insurance should not be made compulsory. It should rather be voluntary and handled by the private market. As later discussed in more detail, this implies that insurers should be allowed to carry out at least some risk-rating. But as European life insurance serves valuable social functions, policies should be formulated so that as many people as possible can obtain life insurance coverage.

There can, however, be contingencies which make life insurance more of a primary than a non-primary social good. One such is, of course, when the welfare systems are less extensive. There might also be other more specific policies that in effect make life insurance less optional. Most people in the United Kingdom, for example, require a mortgage in order to be house owners and virtually all mortgages require some form of life insurance cover.[7] However, in European states which do not have such specific policies and where the publicly guaranteed minimum floor is at a decent level life insurance can be considered a non-primary social good.

The specific problem of adverse selection might arise when participation in the insurance scheme is voluntary and individual risk information is available. Insurance buyers may see themselves as having distinct rather than common interests in sharing risks. Those at lower risk will want to pool their risk only with those at comparably low risk. In contrast, those at high risk will seek the bargain offered by insurance that pools high- and low-risk individuals together. This might, over time, lead to a poor financial situation for the insurance scheme, forcing the insurer to increase premiums, which in turn might lead to the withdrawal of standard risks from the market. The seriousness of this threat is fiercely debated. Adverse selection is a classical problem in insurance theory, but 'little reliable data exist on the *actual* incidence of adverse selection by applicants for life insurance'.[8] Unsurprisingly, insurers hold it to be an absolutely real practical problem. They report that evidence of significant AIDS-related adverse selection has been documented in the USA.[9]

I will now calculate the economical consequences of introducing the no-question policy in Norway. In order to do so, I will first outline the principles of the policy, marshal the relevant data, and make the necessary estimates and assumptions.

Economic consequences of using the no-question policy in Norway

The no-question policy

The no-question policy is inspired by a Dutch solution to problems raised by genetic testing,[10] and has been explored in more detail elsewhere.[11] For cover that is sought above a specific questioning limit, insurers should be allowed to ask about HIV status and to use normal risk-rating procedures. For smaller assured sums, insurers should not be allowed to ask about HIV status. The policy is hence one of limited community-rated private life assurance. The actual limit can be set individually according to the applicant's social and financial circumstances, or it can be a uniform one.

Data about the Norwegian situation

Out of a total Norwegian population of 4.3 million people, by January 1993 1 million people had individual capital life assurance with average yearly premiums of £191 (NK 2,088) per person; and 2.3 million people were covered by group schemes with average premiums of £64 (NK 703) per person.[12] By January 1994 there were reports of 1,337 people with HIV and 369 people with AIDS (of whom 294 had died) in Norway. (There were reports of 90 new HIV infections in 1990; 140 in 1991; 106 in 1992; and 112 in 1993. The numbers of newly diagnosed AIDS cases were 52 in 1990; 62 in 1991; 52 in 1992; and 58 in 1993).[13] Insurance claims related to AIDS are reported to the Insurance Industry's Committee for Health Assessment, which by June 1992 had received 37 such claims. The amounts claimed so far are characterized as small or medium.

The Norwegian insurance industry concludes that there are no signs of AIDS-related adverse selection in the Norwegian life insurance industry so far.[14] They do, however, point out that claimants now, to a greater extent than before, can have known that they were HIV-infected at the time of signing insurance/application forms.

Estimates and assumptions

The 'best estimate' of the number of HIV-positive persons in Norway as of January 1992 was estimated to be 1,500.[15] But since this is so close to the number of known people with HIV (1,337 as of January 1994) I will use the latter figure in the following calculations. The Norwegian insurance industry estimated in June 1992 that about one-third of those known to be HIV-positive already had group or individual life insurance.[16] Using that estimate, the no-question policy for individual insurance can be estimated to be relevant for roughly 900 people known to have HIV by January 1994. But how many of these would really buy life insurance if not questioned about HIV? A maximal assumption is that all 900 would buy insurance of the maximal non-questioned size. A lower assumption could be obtained by subtracting those 340 HIV-positive people who are injecting drug users, reasoning that they would not buy life insurance even with the alternative policy. This gives a minimum estimate of 560 people.

We must also estimate the number of people that will be identified with new HIV infections in the future, and to what extent these people will buy insurance. Data from the last few years indicate that it is reasonable to expect about 100 newly detected cases of HIV infection per year in Norway. Of these, ten can be assumed to be injecting drug users. As roughly half the Norwegian population belongs to group schemes, quite a large proportion of the newly detected people with HIV will already belong to such a scheme. I estimate their number to be twenty per year. For them, the alternative policy can be considered irrelevant. Following the reasoning above, a high estimate is that there will be 80 newly identified people with HIV that will buy life insurance each year if the alternative policy is implemented, while the lower estimate gives a number of 70.

A difficult factor to estimate is the number and timing of AIDS-related deaths for people with HIV. I will base my estimates on a recent review article by Professor R.M. Anderson.[17] He estimates that the median incubation period of AIDS, defined as the period from infection to the diagnosis of the disease AIDS, is in the order of eight to ten years. Anderson stresses, however, that the incubation period is of long and variable nature, and that the longest cohort studies have only recorded about one half of the full distribution. That is, between ten and twelve years after infection with HIV about 50 per cent of the people have developed

AIDS. The extent of the remaining period is unknown. It is also unknown what fraction of those infected with HIV will actually develop AIDS. Concerning the survival time for people diagnosed with AIDS, Anderson cites a recent British study which reveals an average survival time of 18.3 months.[18]

In order not to get caught up in excessively detailed and difficult calculations, I will now compound the data and assumptions made above. I assume for this argument that with the no-question policy Norwegian insurers will have to cover 60 extra AIDS-related deaths per year for the foreseeable future.

Calculating the economic consequences

The size of the question limit is a key factor, which of course can be debated. I will, for the sake of calculation, fix a high and a low limit: the low limit is set to be twice the 1992 average size of individual Norwegian life assurances, which implies a low questioning limit of £19,414 (NK 212,000). The high limit is set at five times the 1992 average, which implies £48,535 (NK 530,000).

On the basis of the no-question policy, compounded data and assumptions, we can now derive two estimates. Sixty extra deaths per year with the low questioning-limit would give insurers extra costs totalling £1,164,840 (NK 12,720,000). To cover this through increased premiums, each individual premium would have to be increased by £1.03 (NK 11.26). This corresponds to an increase of 0.5 per cent for the average premium of £191 (NK 2,088). The increase for the high questioning limit would be £2.58 (NK 28.15), corresponding to 1.3 per cent.

The very small premium increase is a result of what, compared to other countries' experience, is a small number of AIDS-related deaths and of the limitation in costs per death. The small number of deaths is, of course, a consequence of the relatively favourable HIV situation in Norway. The present known prevalence rate of HIV in the Norwegian population is 0.03 per cent,[19] while the 'best estimate' gives a prevalence rate of 0.035 per cent.[20] This should be compared with the corresponding rate of about 0.1 per cent for the whole of Western Europe – three times the Norwegian rate.[21]

Ethical and practical implications

I will now discuss the ethical and practical implications of introducing the no-question policy in Norway. In so doing, I will first outline the main ethical reasons for restricting insurers' rights to ask about HIV status. I will then discuss some problems of the no-question policy, of which the most difficult one is that, with such a policy available in an open, international insurance market, Norwegian life insurers might be exposed to large-scale adverse selection from HIV-positive foreigners.

Reasons for restricting insurers' rights to enquire about HIV

There are several reasons for arguing that the personal rights of applicants for insurance are under pressure: the request for existing HIV information may have negative consequences for the individual.[22] These concern the personal rights to self-determination and protection of privacy. In exchange for the desired insurance, the applicant has to tolerate a certain measure of infringement of his or her privacy. Having to reveal one's HIV status, however, means a relatively large intrusion into one's privacy since this is very intimate and sensitive information.

There are also societal interests to consider. One is the interest of having a well-functioning and financially sound insurance industry. Another is to avoid excessive 'splits' in society. Others are the interests in finding remedies against AIDS and in preventing the spread of HIV. HIV testing is considered a crucial component for the latter objective. The Norwegian Ministry of Social Affairs has questioned whether disease prevention and privacy concerns give reason to intervene in the current civil law matter between insurer and applicant which allows questioning about HIV status.[23] The Ministry's major objection is that the current policy might deter people from being tested. The weight of this argument is primarily determined by the problem's actual size: how many people really do avoid testing because of the current insurance policy, and how does this influence disease prevention? For the present, in Norway, we do not have any reliable knowledge about the actual size of this problem. The British Market Research Bureau has, however, addressed exactly these questions in a study prepared for the Department of Health and the Association of British Insurers.[24] The Bureau conducted three separate surveys, involving 925 members of the general public, 511 young adults aged 20–34, and 100 AIDS specialists. The overall conclusion is that it is '*definitely the case that there are some people who are put off taking an HIV test because of the questions on insurance proposal forms.*'[25] The researchers point out that the project was not set up to attempt to arrive at a specific estimate of the size of this group, which would be a very difficult task. They are, however, confident that in percentage terms it will be very small, probably considerably less than 1 per cent. But this would still give a gross number 'certainly in the thousands, possibly in the tens of thousands', and many of these are people 'whom it is desirable should be tested'.[26]

Problems with the no-question policy

The proposed policy does not allow the marketing of life policies that are self-interest optimal for the majority of customers, that is, for everyone who is not known to be HIV-positive. It hence includes an element of subsidizing solidarity. It also means that AIDS in the insurance context is 'positively favoured' compared to several other diseases, for which risk factors are assessed. The costs of subsidizing solidarity and positive discrimination will, in one way or another, have to be financed by the other insurants through increased premiums. And as de Wit argues, 'when private insurers create subsidizing solidarity the outcome is always arbitrary. Who will carry the burden?'[27] In the solution proposed here, the burden of subsidy is borne by everyone who buys life insurance. Alternatively, policies could be designed where it is borne by all society members, or by subgroups determined by some risk property. The calculations above show, however, that the premium increase that each customer will have to pay with the no-question policy is very small. In fact, the increase might be even smaller as companies will save administration costs from not having to handle HIV information for the majority of applicants.

The problematic European dimension

I will now turn to the European dimension of the no-question policy. In this discussion, I will treat Norway as being a full member of the European Single Market, although at the time of writing it is unclear to what extent this actually will become true.

The threefold difference in HIV prevalence between Norway and Western Europe constitutes an obstacle to introducing the no-question policy in Norway. Another serious problem is the large difference between European countries, most drastically shown in France, Spain and Switzerland, where the HIV prevalence rates are estimated to be about ten times the Norwegian one. At a time when European insurance markets are becoming more transnational, it is possible that a number of HIV-positive Europeans would

buy life insurance in Norway if it became possible for them to do so. The number of extra AIDS-related deaths that Norwegian insurers then would have to cover could very well be 600 or 6,000 per year, rather than the estimated 60. And consequently, the premium increases could then rather be 5 per cent or 50 per cent for the low limit, and 13 per cent or 130 per cent for the high limit.

This blurs the prospects for the no-question policy in Norway. As participation in life assurance markets is voluntary, customers can always leave a specific insurance scheme if they are unhappy with some condition, for example when they feel that some other group is unfairly favoured. Furthermore, no one would want to buy insurance from a scheme with policies of such a kind that its short- and/or long-term sustainability is seriously questioned. Insurers are entrusted to look after people's money, and if they neglect to watch out for 'rip-offs' they are simply not doing their duty towards their customers. A feasible policy must therefore include precautions against excessive adverse selection of the kind sketched above.

Such a precaution against internal Norwegian adverse selection is provided in the no-question policy by the limitation in size of non-questioned insurance. It also seems necessary to prohibit the purchase of more than one non-questioned life insurance policy per individual to protect against excessive adverse selection by known high-risk people buying insurance from multiple sellers. Another topic to be regulated is the relative pricing of insurances of different sizes. Without such regulation, insurers might very well market risk-rated, larger-than-limit insurances which are cheaper than community-rated limited insurances. When the larger insurances are cheaper, or not very much more expensive, low-risk customers will wander away from the small insurances, and an 'assessment spiral phenomenon' – potentially resulting in market dissolution – might arise.

Precautions against transnational adverse selection

But these restrictions do not provide strong enough precautions against large-scale transnational adverse selection. They must therefore be complemented with some further policy. I will discuss two such alternatives:

- Norwegian insurers should be allowed to treat foreign applicants differently from Norwegian ones.
- The no-question policy should be implemented for the whole European Single Market.

The first alternative could be very simple: Norwegian insurers should be allowed to sell insurances to foreigners according to the present policy, that is, by asking about HIV status and rejecting those who are HIV-positive. For Norwegian applicants, however, they should have to follow the no-question policy of not asking about HIV status for small insurances.

Although simple in principle and seemingly feasible in practice, such a policy would be at odds with the present trend towards a single European market with common rules covering the insurance industry. Nys et al. have recently reviewed the present state of the European Single Life Insurance Market.[28] While concluding that each member state has a fairly broad margin to implement protective measures against genetic discrimination on its own initiative, they also point out that Article 7 of the Treaty of Rome, which prohibits discrimination on the basis of nationality, rules out the specific policy here discussed.[29] So, in order for Norway to implement a policy of treating foreign insurance applicants differently than Norwegian ones, Norway would also have to distance itself from the European Single Life Insurance Market.

Although discrimination based on nationality is disallowed, it is possible for members of the European Union to introduce specific restrictions. Policies say that all European citizens should be free to shop for insurance within the whole single market and that each member state is obliged to allow all life insurance products offered for sale in the Union to be marketed in its territory, as long as they do not conflict with the legal provisions protecting the general good in force in that member state. In order for 'protection of the general good' to count as a valid reason for specific policies, the good in question must not be already protected by the rules in the insurer's home member state, the provisions must be applied in a non-discriminatory manner to all insurers, and they must be objectively necessary and proportional to the desired objective.[30] When discussing the use of genetic information in insurance, which I have elsewhere argued is similar to HIV information,[31] Nys et al. say that some member states are on guard against infringements of privacy and adverse public health consequences, and will take legal action if necessary, while other member states at this moment see no reason for specific regulation. This might lead to different levels of consumer protection and create varying restrictions on the free insurance market in the various member states. To overcome such problems and distortions, common action is required.[32]

There is hence reason to explore the second option further: that the no-question policy should be implemented for the whole European Single Market. I will not be able to go into all the details of such a policy. However, it would have to decide on whether to set a single standards premium level (i.e. set in ECUs), or whether there should be different premiums across countries and/or regions set according to local factors. I am inclined to believe that the first option would be the best protection against large-scale transnational adverse selection.

With some version of the no-question policy implemented for the whole of Europe, European people living with HIV would then be able to buy life insurance in their home country and would therefore, in principle, not gain anything from buying life insurance in Norway. This could provide a kind of market equilibrium protection against transnational adverse selection. But is this a feasible policy for Europe? And is the protection for Norwegian insurers good enough?

A very rough indication of the probable European premium increases that would result from adopting the no-question policy can be obtained by remembering that the overall European prevalence of HIV is estimated to be three times the Norwegian one. Multiplying the calculated Norwegian premium increases by three gives an increase of about 1.6 per cent for the low questioning limit, and 4 per cent for the high limit. While remembering that this is a crude overall European estimate, and that there is also considerable variation between and within European countries, we see that these premium increases are of quite some size. And consequently, the alternative policy is less feasible for Europe than for Norway as its success is dependent on acceptance by the customers.

But what would the effect for Norwegian insurers be if European authorities actually implemented the no-question policy? Well, protection against transnational adverse selection is here to be obtained through a market equilibrium. It therefore hinges upon an assumption that people with HIV will not flock to buy insurance in one particular country or from one particular insurer, but will either buy insurance in their home country or buy it uniformly over the whole market. With the first of these alternatives, Norwegian premium increases would be in the order of the initial calculations (0.5–1.3 per cent); if the second takes place, they would be of the overall European order (1.6–4.0 per cent). The assumption of market equilibrium is, however, a very vulnerable assumption, and those who have most reason to fear from market non-equilibrium are the small insurance companies, a category which includes all the Norwegian ones. A possible way to counteract these adverse effects of market non-equilibrium could be some kind of pool system, where insurers redistribute funds to those among themselves who have faced a disproportionate number of AIDS-related claims.

Conclusion

I have explored some of the advantages of, and problems with, a policy where insurers are forbidden to ask about applicants' HIV status for small life insurance policies. This no-question policy would create a voluntary, limited, community-rated private life insurance submarket. It is a market solution that incorporates the ethos of solidarity, and is hence a third alternative to compulsory community-rated insurance and voluntary risk-rated 'free market' insurance. With Norway as a case-study, I have shown that the no-question policy is absolutely feasible economically, as long as the insurers can be protected against large-scale transnational adverse selection. And with the present trend towards a single European insurance market, such a protection could really only be attained by having the no-question policy implemented for the whole of Europe.

Acknowledgments
I would like to thank Charles Erin, Reidar K. Lie, Udo Schuklenk, Peter Singer and Flavio Braune Wiik for valuable comments.

1 H. Nys et al. Predictive Genetic Information and Life Insurance: Legal Aspects: Towards European Policy?. University of Limburg, Department of Health Law, Maastricht, 1993.

2 L. Bergelv, 'Livförsäkringens anpassning till nya risker', prepared discussion address at the 20th Nordic Life Insurance Congress, Helsinki, 1989.

3 D.W. Light, 'The practice and ethics of risk-rated health insurance', Journal of the American Medical Association, 267, 2503–2508, 1993.

4 P.S. Harper, 'Insurance and genetic testing', Lancet, 341, 224–227, 1993.

5 N. Daniels, 'Insurability and the HIV epidemic: ethical issues in underwriting', The Milbank Quarterly, 68, 497–525, 1990.

6 H. Ostrer et al. 'Insurance and genetic testing: where are we now?', American Journal of Human Genetics, 52, 567, 1993.

7 Nuffield Council on Bioethics, Genetic Screening: Ethical Issues, p. 65–74, London, 1993.

8 J.E. McEwen, K. McCarty, P.R. Reilly, 'A survey of medical directors of life insurance companies concerning use of genetic information', American Journal of Human Genetics, 53, 53, 1993.

9 K. A. Clifford, R.P. Iuculano, 'AIDS and insurance: the rationale for AIDS-related testing', Harvard Law Review, 100, 1817, 1987.

10 The Health Council of The Netherlands, Heredity: Science and Society, pp. 131–141. The Hague, 1989.

11 P. Sandberg, 'Genetic information and life insurance: a proposal for an ethical European Policy' accepted for publication in Social Science and Medicine.

12 Statistics from the Norwegian Insurance Association.

13 MSIS-Rapport Week 3, Folkehelsa, Oslo, 1994.

14 Program for Fellesmøte for Helsebedømmelse 18 Juni 1992, pp. 23–24. Oslo, 1992.

15 J. Mann, D.J.M. Tarantola and T.W. Netter (eds.), AIDS in the World, pp. 48–49. Harvard University Press, Cambridge, 1992.

16 Program for Fellesmøte for Helsebedømmelse 18 Juni 1992, pp. 23–24. Oslo, 1992.

17 R.M. Anderson, 'Epidemiological patterns of AIDS and HIV transmission in Europe', Report of the 1993 Conference of European Community Parliamentarians on HIV/AIDS, pp. 7–8. All-Party Parliamentary Group on AIDS, London, 1993.

18 S.E. Whitmore-Overton et al. 'Improved survival from diagnosis of AIDS in adult cases in the United Kingdom and bias due to reporting delay', AIDS, 7, 415–420, 1993.

19 MSIS-Rapport Week 3, Folkehelsa, Oslo, 1994.

20 J. Mann, D.J.M. Tarantola and T.W. Netter (eds.), AIDS in the World, pp. 48–49. Harvard University Press, Cambridge, 1992.

21 Ibid.

22 E.T.M. Olsthoorn-Heim, 'HIV testing and private insurance', Medicine and Law, 12, 11–14, 1993.

23 Norwegian Ministry of Social Affairs, Norwegian Public Report NOU 1990: 2, Lov om vern mot smittsomme sykdommer, Oslo, 1990.

24 Department of Health, AIDS and life insurance. HMSO, London, 1991.

25 Ibid. p. 35.

26 Ibid.

27 G.W. de Wit, 'Genetics: An insurance problem?', The Social Consequences of Genetic Testing, pp. 51–59. Netherlands Scientific Council for Government Policy, The Hague, 1990.

28 H. Nys et al. Predictive Genetic Information and Life Insurance: Legal Aspects: Towards European Policy?. University of Limburg, Department of Health Law, Maastricht, 1993.

29 Ibid. p. 30.

30 Ibid. pp. 26–27.

31 P. Sandberg, 'Limited community-rated private life insurance: an ethical and feasible European solution to problems raised by genetic testing', manuscript submitted for publication.

32 H. Nys et al. Predictive Genetic Information and Life Insurance: Legal Aspects: Towards European Policy?, p. 32. University of Limburg, Department of Health Law, Maastricht, 1993.

Employment, the Law and HIV: An Overview of European Legislation

Anne-Sophie Rieben Schizas

Staff Legal Adviser, Swiss Institute of Comparative Law, Lausanne, Switzerland

This chapter looks at some of the legal questions surrounding HIV, AIDS and employment, together with the answers given under current legislation in different European countries.[1] For practical reasons (language and access to information), the countries considered are Austria, Belgium, France, Germany, Italy, The Netherlands, Spain, Sweden and Switzerland. I will not be going into a precise description of national laws, but will indicate some of the general tendencies that can be observed. However, one country, France, will receive particular attention as it is the only European country to have recently enacted legislation which deals specifically with health-related discrimination in the field of employment.[2] (Also worth mentioning is the introduction of collective labour agreements, as these could prove to be very useful tools in protecting the employment rights of people with HIV or AIDS. However, it is beyond the scope of this study to investigate these further.)

Before tackling the issue of HIV/AIDS and employment, some characteristics of HIV disease need to be pinpointed.

First of all, it must be remembered that an infected individual can live many years before actually developing AIDS. The time lapse between infection with HIV and the development of AIDS-related illnesses – the so-called asymptomatic period – may well be ten years or more. And as treatment improves, this period will expand. During this first phase of the infection, the person is fit for work.

Secondly, before reaching the terminal stage of AIDS, the patient may develop various related illnesses that *can* be treated. He may be intermittently incapable of working, but for the rest of the time he may have a life compatible with the pursuit of his employment.

Third, one must note that the majority of infected people are between 20 and 40 years of age. In other words, they are at the prime of their working life. Given the scale of the infection, HIV and AIDS presents a new social phenomenon in comparison to other diseases.

Last but not least, it must be remembered and emphasized that no risk of infection exists through everyday social contact. HIV is not a highly infectious disease; generally speaking, it is transmitted through blood and semen. Consequently, there is very little or no risk of transmission at work.

The recruitment interview and medical examination

What kind of information can an employer legally ask of a prospective employee? Is he allowed to ask questions about the health status of the candidate and more precisely about his serological status? In the case of a pre-recruitment medical examination, could a candidate be required to have an HIV test? What if the employer, knowing the health status of the candidate, refuses to hire him?

Generally speaking, legal provision for routine HIV screening is rare. An employer may only ask questions directly and necessarily related to the post applied for, that is, if they are relevant to the nature and conditions of the job.[3] In view of the characteristics of HIV infection, serological status is not seen as pertinent for the vast majority of posts.

In Italy, for example, specific provisions have been adopted prohibiting employers from taking measures aimed at identifying HIV infection in candidates for employment.[4] Any violation of that rule is subject to prosecution. In Spain, the Catalonian Parliament has passed a resolution according to which any discrimination as to access to work for infected people is forbidden.[5] In most of the other countries studied, the law considers that matters concerning health relate to the job applicant's private life and thus merit protection. Consequently, the applicant, when questioned, has the right to remain silent or to lie. The employer has no right to terminate or annul the contract on the grounds of a false reply.[6] In the case of appeal, a judge will refer to the general provisions on privacy as provided by the Civil Code or the Constitution or both.

There is, however, some debate as to whether questions on full-blown AIDS are permissible because of their pertinence to a candidate's fitness for a job. Such a procedure is allowed in Germany and Austria, and may not automatically be excluded in the other countries, as questions about an applicant's private life, that is, about his state of health, are justified if they are pertinent to the nature and conditions of the job.[7]

Since, in principle, an employer cannot ask if an applicant is HIV-positive, he cannot require him to take an HIV test. In situations where a medical examination is required – by law[8] or if the employer may so require – the same principle applies: an HIV test may only be performed if it is relevant for the post. Doctors must tell their patients what kind of examination they undertake and they must obtain their patients' consent. They may only report as to whether the candidate is fit or not, but cannot give any further information.

It has occasionally been argued that, for some activities, a test must be required for safety reasons. The traditional example is that of the airline pilot whose acute neurological symptoms could imperil passengers' lives; more commonly, it has been suggested that healthcare workers should be tested on the basis of a potential risk of transmission. However, even if the issue has attracted some public attention, perhaps as a result of an inaccurate understanding of the infection, the possibility of listing some professions as 'at risk' so as to justify compulsory testing has been rejected. This is the attitude that generally prevails in the different countries considered. More precisely, it was the one adopted by the French body, the Council of Prevention of Professional Risks,[9] and also the attitude that can be deduced from some German rules on the prevention of accidents: these provisions, listing the medical examinations compulsory for certain professions such as medicine, do not include HIV testing.

In practice, though, it is not uncommon for job applicants to be screened for HIV infection. Why else, for example, would a

Swiss medical association have to be reminded that 'any decision by employers which requires applicants for employment to undergo an HIV detection test must be strongly opposed'?[10]

Although clandestine HIV testing is liable, in many countries, to prosecution for physical assault, one can only deplore the much too frequent resort to this kind of practice. Very few countries explicitly censure refusal of employment on the grounds of HIV infection. In 1990, Italy introduced a law which stipulated that identification of HIV infection *might* not be a ground for discrimination against someone applying for a job.[11] This year, however, the Italian Constitutional Court essentially repealed this part of the Act by declaring it unconstitutional. France explicitly punishes any refusal of employment on the grounds of health or disability by imprisonment and/or fines, *except in cases where unfitness for employment is medically certified*.[12] Similarly, a person seeking employment in Spain may not be discriminated against on the grounds of physical, mental and sensory handicaps *'whenever the worker is able to work'*.[13] In the other countries considered, there are general provisions prohibiting discrimination, although few of them specifically prohibit all forms of discrimination on the grounds of health.[14] And in Sweden, an employer actually has the right to refuse to employ HIV-positive persons: S.A.S., an airline, is one such employer.[15] Although the Swedish social security scheme will cover persons who, because of HIV infection, are prevented from working, such a social policy choice is questionable as it might in fact might lead to the social exclusion of someone fit to work.

In the final analysis, if no reference to health is made in the refusal of employment, it is very difficult to challenge the decision. Although the right to work appears in the different countries' Constitutions and in several international conventions, it is formulated very broadly and cannot be invoked against individuals.[16]

Stricter controls should be exercised over HIV testing. Unacceptable in themselves, their use might constitute a first step toward the common use of tests, such as genetic tests, to check the fitness of applicants.

Situation of people with HIV or AIDS during employment

Does an employee have a duty to inform the employer of his health status or may he be required to undergo regular medical examinations including an HIV test? To what kind of protection is an employee entitled if he is transferred against his will from one job to another? On the other hand, does a sick or incapacitated employee have the right to be offered an alternative position of a less strenuous or otherwise more suitable nature? What happens when the employee, due to his illness, is often on leave: is he entitled to his salary? How can an employee, suspected by his fellow workers of being HIV-positive, be protected from harassment and exclusion?

Duty to inform an employer

The obligation by an employee to inform an employer of HIV infection does not appear to be specified in any legislation. As asymptomatic seropositivity does not prevent fulfilment of a contract of employment, there is no justification for this. On the contrary, such information belongs to the individual's sphere of privacy and thus benefits protection.

In Spain, for example, the Catalonian Parliament passed a resolution prohibiting action to force an HIV-positive worker to inform the employer of his condition. More generally, the French Conseil d'Etat (last instance court of public law) clearly laid down the principle that no employee is obliged to inform his employer of symptoms of an illness from which he himself or any other employee may be suffering.[17]

Checks by the employers during the period of employment

In the majority of the European countries examined, the principle is that employers are not authorized to carry out health checks. If medical examinations are nevertheless carried out, it is usually at the worker's request or at least with his consent. Such checks should only be conducted by registered medical practitioners. In Italy, health checks have to be made through the public social security system, following a request by an employer.[18]

The information obtained should not be used to the detriment of the worker or for discriminatory purposes. In addition, the information should only be accessible to medical practitioners monitoring the worker's health and should therefore be protected under the provisions on medical confidentiality.[19] More generally, one can infer that HIV testing during one's period of employment is illegal: both in civil law and under the provisions of his National Constitution, an employee has the right to privacy.[20]

An exception, however, is Sweden. Here, an employer is considered to have the right to include in the worker's contract an obligation to undergo regular screening examinations.[21]

Transfer of a sick employee

In the countries considered, no existing legislation regarding working arrangements has been modified to provide for the transfer of an HIV-positive employee when he develops AIDS-related illnesses.

In France, an amendment to a provision of the industrial code limits the employer's disciplinary powers and makes it an offence to take disciplinary action on grounds of morals, health or disability.[22] Furthermore, in The Netherlands and in Sweden, it has been agreed that being HIV-positive or having full-blown AIDS is not a legitimate ground for transferring an employee.

In other countries, labour law forbids discriminatory acts on the part of the employer, in general, and in relation to the transfer of employees.[23] One should mention that in The Netherlands a provision has been recently introduced to the Criminal Code in order to prohibit any discrimination between persons in an occupation or in the workplace on grounds of race, sex or sexual behaviour.[24] However, no reference is made to discrimination on grounds of health.

Reclassification

In this matter too, it is mostly the existing labour legislation that is applied. In general, requests and proposals to adapt, modify or change a post may only be made by the company doctor. It is then up to the employer to consider the request and to implement it, if at all possible.

Attention must be drawn to the fact that, when the law provides for regrading, there is a risk that this may lead to the downgrading of the employee, who may find himself offered an inferior post. Such cases exist: a certain anaesthetist was regarded as a laboratory assistant, and a teacher as a secretary.[25]

Moreover, in contrast with other illnesses, it is more difficult to rearrange working hours without risking a breach of confidentiality where an HIV-positive employee is concerned.

Payment of salary and problems of repeated absences for treatment

In the countries considered, national legislation on sickness is commonly applicable in these cases. No country has enacted special provisions for HIV-positive workers needing frequent treatment. In principle, while the employment contract is in force, a worker who falls sick is paid a guaranteed wage by the employer (Belgium) or is indemnified by social security (France) or is paid his wage by the employer for a certain period and then by public health insurance (Germany). The employer is only entitled to satisfy himself that there is a genuine unfitness for work. He cannot ask the medical officer to divulge the precise nature of the unfitness.[26]

Disclosure of the infection

If the worker's infection is known to the employer, the latter must refrain from disclosing it, at least without the previous consent of the worker. This brings us back to the questions of privacy and confidentiality. One example can be found in the French case law: in the case of Burke Marketing Research, the Director-General had put up a note saying that one of his employees, Marcel D, was suffering from AIDS and that prognosis for the disease was inevitable death. Moreover, when the employee went back to his job after a sick leave, the Director-General did not let him resume his job, even though he was officially certified fit by the company medical officer. The company was ordered to pay him compensation, which included a sum of FFr 70,000 for moral prejudice, the Court finding that his dismissal had occurred under very cruel and painful conditions.[27]

Unfortunately, confidentiality is often not well respected and numerous instances of rejection or avoidance by colleagues have been reported. It appears from a French enquiry entitled 'Living with AIDS in the workplace' that 20–25 per cent of the persons interviewed feared using the same working tools as HIV-positive people working with them. And more than 55 per cent would stop eating in a canteen where they knew an HIV-positive person was working.[28]

Issues of harassment are not dealt with in the national laws in consideration.

HIV/AIDS and dismissal

In most of the countries examined, protection against dismissal on the grounds of HIV/AIDS will largely depend on the remedies that the general legislation provides against wrongful dismissal. No legislation authorizes dismissal solely on the grounds of an employee being HIV-positive. In principle, if the employee's state of health does not affect his work, it does not constitute an acceptable cause for dismissal. Some countries, like The Netherlands, provide high standards of protection: an employer who wishes to terminate an employment contract must obtain the permission of the Regional Department of Employment. The latter does not consider being HIV-positive as a ground for dismissal. Furthermore, a Dutch court may terminate an employment contract at the request of either party. It may do so only in cases of 'considerable difficulty'. HIV is not considered a 'considerable difficulty'.[29]

Others, like Belgium, provide very low standards of protection, as dismissal is at the employer's discretion and the employer is not obliged to give any reason for a dismissal.[30]

Some countries have enacted special provisions prohibiting any dismissal on grounds of seropositivity or of health. In France, for example, the law punishes by imprisonment and/or fine any dismissal on the grounds of health or disability, except in cases where unfitness for employment is medically certified.[31] Even before specific rules were enacted, the French courts had judged that dismissal on the grounds of being HIV-positive was unacceptable. In one case, a kitchen worker had been dismissed for being HIV-positive. The dismissal letter expressly stated HIV to be the reason for the employer's decision, despite a company medical officer having classed the employee as fit to work. The Industrial Tribunal of Paris held the dismissal to be without serious grounds.[32] In another case, an employee of a religious association was dismissed after revealing that he was homosexual and HIV-positive. The case reached the French Cour de Cassation (last instance court of private law), which found the grounds of dismissal unacceptable, the judge referring to the provisions on protection of privacy.[33]

If the employer dismisses an HIV-positive employee on the grounds that he was under pressure from the other employees who had refused to work with the infected person, the employer could be liable for unfair dismissal. This was the holding of a German court which further said that the employer is responsible for controlling the irrational fears of his employees and for providing them with the relevant information on the issue of HIV/AIDS in the workplace.[34]

When the dismissal does not expressly mention HIV or AIDS as a ground, but other unrelated reasons, it will be much more difficult to challenge it successfully. A bank employee in Marseilles tried to dispute his dismissal, but as the decision had not mentioned his health status as a ground for dismissal, the Industrial Tribunal of Marseilles found the dismissal to be justified by real and serious motives independent of his health status.[35]

Full-blown AIDS as such is no more a valid ground for dismissal than being HIV-positve under the legislation studied. The current provisions on illness in employment are applicable in this case. Dismissal is justified if the employer can prove that the sick employee's presence is prejudicial to the business: in other words, where the employee is no longer able to fulfil his duties and prejudices the interests of the firm.[36]

Conclusions

In very few countries have legal texts been enacted to give special protection to workers with HIV/AIDS in their relations with their employer. One country – France – has passed a law to forbid discrimination on grounds of health or disability. For the rest, it is the general rules of labour law, supplemented by the provisions on privacy, that are applicable.

Even if there exist provisions, specific or general, upon which workers with HIV may rely, one wonders how effective they can really be.

First of all, rights must be enforced. The existing mechanisms are often not suited to the distinctive features of discrimination on grounds of health. One of the main problems is the slowness and inflexibility of the procedures. The HIV-positive worker or applicant has to bring an action in court, and legal proceedings take time. It may be months or more often years before a decision is taken. The burden of proof will be on the worker or applicant who claims that discrimination has occurred and it is not always easy to bring the necessary evidence.

Additionally, the claimant will have to cope with the effects of his infection. And, with the exception of the French law on the protection of individuals from discrimination on the grounds of their state of health and disability, no other legislation recognizes the various associations defending the interests of people with HIV or AIDS as having the capacity to take legal proceedings on their behalf. This is critical because HIV-positive people subjected to discrimination very frequently do not wish to take legal proceedings because they do not want their infection to become public knowledge and/or because they do not want to engage themselves in long and arduous proceedings.

Furthermore, discrimination against HIV-positive workers or job applicants is often very insidious and the available legal remedies not very helpful in combating social exclusion. For instance, if pressure is put on an HIV-positive worker by colleagues who know of his infection and he resigns because he feels ostracized, legal rules might be of no assistance. Again, if an HIV-positive worker is dismissed but the decision mentions wholly different grounds, such as some professional failing on the part of the employee, legal rules are likewise of little use.

My intention is not, however, to dismiss the protection offered by law. On the contrary, I think that existing legislation should be strengthened. The French law on the protection of individuals from discrimination on the grounds of their state of health or disability constitutes an interesting model for at least two reasons: first, it is not restricted to HIV/AIDS issues and, second, it gives associations the right to take action, which, in my view, is one of its main achievements.

I would nevertheless suggest that the development of more flexible mechanisms than legal proceedings could be another course of action, especially for disputes between individuals in their working relations. Such a mechanism could take the form of an independent arbitrator trained to promote dialogue and negotiated solutions. Last but not least, one should not forget the significance of informing and educating people about HIV infection, especially at business level, in order to combat irrational fears.

---

1 This chapter is largely based on a study that the Council of Europe commissioned from the Swiss Institute of Comparative Law on 'Discrimination Against Persons With HIV or AIDS', Strasbourg, 1993.

The author is a staff legal adviser at the Swiss Institute of Comparative Law. The views she expresses are her own.

2 Law no. 90-602 of 12 July 1990 on the protection of individuals from discrimination on the grounds of their state of health or disability, *Journal officiel de la République française*, 13 July 1990.

3 **France**, Judgment of the Cour de Cassation, Chambre sociale of 17 December 1973. The position has not altered since.

Belgium, Art. 11 of the Collective Agreement on Employment No. 38, concluded by the National Employment Council on 6 December 1983, relating to recruitment and selection of employees and given mandatory force by Crown Decree of 11 July 1984.

Germany, the Federal Labour Court (Bundesarbeitsgericht), on the questions relating to health which the employer has the right to ask on engagement, has decided that the questions may relate only to points directly connected with the position offered.

4 Art. 6(1) of Law no. 135/1990 'Programa di interventi urgenti per la prevenzione e la lotta contro l'AIDS', *Le Leggi 1990*, p. 1038.

5 Art. 3 of the Catalonian Parliament's Resolution 103/III.

6 Germany, W. Hinrich, 'AIDS und Arbeitsrecht', *HIV/AIDS und Straffälligkeit*, p. 59–64, Bonn, 1991.

Austria, A.M. Walter, 'AIDS am Arbeitsplatz', *Arbeit & Wirtschaft*, p. 42, 1991.

France, AIDES, *Droit et Sida*, p. 58. Librairie Générale du Droit et de la Jurisprudence, Paris, 1992.

Switzerland, R. Pedergnana, *HIV-Infektion und Aids: Arbeitsrechtliche Fragen*, p. 56, 1989.

7 Swiss Institute of Comparative Law, *Discrimination Against Persons With HIV or AIDS*, p. 111. Council of Europe, Strasbourg, 1993.

8 France, Article R 241–48 of the Labour Code provides for a medical examination with the object of investigating whether the employee is suffering from an infectious disease; HIV is not in this category because of its mode of transmission.

9 Ph. Auvergnon, 'Le droit des relations de travail interrogé par le SIDA', *Le Droit social à l'épreuve du Sida*, p. 56, 1992.

10 Swiss Institute of Comparative Law, *Discrimination Against Persons With HIV or AIDS*, p. 112. Council of Europe, Strasbourg, 1993.

11 Art. 5(5) of Law no. 135/1990 'Programa di interventi urgenti per la prevenzione e la lotta contro l'AIDS', *Le Leggi 1990*, p. 1038.

12 Art. 416 of the Penal Code, in its revised version, dated July 1990 (introduced by Law no. 90-602 of the 12 July 1990).

13 Art. 4(2) of the Spanish law 8/1980 of 10 March 1980 on status of workers.

14 Although not mentioning health, Art. 1 of the Dutch Constitution prohibits any form of discrimination on grounds of religion, political opinion...or for *any other reason*.

A general prohibition of discrimination can be found in Art. 7 of the **Austrian** Constitution, Art. 6 and 6(a) of the **Belgian** Constitution, Art. 3 of the **German** Fundamental Law, Art. 2(1) of the **French** Constitution, Art. 3 of the **Italian** Constitution, Art. 14 of the **Spanish** Constitution, Art. 4 of the **Swiss** Constitution; uncertainty remains as to the horizontal effect of such provisions.

15 Swiss Institute of Comparative Law, *Discrimination Against Persons With HIV or AIDS*, p. 112. Council of Europe, Strasbourg 1993.

16 Cf. Art. 18 of the **Austrian** Constitution, Art. 12 of the **German** Fundamental Law, Preamble to the **French** Constitution, Art. 4 of the **Italian** Constitution, Art. 35 of the **Spanish** Constitution, Art. 23 of the Universal Declaration of Human Rights, Art. 1 of the European Social Charter, Art. 6 of the International Covenant on Economic, Social and Cultural Rights.

17 A. Lyon-Caen, 'Droit du travail et protection sociale', *Sida: enjeu du droit*, p. 184, 1991.

18 Art. 5 'Statuto dei lavoratori', in F. Carinci *et al. Le norme essenziali del diritto del lavoro*, p. 21, 3rd edition, Turin, 1992.

19 Cf. for example, the Spanish draft law on the prevention of occupational risks.

20 For example, **Italy**, Art. 8 'Statuto dei lavoratori' embodies the right of workers to privacy. **Switzerland**, Art. 328 Code of Obligations stipulates that employees are entitled to employers' observance and protection of their personal rights.

21 L. Westerhall and A. Saldeen, 'Some reflections on HIV/AIDS in Swedish Law', *Law and AIDS: An International Comparison*, p.36. Centre Nationale de la Recherche Scientifique (CNRS), Paris, 1991.

22 Article L 122-45 of the Industrial Code as supplemented by Section 9 of Law no. 90-602 of 12 July 1990 on the protection of individuals from discrimination on the grounds of their state of health or disability, *Journal officiel de la République française*, 13 July 1990.

23 For example, **Italy**, Art. 15 'Statuto dei lavoratori'. **Spain**, Art. 4(2) of Law 8/1980 of 10

March 1980 on the status of workers.

24 Article 429 quater of the Dutch Criminal Code is in force since 1st February 1992.

25 *Le Livre blanc des états généraux, Vivre le SIDA*, pp. 96–108. Cerf, Paris, 1992.

26 Swiss Institute of Comparative Law, *Discrimination Against Persons With HIV or AIDS*, p. 112. Council of Europe, Strasbourg, 1993.

27 Judgement of 24 October 1989 of the Conseil des Prud'hommes de Bobigny, confirmed by the Paris Court of Appeal, 10 April 1991. Cited in AIDES, *Droit et Sida*, p. 63–64, Librairie Générale du Droit et de la Jurisprudence, Paris, 1992

28 From: *Documents pour le médecin du travail*, 46, 2nd quarter 1991.

29 Section 1639h and 1639w of the Dutch Civil Code.

30 Secton 32 of the Contract of Employment Act of 3 July 1979, *Moniteur belge*, 22 August 1979.

31 Art. 416 of the Penal Code, in its revised version, dated July 1990 (introduced by Law no. 90-602 of the 12 July 1990).

32 Judgement of 23 July 1990, Conseil des Prud'hommes de Paris, cited in AIDES, *Droit et Sida*, Librairie Générale du Droit et de la Jurisprudence, Paris 1992, p. 63.

33 Judgement of 17 April 1991, Cour de Cassation, Chambre sociale, cited in Ph. Auvergnon, 'Le droit des relations de travail interrogé par le SIDA', *Le Droit social à l'épreuve du Sida*, 1992, p. 58.

34 Judgement of 16 June 1987, Arbeitsgericht Berlin, cited in W. Hinrich, 'AIDS und Arbeitsrecht', *HIV/AIDS und Straffälligkeit*, Bonn, 1991, p. 75.

35 Judgement of 15 March 1989, Conseil des Prud'hommes de Marseilles, cited in AIDES, *Droit et Sida*, Librairie Générale du Droit et de la Jurisprudence, Paris 1992, p. 64.

36 Swiss Institute of Comparative Law, *Discrimination Against Persons With HIV or AIDS*, p. 119. Council of Europe, Strasbourg, 1993.

Discrimination in the Workplace: Protection and the Law in the UK

Petra Wilson

Law Faculty, University of Nottingham, England

The object of this chapter is to explore the way in which law and legal regulation can meet the challenges of HIV in the workplace. It begins with a brief overview of the provisions in the law of England and Wales that are most pertinent to AIDS and employment, to set the backdrop for a discussion of three cases of HIV infection in the work place related to the author in the course of recently completed fieldwork. The impact of the current law on the cases is then analysed in order to evaluate the legal construction of the rights of the HIV-positive worker.

AIDS and employment law [1]

As might be expected, the problem arising most frequently in the pre-employment setting centres around testing for HIV infection: that is, employers require an HIV antibody test as part of pre-employment health screening and are often unwilling to employ someone who tests HIV-positive. Legally employers are quite entitled to demand such pre-employment tests and entitled to refuse employment without giving any reason for their decision, whether the applicant tests negative or positive for HIV antibodies, since according to *Allen* v. *Flood* an employer may refuse to employ anyone on whatever grounds:

'an employer may refuse to employ [a person] from the most mistaken, capricious, malicious or morally reprehensible motives that can be conceived but the workman has no right of action against him ' (per Lord Davey in the House of Lords in Allen v. Flood [1898]).

Note, however, that this is old authority predating the Sex Discrimination Act 1975 and Race Relations Act 1976 according to which 'the most mistaken, capricious, malicious or morally reprehensible motives' may no longer include motives based on sexual or racial discrimination.

HIV tests and discrimination

Although the legality of discrimination on the basis of HIV testing has never been ascertained in the courts, the Equal Opportunities Commission (EOC) has conducted an inquiry into the recruitment policies of the former airline Dan Air, which refused to recruit male cabin staff. Dan Air attempted to justify their policy by the production of statistics which purported to show that over 30 per cent of male applicants for cabin staff posts were gay. Dan Air argued that they were entitled to discriminate against men on the grounds of health and safety at work, since HIV statistically affected more men than women. However, the EOC obtained evidence from two senior medical officers that no significant health risk was posed to passengers by HIV-positive staff, and accordingly the EOC issued a non-discrimination notice under S. 67 Sex Discrimination Act 1975.[2]

While it will be difficult to bring an action for discrimination in recruitment HIV testing, similar testing of existing employees gives rise to many more possibilities for action. First, such a test would have to be done with the employees' explicit consent to taking the blood, doing the test and disclosing the result. More importantly every contract of employment has an implied term that an employer will not act in such a way as to undermine the mutual trust and confidence between employer and employee. If no express term allowing for HIV screening has been written into the contract, such a request by an employer could be interpreted as a breach of the implied term of trust. However, breach of contract is not decisive in establishing whether a dismissal was fair or unfair: thus a Tribunal would still have to decide separately if an employee who resigned because of a request for a blood test could claim constructive unfair dismissal, although it might be possible to prove wrongful dismissal. It is important to note here that an employee will only be able to claim unfair dismissal after two years service. There are no similar time limits imposed for claiming wrongful dismissal.

There is no implied right of the employer to require an employee to undergo any form of medical testing. In *Bliss* v. *South East Thames Regional Health Authority* (1985) the court held that if an employer requires such testing he or she might be in breach of his or her duty of mutual respect and confidence. Even if a clause in the contract gave the employer an express right to require such testing it might be difficult to enforce it. The Employment Protection (Consolidation) Act 1978 S.

57(3) states that an employer must not be unreasonable in asking for the term to be enforced. This section would apply where the employee is dismissed for refusing to undergo the examination or test.

Dismissals

It is to be expected that employers will, with increasing frequency, find themselves in a position where they will face pressure to dismiss an employee who is, or is suspected of being, HIV-positive. Such pressure might arise because the employee is frequently absent from work because of ill health, or might originate from the fears and prejudices of other employees. In some cases the pressure to dismiss might be based on the supposed prejudicial reaction of customers and clients. As noted previously there is no legislation specifically regulating the relationship between the employer and the HIV-positive (or supposedly positive) employee. As a result both employees who are having problems at work because they are or are perceived to be HIV-positive and their employers will have to rely on other already existing legislation.

As noted above there is very little reported case law on HIV in the workplace on which to rely, as a result of which most employees and employers will have to rely on the provisions contained in the Employment Protection (Consolidation) Act 1978 (EP(C)A), when dealing with an HIV-related problem.

The EP(C)A requires employers to establish both a fair reason for the dismissal of an employee, and that they acted reasonably in the execution of the dismissal. Although there is no case law that holds dismissal solely on the grounds of HIV to be unfair, some principles established by case law [3] would suggest that the employer who dismisses simply on the basis of an employee's HIV infection (real or suspected) could persuade a Tribunal that he or she were acing reasonably. First, a Tribunal will have to judge whether the dismissal was a reasonable response on the part of the particular employer in question. It is therefore a subjective test which will place the dismissal within its particular context. Secondly, a Tribunal assesses the reasonableness of the employer's action within the employment context, not the justice of his or her conduct from the employee's perspective. Thirdly, it has been accepted by the courts and Tribunals that it is not unfair for an employer to dismiss a person on the basis that an important customer or client would object to a particular employee, however irrational the customer's objection might be. It would seem therefore that in the right circumstances an employer would not be acting unfairly if he or she dismissed someone solely on the basis of a real or supposed HIV infection.

Furthermore two statutory provisions exist according to which an employer may be able to justify a dismissal on the grounds of HIV infection: capability and 'some other substantial reason' under S. 57(2) and S. 57(1)(b) of the EP(C)A 1978 respectively.

Dismissals on the grounds of capability

A person suffering from AIDS may be absent from work either for short or substantial periods of time, either of which could constitute grounds for fair dismissal on grounds of capability. It is important to note, however, that no hard and fast rules regulate the dismissal of an employee on the grounds of capability; each case will be judged on its own specific facts, taking into account both the employer's and employee's specific circumstances. Accordingly, an employer with a very small workforce may be held to have acted reasonably in dismissing an employee after weeks of continual sick leave, while a larger company might have to show months of absence. However, some guidelines for ill health dismissal were laid down by the Employment

Appeals Tribunal for employers dealing with long-term sickness in *East Lindsey District Council v. Daubney* :

• Employers must take appropriate steps to inform themselves of the true medical position. This will normally involve getting a medical report from the employee's treating doctor.

• Except in highly exceptional circumstances employers must personally consult the employee because discussion will often bring to light facts of which the employer was unaware.

• The employer should consider the opinion of an independent medical advisor if asked to do so by the employee.

If an employer fails to satisfy these requirements before dismissing an employee whom he or she suspects of having an HIV-related illness, a case for unfair dismissal may lie. Accordingly it is imperative that an employer makes proper and extensive enquiries of the physician caring for his or her employee. It should be noted also that a refusal to allow the employer to contact the employee's doctor would not be sufficient grounds for dismissal, although successive refusals coupled with periods of illness could make a dismissal based on the assumption of incapacity fair.

Dismissal of an asymptomatic HIV-positive employee would only be fair within the rules of S. 57(2)(a) of the EP(C) Act if the HIV-positive status of the employee affected his or her ability to do the job. It is unlikely that an employee in the asymptomatic stages of HIV infection will be truly unable to fulfil his or her job requirements; accordingly it is unlikely that an employer would be able to justify a dismissal of such a person on the grounds of capability.

Dismissals for some other substantial reason

The stories of the people interviewed by the author suggest that employers will frequently respond to the adverse reaction of their workforce or customers to HIV-positive employees with a dismissal for 'some other substantial reason' of the HIV-positive employee or suspected HIV-positive employee.

Adverse reactions might include a refusal to work with the HIV-positive individual or pressure on the employer to dismiss the HIV-positive employee. On a straightforward reading of the EP(C)A it would seem that an employer is not entitled to dismiss an employee because others refuse to work with him or her; since the employer is under a duty to offer reasonable support to an employee who is the victim of harassment from colleagues. Failure to offer such support could allow the employee to resign and claim constructive unfair dismissal.[4] However, some employers might nevertheless be able to dismiss the victim of such harassment fairly, as shown in *Buck v. The Letchworth Palace Ltd*. Buck was a projectionist at a cinema. He was dismissed after his colleagues found out from a local newspaper that he had been convicted of acts of gross indecency in a public toilet. They feared that they were at a risk of HIV infection from Buck (on the basis that he was homosexual rather than any proof of HIV or AIDS) and refused to work with him any more. Buck was dismissed without consultation on the grounds of his conviction and because of his fellow employees' refusal to work with him. Buck sought legal advice and took his case to an Industrial Tribunal, which found that the dismissal was fair notwithstanding the overreaction of his fellow employees and the lack of proof that Buck actually was HIV-positive.[5] Although the Tribunal emphasized that the employer ought to have consulted with Buck and his colleague, they found that as a matter of fact such a consultation would not have been beneficial in this particular case.

However, this almost incomprehensible decision was reversed by the Employment Appeals Tribunal on the basis that the employer had not followed the proper procedure laid down in the House of Lords in *Polkey v. A.E. Dayton Ltd* which emphasizes the importance of consultation with all employees in such a situation. It is important to note, however, that the Employment Appeals Tribunal did not find that the employers had acted unfairly prima facie, simply that they had not followed the correct procedure for co-worker pressure to dismiss.

A similar reluctance to support the HIV-positive employee was displayed by an Industrial Tribunal in *Cormack v. TNT Sealion*. In that case a ship's cook claimed he had been unfairly selected for redundancy on the basis that his fellow workers did not want to work with him because they believed him to be an 'AIDS carrier'. The Tribunal found that the employer's selection for redundancy was reasonable on the grounds that the ability of the applicant to fit in well with other employees was a material fact for consideration in the redundancy selection process, since the ship's crew were required to work and live in close proximity. They added, however, that a good employer must act promptly to lay at rest all unfounded suspicions in cases of suspected or real HIV infection.

It may be surmised from the two cases discussed above that the adverse reaction of colleagues may justify the dismissal of an HIV-positive person. However, these cases should be understood within the broader framework of general employment law. Although the Tribunals in Buck and Cormack found that dismissal on the grounds of HIV was not prima facie unfair, there is well-established case law which suggests the reverse. Moreover, the case law suggests that employees refusing to work with another employee or employees could themselves fairly be dismissed for such a refusal. The principle of dismissing the perpetrator rather than the victim of harassment was explored in the case of *Philpott v. North Lambeth Law Centre*. In that case a Tribunal held that an employer had acted fairly in dismissing two solicitors who had harassed a third newly engaged solicitor. The new solicitor had worked previously for Gay Switchboard: the two later to be dismissed solicitors claimed publicly that he would introduce AIDS into the Law Centre. They were dismissed for, among other things, the malicious way in which they had reacted to the new appointee.

Three cases of discrimination[6]

I should like to continue now by looking at three cases of discrimination in the work place which were related to me by the respondents in my recent study. I will look at each case in turn and consider the possible legal solutions that the people could have used. I will then look at the deeper implications of the experiences of these three people and at the way in which the law has failed to address their needs.

Steve's case

Steve had been employed as a wages clerk in a company for many years. His employers knew that he was a haemophiliac and knew that his bleeds tended to occur in his knees and ankles. Accordingly he had always delivered the wages to the many outlets of the company by car. In 1986 he was diagnosed as HIV-positive. There was no reason to suggest that this status should affect his ability to do his job for many years. However, Steve began to experience a change in attitude from his employers: it seemed to him they wanted him to leave. One day he was called to the manager's office and told that the company could no longer supply him with a car; accordingly he would have to deliver the wages to the various city outlets on foot. Steve undertook one such journey. He had severe bleeds and had to have a long time off work. Eventually he was dismissed on grounds of ill health.

The prima-facie reason for Steve's dismissal, and indeed the one given to him when he was told he should not return to work, was his recent ill health and his inability to do his job. Lack of capability to do a job is a fair reason for dismissal, such capability being assessed by 'skill, aptitude, health or any other mental or physical ability'

(S. 57(4) EP(C)A 1978). Steve was, under the new regime of walking wage rounds, indeed unable to do his job since he is physically unable to take the strain of walking the wage rounds.

Yet to almost any third party looking in on the events of Steve's dismissal, the state of affairs is not as straightforward as it might at first appear. Steve's lack of capability would appear to be materially connected to the way in which he had been expected to execute his job in the recent past.

The question that must be asked therefore is: to what extent are Steve's employers able to claim that he is incapable of doing the job for which he was employed? When Steve was first employed his health status was made known to his employers, who accordingly provided him with a car so that he was fully capable, despite his medical condition, of meeting the demands of the job. This would suggest that a haemophiliac man was, in the eyes of this employer, capable of performing the job in question. Yet it would seem that an HIV-positive haemophiliac was not.

It would seem that two courses of action were open to Steve. First, he could have tried to sue his employer for a breach of contract, since one of the material terms of his contract (the provision of a car) had been changed without due consultation. Second, it could have been argued that the removal of Steve's car amounted not only to a breach of contract, but also to such a significant change in his terms that he could have resigned and claimed constructive dismissal on the basis that such a change was a breach of the implied term of mutual trust.

Furthermore, it might be argued that Steve could reasonably have expected his employers to find him alternative work if they felt he was no longer capable of satisfying the demands of his current job. An Industrial Tribunal in Tiptools v. Curtis held that if an employee is beginning to find his or her work too hard he or she should be given the chance of doing something less demanding. However, such a claim to transfer to another sort of work could, of course, only succeed for Steve if some appropriate alternative work had been available. An employer cannot be penalized where he or she honestly has no work to offer the employee.

However, from the position of Steve's employers the state of affairs might seem somewhat different. He had had a substantial period of time off work (the exact amount of time was never made clear). They could argue therefore that a dismissal on the grounds of ill health was entirely fair. It is important to note here that the reasonableness of a decision to dismiss on the basis of ill health is measured on a management, not medical, basis. Therefore if an employer, in his or her own particular business circumstances, is not able to accommodate a period of illness it may be fair for him or her to dismiss the employer. In the case of *Spencer v. Paragon Wallpapers Ltd*, Spencer had been absent from work for a period of two weeks, when his employer, with his consent, contacted his doctor and discovered that he would not be able to return to work for a further four to six weeks. The employers decided that the business could not survive with such a period of absence and that they would therefore have to dismiss Spencer and take on a new employee. The Employment Appeals Tribunal found that the company had acted fairly, stressing that such a decision to dismiss must be a management deci-

sion; the role of a Tribunal is only to see that the employer acted fairly in his or her decision-making. This decision was echoed in *East Lindsey District Council v. Daubney* where the EAT held: '...the decision to dismiss or not to dismiss is not a medical question, but a question to be answered by the employers in the light of available medical advice.'

Fiona's case

Fiona had worked for some years for a small company; she felt happy there and felt safe to tell her employers that she had tested HIV-positive. Shortly after this she was told that her job would entail travel to the Soviet Union (as it then was), and that arrangements for her visa were being made. Fiona sought advice about travel to the Soviet Union and found that she would have to show evidence of an HIV-negative test. Fiona felt she had no option but to give in her notice.

When Fiona sought advice from an HIV advice agency about travel to the Soviet Union and discovered that she would have to provide a certificate of an HIV antibody negative test result, she felt that her employers were manipulating her into giving in her notice. Her employers, on the other hand, might have argued (had the occasion arisen) that commercial developments meant they would have to require Fiona to travel to the Soviet Union, and deny that any other agenda had ever existed.

It is of course impossible to know whose version of the events was more correct. The nature of business conducted by Fiona's employers was indeed such that it would not have been unreasonable for them to expect her to travel to the Soviet Union; yet at the same time one can understand that from Fiona's point of view that the need for her to travel to the Soviet Union had arisen at a very (in)convenient time.

Defending Fiona at a Tribunal one could have argued that her resignation amounted to a constructive dismissal by her employers. It could have been argued that her employer's requirement that she travel to the Soviet Union, in the light of the information she had given them, amounted to a demand from the employer that she resign or be dismissed. If such an allegation could be proven then a Tribunal could find that her resignation amounted to an unfair constructive dismissal. It could also be argued in favour of Fiona that in requiring her to travel to the Soviet Union, without prior consultation, her employers were frustrating the contract of employment, again justifying a claim of unfair constructive dismissal. However, this point would be extremely difficult for Fiona to prove, since a need to travel was an express term of her contract. Furthermore, frustration of a contract will only occur where neither party is to blame for the event which renders the contract impossible to perform. The employer could thus argue that they were not frustrating the contract, but rather that they have no option but to dismiss Fiona since she is now unable to fulfil her contract of employment.

From the employer's side, it could be argued that while Fiona's resignation came as a complete surprise, her inability to obtain a visa to travel to the Soviet Union would have justified a dismissal on the grounds of capability. They might have argued that she had been employed on the express terms that she might be required to represent her employers overseas and that her current inability to do so meant that she could no longer fulfil her contract of employment. It should be noted, however, that capability, even when the employee can no longer do the job for which he or she was originally employed, might not justify dismissal. As discussed in Steve's case, a Tribunal might find that an employer had a duty to find alternative work for his or her employee. However, since this case concerns a small firm, such a duty might be impossible to satisfy.

Clearly the situation presented by Fiona is very difficult and may lead one to argue that some of the difficulties which arise in the employer/employee relationship can be settled only according to conscience, not legal process.

John's case

John had worked for a large supermarket for four years when he was diagnosed as HIV-positive. John used cutting machinery in his work and was worried that he might be a risk to other people's health if he had an accident at work. He had always got on well with his line manager and decided to confide in him. His manager responded calmly, deciding with John's consent that he should move from machine-related work to shelf stacking. John was happy with the arrangements. Eventually John began to suffer from occasional bouts of HIV-related pneumonia and was off sick for long periods one winter. On arriving back at work after such a period of sick leave he found a new manager in post. He did not get on well with the new manager, who made it clear that he knew about John's condition and wanted him to leave. One day John came to work to find that his duties had been changed. Despite his recent case of pneumonia his new job meant he had to work for several hours at a time packing in the freezer storage room. He complained that the constant inhalation of very cold air was affecting his health, but was told that there was no possibility of change. After several months working in freezer storage John was forced to quit his job because of the deterioration in his health.

When John first contacted an HIV advice agency, some months after he had resigned from his job, he was very angry. He, like Fiona, felt forced to resign from his job as a result of changed working conditions. John felt that he had behaved reasonably and fairly, telling his employers that he might represent a risk to his co-workers and accepting a move to a job he felt was less satisfying. He believed also that his employers had treated him fairly, respecting his confidentiality and keeping him in employment. When his new line manager forced him to work in conditions which John believed to be detrimental to his health he felt betrayed, he believed that he had been manipulated into resignation.

Like Fiona, John would have been in a very difficult position if he had tried to prove the malice that he believed existed. Like Fiona's inability to travel to the Soviet Union, John's health condition could be said to make him incapable of fulfilling his new job requirements; an incapability which John's employers could have argued justified his dismissal. In theory John could have claimed unfair constructive dismissal – being forced to work in freezing conditions has upheld a claim for unfair dismissal (*Oxley v. Firth*) in a case where the claimant's health was in no way compromised by the conditions. John's employers for their part might have argued that the economic conditions of the business were such that John's move to freezer packing was unavoidable and a move to another job impossible.

In reality, however, the advice agency to which John had turned could do nothing to help him fight his employers, because by the time he sought their advice the three-month limitation period (S. 67(2) EP(C)A 1978) for bringing a case to Tribunal had elapsed.

In search of a useful anti-discrimination law

The three cases above have shown that the law, while useful in theory, is rarely a practical tool which people affected by the virus can use to address their needs. But why should this be the case? Why should the law not be useful?

To begin to answer this question we must look at the various *functions* of the law.

Law has a wide range of functions: it can be *enabling*, giving people access to services such as education, social support and healthcare . This enabling function of law has been embraced widely with respect to HIV, especially in terms of access to education and counselling on HIV for a very wide group of citizens, if not all citizens. It can be *regulatory* – that is, regulating the behaviour of certain people at certain times. This again is evident in HIV and can be seen in the compulsory collection of data under the AIDS Control Act 1987, the segregation of HIV-positive prisoners under Viral Infectivity regulations and the general extension of public power over people with HIV via the Public Health (Control of Diseases) Act 1984. All these provisions illustrate the *coercive* role of law, with its emphasis on control, compulsion and punishment of those with HIV who are deemed to be a risk to broader society.

However, these three functions are not the only functions of law. There is one, perhaps the most significant function of law, which is significantly absent from most of the statutory and case law pertaining to the specific needs and experiences of people affected by HIV. That is the *protective* function of the law. From the perspective of the so-called 'general public' the law has been very protective, protecting the majority of the supposed uninfected from the minority of the known infected population. The cases above demonstrate admirably that if employers want to discriminate unfavourably against someone who is or whom they perceive to be HIV-positive, they can do so with relative impunity. That is, in practical terms, there is little most employees could do in response. But from the perspective of the HIV-positive person, those same laws seem to be far from protective, for the protected ones are those believed to be infection free, not the infected.

I would argue therefore that the bedrock of the legal institution on which 'AIDS

Law' was built is in itself faulty to the extent that it would be impossible to construct any system of rules that could really be protective to the interests of those affected by HIV. If one considers again the cases of Steve, Fiona and John one can see not only the cases of men and a woman who have lost their jobs because of an aberration in otherwise normal lives, but also people who are seen by others, their colleagues and employers, as single issue entities, that is, as a person with HIV. Not as John, who happens to be a haemophiliac who has contracted another illness, but John, the carrier of a frightening disease. Law, however, treats acts of discrimination as aberrations in otherwise normal lives of equal people.[7] It denies the fact that single acts of discrimination are often impossible to disentangle from a day-to-day reality of continual acts of minor discrimination. In demanding substantive acts of discrimination the law thus ignores the realities of the lives of the powerless. It is within this construction that I would argue the funda-mental flaw of all attempts at anti-discrimination, or protective legislation for people affected by HIV, lies.

The law, it may be argued, is therefore constructed by the well, from their vantage point, and largely to their advantage. Moreover, the laws are couched in terms of the abstract rather than the substantive. That is, the abstract right of equality is granted through the vague words and direction in cases such as *Daubney* v. *East Lindsey*, and *Buck* and *Cormack*. But the substantive realities of HIV discrimination are not addressed from the perspective of the affected. MacKinnon argues that abstract rights granted to women in current legislation authorize and legitimate the male experience of the world.[8] Substantive rights framed from the perspective of the real experiences of women would, on the other hand, challenge that epistemological power, granting women a chance to construct their own reality from within, rather than living the role defined by men.

Conclusion

It can be seen from these examples that fear of HIV is legitimated in both the common law and in the statutory law, where all rights granted to the affected are couched in the terms of public health, that is in terms of their potential effect on us, rather than in terms of the substantive rights of an infected individual. I would argue that if the law is going to respond effectively to HIV discrimination it has to take on board the full reality of that discrimination: its location in the whole and complete lives of people rather than looking at just their working lives.

It may be argued then that we need to re-develop anti-discrimination law from its conceptual roots. At present, it is grounded in utilitarian principles: that is, in terms of what is good for a workforce in general. The good of the individual is decided on a case by case basis within a utilitarian framework of the greatest good of the greatest number. Thus if the greatest number feel irrationally scared of working with someone who is HIV-positive, then that person may lose his or her job (*Buck* v. *Letchworth Palace*). If, however, the basis of the law lay in a deontological respect of the individual's rights, such a response would not be possible. The effect of an anti-discrimination law based on a deontological construction of rights could be both symbolic and practical. A legislative response which begins from the premise that the right to fair treatment is an absolute right, would symbolically strengthen all potential victims of discrimination. It would, of course, be naive to suggest that such a construction would make the right to fair treatment inviolable, since the exact nature of fairness will still be undecided, but it would put the potential victim of discrimination in a much stronger starting position.

I would argue that it is only through such a construction of discrimination that the HIV-positive worker could be seen as an equal colleague, rather than as the vector of infection.

Further reading

Department of Employment and Health and Safety Executive, *AIDS and Employment*, 1986.

Department of Employment and Health and Safety Executive, *AIDS and the Workplace: A Guide for Employers*, 1990.

Grubb, A. and Pearl, D. 'Blood testing, AIDS and DNA profiling', *Family Law*, London, 1990.

Harris, D. and Haigh, R. (eds.), *AIDS: A Guide to the Law*. The Terrence Higgins Trust/Routledge, London, 1990.

MacKinnon, C. *Towards a Feminist Theory of the State*. Harvard University Press, 1989.

Problems Associated with AIDS, Response by the Government to the Third report of the Social Services Committee Session 1986–7, Command Paper 297.

Cases cited

Allen v. *Flood* [1898] AC 1

Bliss v. *Southam Thames Regional Health Authority* [1985] IRLR 404

Buck v. *Letchworth Palace* [3.3.87 and 3.4 87] case no. 36488/86

Cormack v. *TNT Sealion* [25.11.86] COIT 1825/126

East Lindsey District Council v. *Daubney* [1977] IRLR 181

Gardiner v. *Newport County Borough Council*

(1974) IRLR 262

Oakley v. *Labour Party* [1980] IRLR 34

Oxley v. *Firth* [1980] IRLR 135

Philpott v. *North Lambeth* (case no. 11212/86)

R v. *Fisher* [1987] Crim. L. R. 334

Saunders v. *Scottish National Camps Association Ltd* (1980) IRLR 174 EAT

Spencer v. *Paragon Wallpapers* [1977] ICR 301

Terry v. *East Sussex* [1976] ICR 356

Tiptools v. *Curtiss* [1973] IRLR 276

Statutes cited

Sex Discrimination Act 1975

Employment Protection (Consolidation) Act 1978

Public Health (Control of Diseases) Act 1984

Public Health (Control of Disease Regulations 1985

AIDS Control Act 1987

1 For general discussions of AIDS and employment law see:

N. Fagan and D. Newell, 'AIDS and Employment Law', vol. 137, *New Law Journal*, p. 752, 1987.

S. Southam and G. Howard, *AIDS & Employment Law*. Financial Training Publication Ltd, London, 1988.

B. Napier, 'AIDS, discrimination and employment law', *Industrial Law Journal*, vol. 18, p. 84, 1989.

K. Widdows, 'AIDS and employment law: some aspects at the national level', *International Journal of Comparative Labour Law and Industrial Relations*, vol. 4, p. 140, 1988.

R.A. Watt, 'HIV, discrimination, unfair dismissal and pressure to dismiss', *International Law Journal*, vol. 21, p. 280, 1992.

2 Equal Opportunities Commission, *Formal Investigation Report: Dan Air*, January 1987.

3 See particularly *Saunders* v. *Scottish National Camps Association Ltd* (1980) IRLR 174 EAT in which a gay man was employed to maintain the plant and fittings of a children's holiday camp. His homosexuality became known to his employer who dismissed him on the basis that parents would not send their children to the camp if they knew of his sexuality because they would believe he was a threat to their children. There was no objective evidence that Saunders would cause any harm to the children, but the Tribunal and Court of Session accepted that his dismissal had been fair because his employer feared irrational fear on the part of customers.

4 *Wigan Borough Council* v. *Davies* (1979) ICR 411.

5 It should be noted, however, that the Tribunal found that the dismissal was reasonable on the basis of Buck's conduct (i.e. acts of gross indecency) rather than simply on his colleagues' refusal to work with him. Similarly, it was held in *Gardiner* v. *Newport County Borough Council* (1974) that the dismissal of a man on the basis of a similar conviction was not unfair.

6 These three case studies also appear, with two further studies, in: P. Wilson, *HIV and AIDS in the Workplace: An Examination of Cases of Discrimination*, National AIDS Trust, 1992.

7 For further comment on this argument see:

P. Fitzpatrick, 'Racism and the innocence of law', *Journal of Law and Society*, vol. 14, 1, pp. 119–132, Spring 1987.

N. Lacey, 'Legislation against sex discrimination: questions from a feminist perspective', *Journal of Law and Society*, vol. 14, 4, Winter 1987.

C. MacKinnon, *Feminism Unmodified*. Harvard University Press, 1987.

8 *Ibid*.

Assessing Fitness for Work: Case Studies of HIV and AIDS from the GAK/GMD Medical Advisory Service, Amsterdam

Dr Willem Faas

GAK/GMD Medical Advisory Service, Amsterdam, The Netherlands

The past years have seen a steady increase in the number of HIV-positive patients in The Netherlands. It is therefore to be expected that, within the framework of the AAW (National Disablement Insurance Act) and the WAO (Disablement Benefits Act), the medical advisor will see a growing number of workers at his surgery who have become fully or partially incapable of work because of symptoms associated with HIV infection. This concerns not only incapacity for work caused by the physical effects of the disease but also the impact of HIV infection in the psychological and socio-economic field. Incapacity for work (if any) may be involved in all stages of HIV infection; the classifying method most commonly used for HIV-infected patients is a classification according to 4 stages, defined by the Centers for Disease Control and Prevention (CDC) in Atlanta, USA (p7). Classifying the disease into stages is of importance in determining the treatment strategy, the comparability of patients in research and in relation to the prognosis. It is also of importance to the medical advisor as a weighing factor in his assessment of the degree of incapacity for work and the decision whether the patient is eligible for reinstatement at work.[1]

Assessing capacity for work

The medical adviser's assessment of incapacity for work is not only based on legal criteria concerning sickness or infirmity. Although sickness plays a major role in the determination of the patient's remaining working capacities, it is not a decisive factor. Obviously, this does not apply solely to HIV infection but to all ill health. Factors other than purely sickness-related ones may seriously affect a person's capacity for work: for example a patient's ability to accept and deal with the disease, his personal circumstances and the conditions at work. In case of HIV infection, the latter include the physical and mental workload, the potential for making adjustments to this workload as well as acceptance of the disease at the workplace. These factors could be so vitally important that even patients who do not have any HIV-related somatic complaints (CDC group II) may still be fully incapable of work. On the other hand, a patient for whom an diagnosis AIDS has already been made, may still be partially or even fully fit for work. One should therefore be careful not to make general statements such as 'HIV-positive means fit for work, AIDS means unfit for work'.

Case studies

The following examples from the experiences of the Amsterdam HIV/AIDS team of the GAK/GMD medical advisory service[2] dealing with HIV-positive patients clearly illustrate this. It should be noted that patients referred to the GAK/GMD have already been on sick leave for a considerable period of time. On average, these patients have been eligible for benefit payments under the ZW (Dutch Sickness Benefits Act) for approximately six months. The fact that such a long time has passed, seriously interferes with finding an adequate solution, that is, successful reinstatement in gainful employment.

Statistics from a study of GAK/GMD files concerning 185 HIV-infected patients give an impression of the degree of incapacity for work in relation to the different stages of HIV infection. In addition, a few important points of attention will be mentioned with respect to the GAK/GMD case management of HIV-positive patients. To date the HIV/AIDS team has managed more than 850 cases (since 1989).

Patient A is a 33-year-old sound engineer who suffers from depression following confirmation of a positive HIV test result. The results of previous tests carried out one and two years earlier were HIV-negative. After five months he reports sick because he is no longer able to function properly. He claims to suffer from serious sleeping disorders, concentration problems, tension and gloominess. He also has intense feelings of shame and guilt; he was probably infected one year earlier despite all his good intentions around safe sex and he may possibly have transmitted the disease to others. He isolates himself and becomes apathetic. He has a gloomy picture of his future but no suicidal tendencies. He appears to be gradually drinking to excess. About a year after the positive test result, the patient admits his alcohol abuse. His temporary employment has meanwhile terminated. At that time, the patient's case is reported to the GAK/GMD. He has received sickness benefit under the ZW (Sickness Benefits Act) for six months. During his examination by the GAK/GMD it transpires that during a previous hospital examination that his CD4 cell count had been normal. There are no physical HIV-related symptoms whatsoever. The medical advisor concludes that the patient should be considered fully incapable of work mainly on account of psychological problems or, in other words, because of a reactive depressive condition involving alcohol abuse. It is pointed out to the patient that he himself is responsible for making the best of his situation, for example by getting treatment for which he is referred to a specialized institution. Finally, an appointment is made for a further medical re-examination in due course.

Patient B is a 31-year-old administrative worker. He reports sick stating complaints of fatigue and dejection. He frequently has a slightly feverish temperature. He suffers from diarrhoea and weight loss. He has known for some time that he is HIV-positive. At the time of his visit to the GAK/GMD he has been receiving sickness benefit for six months. During this period his condition has improved. The GAK/GMD medical advisor is advised by the patient's hospital physician that the patient is classified as group IV-a in accordance with the CDC (comparable to the former 'AIDS-related complex'). His cellular resistance is disturbed, complications are to be expected in the near future and will result in an AIDS diagnosis. Zidovudine treatment is started (it appears that these details had not been collected during the first six months).

Nevertheless, the patient would like to resume work. It is evident that full-time work is out of the question considering his deteriorating condition marked by rapidly occurring signs of fatigue. The medical officer concludes that the patient is fit to do part-time (50 per cent) administrative work without pressure of time and pace. If a solution is therefore to be found at his former workplace, his duties need to be adjusted. The aim is to create a light job for him in which he can work 50 per cent of his usual working hours.

As the patient works for a large company, it seems that this can be easily organized. His colleagues and superiors are aware of patient's disease. Making appointments for the medical adviser and the occupational adviser of the GAK/GMD with personnel officers of the company proves to be unexpectedly problematic. From informal talks it becomes clear that people working at his department have raised serious objections to his return. However, the ins and outs of the matter are left unsaid. The planned reinstatement at work takes such a long time that the patient starts to suspect that the nature of his disease forms the main obstacle. He loses his motivation and after some time he does not want to resume work any longer: 'if things have to go like this I am not interested any more'. Shortly afterwards, his intestinal complaints get rapidly worse and a microsporidal infection is established which confirms an AIDS diagnosis. Attempts to reinstate the patient in employment are cancelled.

Patient C is a 38-year-old financial director of a private company who falls ill in the course of 1989 as a result of *Pneumocystis carinii* pneumonia (PCP). This confirms his AIDS diagnosis. He receives treatment. After two months he resumes part-time work (50 per cent) and after three months his working hours are extended to 80 per cent. It is agreed that he will not work full time so that he has an extra day of rest. These arrangements are made in close consultation with the medical adviser. Early in 1990, he claims that he is doing well and he hopes to be able to continue his work for a long time. Except for tiring very quickly, he has no further physical complaints. At work he

has informed everyone of his disease. No problems have occurred in connection with the disease or the fact that he works part-time (80 per cent). In December he still works 80 per cent of his former working hours. However, his complaints of fatigue are increasingly bothering him. Gradually he has to reduce his working hours to less than 50 per cent. The company arranges a replacement for him. In May 1991, he has to cease work completely owing to serious recurring HIV infection-related complications; two months later he dies.

Patient D, a 40-year-old executive of an Arabian company has to discontinue his work because of acute symptoms associated with a cerebral toxoplasmosis. He has known for two years that he is HIV-positive. The cerebral toxoplasmosis is clinically confirmed resulting in an AIDS diagnosis. After a relatively short period of time, patient resumes full-time work but he has to stop two months later on account of a recurrent *Toxoplasma gondii* infection. He recovers and wishes to resume full-time work again. He refuses to follow the advice to start working part-time, for example 50 per cent of his usual working hours. The employer must not suspect anything about his disease because the patient is convinced that he will be fired as soon as the diagnosis becomes publicly known. He refers to the Arabian background of the firm, for which he has already worked for more than ten years. At work he told his colleagues that he had suffered from meningitis. He resumes work for about a month. It is evident that patient is no longer able to work for the 40-hour-week required by his hectic job. Attempts are made to persuade him to inform his employer about his disease, so that the possibility of adjusting his work could be made a subject of discussion. He cannot summon the strength to do so. Although he has always enjoyed his work he decides to stop for good. After he finally stops work he still lives for more than a year.

Patient E is a 45-year-old male who has known since 1987 that he is HIV-positive. Before 1987 he had also suffered from various complaints, in particular fatigue and respiratory infections. In 1989, he claims he has been incapable of work since 1984 – significant if he is to claim retrospective benefits. He has been unemployed for years. As a participant in an epidemiological research project he was informed in 1984 about a decreased number of CD4 cells. At the time the meaning of this was less clear than today. From information obtained from his current hospital physician it appears that he was referred to a hospital consultant in early 1987. He appeared to be positive for both HIV antibodies and the HIV antigen and he had a *Candida* infection in his mouth. His main complaint was fatigue. This was followed by diarrhoea. In 1987, the patient suffered from HIV-related complaints, without any opportunistic infection being involved which would have led to an AIDS diagnosis. Since April 1987, the patient's disease has been classified as group IV-a. It is important to note that the patient, in view of his unemployment, had been covered by insurance until 1985 under the WAO (Disablement Benefits Act) on the basis of his benefit having been granted under the WWV (Unemployment Allowance Act). His insurance cover was cancelled when this benefit was converted to a benefit granted under the RWW (National insurance Scheme for Unemployed Workers) – a less generous scheme.

Lessons from the experience of GAK/GMD

In relation to the assessment of incapacity for work of patients with HIV infection as well as the assistance rendered to these patients in finding employment, it is sensible from a medical adviser's point of view to make a distinction between patients with a relatively favourable prognosis (CDC group II and III) and patients with a relatively bad prognosis (group

IV). The latter group includes patients showing specific HIV-related symptoms but who have not yet been diagnosed as having AIDS (group IV-a and IV-c2) and patients having AIDS.

As a rule of thumb it can be said that purely on physical grounds, patients from group II and III still have a remaining capacity for work. Most patients from this group do not have functional limitations resulting from HIV-related somatic disorders. According to current insights, it may take years before patients of this group develop the full symptoms associated with AIDS. Consequently, these patients cannot be considered incapable of work on somatic grounds from the very start.

There are, of course, various non-somatic grounds which may result in patients from group II and II being considered incapable of work. These limitations mainly relate to psychological aspects and are often temporary; some patients, for example, recover following a reactive period marked by adjustment and mood disorders and still succeed in finding a mental balance. Others, however, remain definitely unfit for work: the adjustment fails or the patient becomes chronically depressed or suffers from anxiety.

As far as patient A is concerned, time will tell what will happen to him. However, one should keep in mind that as time goes by, the next stage of his HIV infection may result in additional functional limitations of a more somatic nature.

In our medical advisory practice, it frequently occurs that having been notified of a positive test result (whether or not followed by a period of sickness) patients from group II and III do not want to resume (full-time) work, because they feel that certain job aspects will adversely affect their health: for example shift work, night shifts (hospital, hotel, bar), work involving a great deal of travelling (purchasing/selling, public relations, working for a tour operator) and jobs involving heavy physical duties. Occasionally, this becomes the subject of very difficult discussions because it is absolutely unknown what circumstantial factors will speed up the development of the HIV infection. During these discussions an element of negotiation will therefore inevitably creep in when it comes to the assessment of the degree of incapacity for work. Practice has taught us that a forced resumption of employment in a workplace similar to that of the described patients has very little chance of success as long as the patient is convinced that he is putting his health at risk.

Also, less obvious physical stress factors may result in mental strain. Do HIV-positive patients from group II and III have to be protected against this? So far, it has not been convincingly demonstrated that these symptom-free patients would be unable to fulfil positions setting high demands to their intellectual powers, abilities to react, etc. Literature on this subject is not unanimous. Until now, it has not been necessary for GAK/GMD medical advisers in Amsterdam to consider the possibility of a minor AIDS dementia complex in the case of stages II and III (before the patient is showing other symptoms). However, because of this possible complication the advice in countries such as Germany and the United States has been to consider specific professional activities unsuitable for certain symptom-free HIV-positive persons: for example, civil aircraft pilots, persons doing important monitoring duties (such as radar installations), persons with high responsibilities in nuclear plants and military staff with far-reaching powers.

It cannot be emphasized too often that fear of infecting others (particularly in jobs in the food industry and in bars and restaurants, as well as when working as hairdressers, beauticians and chiropodists) is never a reason for incapacity for work, neither in the employer's opinion nor in that of the patient. In these situations, the medical adviser should, therefore, not decide to consider the patient incapable of work if there are no other grounds for this.

If patients fall under group IV-a or IV-c2, it has to be assumed that an AIDS diagnosis will be made within one or two years. As the average life expectancy after this diagnosis is currently about two years, it is standard policy within the Dutch social system not to demand that the patient works even if he was capable of physical activity. As the prognosis of an illness becomes worse the 'excusability' increases. Obviously, this applies in particular to patients diagnosed with AIDS. Here, a comparison can be made with cancer patients with a poor prognosis: those who wish to work may do so (provided it is not irresponsible); those who do not want to work, do not have to.

The HIV/AIDS team in Amsterdam offers assistance to all patients from group IV who wish to find suitable employment. It is never assumed that supervising these patients would be pointless. In fact, the case of patient C shows that a successful reinstatement at work can be reached. The cases of patients B and D, however, show that reinstatement at work is not always successful. It is not always easy to indicate a single reason why attempts at work rehabilitation sometimes fail. The motivation of patient B died away because of the poor response from his employer and colleagues. The patient lost his resilience out of fear, whether justified or not, of negative reactions to the disease itself. He could not accept the fact that he was seriously ill and that he had no choice but to adjust his work schedule in order to be able to continue working. Rather than make his illness the subject of discussion which might have enabled him to continue his work in a part-time job, he preferred absolute secrecy as a result of which he quietly disappeared from the workplace. Because this situation frequently occurs, relatively few conflicts about AIDS and HIV arise at the workplace between HIV-positive workers on the one hand and their colleagues and employers on the other.

The example of patient E illustrates the difficulties encountered by the medical adviser when he has to answer retrograde questions that can easily have legal implications – another case management dilemma for the medical adviser. This concerns patients who report sick, claiming that they must have been unfit for work for quite some time, now that it has been confirmed that they are HIV-positive or have AIDS. Obviously, the object of their claim is to become eligible for a more favourable benefit scheme; at the time of their assessment patients are no longer insured under the WAO (Disablement Benefits Act), so they try to get themselves declared unfit for work with retroactive effect to a date on which they were still covered by the WAO insurance scheme.

In the case of patient E, it was decided that he probably had been incapable of work since early 1987 on account of his HIV-related complaints and symptoms but not from 1984, as the patient claimed. But the details covering the period before 1987 were insufficient to serve as proof that he was already incapable of work at that time. The patient, by the way, did not agree with this conclusion.

During the above study of the GAK/GMD files, attention was focused on the (in)capacity for work of patients reported to the GAK/GMD in the different stages of HIV infection. A distinction has been made between incapacity for work due to physical limitations and due to psychological limitations. The percentages in Table 1 have been rounded off and cover 27 patients in groups II and III, 48 patients in groups IV–a and IV-c2 and 110 patients with AIDS.

These figures clearly show that the physical impediments increase as the HIV infection develops and that incapacity for work in CDC groups II and III is mainly caused by psychological complaints. Anxiety disorders, affective disorders and adaptation disorders are mentioned most frequently.

From case management experiences in Amsterdam it appears that, irrespective of the stage of the disease, the following factors are of essential importance:

Table 1
Incapacity to work in relation to CDC classification of HIV disease

Assessment of:		
1. Physical condition		
CDC-II/III	incapable of work	10%
CDC-IVa/IV-c2	incapable of work	50%
CDC-IV (AIDS)	incapable of work	75%
2. Mental condition		
CDC-II/III	incapable of work	55%
CDC-IVa/IV-c2	incapable of work	15%
CDC-IV (AIDS)	incapable of work	5%

- acceptance of the disease by the patient;
- the extent to which family and friends are expected to accept the situation;
- the actual acceptance by these persons;
- disease of the partner in particular;
- the extent to which the employer and colleagues need to accept the situation;
- the actual acceptance by these persons;
- work orientation;
- possibilities to adjust the work.

It appears that incapacity for work in all stages of HIV infection is affected and determined by a large number of factors.

The decisive factor in the patient's decision to continue work concerns their physical capacities, the extent to which the disease is accepted and the orientation towards work. As far as people from CDC group IV are able to continue their jobs, experience shows that working part-time (50 per cent) is usually the most effective way to ensure that they continue to work for as long as possible. Patients who continue work for one to two years after AIDS was diagnosed are no longer exceptions to the rule: 20–30 per cent of these patients manage to continue work in one way or another.

Conclusion

The conclusion of this contribution is that assessing incapacity for work in the case of HIV-positive people and supervising these patients in connection with reinstatement at work, requires a tailor-made approach in all stages of HIV infection. It is certainly true that physical capacities decrease as the HIV infection develops (this particularly applies to patients from CDC group IV) and that, relatively speaking, more symptom-free HIV-positive people are engaged in employment than those who are not symptom free. However, this should not lead to the conclusion that HIV-positive patients are per definition fit for work without any restrictions and patients with HIV-related symptoms or AIDS are incapable of doing any work at all. In addition to somatic factors, psychological and situational factors play an important, if not decisive role in both the assessment of incapacity for work and the question whether reinstatement at work will succeed or fail.

Obviously, a patient is more concerned about the threat of losing his life than his participation in gainful employment. Experience has taught us that as time goes by, this participation easily disappears as a result of the patient's preoccupation with his disease.

I would therefore recommend the medical adviser to start counselling the HIV-positive person as soon as possible after this patient has been reported to organizations such as the GAK/GMD. For this purpose, the medical adviser should look into the stage of the patient's HIV infection and his psychological condition; he should also form an idea of the problems that may occur as regards the acceptance of the disease and the orientation towards work.

Moreover, it is important that nothing is left undone to promote the acceptance of HIV-positive persons at the workplace and that all parties involved should do their utmost to enable people with HIV infection or AIDS to participate in employment for as long as possible.

1 The contents of this chapter are partly based on a previously published paper in *Nederlands Tijdschrift voor Geneeskunde*, p. 136, 1992.

2 GAK/GMD (formerly the GMD) is an institution, funded by employers and employees, that assesses individuals for state benefits and fitness for work.

Preconditions for Policy Development: Workplace Attitudes Towards HIV/AIDS

Dr David Goss and Derek Adam-Smith

Centre for AIDS and Employment Research, Portsmouth Business School, England

'Rules are meaningless if people's attitude towards someone with HIV is not a very positive one.'

Paul, clerical worker.

Introduction

As an issue, HIV confronts organizations with the decision whether or not to adopt a positive stance towards people affected by the virus. In the absence of UK or European employment legislation aimed specifically at the protection of people with AIDS the development of a constructive stance is essentially a *choice* for senior management. Where this choice has been made it usually takes the form of an HIV/AIDS policy.[1]

The context of organization policy development in the UK has largely been one of piecemeal initiatives based on voluntary rather than statutory principles. The most widely circulated guidance was provided by the Department of Employment and Health and Safety Executive in the 1986 and 1990 booklets *AIDS and Employment* and *AIDS and the Workplace: A Guide for Employers* (respectively), emphasizing the duty of employers not to discriminate against employees carrying the virus and to provide education and training for all employees. This has been supplemented by material provided by various public/voluntary sector bodies such as Lesbian and Gay Employment Rights (LAGER)[2] and health authorities (e.g. North West Thames),[3] usually providing a stronger emphasis on equal opportunities issues. The adoption of policies by UK organizations is difficult to determine with any degree of accuracy because of lack of representative surveys, although evidence from Incomes Data Services suggests that policies are more common in the public sector, and in the private sector are restricted to larger companies.[4] Local studies by Whelan[5] and Gadd[6] broadly support this picture.

More recently, however, developments in this field have taken a more sophisticated turn with the launch in 1992 of the National AIDS Trust's (NAT) 'Companies act!' and in 1993 of the Terrence Higgins Trust's (THT) 'Positive Management Programme'. The latter is concerned with protecting employment on the grounds that work, for people with HIV/AIDS, guarantees money and therefore safeguards standard of living. It provides training materials, guidance and a training video based on the good practice of major companies. The NAT scheme,

'Companies act!', is based on a national charter setting out not only good practice but also committing companies to a public stand in supporting the fight against AIDS, and encouraging signatories actively to promote constructive work in the AIDS field. At the time of writing there are around 43 signatories to the Charter, including companies such as Marks and Spencer, IBM and National Westminster Bank. The philosophy of 'Companies act!' suggests that 'HIV should be on every personnel manager's agenda; a non-discriminatory policy is the only practical approach. HIV and AIDS are equal opportunities issues, not exclusively health and safety ones.' [7]

While policies which follow the guidelines set out by NAT are to be welcomed as a constructive step in the fight against AIDS and viewed as something to be encouraged,[8] it is also worth asking what barriers may be faced by managements concerned to implement such an initiative. Indeed, a perennial problem with any organization policy, especially one which does not have the force of law behind it, is to translate its objectives into a meaningful and active practice – as opposed to an empty formality that can safely be ignored. In this respect experience often contradicts the rationalist assumption that 'practice follows policy' (i.e. the latter is a guide for the former) and seems rather to support the proverb that 'you can lead a horse to water but you cannot make it drink'.

The exact causes of this type of problem are numerous, but common to most instances seems to be the overestimation by policy-makers of the understanding and interest that 'ordinary' organization members have in the issue concerned, and an associated failure to consider the possible need to inform, and even educate organization members of the need for a policy prior to its implementation. Such considerations are of special importance when dealing with an issue such as AIDS where opinion is openly divided and the nature of the disease such as to evoke strong, emotional and frequently irrational responses.

For an AIDS policy to be successfully implemented, therefore, it is necessary to have some understanding of how it is perceived as a workplace issue. It is only on the basis of such an understanding that likely barriers to effective policy adoption can be identified and appropriate implementation strategies and tactics developed. Surprisingly, there seems to be very little systematic research that provides an insight into the profile of the problem that AIDS poses for organizations. The research reported in this chapter was intended to go some way towards filling this gap and the following account provides a preliminary sketch of important dimensions of employees' understanding of, and concerns about, AIDS at work.

To this end, data is presented under five distinct but interconnected headings: Relevance of HIV/AIDS; Perceptions of risk; Employer regulation and procedures; Working relations; and Training and education. The main issues for practice are extracted and discussed in the final section. The approach of the chapter is primarily descriptive, the intention being to lay before the reader as much of our data as possible.[9]

Eleven organizations were investigated with an average of ten employee interviews per organization, a total of 106 respondents. Each interview lasted between half an hour and two hours, was tape-recorded and transcribed in full. Wherever possible interviews in each organization covered senior managers, line managers, clerical and manual workers. The organizations studied were drawn from the manufacturing, health care, voluntary/charity, hospitality, and public sectors and were located across the UK, although predominantly in the South East. Clearly this research has generated a vast pool of data (some 500,000 words) and the present chapter is one of the first analyses undertaken. As such the results must be regarded as provisional and subject to refinement as the analysis proceeds. In this paper we have concentrated on those issues which appeared to operate relatively independently of differences between organizations and sectors. Details of the organizations, interviews and coded identifiers are given in Table 1.

The relevance of HIV/AIDS in the workplace

Responses to the question of the relevance of HIV/AIDS to normal workplace life tended to take one of three forms: irrelevance (approximately 80 per cent of respondents); injury (10 per cent); and social impact (10 per cent). We will consider each in turn.

Irrelevance

Respondents tended to give one of two explanations for their view that AIDS was irrelevant to their working life. On the one hand, were those who asserted that they

were well informed about AIDS and, as a result, understood that the risk of transmission through work-related activity was negligible (hence irrelevant); this we term 'considered irrelevance'.[10] For example:

> 'I know all I really need to know. It's contracted through sex and it's contracted through blood, but as long you keep your head and show common sense, use protection. I don't need to go into detail about this or that.'

> (nightclub waiter F6)

> 'Because of the nature of our job we don't really have any contact with blood products. It's not that sort of job. We don't have that kind of intimate contact...'

> (clerical assistant, local authority H3)

On the other hand, were those who confessed to not having given the issue any serious consideration (as one respondent put it: 'I'm a clean person so I know I'm okay!'). This response we label 'spontaneous irrelevance'. Of 'spontaneous irrelevance', it can be noted that when

Table 1

Number of interviews, by organization

Organization	Sector	Managers	Non-managers	Total
A	Hotels	3	8	11
B	Man./Distribution	3	8	11
C	Public	3	5	8
D	Voluntary	5	6	11
E	Health	2	3	5
F	Pubs & Clubs	4	6	10
G	Manufacturing	3	8	11
H	Public	3	7	10
J	Voluntary	5	4	9
K	Health	9	2	11
L	Nightclubs	3	6	9
Totals		**43**	**63**	**106**

respondents claimed HIV/AIDS to be of little or no *relevance* to their work situation, this did not mean that it was not discussed at work; rather discussion tended to be restricted to non-work issues such as the infection of celebrities and scares in the popular press. For example:

'Nobody's ever talked about it specifically. Some years ago when there was more of a scare we would talk about children in the schools and what was the potential likeliness of problems. There were a lot of stories but none of us had any knowledge.'

(clerical assistant, charity D3)

We are not, therefore, talking about a total absence of AIDS discourse; indeed the 'working out' of such secular ideas may contribute to a 'background understanding' or latent meaning framework capable of influencing behaviour should events force HIV/AIDS onto the workplace agenda.[11] Thus, in both the 'considered' and 'spontaneous' forms of response, an initial assertion of irrelevance did not mean that respondents had no views about how employers and fellow employees should respond (as will be seen in subsequent sections).[12]

Injury

As would be expected, concern about blood was more frequently voiced in work situations where injury, especially cuts, were a common occurrence (the manufacturing shopfloors and the hotel and catering establishments). In non-physical work settings where such concerns were raised it tended to be in the context of First Aid. Few respondents in this category had received any information or training about HIV/AIDS from their employer and most relied upon an often hazy knowledge acquired from public health broadcasts and the media. Certainly in the absence of relevant information and of clear procedural knowledge for dealing with blood spillages, there were cases where such

eventualities were the subject of some anxiety. For example:

'...say a guy got his hand stuck in the machinery, then it would be the job of the maintenance fitter to free him...If you see blood, it suddenly pops into your mind, "God! HIV! AIDS!", and your job is to release the hand.'

(metal worker G1)

'I have been involved in areas where there is likely to be a violent situation and sometimes one has to go in and, should we say, sort out the problems of violence where someone has been injured. There has been times when the doubts have crept into my mind: should I be wearing gloves, should I be doing this?...to a certain degree it's on one's mind.'

(nightclub manager L2)

'I'll tell you what I have thought about, somebody said to me, "Wouldn't you like to be a First Aider?" and I said, "No I wouldn't", because I am not very keen on blood, and I don't think I could give resuscitation to anybody who had AIDS. But I mean there's probably ways and means where you wouldn't catch it but I wouldn't know without somebody giving some sort of information on it.'

(supervisor, charity D2)

This is not to say that these organizations had not provided information relating to HIV/AIDS at some point in the past; rather individual uncertainty was usually the result either of a failure of communication and/or of infrequent or ineffective dissemination, a particular problem where there was a high labour turnover. There was, however, a discernable contrast between the effects of apparently *ad hoc* approaches to information provision and those of the more comprehensive training and education programmes which had influenced many of those who saw the relevance of HIV/AIDS in terms of social impact within the organization.

Social impact

Most of the respondents who regarded HIV/AIDS as an issue of wider relevance to workplace activity were in managerial positions and/or had received specific awareness training. In several cases concern about HIV/AIDS had been the stimulus to seek training whereas in others it had been sparked by first hand experience of dealing with employees or clients with the virus. The following are illustrative:

'I thought it was foolhardy to work on the assumption that it was never going to happen here. By the law of averages, I guess it's going to happen in most organizations at some point, and I am also perfectly aware of the fact that if we do get a member of staff with AIDS then the person that they come to to say, "What do we do now?", is me. I thought probably I ought to be better aware than I was.'

(personnel manager, charity D9)

'Because I am a counsellor and I go through continuous training sessions, and quite often you were talking about HIV and AIDS, and we've had many workshops dealing with HIV and AIDS. And it was from that I used to come back [to work] and say, "Hey, come on, we've got to be doing something!" Sooner or later somebody is going to knock on the door and say, "I have a problem which I think you need to know about and how are we going to deal with it?".'

(welfare manager, manufacturer/distributor B1)

'Given the strength of the education we got last year, I did have to think about it, because we had to be prepared for somebody to come into the department who might be HIV-positive, we might not know, but we had to think about the safety precautions we should take.'

(packer, manufacturer/distributor B2)

Taking the overall response to the issue of relevance it was notable that the definitions provided by those in the third group demonstrated a broader grasp of potential social/human issues and a more balanced conception of risk. However, as this was very much a minority response the notion of risk demands more detailed exploration.

Perceptions of risk

On the subject of risk Sim[13] identifies three factors associated with any given hazard – 'magnitude', 'probability', and 'acceptability' – which together contribute to shaping individual responses to that hazard. In relation to HIV/AIDS it seems that the factors of magnitude and probability are, in theory, amenable to relatively objective categorization. The *magnitude* of this particular hazard (that is the likelihood of it proving fatal to an individual in contact with it) is known to be extremely high to the extent that the link between contracting HIV, developing AIDS, and resulting death is strong, albeit of variable duration. This conclusion is generally subject to little dissent and appears to be widely accepted. In contrast, the *probability* of an individual contracting HIV through occupational activity of any sort is extremely low.[14] Probability, however, is (as we show below) subject to widely differing 'lay' interpretations despite the existence of clear expert opinion. The third factor – *acceptability* – is even more nebulous: it relates not to objective or verifiable fact, but to questions of moral choice and subjective judgement. This is especially relevant in the case of AIDS because it is a disease which is defined not merely through medical/physiological concepts, but also through numerous 'layers' of moral meanings, in particular the notions of deviance and homosexuality.

For the present analysis we concentrate on 'probability' and 'acceptability' and the apparent negative relationship between these two dimensions (i.e. as one increases the other declines). Thus, on the one hand were respondents who possessed a realistic assessment of the risk posed by HIV in the workplace (i.e. high acceptability and low probability). Very often this implied an 'inversion' of the conventional notion of risk (transmission of the virus from an infected to healthy person); rather, the risk was that of discrimination and prejudice *against* the infected. For example:

'The risk of passing it on to anyone must be fairly remote so there is no one at risk. Most people are paranoid about people who are different...I think we all know how the system works, in that if you declare that you are HIV, most people accept that you will be penalised in some way...because you can't avoid the stigma.'

(local authority officer H6)

'...it's just a condition, the same as any other...but I mean it's not contagious in the workplace...[people with HIV] are only really at risk to themselves perhaps it wouldn't be beneficial for them to keep coming in to the office from their own personal health point of view.'

(clerical worker, manufacturer G5)

In contrast, those responses which exhibited an exaggerated perception of probability tended to favour some form of employer regulation to control what they feared to be the likely adverse and unacceptable effects of HIV in the workplace. Thus:

'I wouldn't like anybody behind the bar to be employed who is HIV-positive, if cuts happen, constant contact with liquids that are drunk by customers, coming into contact with customers...I wouldn't expect them to be handling the glassware...[Testing] wouldn't be a bad idea, I personally wouldn't give objections if someone tested me...Yes I would think that would be a pretty good thing actually. Yes, that would be good.'

(manager, nightclub F6)

'I mean even in my kind of job you are always cutting yourself on the metal. When you cut yourself you leave blood on the metal and the next person picks it up...unless I'm ignorant of that part but I think blood is one of the main factors...They should perhaps find him a job where perhaps you minimize the risk, in a way that you can't catch it. I know it's a sorry state, but that's it. I mean if you have got anything they put you in hospital and keep you away from other people, whatever it is, not only that, any disease, that's contagious, they keep you away.'

(metal worker G2)

'When it comes to people dealing with food and say for example, to keep an employee in the kitchen who had AIDS, if she cut her finger and is sort of mixing some dough and some blood was getting into the dough then that person would get AIDS, then she is basically killing someone, isn't she?'

(nightclub waitress L3)

'How can it be transmitted? If it can be transmitted on money, you know things like that...maybe it can be transmitted through food, maybe it can be transmitted through something else...obviously we're prone to say cuts and things like that in the kitchen, I'm in contact with raw meat and things like that so there's cross-contamination there...if I knew there was a drug user here, or a homosexual here, then I would possibly, certainly protest slightly. I would turn around and I definitely wouldn't work with the person. It might sound nasty.'

(chef, local authority H10)

It should be noted that the quotations used thus far in this section represent the extremes of such responses with most respondents falling somewhere between. Indeed, it was not uncommon for probability and acceptability to be, in a sense, 'equalized': respondents claimed that they would be prepared to accept colleagues or clients with HIV as long as they were aware of their condition and 'appropriate' precautions ensured. Consider the following:

> 'It depends where I was going to put them at work. Like I said, it's ignorance...If I thought I could do something then I would want to know. If there was like a leaflet and instructions and I knew that whoever I put them with was never going to catch it then that's fine by me, but if I thought in the situation whereby you could transmit it by cuts and things then I think I would want to know and I probably wouldn't put them in that area anyway. I would put them somewhere, where they were totally on their own, not on their own exactly, but on their own.'

> (supervisor, charity D2)

In this respect (i.e. away from the extremes), as the last quotation demonstrates, the perception of risk was an inherently unstable phenomenon and many respondents pointed to their felt need for more information and education if they were to achieve what to them seemed a desirable balance of acceptability and probability.

However, before focusing directly on training and education, it is necessary to consider two closely related areas (already alluded to briefly above) where this unstable and ambivalent assessment of risk appears to exert an influence, namely, desire for employer regulation, and working relationships.

Employer regulation

Overall there was little unequivocal support for employer measures to identify people with HIV, either at the point of recruitment via testing or through self-disclosure. Where this did occur it tended to come from respondents who held a high perception of probabilistic risk and who (also) worked in areas where the chance of injury and spillage of blood was greatest. Even so, with the exception of a

few 'extreme' cases, most respondents' views on testing and disclosure were again ambivalent and highly conditional. The following quotations illustrate the *range* of opinion (i.e. from outright opposition, through ambivalence, to support):

> 'Definitely not [testing]. Particularly not medical work because it's obviously going to be used against them. First of all it's damaging to the individual concerned, there are all sorts or reasons to undergo HIV testing but there are all sorts of reasons not to as well. They shouldn't be forced to take one by an employer or an insurance agency whatever. They would have to deal with the upshot of that. Also it could only be used to work against them. If you test positive it isn't exactly going to work in your favour.'

> (social worker C5)

> 'I mean I wouldn't object to it if it was part of the basic contract, but I would have to have a very good answer as to why they wanted it done, but if it was on a medical side and I was going say as a sick berth attendant I would expect it almost as a mandatory question. Mostly because of the close physical contact...If you were a prospective employer and you knew that the guy, or girl, that you was employing was HIV free, and the nature of the job might be delicate, then it would probably give you more confidence, or choice to employ them. Not that I'm saying you should not employ HIV-positive people, it just depends on the context of the job, doesn't it?'

> (metal worker G1)

> 'Maybe we should introduce a medical and incorporate that into it. Yes I guess, my personal opinion is that if somebody is HIV-positive, they ought to declare that they are. I think it should be a statutory regulation that people should declare if they are HIV-positive...I don't think we should employ people who are HIV-positive...it's a contagious illness/disease whatever you want to

call it. It may not be contagious in the same way that the plague is or TB, something like that but it is still contagious so therefore you shouldn't be in contact with the public.'

(nightclub worker F1)

However, apart from those respondents who had strong objections to testing and employer surveillance on principle, a clear majority of respondents felt that workers involved in medical fields and close personal contact should be subject to testing (even if they did not see this as appropriate to their own workplaces). The following responses were typical:

'Catering, nursing, where you are dealing physically with either food, well obviously with food you are dealing with instruments that you could cut yourself with or whatever, then nursing obviously, being at the doctor and dentist I think they are quite important.'

(clerical assistant, charity D7)

'Yes, like nursing, doctoring, any kind of job where accidents might happen. Well if people don't know they had it, then they wouldn't be able to take measure to prevent any kind of accidents would they. I think it's a good thing for everybody to be tested, I think the entire country should be.'

(clerical assistant, medical centre K5)

For most non-medical organizations, however, the bulk of respondents were in favour of some form of employer protocol for dealing with AIDS-related issues, seeing this as a more realistic and practical solution than either testing or mandatory self-disclosure. Here again though, uncertainty and ambivalence were apparent, some respondents wanting formal rules to establish and safeguard the rights *of* people with HIV, whilst others envisaged rules designed to protect individuals and the organization *from* them.

Working relations

Very few respondents had, knowingly, worked with colleagues or clients who were HIV-positive and, as such, their responses must be seen in this light (i.e. as based on intention rather than experience). When asked about their expected reactions to working with someone known to be HIV-positive a range of responses similar to those previously discussed emerged: from a (single) refusal to mix with such a person to a commitment to provide help and support. Illustrations of this mix are provided below (note the third quotation where the issue of acceptability is again present, linked here to perceptions of 'guilt' and 'innocence'):

'They wouldn't work here. They would be fired straight away...there would just be an atmosphere in there all the time...I would keep away.'

(manager, nightclub F10)

'I don't know it is hard to say until something like that happens. Working colleagues? I don't know whether I could accept it. It's like I suppose taking your child into a house where you know someone has HIV...with your own kid it's the last thing you'd want.'

(chef, local authority H10)

'It would be silly to say it wouldn't unnerve me because it would. I wouldn't want to work with someone who is HIV-positive. I've got a lot of sympathy for those who are heterosexual, but I haven't got much sympathy for homosexuals because they know what they are getting involved with. I wouldn't want them touching me, well it's silly to say that, I would feel sorry for them depending totally on the circumstances. If he was known to be very promiscuous, I wouldn't feel too sorry for him as he brought it on himself.'

(nightclub waitress F6)

'If you know someone's got the potential to giving you a serious illness, it's human nature that there is that threat...I don't think you can lose that stigma. Once you know that someone has got it, they've got the potential, the disaster, they can give it to you, even if you only perceive it as a threat. You might not like being in close proximity to them, you'd be quite happy sit at a desk together but when it comes to physical contact.'

(local authority officer H6)

'The one experience I have had that was memorable, it surprised everybody. The initial reaction was shock, horror and the disbelief that Nigel was gay. Then some embarrassment, then some guilt, like why he didn't tell us, then it goes back to shock again, because then you realize that he has got HIV and potentially that he could be dead in a certain length of time. Then there is a tremendous feeling of what can we do. When the guy did die the reaction from the staff was considerable.'

(hotel manager A8)

Other than a few examples of clearly articulated intolerance, there was little in our data to suggest that employees with HIV/AIDS would, a priori and automatically, be the subjects of prejudice and discrimination. At the same time, however, neither was there overwhelming evidence that they would be treated like any other employee with a medical condition, although the latter seemed more likely than the former – at least in intention. Certainly for many respondents their uncertainty on this issue was coupled to a self-confessed lack of understanding of the virus and its implications. It is in this respect that workplace education and training may have an important role to play.

Employer-provided education (EPE): need and demand

As already stated the issue of EPE (which here we take to include both training courses and information provision) was presented by many respondents as the linchpin of desired workplace responses to HIV. Here again, however, there was a variety of ways in which the nature and effectiveness of EPE were articulated. One pattern to emerge was a rudimentary hierarchical ordering of the type of information that respondents wanted. In general those who felt themselves to be fundamentally ignorant and/or perceived a high probability of risk were most concerned to receive material focusing on basic practical/medical 'facts' about transmission, located clearly within the context of their work. In contrast, those already equipped with such an understanding were more concerned to have information relating to the human and social implications at work, coupled to regular reviews of medical developments. Significantly, the potentially limiting effects of a 'disconnection' between the 'biological' and the 'social' approaches to education were raised by one respondent who felt that AIDS education should be closely allied to issues of equal opportunities rather than given a purely 'medical' perspective on the grounds that to emphasize the latter in isolation could result in a 'reversal' of the real priorities arising from HIV. In short, that 'medicalization' was often *perceived* as emphasizing risk and threat – which in the workplace are practically insignificant – instead of providing assistance to those likely to be affected by the disease. Thus:

'There is nothing here about what do you do if you've got it, and who you go to. These are all about how you catch it, what you do to clean up blood or vomit, wear rubber gloves, it's about precautions, it's preventative risk but not on how to deal with it if you've got it.'

(manager, local authority H2)

It was certainly the case that the education sessions that were most easily recalled and which had made the deepest impact on respondents were those that had tackled the issue 'experientially', using 'real' cases with which trainees could identify. For example:

> '...when I went there I was expecting an in-depth approach, an educational view about AIDS, but it wasn't it was really about attitudes...that was what I was looking for, it was helpful to learn things about attitude, you learn your own prejudices that you think you don't have, and then we had some one with full-blown AIDS come in and talk to us all which was very moving...'
>
> (nurse K2)

From the responses of those who had experienced EPE specifically aimed at workplace issues, two significant findings emerged. First, it was that amongst those respondents who had previously received education there was a demand for updates and ongoing information:

> 'I would say more regular updates, there's conflicting reports all the time, and especially in people's letters in the safety journals where people write in and ask questions, quite often there's a question so it would be handy to have regular information though as to what is correct and what actually isn't.'
>
> (supervisor, manufacturer/distributor B3)

Second, the response to EPE was overwhelmingly positive: virtually all respondents regarded it as having been helpful, both in terms of providing information and, perhaps more importantly, helping to allay fears or anxieties. The following were typical:

> 'It made you understand, it made you aware that there's not really any danger of actually getting it unless you have some sort of blood contact, so if you touch someone, or drink out of the same glass, there is no chance of getting it. I think it made me feel a lot better about HIV than I otherwise would have done. This leaflet backed up what the government said...'
>
> (secretary, charity D5)

> 'Very useful because through my employment it's the only way I've known about it. Being employed in social services I've learnt a lot more than in general. Well I suppose because when we first knew about AIDS, it was all shock, horror, we're all going to catch it. But when you know more about it you find you're not so afraid.'
>
> (secretary, social services C3)

There are, however, two important cautions to be made about EPE provision. First, there emerged a scepticism on the part of many respondents towards generalized public health information campaigns that were seen either as too abstract and/or 'tainted' by apparent disagreement between experts. In several cases, for instance, there was a high sensitivity to inconsistency in the 'official' message, as one respondent explained:

> 'The only qualm I'd have is that professional opinion seems to change from time to time, like we are seeing now, the forecast of heterosexual AIDS. The prediction of masses of people being infected has not started to happen. So obviously you take everything with a pinch of salt. Professional opinion might change.'
>
> (local authority officer H6)

Second, there was a more practical concern with the provision of training, namely, what could be described as the danger of 'P(olitical) C(orrectness) fatigue':

> 'I've no objections to making it specifically AIDS but I think that people have to see it as part of a wider context. Already with race awareness they are coming in and saying do you think I am racist is that why I am going on the course. So they will either come in and say do you think I've got AIDS or do you think I've got a problem with people who have AIDS.'
>
> (manager, local authority H2)

Taking these findings together, it seems clear that good employer information is likely to be welcomed by employees, but that to really 'connect' it must be tightly focused on workplace issues that are perceived as relevant and provide a balance of medical and social concerns. As the last quotation illustrates the issue of proportion may also be important. Our data suggests that the 'panic response' to AIDS is no longer as strong as it was in the mid 1980s and a more 'low key' (yet sustained) approach to education may be received as more 'realistic'. Taken overall, this would seem to be a vindication of the approach adopted by the Terrence Higgins Trust and the National AIDS Trust to develop specific workplace training/education initiatives rather than to rely on the non-specific health education materials (although this can clearly have an important constituent role).

Conclusions

The intention of this chapter has been to use detailed qualitative data to give a 'feel' for the ways in which HIV/AIDS is understood within workplace situations. Although we can make no claims to statistical representativeness, the research does suggest a series of conclusions that bear upon the issue of policy implementation and effectiveness with which we opened our discussion.

Thus, despite initial assertions by respondents that HIV/AIDS was not a major issue in their working lives, it emerged that such views generally derived from a limited understanding of the virus and its effects. Although at first sight a peripheral concern of most respondents, there remained 'beneath the surface' a residual apprehension and uncertainty. What clearly emerges from our data is that although most respondents had gleaned an understanding of the 'big picture', there was a surprising uniformity in the lack of assurance with which they approached the issue of AIDS at the level of practice.

On this basis, it seems inescapable to conclude that if such policy is to be genuinely effective in changing the attitudes and behaviour of organization members then it must either be built upon or involve from the outset some form of education and information provision relating to the virus. The nature and complexity of the AIDS issue and the uncertainties that surround it at 'grass roots' level are such that without such information support there is every probability that policy will quickly become nothing more than an empty rhetoric.

Acknowledgements
The research presented in this chapter was supported by the Economic and Social Research Council, grant no. R000 234131.

1 D. Adam-Smith, D. Goss, A. Sinclair, G. Rees, K. Meudell, 'AIDS and employment: diagnosis and prognosis', *Employee Relations*, 18, 3, pp. 29–40, 1992.

2 LAGER, *HIV and AIDS: Policy Guidelines*. Lesbian and Gay Employment Rights, London, 1990.

3 North West Thames, *HIV Infection and the Workplace*. NWT HIV Project, London, 1989.

4 Incomes Data Services, *AIDS and Employment*, IDS Study 393, 1987.

Incomes Data Services, *AIDS Returns to the Agenda*, IDS Study 528, 1993.

5 C. Whelan, 'Managing a crisis', unpublished report, North Nottinghamshire Health Authority, 1992.

6 K. Gadd, Report to Portsmouth AIDS Forum, unpublished, Centre for AIDS and Employment Research, Portsmouth Business School, 1993.

7 National AIDS Trust, *Companies act! The Business Charter on HIV/AIDS*, p.2. NAT, London, 1992.

P. Wilson, *HIV and AIDS in the Workplace: An Examination of Cases of Discrimination*. National AIDS Trust, London, 1992.

8 For an analysis of 'less desirable' policies see:

D. Goss, D. Adam-Smith, A. Sinclair, G. Rees, 'AIDS policies as data: possibilties and precaution', *Sociology*, 27, 2, pp. 299–305, 1993;

D. Goss and D. Adam-Smith, 'Empowerment and disempowerment: the limits and possibilities of workplace AIDS policy', *AIDS: Foundations for the Future* (eds. P. Aggleton *et al.*). Falmer, London, 1994.

9 More theoretical treatments can be found in:

D. Goss and D. Adam-Smith, 'Framing difference: AIDS, sexuality and organization', paper presented at the British Sociological Association Conference, University of Central Lancashire, March, 1994;

D. Goss, 'Writing about AIDS: framing policy', paper presented at the EIAMS Conference on Writing Rationality and Organization, Brussels, March, 1994;

D. Goss and D. Adam-Smith, 'Empowerment and disempowerment: the limits and possibilities of workplace AIDS policy', *AIDS: Founda*

tions for the Future (eds. P. Aggleton *et al.*). Falmer, London, 1994.

10 'Considered Irrelevance' tended to be prevalent among respondents with a 'narrow' understanding of the medical aspects of AIDS (often acquired through First Aid training or former 'medical' employment) and a view of the virus's impact in biological rather than social terms. This type of response suggests a potential for strongly biologically oriented training alone to 'close down' consideration of the more contingent 'human' issues to which HIV/AIDS can give rise in the workplace. (While not inevitable, this is something that educators should bear in mind: depending on the audience and situation, such 'closure' may be more or less desirable; but it is not something that should be allowed to happen unintentionally).

11 This possibility concerned several of the respondents (in our third relevance category, see below) who were involved with HIV/AIDS training on the grounds that much of the information culled from the tabloid media was often inaccurate and far from helpful. As one put it:

'People were not happy because they did not understand...If you look around at this organisation and see people reading the broad sheets it's a very small number of people – the rest read the tabloids. What we were trying to address was ignore what you read in the press, these are the experts and they will answer straight any questions which you may have.'

H1

12 This, of course, raises a methodological issue for investigators who seek to tap employee attitudes via self-administered questionnaires. Using the criteria of 'relevance' as the basis for questions, it would be quite conceivable to get an overall response that suggests AIDS to be a non-issue, masking deeper concerns and potential areas of difficulty or concern.

13 J. Sim, 'AIDS, nursing and occupational risk', *Journal of Advanced Nursing*, 17, pp. 569–75, 1992.

14 It is well established that the virus can only be transmitted through bodily fluids, most likely through blood to blood contact or unprotected sexual intercourse with an infected individual.

HIV and AIDS: A Personal Consideration of the Principle of Employer Interest

Julian Hussey

Associate of The Industrial Society[1] and freelance consultant

Where is the bottom line?

'Employers are only interested in the bottom line. So to argue successfully for employer action on any new issue you must make yours a financial argument.'

I have heard this theory of employer motivation, or less direct versions of it, used repeatedly by campaigners for employee training and development, for equal opportunities (and their more anonymous cousin, managing diversity), and now for action on HIV and AIDS. But I question its accuracy. If all the important decisions in society today were economic they would be more straightforward than experience tells us they are. Management training quoting Herzberg's theories of motivation – which rate responsibility and job satisfaction as higher motivators than remuneration – would be redundant.[2] Sales training that emphasizes quality, personality and client need over price would fail consistently. And the advertising industry could slim down its activities to the production of monthly updated price-lists of all available goods.

For most employers the real bottom line is to do what they do as well as possible. Doing it well means staying in business or avoiding rate-capping or a public enquiry

and these are certainly economic concerns. But if economic success becomes the overriding objective it often becomes unobtainable: it is objectives like making quality motor cars people want, providing quality and choice people want, and responding to issues people really care about that have brought economic success to Land Rover, Waterstones and The Body Shop International.

Appointing on principle

These three companies share the not-so-privileged information that you are only as good as your employees make you. And that if you want the best possible job done, you need the best possible people in the jobs. For a while, as manager of a project promoting equal opportunities practice and positive action, I thought that the definition of 'best' was becoming less subjective over the years. Now I'm not so sure.

For while, on one level, the equal opportunities interpretation of recruitment and selection sought to emphasize its science and not its art, on another level it invited a more detailed consideration of what employers really sought to achieve by their recruitment, management and leadership styles. Many of the challenges made by workforces to some of the assertions of equal opportunities trainers like myself were actually clues to both the real nature of employer cultures and the attitudinal obstacles that managers and employees were prepared to promulgate in direct opposition to company line.

Racism and sexism are still encountered daily in workforces across the country. Employers who deny that are naive. But employers who have recognized the dangers of discrimination and harassment, and responded to them with policies and procedures and training, have given their workers some leadership on the issue and the chance to flag up their problems. In practice it is the leadership that is crucial in bringing about change to organizational culture: but failure to carry that leadership through all managers and supervisors can make a mockery of any policy. Unfortunately, the 'best' managers and supervisors recruited for the job may be better at some aspects of that job than others. Perhaps managers who think they can act out of prejudice should not have been appointed in the first place.

Managing cultures

What even the most bigoted manager or worker must contend with in the UK is that racism and sexism in employment have been legislated against. The quantity and quality of employer action in these areas, compared with others that fall outside UK anti-discrimination law (like disability and sexual orientation), is surely not coincidental. Does the law ensure more policies? Certainly the Codes of Practice issued by the Commission for Racial Equality and the Equal Opportunities Commission as guidelines for responding to the law have had great though not universal influence. Does the law ensure more employer action? If publicity around successful prosecution of the law continues, and the laws themselves

remain on the statute book more companies will accept their responsibilities and see the advantages of changing work cultures. But has the action to date really achieved anything? Many individuals would answer a clear 'yes', while others will have seen no change, and some may have suffered different humiliations because of unchallenged reactions to change from the media and their colleagues. Even the most positive changes to workplace cultures are sometimes so necessarily slow that we must make very long-term comparisons to detect them.

When the leadership says 'We shall not discriminate on the grounds of HIV or AIDS' have they devised a response to the objections their employees might raise? Can they differentiate between discrimination based on fear and discrimination based on prejudice? Do they realize that they are, in effect, attempting to legislate against anti-gay prejudice without having any idea of the extent of that prejudice amongst their managers, supervisors and workers? And without any specific support from the UK legislature.

Many employers have considered all of these questions, but there remains a number content to see the job only half done, and a greater number still who are happy to refrain from any action at all on HIV and AIDS. Only those with the strongest convictions can send the strongest messages. In an organization where policy is not adopted will-nilly, employees are more likely to understand the seriousness of their leaders' intent. But will that change only their actions or will it also challenge some of their beliefs and attitudes? Organizations that really want to take their cultures in hand and manage them need to know their starting point and have clear goals.

Training for change

I recently undertook a programme of training for a large company keen to see its new HIV and AIDS policy communicated effectively to the whole workforce. Sixty-four people were trained over a three-week period with the objective that they should understand the company's decision to adopt and implement the policy so that they should be able to communicate this and its implications to their colleagues. Most of those trained were not managers or supervisors but had some nominal responsibility for training in addition to their other roles. Most were sent on the courses rather than volunteering. I took the opportunity to survey their views on six statements, both before and after the training. The results *after* training are shown in Table 1.

These show that the majority could see some value in HIV and AIDS information: both before and after the course, 94 per cent agreed that 'learning about HIV and AIDS was necessary to people's health and safety at work'. Interestingly, the one area where there was a great divergence

of views (the issue of safer sex information in the workplace) was the area most influenced by the training: those agreeing that HIV and AIDS information in the workplace should include guidance on safer sex increased from 44 per cent before the course to 63 per cent after the training.

There was agreement by 88 per cent of the participants that most people still do not understand the basic facts about HIV and AIDS. And 95 per cent agreed that employers need to address the issues about HIV and AIDS by developing or reviewing their policies and procedures. But many people expressed concerns about their next task: to brief staff teams who they feared would respond negatively because of anti-gay prejudice. As long as HIV and AIDS continue to affect a disproportionate number of male homosexuals in the UK population the issues of anti-gay prejudice and HIV/AIDS discrimination remain inextricably linked. None of my trainees knew of any openly

Table 1
Survey of 64 delegates selected for HIV/AIDS training by the personnel department of a large company

	Agree	Disagree	Don't know
Learning about HIV and AIDS is necessary to people's health and safety at work	94%	6%	
HIV and AIDS training should be recognized as developing transferable skills for staff at various levels.	77%	17%	6%
HIV and AIDS information in the workplace should include guidance on safer sex.	63%	36%	1%
Most people still don't understand the basic facts about HIV and how it can be transmitted.	88%	11%	1%
Employers need to address the issues surrounding HIV and AIDS by developing or reviewing their policies and procedures.	95%	5%	
A workforce informed about HIV and AIDS may be more understanding when faced with illnesses of all kinds.	90%	9%	1%

gay or lesbian employees in the organization (in a workforce of over 4,000); in fact the prospect of anyone coming out at work was so unlikely it was laughable.

Good practice means action

Legislation on employment and social discrimination due to disability may ultimately be the UK's way of equalizing the rights of disabled people and may protect people with HIV and AIDS from discrimination on grounds of their medical condition. Employers here might then redouble their efforts to make policy and train and grow appropriate organizational cultures. But similar legislation enshrining the rights of homosexuals in Britain is likely to remain only a lobbyist's dream for a few years yet. In the meantime campaigners, health educators and employers have to get on with it without the support of specific legislation.

Campaigners for good employer practice on HIV and AIDS have learnt that established good practice in recruitment, ill health and welfare procedures, employee training and information, First Aid, and confidentiality provides the structure, the skills and habits required for the appropriate handling of this new disease. So, unlike the original equal opportunities campaigners, they can often find all the necessary mechanisms in place. But

whereas objections to equality of opportunity on grounds of sex and race can be met with straightforward appeals to common decency and even the law, objections to equal treatment for people affected by HIV and AIDS open up a can of worms that most employers would rather leave closed. But many employers have faced these problems head on and while the majority of those who are prepared to include sexual orientation in their equal opportunities policies are still in the public sector, we are witnessing the start of some exciting moves in the private sector.

The people who lead organizations have a responsibility to share their vision with all those they expect to help them achieve it. If the principled response of the Chief Executive is to condemn discrimination on the grounds of HIV and AIDS, race, sex, sexual orientation or disability, then the principled action of the executive must be to lead their workforce to do the same. Action and not lonely policies will convert a workforce. I am sure that all policy-makers hope that their principled efforts will open the door to raised awareness and appropriate action throughout the organization. But if that were really the case, exponents of good practice would not make such a fuss about the handful of examples we do have of companies and organizations where the policies and the culture experienced by the workers actually coincide.

Conclusion

A workplace culture cannot be imposed, but it can be worked for if you first establish what you want. The adoption of good practice and the appointment of good managers are vital steps towards implementing principled decisions. But condemning fear and prejudice without offering sound information and advice cannot change hearts or minds. In years to come more and more employers will find themselves tested by real cases of HIV and AIDS: only those that have taken their workforces' culture and level of information in hand will face that challenge with any confidence.

Those who do believe in challenging discrimination in their organizations must make their position public and thereby lead by example. Otherwise, the misguided efforts of those who fear HIV and AIDS to the extent that they will unnecessarily test their current and prospective employees for the virus will continue to grab headlines, and make the public wonder 'Why not?' Real progress in the UK has been made over the last ten years: you no longer hear repeated calls for AIDS to be made a notifiable disease; public services are widely offered within anti-discrimination frameworks; and information is available to anyone with the initiative to ask for it. Every employer and every service provider that takes informed and positive action on HIV and AIDS helps to cement the building blocks of change that others have struggled to put in place. So we must encourage employers to legislate for themselves, to create the cultures they want, and to do it not to avoid prosecution or to save money, but as a matter of principle. That is the sort of commitment that lasts.

1 The Industrial Society is the UK's foremost independent training organization, promoting good practice at work and the development of the individual.

2 F. Herzberg, The Harvard Business Review, January–February 1968.

AIDS in Africa: Signs of Hope from the Workplace

Glen Williams

Series Editor, *Strategies for Hope*, ACTIONAID, London, England

Dr Sunanda Ray

Department of Community Medicine, University of Zimbabwe

The widespread prevalence of HIV and AIDS in sub-Saharan Africa will have a significant impact on European financial institutions and companies investing or operating directly in the region. Yet there is no justification for pessimism, defeatism or despair. Investment now in AIDS education programmes in the workplace could help to curb the spread of HIV and reduce the impact of the AIDS pandemic on the health of the working population and on economic productivity.[1]

Zimbabwe, where about 15 per cent of the working population is estimated to be infected with HIV,[2] is only one African country where AIDS has profound implications for all sectors of the economy. A number of workplace-based AIDS education programmes in Zimbabwe, however, have been remarkably successful. In a wide variety of situations, such programmes have succeeded in making information about HIV and AIDS widely available, in encouraging informed, supportive attitudes towards co-workers infected with HIV, and in promoting changes in sexual attitudes and behaviour. The educational strategies used in these programmes can be adapted and applied to many different types of workplaces, not only in sub-Saharan Africa, but also in parts of the industralized world. This chapter describes and analyses some of the most successful of these programmes, and examines key policy issues associated with HIV/AIDS and employment.

AIDS and the workplace

The effects of HIV and AIDS on the workplace in Zimbabwe are already apparent. Growing numbers of employees are taking more sick leave because of AIDS-related illnesses. Some companies are also starting to observe sharp increases in the mortality rates of their employees. The Anglo American Corporation – with over 15,000 employees working in fields as diverse as mining, agriculture, forestry, manufacturing industry and financial services – saw deaths in service increase by 183 per cent between 1987 and 1992.[3] Medical insurance, life assurance and pension funds are also affected by HIV and AIDS. The indirect effects of the pandemic on the workplace are also starting to be felt, as growing numbers of employees take days off to attend the funerals of colleagues and family members, or to nurse sick relatives.

Despite the current harsh economic climate and massive retrenchments in some industries, employers in Zimbabwe are generally retaining workers known or believed to be HIV-positive, as long as they are able to perform their duties. In many firms, employees who are no longer well enough to carry out their normal jobs are often placed on light duties. Inevitably, however, the number of light duty jobs is limited, and growing numbers of workers with AIDS are being retired on health grounds.

In the second half of the 1990s, AIDS will claim the lives of many more of Zimbabwe's most highly trained and productive professional people. Equally serious will be the loss of thousands of skilled and semi-skilled workers. Recruiting and training staff to replace all those lost to AIDS will be both time-consuming and costly. Employers also face the prospect of higher medical costs and increased contributions to medical aid societies. AIDS is therefore a real threat to the productivity – and even the survival – of many local companies and businesses. European financial institutions and companies investing or operating directly in Zimbabwe – and in many other countries of sub-Saharan Africa – will also be affected by the social and economic consequences of the AIDS pandemic.

Employers' responses

Most employers in Zimbabwe have not yet developed an effective response to the AIDS pandemic. Few workplaces even have an AIDS poster on display. Some Zimbabwean companies, however, have developed imaginative and effective workplace-based AIDS education programmes, which are impressive by any standards.

David Whitehead Textiles (a member of the Lonrho Group), with a workforce of 4,500 at its factories in the towns of Kadoma, Chegutu and Gweru, has led the way with an innovative AIDS education programme. In 1989 the company trained all 64 Health and Safety representatives in HIV/AIDS awareness and communication skills, produced 20,000 copies of a comic book *AIDS: Towards Greater Understanding*, and began providing free condoms to employees. The company also funded a theatre group which performed an AIDS play in factory canteens, theatres and school halls. The programme appears to have influenced the sexual behaviour of many members of the workforce, evidenced by a sharp fall in sexually transmitted diseases (STDs) treated at workplace clinics. At the Kadoma factory, for example, the number of STD cases fell by 53 per cent between 1989 and 1992. At the Chegutu factory the fall was even greater: 75 per cent during the same period.

Rio Tinto Zimbabwe, with 3,500 employees, began its AIDS programme in 1990. The first step was to train volunteers who later established AIDS Action Groups, which are responsible for planning and implementing AIDS educational activities at the workplace and the surrounding communities. Members of the Groups also distribute free condoms at their places of work, and ensure that condoms are available free of charge in changing rooms and at bars, beerhalls and social clubs on company premises. The numbers of condoms distributed at the company's three mines and a nickel refinery increased dramatically – by an average of 63 per cent between 1990 and 1992 (see Figure 1).

The number of STD cases treated at the company's four clinics fell dramatically during the same period, the declines ranging between 47 per cent and 78 per cent (see Figure 2), although the numbers of employees remained static.

Eastern Highlands Tea Estates, which employs about 3,000 men and women on a tea and coffee plantation near the Mozambican border, trained 48 supervi-

Figure 1
Condoms distributed by Rio Tinto Zimbabwe clinics 1990–1992
Source: Rio Tinto Zimbabwe Limited

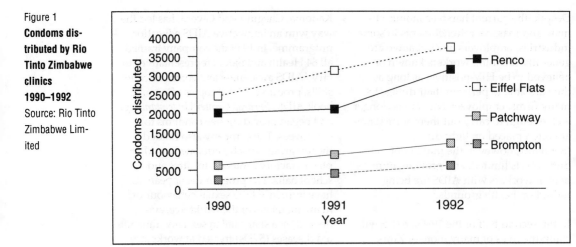

sors, foremen and other influential members of the workforce as AIDS educators in 1991. The company also made free condoms (supplied by the National Family Planning Council) available at offices, beerhalls and clinics. At the same time, 'campfire counselling' meetings organized by the company's industrial relations officer and community leaders gave people the chance to talk more openly about sexual behaviour, family planning, STDs and AIDS. The programme appears to have had a marked effect on sexual behaviour. During the first half of 1993 company clinics treated exactly one hundred STD patients, compared with 243 during the same period in 1991 – a fall of 59 per cent.

Trade unions

The Zimbabwe Congress of Trade Unions (ZCTU) consists of 38 affiliated unions with a combined membership of about 250,000. The ZCTU's AIDS programme focuses mainly on AIDS information and awareness, and on workplace-related human rights issues. It is also concerned about occupational exposure to HIV infection, particularly among health workers.

The ZCTU has endorsed the policy guidelines of the World Health Organization (WHO) and the International Labour Office (ILO) on HIV/AIDS in the workplace, and has proposed that they become legislation. At special AIDS workshops in 1989 and 1991, the ZCTU resolved to stand firm against compulsory HIV testing, breaches of medical confidentiality, the dismissal of HIV-positive workers, and discrimination against HIV-positive workers with regard to promotion, pensions, medical insurance and other employment-related benefits.

The ZCTU has developed its own AIDS training materials, and in March 1993 began a series of four-day training workshops for National Health and Safety Officers, who will train up to 700 Health and Safety representatives at branch and shopfloor level. These in turn will train groups of cadres selected by other union members from the shopfloor. By the end of 1994, the ZCTU expects to have trained several thousand Health and Safety cadres in basic AIDS awareness, workplace-related human rights issues, and how to mobilize workers to combat the spread of HIV and AIDS.

The training workshops focus especially on gender issues and their relevance to the spread of HIV infection. Women trade unionists are actively involved, and are beginning to see themselves in a better position than other women to negotiate safer sex. The ZCTU uses participatory training methods including discussions, drama, role-playing, films and videos, and emphasizes the use of plain, straightforward language and colloquial expressions when discussing HIV/AIDS and sexuality.

The ZCTU is also involved in discussions with the Ministry of Health and the Employers' Confederation of Zimbabwe to define a code of conduct on HIV/AIDS in the workplace. These discussions began after some companies began pre-employment HIV screening, to which the Ministry of Health is strongly opposed. Individual unions are also negotiating for the inclusion of HIV-related clauses into their collective bargaining agreements with employers. The Agricultural and Plantation Workers Union, for example, has successfully negotiated a clause on the confidentiality of health information (including the results of HIV tests) in its agreement with employers.

Lessons from experience

Although the workplace AIDS education programmes described in this chapter are not typical of the situation in Zimbabwe as a whole, they – and similar successful initiatives elsewhere in Zimbabwe – do offer a vision of hope for the future. The success of these programmes is due to a number of common factors, which can be summarized as follows:

Management commitment: For any workplace AIDS education programme to succeed, strong backing from senior management is essential. In order to be motivated to provide such backing, however, management must first be convinced that the AIDS pandemic poses a real threat to the output and productivity of their operations, for example through low employee morale, lost working time through increased sick leave and accidents, damage to machinery and increased costs of employee benefits.

Workforce participation: Workers need to be actively involved in the design and day-to-day implementation of programmes, rather than being passive participants in occasional lunch-time lectures.

Continuity: Workplace programmes require a continuous effort over a long period of time; 'one-off' or occasional events are insufficient.

Appropriate 'messages': Health 'messages' need to be culturally sensitive, socially acceptable and realistic, leaving

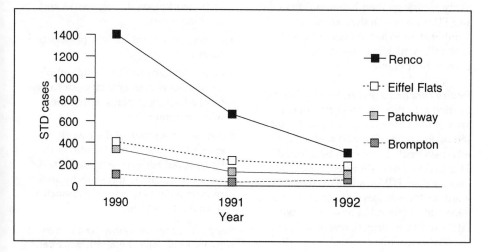

Figure 2
STDs treated at Rio Tinto Zimbabwe clinics 1990–1992
Source: Rio Tinto Zimbabwe Limited

the individual to make an informed choice. The two main themes of successful workplace AIDS programmes in Zimbabwe are: first, that mutual faithfulness between two uninfected partners is the most effective way of preventing the spread of HIV and other STDs; second, that the correct use of condoms, with every act of sexual intercourse, can provide a very high level of protection against HIV infection.

Condom availability: Free, readily available condoms are vital to the success of workplace AIDS education programmes. They are essential for people who have more than one sexual partner, and also for couples where at least one partner is HIV-positive.

STD control: Linking AIDS education to STD control has three main advantages. First, since the presence of an STD increases the likelihood of HIV transmission, treating people for STDs will, of itself, help to reduce the spread of HIV. Second, changes in the prevalence of STDs can also provide useful feedback on the effectiveness of HIV/AIDS programmes in changing sexual behaviour. Third, many people practising high-risk sexual behaviour have already experienced an STD, and wish to avoid becoming re-infected. They are often more likely to change their behaviour to avoid an STD with which they are already familiar than to avoid being infected with HIV, which may be outside their personal experience.

Health care and support: HIV/AIDS prevention activities are most effective in association with medical care and counselling for people infected with HIV, or who believe themselves to be infected. This makes it easier for people who suspect they are HIV-positive to come forward for the services and support they need and – if found to be infected with HIV – to live informed, responsible and socially useful lives.

Supportive policies: The most successful workplace AIDS programmes operate in an environment in which the basic human rights of HIV-positive employees are respected. These rights include, for example, continuation of employment, confidentiality of medical information, and non-discrimination in relation to benefits such as medical care and pensions. Most employers in Zimbabwe, however, have yet to formulate explicit, comprehensive policy statements on the rights of HIV-positive employees.

Peer education: The most effective AIDS educators at the workplace are members of the workforce who are trained to provide their colleagues with basic information about HIV and AIDS. With only a limited amount of basic training, 'peer educators' can be remarkably successful in providing basic information, in promoting safer sexual behaviour, and in encouraging supportive attitudes towards people infected with HIV. The effectiveness of peer educators depends to a large extent, however, on the support they receive from their employers. They need, for example:

- time off work to attend training courses, workshops and follow-up meetings with trainers and other peer educators;
- the opportunity to talk about HIV and AIDS with individuals or small groups at the workplace, during breaks and working hours;
- stationery to print leaflets, posters and other materials;
- help with transport to attend out-of-town meetings, to give talks, or to perform educational plays within the wider community;
- official recognition of their work, for example, in the form of T-shirts or badges, publicity in company newsletters or magazines, and visits by senior management to special events such as drama productions.

Support of this kind does cost money. It is likely to be repaid many times over, however, by helping to prevent high rates of HIV infection and the resulting negative consequences for the output and productivity of companies.

Policy issues

The AIDS pandemic raises a host of issues concerning workplace policies and employment-related benefits. Like most other countries, Zimbabwe has no laws specifically covering issues such as HIV screening, confidentiality of medical information, medical insurance and pensions for HIV-positive employees. However, the Zimbabwe Government endorses the policies recommended by the WHO and the ILO.[4]

HIV screening and testing: The extent to which HIV screening takes place at the workplace in Zimbabwe is unclear. In March 1990, a survey of senior managers from ninety four companies found that 41 per cent thought pre-employment HIV screening was justified, and 22 per cent had already initiated screening of all or some job applicants, or of current employees.[5] The Minister of Health and Child Welfare has since declared that, in the Government's view, HIV screening cannot be justified on moral and practical grounds, and should not be carried out. The Employers' Confederation of Zimbabwe and the Confederation of Zimbabwe Industries have also announced their opposition to HIV screening.

Some of Zimbabwe's largest companies, such as Delta Corporation, have declared themselves opposed to HIV testing of job applicants or employees, except for clearly defined medical reasons or if required for life assurance purposes.[6] Some companies, however, carry out HIV testing of job applicants and employees, with or without the knowledge of the persons concerned, as part of the process of selection for employment, training or promotion. Apart from the questionable ethics of testing people for HIV without their knowledge or consent, this practice is expensive – about US$10 per test – and generally of little or no practical value to employers.

A negative test, on the one hand, does not guarantee that a person will not become HIV-positive at some time in the future. A positive test result, on the other hand, will not necessarily help the employer decide whether or not to hire or promote a particular individual. Graduate employees – the main candidates for further training and promotion – are generally on the look-out for better employment opportunities, and normally stay with the same company for only a few years. An HIV-positive person who is otherwise healthy may be able to work normally for five to ten years, by which time the company's investment in recruiting and training him or her will have paid off.

Confidentiality: Most people with HIV do not wish their workmates and employers to know about their HIV status, and with good reason. Not only in Zimbabwe, but in many other countries, fear of rejection by their workmates and of discrimination by their employers prevents many people with HIV from coming forward for the information, care and support they need.

In Zimbabwe, where the transmission of HIV among adults is almost entirely heterosexual, negative attitudes towards HIV-positive workmates or employees are usually based on misconceptions about how HIV is transmitted. The risk of passing on HIV to co-workers at the workplace is either non-existent or extremely small. The virus is not passed on through shared equipment, tools, furniture, toilet and bathroom facilities, or cooking and eating utensils. Nor is it transmitted by shaking hands, through the air or by mosquitoes. There is therefore no reason, in virtually all workplace situations, why colleagues, supervisors, line managers or personnel officers should know a person's HIV status.

Some employers in Zimbabwe have endorsed the policy recommended by the WHO and the ILO that the confidentiality of all medical information, including employees' HIV status, must be maintained. Many also observe this policy in practice. Yet breaches of medical confidentiality, especially the results of HIV testing, do occur. In some companies, personnel officers and timekeepers check employees' clinic cards, which contain confidential medical information. Some companies require that doctors record the diagnosis on their employees' sick leave forms, although this practice is condemned by the Ministry of Health and the Zimbabwe Medical Association.

The responsibility for maintaining medical confidentiality rests mainly with health professionals, who are bound by codes of practice that include the principle of confidentiality. Most health professionals in Zimbabwe appear to be holding the line on confidentiality where HIV testing is concerned. They are likely, however, to come under increasing pressure from senior management to divulge the HIV status of particular individuals, especially if they themselves are employed directly by the company.

In order to minimize the possibility of a breach of medical confidentiality, the Ministry of Health and Child Welfare advocates the principle of informed consent. In other words, health personnel should not pass on sensitive medical information – including an employee's HIV status – to any other person without the employee's agreement. This principle aims to ensure that the number of people at the workplace who have access to sensitive medical information is kept to an absolute minimum, thus protecting the right of the individual to confidentiality, and helping to maintain a harmonious and productive working environment.

Medical insurance: Most medical insurance policies are funded by equal contributions from employers and employees. About 600,000 people in Zimbabwe are members of a medical aid society. The largest, CIMAS, has a membership of 270,000. CIMAS has established an AIDS Research Unit to determine the cost of claims from its members being treated for AIDS-related illnesses, and to forecast the likely impact of the AIDS epidemic on the finances of the organization as a whole.

CIMAS estimates that the average cost of treating a person with AIDS in hospital during the last eighteen months of life is about US$580, with 60 per cent of costs occurring in the last two months.[7] During 1992, CIMAS spent approximately US$423,530 on hospital treatment for 734 patients with AIDS-related illnesses. In view of the rapidly escalating numbers of people with AIDS being treated in hospital, CIMAS expects its AIDS-related expenditure to exceed US$2.8 million per year by 1996.[8] Without changes in its policies, CIMAS cannot afford to meet these costs.

CIMAS rejects discrimination against patients with AIDS as a means of overcoming this problem, and is currently examining five main policy options to cope with the impact of AIDS:

1. Limiting medical aid to cover eighteen days hospital treatment per membership year.
2. Introducing more effective, standardized treatment regimens as early as possible after HIV diagnosis, especially treatment for TB and STDs.
3. Establishing hospices run by nurses and visited regularly by doctors.
4. Expanding the existing 24-hour nursing home-care scheme, which operates at only one sixth of the cost of hospital-based care.
5. Providing each terminally ill patient with a lump sum and allowing them to choose between hospital care, hospice, home nursing or family care.

Theoretically, CIMAS and other medical

aid societies could also increase their premiums to meet increases in costs due to AIDS, but Richard Hore, Chief Executive of CIMAS, rejects this option:

'The premiums are already quite high, and to increase them further would make medical aid something available only to the very rich, which we don't want.'[9]

Life assurance: Some employers provide life assurance as part of a package of social security benefits to senior staff. The Government of Zimbabwe permits HIV screening of people wishing to take out life assurance policies for US$11,765 or more, or from anyone whose medical history indicates a likelihood of HIV infection. If the result of the test is positive or the person refuses to undergo the test, insurance cover is denied.

Pension funds: Pension funds operate quite differently from life assurance or medical insurance funds, but they are also affected by the AIDS epidemic. A number of employers, fearing that a sharp rise in AIDS-related deaths will over-stretch the resources of their pension funds, have adopted discriminatory measures against new employees found to be HIV-positive. A few companies now use the results of HIV screening to exclude new HIV-positive employees from joining their pension funds. Some other companies allow new HIV-positive employees to join, but reduce the benefits to which they are entitled.

These discriminatory measures, however, are neither rational nor appropriate to the circumstances. The primary purpose of a pension fund is to provide a regular income to ex-employees and their families in old age or ill health. In addition, many funds also pay out a lump sum upon retirement or death in service. The AIDS epidemic has caused an increase in the numbers of ill-health retirements or deaths in service, leading to greater lump sum payments, which in turn could threaten the viability of some pension funds. In order to maintain a healthy balance between lump sums and regular payments, some employers have changed the rules of their pension funds to reduce the size of the lump sums payable on ill-health retirement or death in service. A few have also increased the amount of regular pension payments in order to compensate. These changes apply to all members of the pension funds concerned, regardless of their HIV status.

There is now a growing realization among employers, pension fund managers and trustees in Zimbabwe that the direct effects of AIDS on pension funds are manageable, without the need for discrimination against HIV-positive employees. The level of contributions by members and their employers need not necessarily be affected by the epidemic. Simon Gilliat, an actuary whose firm advises many pension funds in Zimbabwe, estimates that the effect of AIDS on total contributions will be either an increase – or perhaps even a decrease – of no more than 2 per cent, depending on the type of pension scheme involved.[10]

It is clear that pension funds will continue to evolve in response to the AIDS epidemic. In the past, for example, many funds insured regular pension payments by means of a capital payment to an insurance company on the retirement or death of each individual member. Many people with AIDS, however, die soon after ill-health retirement, and this is often followed by the death of their spouse. This results in un-utilized capital, which remains with the insurance company, not the pension fund. Growing numbers of pension funds are now avoiding this problem by paying pensions directly from their own resources, rather than through an insurance company.

Although the direct effects of the AIDS epidemic on pension funds are manageable, the indirect effects may be damaging. With the domestic economy in a state of recession and inflation eroding the value of capital, it is already very difficult for pension fund managers to invest their assets at a decent rate of return. Given that AIDS may have a negative impact on the productivity of the Zimbabwean economy, pension fund managers may find it even more difficult in future to invest their assets at a return higher than inflation. This would further reduce their capacity to provide their members with a level of income sufficient to support either themselves or their dependents after retirement or death in service.

The future

During the 1990s and well into the next century, the AIDS pandemic will have a profound impact on the workplace, not only in Zimbabwe but in many other countries throughout the world. In the immediate future, companies will see the numbers of AIDS deaths among their employees continue to rise because of the high prevalence of HIV infection within the working population.

There is nothing inevitable, however, about the apparently relentless advance of the pandemic. AIDS is preventable, mainly through changes in sexual attitudes and behaviour. In Zimbabwe several workplace programmes, including those described in this chapter, have been successful in promoting safer sexual behaviour and in encouraging more supportive attitudes towards people infected with HIV. The educational strategies used in these programmes can be employed in many different kinds of workplaces, not only in sub-Saharan Africa but also in other regions of the developing world. They are also relevant to various types of workplaces in Europe and other parts of the industrialized world.

The underlying reasons for the spread of HIV and AIDS in Zimbabwe – as in other countries – are closely related to the nation's political, social and economic development. Yet the complex nature of the AIDS pandemic should not be a cause for fatalism, confusion or inaction. There is a tremendous amount that can be done, by all sections of society, to prevent the further spread of HIV and to cope with the effects of AIDS on individuals, families and communities. The workplace can – and must – play a frontline role in promoting safer sexual behaviour, and in creating a social environment in which people with HIV and AIDS can live and work without fear of discrimination.

1 This chapter is based on the book *Work Against AIDS: Workplace-based AIDS Initiatives in Zimbabwe*, by Glen Williams and Sunanda Ray, published by ACTIONAID, London, 1993; available from TALC, P.O. Box 49, St Albans AL1 4AX, UK.

2 Helen Jackson, *AIDS: Action Now*. AIDS Counselling Trust and the School of Social Work, second edition, 1992.

3 A.C. Devlin, Group Personnel Manager, Anglo American Corporation Services Ltd, personal communication, January 1993.

4 World Health Organization/International Labour Office/League of Red Cross and Red Crescent Societies, *Guidelines on AIDS and First Aid in the Workplace*, WHO AIDS Series No. 7, 1990.

5 H. Jackson, M. Pitts, 'Company policy on AIDS in Zimbabwe', *Journal of Social Development in Africa*, 6, 2, pp. 53–70, 1991.

6 'Zimbabwe's Delta Corp. sets its face against testing', *AIDS Analysis Africa*, May/June 1992.

7 R. Hore, 'Impact of Aids on direct health care costs: Zimbabwe', unpublished paper, November 1992.

8 R. Hore, personal communication, May 1993.

9 *Ibid.*

10 *Focus*, Harare, October 1992.

One Employer's Approach to Employee Education

Sue Belgrave

General Manager of Company Culture, The Body Shop International PLC, Littlehampton, England

The Body Shop International PLC is a company which manufactures skin- and haircare products and retails them in more than 1,000 shops in 45 countries around the world. Our philosophy is to take out no more than we put back and to leave the world a better place. We are totally opposed to the use of animals for testing of cosmetics, are active in our determination to reduce our environmental impact and are looking to expand our Fair Trade relationships with the majority world.

Why the Body Shop is concerned about HIV and AIDS

HIV/AIDS is one of the most alarming illnesses facing the world, alarming because the virus is so mutable, because there is no cure and because prejudice and ignorance stand in the way of prevention.

The Body Shop is a company committed to the education and empowerment of our employees and to the creation of active citizens in the workplace. As such, we are well placed to provide information to our employees on a wide range of issues.

We are committed to a high standard of care for our employees. On a practical level, we provide a workplace nursery and family care programme and have a full-time counsellor and occupational health advisor. We also offer a flexible benefits package including a pension scheme and permanent health insurance. We are a family company – we try to be like a family in the way we relate to each other, care for each other and celebrate together.

The Body Shop is also a company with a young workforce and young customers, many of whom we can assume are sexually active and therefore potentially at risk of HIV infection. Quite simply, we are concerned for the health of our employees.

And we are aware that sooner or later, in one way or another, our lives will be affected by HIV and AIDS both in a personal and corporate sense. To a company with a large workforce such as ours the social and economic risks were obvious. Therefore, rather than face this situation in fearful ignorance, in 1991 we decided to launch an awareness campaign.

The immediate aims were:

- to give our employees the information and understanding to protect themselves and their families;

- to create an atmosphere in which people would feel safe to ask questions and within which tolerance, sympathy and support could grow;
- to provide some corporate protection for The Body Shop.

What was less obvious was how to do it

We started at the top and the response from the Board of The Body Shop was one of total support. The only question was: why hadn't we done something sooner?

From the beginning we wanted to be sure that HIV and AIDS was seen in the context of our overall approach to caring for our employees and not as an isolated issue. We therefore sought out a general health education consultant with special expertise in HIV/AIDS to advise us throughout our programme. In the event, during our awareness sessions conversation frequently moved into other areas of concern unrelated to AIDS and it was extremely useful to be able to answer those questions as they arose.

Two steps were then taken:

- In March 1992 we issued a general questionnaire to all our employees with the aim of establishing the level of understanding of a number of health topics, identifying areas of concern across the company and raising the profile of health as an issue within the company.
- At the same time we started work on our HIV/AIDS policy, believing it was essential to make our position clear on a number of key issues – rejection of compulsory testing, support of confidentiality – before starting work on our awareness campaign. We wanted to be absolutely sure that our employees felt confident about where they stood in relation to HIV/AIDS before we ran the awareness sessions.

The Body Shop HIV/AIDS policy

We arrived at following policy, which was issued to all staff:

- We recognize that HIV and AIDS constitute a new and still misunderstood threat to health.
- We will provide a programme of education and training for all employees that will help them to safeguard their own health and that of their families and friends.
- Through this programme, we aim to create an atmosphere of understanding in which anyone who is HIV-positive or has an AIDS-related illness will feel free to come forward in the knowledge that they will meet with care and sympathy and that appropriate support will be offered.
- There is no obligation on any member of staff to disclose their HIV status, but if disclosure is made that information will be treated in strict confidence unless the individual wishes otherwise.
- No member of staff will be dismissed or redeployed because they are HIV-positive and/or have an AIDS-related illness, unless they request it or medical advice suggests it is in their best interests.
- Disclosure of confidential information relating to HIV status or continued discrimination of any kind against an employee who is HIV-positive or who has an AIDS-related illness will lead to dismissal.
- The Body Shop is determined to lead by example. We will campaign internally to dispel the myths that are contributing to the continuing escalation of the AIDS epidemic and to improve conditions for those who are part of the epidemic.

The awareness programme

With the policy in place we were able to move to the next phase – the awareness programme.

HIV/AIDS: the facts

We began with a programme for heads of departments and general managers because we wanted them to feel comfortable about handling any questions that might arise from the process. The programme established the pattern eventually used for the whole company: namely, the consultant asked participants for information in three areas:

- 'Things which you know to be true about HIV/AIDS'
- 'Things which you know to be untrue'
- 'Things which you are not sure about'

This format proved very non-threatening, allowed areas of uncertainty to be easily identified and allowed plenty of opportunity for our consultant to go through the basic facts.

The initial session, which lasted for two hours and which was well attended (including some Board members), was followed at a later date by role-play allowing the same individuals to explore hypothetical workplace situations in a safe environment. While our HIV/AIDS policy seemed straightforward enough in writing, it was only in pursuing the detail that we really came to understand the difficulties we might face.

We then moved on to offer two-hour sessions to all staff at head office and offices/company shops in London (a total of 700 employees). We offered all employees the choice of attending sessions with or without their colleagues and of attending single sex groups. Most people chose to attend with their work colleagues which reassured us that, generally speaking, people felt comfortable in their working environments. In only one or two areas, which were predominantly male, did the few female employees choose to join a single sex group.

Attendance at the sessions was compulsory. We took this decision in order to ensure that those who attended did not feel in any way a focus for attention because they had shown interest, and because it attached a high level of importance to the sessions. There was some resistance in the early days – 'it's not relevant', 'I don't want to know '– but curiosity, aided by the extremely favourable response, got the better of most of those who were initially reluctant.

For many it was the first opportunity to understand not just how HIV works, but what a virus is and how viruses work, what blood is and what it does. A chance to get to grips with what immunity means, what infection means and what a vaccination does. And how terrifying HIV must seem if you really have no understanding of what it might be.

The exercise served to highlight many of the inadequacies of our science education system. It was rewarding to see confidence growing within the groups as individuals came to understand the vulnerability of HIV; that you really can *not* catch it from toilet seats; that using a condom does protect you; and that masturbation can be good for both of you. We talked together in ways in which we had never talked before and that too was good.

As confidence grew so too did anger at what people came to see as prejudiced, inaccurate and just plain wrong reporting of AIDS in the media.

Seeing the confidence that came from having created a situation in which individuals could ask all the questions that they had ever wanted to ask was an absolute affirmation of the costly (both in terms of time and money) decision to use a trainer, a person, not leaflets or a video. It was the human contact and the shared feelings which grew within the groups that made the difference.

At the end of the training sessions, each participant was asked to complete an evaluation form. Comments were constructive and positive: 'Perhaps managers need to be more aware of company policy and to be counselled on how to deal with an HIV situation when confronted', 'Thought the presentation was very clear. Opened lots of new avenues of thought!'

(As back-up to the sessions we made the National AIDS Helpline number and additional leaflets available around the company.)

In all, it took nearly four months to complete the groups at head office.

The emotional impact

At that point we moved to the next phase of the programme which was to explore the emotional aspects of HIV. Understanding HIV/AIDS is not just about the facts of the infection: the prejudice surrounding it is almost as significant. To have ignored that aspect would have been to tell only half the story.

For the next phase, with funding from the Healthcare Foundation,[1] we commissioned an interactive theatre workshop from Interactors, a company specializing in the field of HIV/AIDS awareness that had already created a workshop for young people on this subject. We asked them to conceive a programme which would specifically explore the workplace issues – dismissal, confidentiality, ignorance, prejudice – and thus allow us to explore the limitations of our own company policy.

Interactors researched the programme for nearly three months, talking to employers, doctors, people with AIDS, people recently diagnosed and their families. The workshop they produced was unforgettable, and if anyone ever doubted the power of interactive theatre in the workplace all doubts would have evaporated at the first discreetly wiped-away tear: based around four characters, two of whom work in a canteen, fears around food preparation and HIV are

widespread; and one of them – a young woman married with two children – has just tested positive…The workshop develops according to the wishes of the audience via interventions solicited by the actors: 'Shall I tell her I'm HIV-positive?', 'How can I tell him?', 'Shall I tell my boss?', etc.

The opportunity to take part in the workshop was offered to anyone who was interested and more than met our objective of widening discussion away from the biological towards the social context of HIV/AIDS.

First aid

As a further step, we ensured that all First Aiders received updates on dealing with spillages of blood or other substances and that all First Aid boxes were equipped with aprons, gloves and masks for resuscitation.

Awareness nationwide

With a format in place, we then moved on to tackle the physically much harder problem of extending the same programme to our shops throughout in the UK.

We initially trained all business development managers – individuals with responsibility for groups of shops around the UK. This was followed by four features on HIV/AIDS delivered to all shop staff via our weekly communications video, BSTV. Using the same consultant, these dealt with the Body Shop policy, the facts of HIV/AIDS, First Aid and safer sex.

In 1994, we plan to take the full AIDS awareness programme to a further 550 staff at head office. In the meantime, we have actively encouraged shops to link with local expert organizations – a familiar process for Body Shops, nearly all of which have strong ties with their local community. (As part of our belief in personal development and in our responsibility 'to put something back', each BSI employee is entitled to spend half a day per month working on a community project. Projects range from working in a prison crèche, to making tea in a local drop-in centre, to dog walking and tree planting.)

Body Shop International PLC

Globally, we have 1,114 shops, trading in 45 countries and in 23 languages. Some of the initiatives undertaken to help prevent the spread of HIV/AIDS worldwide are as follows:

USA

In the USA, where we have 170 shops, we ran a major in-store campaign around the slogan 'respect and protect'. We ran window posters, provided information and linked up with the US Red Cross to provide detailed training for all shop staff. We linked with other mall users to maximize the use of trainers.

India

In India, where we have an active involvement in a Fair Trade project making footsie rollers and other massage aids, we have worked with local people to combat the disease. We targeted lorry drivers as potential carriers of the disease across the continent by providing condoms and information in tea houses and truck stops.

Nepal

In Nepal, in another Fair Trade project making paper from rags, water hyacinth and lokhta, HIV awareness slide shows were put on at which highly valued matches were given away with condoms.

Campaigning

As we evaluated the progress of our HIV/AIDS awareness programme our conclusions were so positive that we decided to try to share our experiences with other employers. In 1992 The Body Shop became a founder signatory to Companies act!, the business charter on HIV/AIDS. (This is a national initiative sponsored by the National AIDS Trust to encourage companies to address HIV/AIDS in the workplace.) We then collaborated with LWT (London Weekend Television) to put on a workshop for human resource managers from 100 major UK companies as part of our commitment to Companies act! and World AIDS Day 1992.[2]

We have also worked with the Terrence Higgins Trust on their training video – Positive Management. We have provided massage oils for the Ayrshire and Arran Health Authority for its innovative project on sexual health for young people. I have also spoken at conferences around the country and have been interviewed on numerous occasions.

In shops around the country community projects focusing on HIV and AIDS are given continuing support. In Bristol, for example, our shops have a relationship, now three years old, with the Aled Richards Trust, an HIV voluntary organization which provides support and companionship for those living with HIV and AIDS in the area. The Body Shop provides the oils for the massages offered to those using the Trust's services; and Body Shop staff offer care and friendship by making regular visits and providing transport for those in need.

The future?

At The Body Shop our commitment to this issue of HIV/AIDS awareness is long term. While people continue to die from the disease we need to keep our campaign alive. All new employees are offered the awareness programme, and as the understanding of HIV/AIDS increases we will arrange updates to avoid the onset of any complacency. We also use World AIDS Day (1 December) as part of our campaign. In 1993, our staff wore Red Ribbons, the symbol of AIDS awareness, and we wrapped our entire office building in a giant Red Ribbon in a warmly appreciated gesture of solidarity.

When we educate ourselves and our employees about AIDS we talk about saving lives

We talk about reducing uncertainty and fear

We talk about respect for the individual dignity of every employee

We talk about the nobility of work

We talk about doing the right thing...

Robert Goodale
American President, Finevest Foods Inc.

In our HIV/AIDS awareness programme we started to talk to each other in a new way. Our programme was and continues to be an expression of our commitment to our employees and to their families. It proved to be a great way for us to use our resources and the position of trust we hold with our employees 'to put something back'. We hope that in doing so we have started to change some attitudes, challenge some prejudices and answer some questions. But we wish – and *how* we wish, as the tragedy of AIDS continues to unfold with all its numbing, frightening, inevitability – that we did not have to do the job at all...

---

[1] The Healthcare Foundation is a charity set up with profits from sales of Mates condoms. Founder trustees included Richard Branson, Michael Grade and Anita Roddick.

[2] World AIDS Day is an annual day of observance designed to expand and strengthen the worldwide effort to stop the spread of HIV and AIDS. It is coordinated internationally by the World Health Organization's Global Programme on AIDS.

Wellcome's Positive Action in Response to HIV and AIDS

Dr Andrew Revell

The Wellcome Foundation Ltd, Beckenham, Kent, England

The most immediate challenge when a new disease emerges is to help those living with the condition. Wellcome has been at the forefront of viral research leading to the development of vaccines, and introduced the world's most effective anti-viral drug, acyclovir (Zovirax), for the management of herpes virus infections. When HIV was identified as the cause of AIDS in 1984, Wellcome was first to respond: within three years we brought out zidovudine (Retrovir/AZT) and with it much needed hope to people living with this disease. Our primary contribution to the fight against HIV and AIDS will remain in the field of research and development. We will continue to study ways of using zidovudine, either alone or in combination, to bring the maximum benefit to people affected by HIV. We are also committed to the discovery and development of new compounds against HIV. And to this end, Wellcome is currently spending some £1 million per week on HIV research. These are conventional steps for a company in Wellcome's position to take in response to the medical/scientific challenge of HIV and AIDS.

HIV, however, is by no means just a medical issue. Those of us who have been involved in the field for any length of time, especially those who have worked closely with people living with this disease, quickly come to realize that this virus raises a number of other non-medical issues: social and political issues, issues of human rights – issues which challenge all of us to examine our attitudes, beliefs and behaviour. We believe that the scale of this problem and the fundamental questions it poses demands that we all go beyond the cosy, the conventional and the obvious, and seek new and innovative ways of fighting this epidemic. Whether in the statutory, voluntary or private sectors, whether through the help of non-governmental organizations, aid agencies, pharmaceutical companies or individuals, we are all confronted with a global challenge that demands that we leave our preconceptions behind and work together to beat it.

Positive Action

For its part, Wellcome has gone beyond the traditional role and responsibilities of a pharmaceutical company and in 1992 launched an international programme of HIV education, care and community support called 'Positive Action'.

Positive Action is a global programme comprising a wide range of projects undertaken both internationally and nationally by Wellcome Companies around the world. In each case Wellcome seeks to join forces with a project partner with experience and expertise in the area being addressed. Clearly, Positive Action alone cannot provide a solution to the enormous problems we face. What it can do, and seeks to do, is to act as a pathfinder, showing the way towards new and innovative ways of meeting the challenges posed by HIV and AIDS.

The activities within Positive Action are grouped under five main initiatives, each focusing on different needs:

The HIV community support initiative

HIV and AIDS strikes hardest against those on the fringes of society, as well as the disempowered: for example drug users, gay men and people with poor socio-economic standing. Some governments have been slow to respond with the services required. In many, if not all, countries of the world it is the people living with HIV and AIDS themselves or the communities most affected that have responded most dramatically and effectively in providing the necessary prevention, care and support services.

Within this initiative, Wellcome aims to work with and support AIDS service organizations, self-help groups, counsellors and other community-based groups and services to help them build upon their success.

The children and young people initiative

This initiative is designed to help address two different challenges: first, even in industrialized countries where there is a

high level of awareness of HIV and its routes of transmission, the degree to which young people have changed their behaviour has been disappointing. There is clearly a need to develop new and more effective ways of persuading young people to practise safer sex. Second, with predictions of ten million children infected by the year 2000 and a further ten million AIDS orphans, Wellcome seeks to facilitate the provision of services to children and families affected by HIV and AIDS.

To this end, Positive Action – in partnership with the National Children's Bureau[1] and the Institute of Child Health [2] – organized a European Symposium to debate the issue. For the first time, doctors, educationalists, social workers, legal experts and family members with HIV from all over Europe were brought together to discuss the problems and sow the seeds of a concerted European response. This has now given rise to a European Forum which will take the issues further and in fact is already developing and implementing action throughout the region with support from Positive Action and the European Union.

The workplace initiative

People living with HIV and AIDS are still often subjected to prejudice and discrimination at their place of work. They may be alienated or even lose their jobs. On the other hand, the workplace presents an excellent forum for education, and employers have a duty to use this opportunity to reduce ignorance surrounding HIV and AIDS so that employees are informed, equipped to avoid infection and supportive of those living with HIV and AIDS. Moreover, as the epidemic continues to spread, it is increasingly in the employer's interests to develop and maintain an informed workforce.

In 1987, Wellcome mounted a company-wide education campaign about HIV and how to avoid infection. More recently, it has conducted a survey of all 17,000 employees to ascertain levels of knowledge about HIV and its transmission, and to identify gaps in knowledge and what additional information the company should be providing. It has also conducted a worldwide employment policy audit – as part of Positive Action – to ensure that Wellcome's policies adequately support employees with HIV.

As a result, global policies on chronic, progressive illness (including HIV) have been developed and a company information and training programme is under development.

The developing country initiative

The great majority of HIV infections are in developing countries. Prevention of the further spread of HIV and the care and support of those affected are both critical issues. In the absence of adequate government action, affected communities have responded with great spirit, determination and effect, though severely hampered by lack of resources, and a lack of cross-fertilization of ideas, expertise and mutual support. Moreover, most projects to date have addressed prevention or, less commonly, care. This has created an artificial conceptual gap between prevention and care, which can hinder an optimal response to the epidemic.

This initiative represents a commitment to help address HIV prevention and care in developing countries in an integrated and systematic way, to join with project partners in order to develop and disseminate models of good practice.

The information and policy initiative

A great deal of ignorance about HIV and AIDS remains, and prejudice and discrimination towards those affected continues. Most people obtain their information about HIV and AIDS from the mass media. This includes both factual information about numbers infected, the spread of the virus, routes of transmission and means of prevention, as well as opinions and attitudes that can counter or reinforce stigma and prejudice.This initiative aims to help policy-makers and information providers such as the media develop sound policies and provide accurate information about HIV and AIDS. The objective is to encourage a society which is both well-informed about the epidemic and supportive of those affected so that people with HIV and AIDS can live with freedom, dignity and support.

Conclusion

Wellcome's response to the HIV epidemic has had three elements: to develop the drugs to attack the virus and to continue its commitment to develop new and improved treatments; to educate and inform its workforce; and to take up the challenge of forming new partnerships and developing new solutions to the range of issues presented by the epidemic through Positive Action – the company's international programme of HIV education, care and community support.

From our knowledge of the epidemic and our experience in responding to it I would recommend that all companies, large or small, national or international, should consider taking three important steps in *their* response:

Step one is to provide employees with information about HIV and AIDS, particularly HIV transmission and prevention, as part of an overall health education process. This will assist the workforce in avoiding infection and will encourage a responsible and supportive attitude towards those affected.

Step two is to review employment policies with respect to chronic illness to see if they deal adequately and fairly with the issues raised by HIV and AIDS and then to update them or create a specific policy on HIV/AIDS, if necessary. This will ensure that people affected will not be stigmatized or mistreated and will guard against potential disruption to employee relations.

Step three should be to look for ways in which the company can play a greater role in society's fight against this epidemic. As a company at the very centre of the medical response to the epidemic, Wellcome has already taken many strides down this route and has to date committed in the region of £10 million to the Positive Action programme. But by making AIDS a priority part of *their* community relations, *all* organizations can and should contribute and become part of the solution.

---

1 The National Children's Bureau is a London-based charity which promotes the needs of children through policy research, development and implementation.

2 The Institute of Child Health undertakes research in many areas of child health, including paediatric HIV infection, and coordinates the European Collaborative Study on children born to women with HIV infection. It is based at Great Ormond Street Hospital, London.

Contributors' Addresses

National AIDS Trust
6th floor, Eileen House
80 Newington Causeway
London SE1 6EF
Tel: + 44(0)171-972 2845
Fax: + 44(0171-972 2885
e-mail: julian.meldrum @ posnet.co.uk

Dr Eddy Beck
Academic Department of Public Health
St Mary's Hospital Medical School
Norfolk Place
London W2 1PG
England
Tel: + 44 (0)171 723 1252
Fax: + 44 (0)171 402 2150

Sue Belgrave
General Manager of Company Culture
The Body Shop International PLC
Watersmead
Littlehampton
West Sussex BN17 6LS
England
Tel: + 44 (0)1903 731500
Fax: + 44 (0)1903 726250

Dr Michael Bloor
School of Social and Administrative Studies
University of Wales
College of Cardiff
62 Park Place
Cardiff CF1 3AS
Wales
Tel: + 44 (0)1222 874000
Fax: + 44 (0)1222 874175
e-mail: bloor@cardiff.ac.uk

Dr Saulius Chaplinskas
Director
Lietuvos AIDS Centras
Kairiukscio 2
2021 Vilnius
Lithuania
Tel: + 370 2 35 04 65/76 32 38
Fax: + 370 2 35 02 25/76 58 50

David Cowan
Centre for Legal Studies
Arts Building
University of Sussex
Falmer
Brighton BN1 9QN
England
Tel: + 44 (0)1273 606755
Fax: + 44 (0)1273 678466

Yael Davidson
National Public Health Nursing Supervisor
Department of Public Health
Ministry of Health
20 King David Street
Jerusalem
93591 Israel
Tel: + 972 2 247023
Fax: + 972 2 259218

Jacqueline De Puy
245 rte d'Hermance
1246 Corsier
Switzerland
Tel: + 41 22 751 11 71
Fax: + 41 22 301 37 92

Dr Willem Faas
GAK/GMD
Gatwickstraat 1
1043 GK Amsterdam
The Netherlands
Tel: + 31 20 606 6206
Fax: + 31 20 606 6230

Jonathan Glasson
152 Mayall Road
Brixton
London SE24 0PH
England
Tel: + 44 (0)171 737 4562

Dr David Goss and Derek Adam-Smith
Portsmouth Business School
University of Portsmouth
Locksway Road
Milton
Southsea PO4 8JF
England
Tel: + 44 (0)1705 876543
Fax: + 44 (0)1705 844059
e-mail: gossd@csovax.cso.port.ac.uk

Dr Alastair M Gray
Centre for Socio-Legal Studies
Wolfson College
University of Oxford
Oxford OX2 6UD
England
Tel: + 44 (0)1865 284220
Fax: + 44 (0)1865 284221
e-mail: socleg@vax.oxford.ac.uk

Dr Gill Green
MRC Medical Sociology Unit
5 Lillybank Gardens
Glasgow G12 8QQ
Tel: + 44 (0)141 357 3949
Fax: + 44 (0)141 337 2389
Scotland
e-mail: gill@m.soc.mrc.gla.ac.uk

Dr Bernhard Güntert and Willy Oggier
Research Group for Management in
Health Services
University of St. Gallen
Rorschacherstrasse 103c
9007 St. Gallen
Switzerland
Tel: + 41 71 26 25 86
Fax: + 41 71 25 14 96
e-mail: guentert@sgcl1.unisg.ch

Marlene Gyldmark
Danish Hospital Institute
Landermaerket 10
Copenhagen
Denmark
Tel: + 45 33 11 57 77
Fax: + 45 33 93 10 19
e-mail: dsinmg@vm.uni-c.dk

Mary Haour-Knipe
Group Leader: Migrants & Travellers
Assessing AIDS Prevention
5 rue St-Ours
CH-1205 Geneva
Switzerland
Tel: + 41 22 781 35 50
Fax: + 41 22 781 35 50

Dr Jacques Marquet, Dr Michel Hubert &
Dr Luc Van Campenhoudt
Centre d'études sociologiques
Facultés universitaires Saint-Louis
43 Boulevard du Jardin Botanique
B-1000 Brussels
Belgium
Tel: + 32 2 211 79 70
Fax: + 32 2 211 79 97
e-mail: marquet@fusl.ac.be

Julian Hussey
55 Lower Bristol Road
Bath
England
BA2 3BE
Tel: + 44 (0)1225 334856

Dr Johannes Jager & Dr Maarten Postma
RIVM
PO Box 1
3720 BA
Bilthoven
The Netherlands
Tel: + 31 30 74 28 46
Fax: + 31 30 25 29 73
e-mail: maarten.postma@rivm.nl

Professor John Kyriopoulos
Athens School of Public Health
Department of Health Economics
196 Alexandras Avenue
115 21 Athens
Greece
Tel: + 30 1 64 47 941
Fax: + 30 1 64 44 260

Professor Denis-Clair Lambert
Department of Economics
University of Lyons 3
23 rue Sala
Lyons
690020 France
Tel: + 33 78 42 64 31
Fax: + 33 72 72 20 50

Dr Catherine Le Galès
INSERM Research Unit 357
Hôpital de Bicêtre
78 rue du Général Leclerc
94275 Le Kremlin Bicêtre
France
Tel: + 33 1 49 59 19 69
Fax: + 33 1 46 71 32 70

Dr Reiner Leidl
University of Limburg
PO Box 616
6200 MD Maastricht
The Netherlands
Tel: + 31 43 88 17 27
Fax: + 31 43 67 09 60
e-mail: reiner.leidl@egz.rulimburg.nl

Dr Vlastimil Mayer
Coordinator, AIDS Prevention Programme
Institute of Virology
Slovak Academy of Sciences
Dúbravská cesta 9
842 46 Bratislava
Slovak Republic
Tel: + 42 7 374468
Fax: + 42 7 374284

Dr Michael Merson
Executive Director
Global Programme on AIDS
World Health Organization
1211 Geneva
27-Switzerland
Tel: + 41 22 791 47 70
Fax: + 41 22 791 07 46
e-mail: cherney@who.ch

Dr Christoph Minder
Institut für Sozial- und Präventivmedizin
Universität Bern
Finkenhubelweg 11
3012 Bern
Switzerland
Tel: + 41 31 631 35 11
Fax: + 41 31 631 35 20

Peter Molyneux
Director
AIDS and Housing Project
Livingstone House
11 Carteret Street
London SW1H 9DL
England
Tel: + 44 (0)171 222 6933
Fax: + 44 (0)171 222 6932

John Nicholson
Director
George House Trust
75 Ardwick Green North
Manchester M12 6FX
England
Tel: + 44 (0)161 839 4340
Fax: + 44 (0)161 839 6540

Professor George Papaevangelou
Athens School of Public Health
196 Alexandras Avenue
Athens 115 21
Greece
Tel: + 30 1 64 47 941
Fax: + 30 1 64 44 260

Dr Sunanda Ray
Department of Community Medicine
University of Zimbabwe
PO Box A178
Avondale
Harare
Zimbabwe
Tel: + 263 4 791 631
Fax: + 263 4 732 828

Dr Andrew Revell
Coordinator – Positive Action
The Wellcome Foundation Ltd
Langley Court
South Eden Park Road
Beckenham
Kent BR3 3BS
England
Tel: + 44 (0)181 658 2211
Fax: + 44 (0)181 663 3347

Anne-Sophie Rieben Schizas
Institut suisse de droit comparé
Dorigny
1015 Lausanne
Switzerland
Tel: + 41 21 692 49 11
Fax: + 41 21 692 49 49
e-mail: secrétariat@isdc-dfjp.epfl-ch

Peter Roth
4 Raymond Buildings
Grays Inn
London WC1R 5BP
England
Tel: + 44 (0)171 405 7211
Fax: + 44 (0)171 405 2084

Dr Joan Rovira
SOIKOS
Sardenya 229–237, 6° -4ª
08013 Barcelona
Spain
Tel: + 34 3 2314217
Fax: + 34 3 2313507
e-mail: rovira@riscd2.ub.es

Per Sandberg
Centre for Medical Ethics
Gaustadalléen 21
N-0371 Oslo
Norway
Tel: + 47 22 95 87 80
Fax: + 47 22 69 84 71

Dr Ronny Shtarkshall
The Hebrew University and Hadassah
Braun School of Public Health and
Community Medicine
PO Box 12272
Jerusalem
921120
Israel
Tel: + 972 2 777 110
Fax: + 972 2 434 434
e-mail: shiluv@hadassah.bitnet

Dr Alexandr Stožický
Director of Secretariat
Czech Medical Association J.E. Purkyně
PO Box 88
Sokolská 31
120 26 Prague 2
Czech Republic
Tel: + 42 2 2491 5195
Fax: + 42 2 2421 6836

Keith Tolley
Queen's Medical Centre
School of Public Health/Dept. of Economics
University of Nottingham
Nottingham NG7 2UH
England
Tel: + 44 (0)115 924 9924 ext. 44641
Fax: + 44 (0)115 970 9316
e-mail:
mhzkt@mhn1.phme.nottingham. ac.uk

Glen Williams
Series Editor
Strategies For Hope
93 Divinity Road
Oxford OX4 1LN
England
Tel:+ 44 (0)1865 727612
Fax:+ 44 (0)1865 722203

Petra Wilson
Law Department
University Park
Nottingham NG7 2RD
England
Tel:+ 44 (0)115 951 5722
Fax:+ 44 (0)115 951 5696
e-mail: uzpsw@lln1.law.nottingham. ac.uk

Professsor Władysława Zielinska and
Dr Anna Korczak-Rogoń
Centrum Diagnostyczno-Kliniczne AIDS
ul.Smoluchowskiego 18
80-214 Gdańsk
Poland
Tel:+ 48 58 41 28 87
Fax: + 48 58 41 28 87

Index